Perceptions in Litigation and Mediation

Tamara Relis is a Research Fellow at Columbia University Law School in New York and in the Law Department of the London School of Economics and Political Science (LSE). She holds a PhD in law and an LLM masters degree in law (*with Merit*) from the LSE law department, as well as an LLB law degree (*Hons*) from the University of London. She is a trial lawyer (barrister) with experience in trial court practice and has worked and qualified as an attorney in litigation (solicitor).

Dr. Relis is the recipient of various awards for her doctoral and postdoctoral research, including awards from the British Academy, the Economic & Social Research Council, Columbia University, and the LSE. She has been invited to speak about her research throughout North America, Europe (Italy, Germany, Spain, France, and Croatia), India, and South Africa. She was also invited to Japan through a Japanese government award to speak about her findings, culminating in this book.

Dr. Relis' work has been published in the *Harvard Negotiation Law Review* (2007), the *Pittsburgh Law Review* (2007), *Studies in Law, Politics and Society* (edited by Austin Sarat and Patricia Ewick, 2002), as well as in Japan in *Sociology of Law* (JASL – University of Tokyo, 2004). Her work was also translated into Japanese in Kyoto University's law journal (2004).

She is presently conducting a large-scale empirical study on the permeation of international human rights laws and norms in formal courts versus informal justice processing of violence-against-women cases throughout India. She uses victims', the accuseds, and legal actors' understandings, aims, and experiences as a lens to map, theorize, and critically analyze the theoretical ideas informing these processes (e.g., norm diffusion theory, universalism versus cultural relativism, restorative justice, and feminist critiques of mainstream human rights paradigms) and shows how these ideas are understood by those on the ground.

Perceptions in Litigation and Mediation

Lawyers, Defendants, Plaintiffs, and Gendered Parties

Tamara Relis

London School of Economics, Department of Law, and Columbia University Law School

CAMBRIDGE UNIVERSITY PRESS
Cambridge, New York, Melbourne, Madrid, Cape Town, Singapore,
São Paulo, Delhi, Dubai, Tokyo, Mexico City

Cambridge University Press
32 Avenue of the Americas, New York NY 10013-2473, USA

Published in the United States of America by Cambridge University Press, New York

www.cambridge.org
Information on this title: www.cambridge.org/9780521517317

© Tamara Relis 2009

This publication is in copyright. Subject to statutory exception
and to the provisions of relevant collective licensing agreements,
no reproduction of any part may take place without the written
permission of Cambridge University Press.

First published 2009

A catalogue record for this publication is available from the British Library

Library of Congress Cataloging in Publication data

Relis, Tamara.
Perceptions in litigation and mediation : lawyers, defendants, plaintiffs, and gendered parties /
Tamara Relis.
  p. cm.
Includes bibliographical references.
ISBN 978-0-521-51731-7 (hardback)
1. Mediation. 2. Dispute resolution (Law) 3. Actions and defenses. I. Title.
K2390.R45 2009
347.09 – dc22   2008033580

ISBN 978-0-521-51731-7 Hardback

Cambridge University Press has no responsibility for the persistence or
accuracy of URLs for external or third-party internet websites referred to in
this publication, and does not guarantee that any content on such websites is,
or will remain, accurate or appropriate. Information regarding prices, travel
timetables and other factual information given in this work are correct at
the time of first printing but Cambridge University Press does not guarantee
the accuracy of such information thereafter.

For Coby, my heart and soul

Abstract

Grounded in interpretive theory, this book addresses the question, "How do professional, lay, and gendered actors understand and experience litigated case processing leading up to and including mediation in legal disputes?" Litigation and mediation processes are increasingly well described and understood through a fast-growing literature to which lawyers and other social scientists have contributed. Yet, rather little in-depth empirical data are available on what happens during case processing as well as what occurs prior to and inside mediation sessions, in terms of how these processes are understood and experienced by the actors involved. The different perceptions of professional, legal, and lay actors, and of males and females, particularly require further examination. These differences are explored here through data derived from 131 interviews, questionnaires, and observations of parties, lawyers, and mediators involved in 64 mediated fatality and injury cases in medical disputes (mandatory and voluntary; pre- and intra-litigation).

Attention to the discursive representations of the various actors on issues such as understandings of plaintiffs' litigation aims, all actors' mediation objectives and perceptions of what occurred during mediations reveals significant differences in terms of both language and agenda. It emerges that professional and lay actors, males and females, occupy largely parallel worlds of understanding affecting how conflict and its resolution are perceived. There is some evidence that mediation experience leads lawyers to reconceptualize their roles. This move away from conventional legal thought is further revealed through the discourse of lawyer-mediators, which was frequently distinct from practicing attorneys and more akin to that of non-lawyer-mediators. Nevertheless, in juxtaposing actors' understandings and perceptions on all sides of the same or similar cases, the data reveal inherent problems with the core workings of the legal system, as stark similarities in the discourse of plaintiffs and defendants on the one hand, and lawyers of all camps on the other reveal unlikely conceptual alignments between legal and extralegal actors involved in case processing.

Contents

List of tables	*page* xiii
List of figures	xv
List of abbreviations	xvii
Acknowledgments	xix

1	Introduction		1
	1.1	Book structure	5
	1.2	Findings and recurrent themes	8
		Parallel worlds' theme findings	9
		Lawyers' reconceptualization theme findings	17
		Gender theme findings	22
	1.3	Methodology	26
2	Great misconceptions or disparate perceptions of plaintiffs' litigation aims?		33
	2.1	Lawyers' comprehensions of plaintiffs' litigation aims – group differences	36
		Physician lawyers: It's only about money	36
		Hospital lawyers: It's mostly about money	38
		Plaintiff lawyers: It's mostly about money, but also other issues	39
	2.2	Plaintiffs: "It's not about the money! It's about principles"	42
	2.3	Case studies: Parallel worlds of understanding the meaning of litigated cases	46
	2.4	System conditioning, dispute transformation, and principles intermeshed with money	51
	2.5	Gender differentiations	58
		Female lawyers' extralegal sensitivity	58
		Female plaintiffs' compensatory unease	60
	2.6	Chapter conclusion	61

3		**The voluntary versus mandatory mediation divide**	65
	3.1	Lawyers' world – mandatory versus voluntary mediation divide	68
		Negative lawyer attitudes	72
		Underlying meaning of lawyers' mandatory – voluntary mediation preferences	75
	3.2	Parties' world – no mandatory versus voluntary divide	77
		Just a stage in the litigation process	77
		Same positive attitudes – same eagerness	78
		Same overall understandings, expectations, intentions, and needs	79
	3.3	Chapter conclusion	82
4		**Consequences of power: Legal actors versus disputants on defendants' attendance at mediation**	86
	4.1	The attendance arbiters	88
		Lawyers' experiences with defendants at mediation	89
	4.2	Professionals' reasoning on defendants' attendance	91
		Physician lawyers	94
		Hospital lawyers	96
		Plaintiff lawyers	97
		Analysis of lawyers' views	99
		Mediators	101
	4.3	Facing opponents: Disputants ascribe common meaning to case resolution	104
		Defending doctors' views on attending mediation	105
		Plaintiffs on defendants' mediation attendance	109
	4.4	Gender disparities	119
		Professionals' gender disparities	119
		Parties' gender disparities	120
	4.5	Chapter conclusion	125
5		**Actors' mediation objectives: How lawyers versus parties plan to resolve their cases short of trial**	129
	5.1	Legal actors' mediation objectives	131
		Physician lawyers	132
		Hospital lawyers	134
		Plaintiff lawyers	135
		Lawyers' gender divisions	139
	5.2	Disputants' mediation aims	141
		Plaintiffs' mediation aims	142
		Plaintiffs' gender differences	145
		Defendant physicians' mediation objectives	149

	5.3	The confidentiality premise	150
	5.4	Chapter conclusion	153
6	**Perceptions during mediations**	156
	6.1	Mediation's contextual worlds: Confrontations and representations	158
		Legal actors' confrontations	158
		Conflicts between legal and lay actors	159
		Representations	161
		Surface findings	163
	6.2	Favored and disfavored mediation elements – legal actors	165
		Favored elements	165
		Objectionables	171
	6.3	Favored and disfavored mediation elements – disputants	172
		Favored elements	173
		Objectionables	176
	6.4	Gender disparities	181
		Legal actors	181
		Plaintiffs	184
	6.5	Chapter conclusion	193
7	**Parallel views on mediators and styles**	197
	7.1	Contextual realities and surface findings	199
	7.2	The legal evaluative world on style	204
		The importance of background	205
		The significance of style	207
	7.3	The extralegal facilitative world on style	212
	7.4	Gendered mediator experiences	217
		Overpowered female facilitative mediators	217
		Mediators and female plaintiffs	220
	7.5	Chapter conclusion	223
8	**Conclusion: The parallel understandings and perceptions in case processing and mediation**	226
	8.1	Parallel lay versus legal worlds of understanding and meaning in case processing and mediation	228
		Litigation aims and mediation objectives	229
		Mandatory versus voluntary mediations	230
		Defendants' attendance and the meaning of mediation	231
		Mediation perceptions and assessments	231
		Mediators and their styles	232
	8.2	The reconceptualization of legal actors	234
		The literature	236

	8.3	Parallel worlds' findings – macro-meanings	238
		The formal versus informal justice debates	240
		The role of the legal system	241
		The role of lawyers	242
	8.4	Gendered parallel worlds	245
		Extralegal sensitivity of female lawyers	245
		Disempowered female plaintiffs	248
	8.5	Practical application of the findings	252
	8.6	Recommendations for future research	254

Bibliography 257
Index 281

List of tables

1	Breakdown of dataset (interview/questionnaire) files	*page* 27
2	Respondents' genders and ages	29
3	Disputants' education and previous mediation experience	29
4	Lawyers' medical mediation experience (*not mediation experience generally*)	30

List of figures

1	Physician lawyers' understandings of plaintiffs' litigation aims.	page 37
2	Hospital lawyers' understandings of plaintiffs' litigation aims.	38
3	Plaintiff lawyers' understandings of plaintiffs' litigation aims.	40
4	Claimants' descriptions of their litigation aims.	43
5	Instances of hospital lawyers mentioning plaintiffs' extralegal litigation objectives.	59
6	Instances of all defense lawyers mentioning plaintiffs' extralegal litigation aims.	59
7	Non-disputants' views on defendant physicians' attendance at mediation.	92
8	Non-disputants' reasons against defendants' attendance at mediation.	93
9	Non-disputants' reasons in favor of defendants' attendance at mediation.	94
10	Disputants' views on defendants' mediation attendance.	104
11	Disputants' reasoning on why defendants should attend mediation.	105
12	Extralegal reasons for defendants' mediation attendance by gender.	119
13	Tactical reasons against defendants' mediation attendance by gender.	120
14	Legal actors' mediation aims.	131
15	Disputants' mediation aims.	131
16	Defendants' versus defense lawyers' mediation aims.	133
17	Plaintiffs' versus plaintiff lawyers' mediation aims.	136
18	Lawyers' references to extralegal mediation aims.	139
19	Plaintiffs' mediation aims concerns – by gender.	146
20	Plaintiffs' mediation needs and fears – by gender.	147
21	Surface perceptions of mediations – all actors.	163
22	Mediation's favored elements – legal actors.	166
23	Mediation's favored elements – disputants.	174
24	Plaintiffs' gender disparities at mediation.	185
25	Surface perceptions of mediators and style.	202

List of abbreviations

ADR = alternative dispute resolution

CMPA = Canadian Medical Protection Association

College = College of Physicians and Surgeons of Ontario

Fieldwork Period = 17 months between May 2000 and October 2001 in and around Toronto, Canada

Legal actors = all lawyer groups

Medmal = medical malpractice/medical negligence/medical injury

MMP = Ontario Court Mandatory Mediation Program

Non-disputants = all legal actors together with all mediators

The terms "claimant," "plaintiff," and "complainant" have been used synonymously.

The terms "disputant," "litigant," and "party" have been used synonymously.

The terms "lawyer," "counsel," and "attorney" have been used synonymously.

Acknowledgments

This book would not have been possible without the support of my mentors, colleagues, family, and friends. My husband, Coby Relis, has been the backbone of my work. I am also extremely indebted to Professor Simon Roberts for his support and erudite guidance during the research period and to Professor Nicola Lacey for her advice and assistance throughout the years. I thank Dr. Joseph Relis for his continuous encouragement and strong belief in this work, as well as professors Richard Abel, Michael Palmer, and Carrie Menkel-Meadow, for their insightful suggestions for publication. The London School of Economics has supported my research throughout the years and has graciously acted as my second home. I am also grateful to Columbia University Law School in New York for its accommodation and support during the writing-up stages, and to the University of Toronto and professor Mariana Valverde for their assistance during the Fieldwork Period. The Economic & Social Research Council (Award PTA-026–27-0979) and the British Academy (Award PDF/2006/64) provided me with the financial support that made the transformation from research thesis to published manuscript possible. Finally, and importantly, I offer my deepest thanks to all those lawyers, disputants, and mediators involved in the cases covered in this project and to all those who kindly allowed me access to the research sites. Although their names must remain confidential, without them this research would not have been possible, and for them and others like them I hope to make a difference.

CHAPTER ONE

Introduction

This book is an analytical study exploring through actors' understandings, perceptions and experiences the internal dynamics and realities of case processing in the legal system leading up to and including mediation. By looking at the jigsaw of views, I attempt to infer something about the system of mediation in which all actors have a part, but none knows the whole play. Specifically, the research addresses the question, "How do the diverse professional, lay, and gendered actors understand and experience case processing leading up to and including mediation in legal disputes?"[1] Thus, in terms of theoretical framework, in sharp contrast to many studies to date that have focused on structural features of litigation and mediation – some informed by a neo–systems theory perspective – this book focuses on recovering actors' understandings and meanings affecting their actions within the interface of social structure, here being mediation and related litigation processes.[2]

---

1 I use the term "mediation" as traditionally understood to mean "a nonbinding process in which an unaligned third party works with disputing parties and their lawyers towards resolving or mitigating their conflict in a mutually satisfactory settlement. Parties may consider a comprehensive mix of their needs, interests, and whatever else they deem relevant to the dispute" (Fuller 1971, pp. 305, 308; Folberg and Taylor 1984, p. 10).
2 Looking back ultimately to Max Weber and Alfred Schutz my approach here is an interpretive one, attending to the subjective meaning of human action. Both Schutz and Weber viewed the essential function of social science to be interpretive, to understand the subjective meaning of social action, with action (i.e., all human behavior being overt or passive to which individuals attach a subjective meaning) being defined through meaning and taking account of others' behaviors (Schutz 1967, pp. xxi, xxiii, xxviii; Weber 1922, p. 1). Yet, taking as central to my research the interstitial position of the "knowing social actor" whose action is informed by structure, I draw on the paradigm emerging in the works of Anthony Giddens and Pierre Bourdieu to inform my investigation. Giddens' structuration theory "recognizes human beings as knowledgeable agents, reflexively monitoring the flow of interaction with one another and routinely monitoring social and physical aspects of the contexts in which they move...maintaining a continuing 'theoretical understanding' of the grounds of their activity" (Giddens 1984, pp. 5, 30). In contrast to positivism, for Giddens social reality is the ongoing construction of, and by, knowledgeable actors whose recurrent interactions create, reproduce, and transform the social world (Mouzelis 1991, p. 19). Yet, "the constitution of agents and structures... represent a duality... as structure... organising human conduct... is not external to individuals. Structure is recursively organized sets of rules and resources... comprising the situated activities of human agents, reproduced across time and space" (Giddens 1984, p. 25). Not far from Giddens, Bourdieu's theory of practice stipulates that "each agent... is a producer and reproducer of objective meaning. Yet, only by constructing the objective structures is one able to pose the question of the mechanisms through which the relationship is

1

The findings can be conceptualized as a story about a drama and its actors (Turner 1974). It is a drama entailing different forms of communication, a drama of tactics and strategy as well as one representing highly meaningful and potentially life-altering experiences – depending on which of the actors describes it. Indeed, understandings of the drama's meaning and purpose are divergent. It is a drama of incongruous yet converging interests, perceptions, intrigues, and humanity. It is a drama about money and human lives. The drama offers various opportunities for its actors. Yet, the actors have differing needs and desires. Each performance focuses on resolving a dispute. But the actors do not share the same understanding of what that dispute is about. Nor are there shared comprehensions of how to resolve it. Actors who appear to be on the same side pursue disparate objectives. Who is aligned with whom? Some players have more power, frequently transforming the drama for all. Yet, the actors have very different comprehensions of what is taking place. Still, although it can be said that legal, lay, and gendered actors have disparate conceptions of the good, it appears that the drama is slowly uniting all of its actors to hold similar conceptions of the good.

Professional versus lay roles have been examined for a number of reasons.[3] Professionals such as lawyers and mediators are distinct from lay plaintiffs and

---

established between the structures and the practices or the representations which accompany them." In going beyond the subject/object dichotomy, Bourdieu notes that "agents' habitus acts within them as the organizing principle of their actions, habitus being a system of structured structures acting as principles that organize practices" (Bourdieu 1990, pp. 18, 53). Thus, social practices are fundamental in understanding how social structures are produced and reproduced, as practices constitute structures whilst also being determined by structures (Bourdieu 1977, pp. 21, 72; 1990, pp. 18, 53). This approach accords with anthropologists' shift from analyzing laws as systems of rules or processes to instead utilizing paradigms that focus on actors' individual approaches, preferences, and decisions whilst operating within rule and normative structural systems (Merry and Silbey 1984, p. 159). The works of Garfinkel and Goffman also provided useful insight in relation to the final chapters (*six and seven*), which provide a more detached focus of my situated actors. Thus this research may also be viewed as an ethnomethodological study "setting out to make explicit the truth of primary experiences of the social world" (Bourdieu 1977, p. 3). I have "sought to treat practical activities, practical circumstances, and practical sociological reasoning from within actual settings as topics of empirical study," including "how" things are discussed. This is notwithstanding the fact that in contrast to Giddens and Bourdieu, Garfinkel takes the view that the objective reality of social facts is the ongoing accomplishment of the concerted activities of daily life (Garfinkel 1984, pp. vii–viii, 1). Likewise, predominantly in relation to the final chapters, Goffman's work had a role to play in informing the analysis on perceptions as well as actors' concerns with managing others' impressions, that is, how individuals interact utilizing self-presentation and performances during mediations' interactions. Finally, viewed as a fieldwork monograph from a sociological and anthropological perspective, this research draws on some of Clifford Geertz's insights in cultural hermeneutics in that I aimed throughout to provide "thick description," revealing the complexity of elements within litigation and mediation processes. As Geertz notes, "ethnography relates to the intellectual effort of establishing rapport, understanding your notes, interviews... thinking, reflecting... It is an elaborate adventure in 'thick description'... not just describing what happens on the surface... but providing richly and fully described accounts of what is going on... and setting down the meaning particular social actions have for the actors whose actions they are." Moreover, as "small facts speak to large issues," I aimed to "draw large conclusions from small, but very densely textured facts to support broad assertions... by engaging them with complex specifics" (Geertz 1973, pp. 6, 9, 23, 27–28).

3 Individuals play roles that tell them and others what to expect in their activities. Although the term "role" vacillates when examined carefully and individuals are simultaneously involved in several roles, it can be defined generally as "activities individuals would engage in were they to act solely

defendants in the context of litigation and mediation in various respects. Lawyers and mediators are committed to, and embrace, the professional roles that define them and what they do (Goffman 1961a, pp. 164, 171; Burns 1992, p. 133; Manning 1992, p. 112). Role expectations of these professionals act as both external constraints on them as well as resources that they can manipulate (Manning 1992, p. 177; Lemert and Branaman 1997, pp. 35–36). Moreover, professionals such as lawyers and mediators are "repeat players" in litigation and mediation and are in a position of advantage (Galanter 1974, pp. 97–98, 103, 114), working with clear ideas of what they are supposed to be doing during case processing. In contrast, lay non-corporate actors, such as the plaintiffs and defendants in the cases studied here, are predominantly unsophisticated in litigation and mediation and thus do not know in advance what they should or can be doing during the processing of their cases. Consequently, their understandings and actions, unlike those of legal actors, are generally not affected by prior knowledge of accepted norms or of "how things go" during litigation and mediation.

A second focus of this book involves a comparison of female and male professionals' and lay actors' understandings and experiences during case processing including mediation.[4] Scholars have posited that the influx of women lawyers into the legal profession may alter the nature of lawyering, including negotiations within the adversarial system to being more relational.[5] However, limited empirical data on how the diverse genders actually practice law and whether females contribute to an emphasis on needs versus rights (Menkel-Meadow 1994a, pp. 89, 91, 95). Moreover, no systematic empirical field studies have examined whether gender affects lawyers' approaches to case processing that includes mediation (Klein 2005, p. 792). Nor have gender-based differences in lawyers versus parties been explored (Stempel 2003, p. 312). This is notwithstanding the fact that "disputing may be influenced by the ... genders of those involved" and that "gender-based differences may affect the dynamics of mediation sessions" (Goldberg et al. 1992, p. 139).

In locating my arguments within the literature debates, it became clear that notwithstanding mediation's popularity, exponential expansion, and institutionalization connecting it to formal justice systems in many jurisdictions in North America, the United Kingdom, Europe, Australia, and worldwide (including a number of civil law jurisdictions)[6] and despite voluminous rhetoric and theoretical discourse, there is a dearth of in-depth empirical knowledge (versus survey data) representing any aggregate view of how litigation-linked dispute resolution works in practice; how it is deployed by lawyers and disputants in terms of their

---

in terms of the normative demands upon those in their positions" (Goffman 1961b, pp. 87, 90–91, 106–10, 132–33, 139, 152; 1974; Manning 1992, pp. 127, 176).

4 Other independent variables such as socioeconomic status or ethnicity were not examined for various reasons, including the relatively small numbers in each actor group. Segmentation of the data on the basis of these other independent variables would result in group numbers too small for meaningful analysis.

5 Menkel-Meadow (1985, pp. 50–58), Stempel (2003, pp. 311–12), and Klein (2005, p. 777).

6 Nolan-Haley (1996, p. 100), Palmer and Roberts (1998, p. 148), Alexander (2002, pp. 272–73, 275), and McAdoo and Hinshaw (2002, p. 475).

understandings, perceptions, and goals (as well as their complex interconnections), lawyers' impact; and generally what occurs during the multileveled interactions in mediation processes.[7] Indeed, the social science literature contains only scattered evidence of what it means and feels to undergo mediation (Lande 2000, p. 330).

In particular, although valuable work has been undertaken such as Sarat and Felstiner's research entailing observations of U.S. divorce lawyers and their clients,[8] overall little in-depth empirical knowledge exists from litigants themselves on their dispute perceptions (Guthrie 2001, p. 165), their agendas for litigation and mediation (Relis 2002, pp. 151–52; Jones 2003, p. 284; Sternlight 2003, pp. 298–99), and their evaluations of ADR (Guthrie 2002, p. 129). Yet, "listening to disputants' voices should be particularly important in . . . democracies that proclaim the value and dignity of the individual and in a field that names disputants' self-determination as its fundamental underlying principle. . . . " Listening to disputants' voices "is essential for the maintenance of the legitimacy of the public institutions that embrace mediation" (Welsh 2004a, pp. 578, 605–6). In providing these data, the findings here challenge dominant understandings of how litigation-track mediation works in practice.

The overall shift in focus from adjudication to settlement has been observed in Western legal systems over the last thirty years or so. For instance, Habermas notes the move in the last thirty years of the twentieth century from a mode of command to a mode of inducement, with actors now transacting their legal positions within negotiating modes of decision making, reflecting a shift from "the system" to the "lifeworld" (Habermas 1981, p. 371; Roberts 2002, p. 33). This shift has been discussed and theorized within the literature on civil justice as well as the literature on ADR. In terms of the phenomenon of trials having become more distant prospects (Glasser and Roberts 1993, p. 277), Galanter remarks, "It is accepted that most cases that enter the civil justice system are resolved short of adjudication via a single process of maneuvering and bargaining 'in the shadow of the law' (Mnookin and Kornhauser 1979, p. 959) and not within two separate tracks of adjudication and negotiation. . . . This has been referred to as 'litigotiation'." (Galanter and Cahill 1994, pp. 1341–42). Thus, "the diverse modes of decision-making of adjudication and settlement . . . entailing contrasting values . . . have come to share the framework provided by civil procedure as the primary arena for lawyers' attempts to settle" (Roberts 2000, pp. 739, 742–43).

In terms of the institutionalization of this shift, Roberts notes that "right across the common law world, what appear to be large-scale changes in state management of civil disputes have become visible over at least two decades. At the heart of these changes lies a growing recognition of 'settlement' as an approved, privileged objective of civil justice. The courts present themselves not just as agencies offering

---

7 Stempel (2000a, p. 389), McEwen and Wissler (2002, pp. 131, 142), Hensler (2003, pp. 192, 195), Jones (2003, pp. 290–91), Stempel (2003, p. 353), and Welsh (2004, pp. 575, 597).
8 Sarat and Felstiner (1986, pp. 116–17; 1988, pp. 739–42, 766–67; 1995, p. 406).

judgment but as sponsors of negotiated agreement... with mediation, a third route, now recognized alongside lawyer negotiations and judicial determination" (Roberts 2000, pp. 739, 744). The judicial promotion of settlement, together with the growth of ADR (and particularly mediation) in North America and Europe, have been remarked upon by various academics (Edwards 1986, p. 668; Twining 1993, p. 380; Galanter and Cahill 1994, pp. 1342–43). Moreover, the disparate institutionalized processes for dispute handling now inherent in settlement have been conceptualized by those such as Frank Sander in his vision of the "multi-door courthouse" (Sander 1976, p. 111), Hart and Sacks in explaining the need for cooperation in social interactions in the civil justice system (Hart and Sacks 1994, p. 1), and Lon Fuller in theorizing mediation.[9]

Yet, in juxtaposing the understandings, needs, objectives, and experiences of legal, lay, and gendered actors (plaintiffs, defendants, lawyers, and mediators) on all sides of actual litigated and mediated cases, the findings here illuminate important paradoxes inherent in legal policy initiatives related to the resolution of civil disputes. In providing a unique look into the diversity of prevalent realities, I demonstrate through lawyers' and parties' own discourse that both the formal and informal justice systems are not serving many of disputants' intrinsic, often overriding, needs, and I challenge the notion that disputants and their representatives broadly understand and want the same things during case processing. In fact, the chapter's findings indicate repeatedly that notwithstanding legal benefits, utilizing attorneys to assist disputants in resolving disputes is laden with difficulties, as epistemologically each actor group essentially occupies different, though parallel, worlds.

Although this research utilizes one particular dispute type for methodological consistency, namely, medical injury cases, the matters explored here relate to generic issues inherent in the legal processing of cases leading up to and including mediation. Thus, the findings are arguably pertinent to the bulk of human-oriented litigated and mediated disputes. As such, this work should be of interest to scholars and students of law, law and society, critical feminist studies, sociology, law and psychology, and medico-legal studies. It should likewise be of interest to practicing lawyers, mediators, and to the medical profession, as the data presented here offer elusive insight into disputants', lawyers', and mediators' approaches and strategies. However, more importantly, I hope that the findings act to reorient readers to certain disturbing realities inherent within the legal system and legal practice, and cause them to ask, How can we engage in a system of change?

1.1 Book structure

The chapters examine actors' views and experiences during the processing of their cases in a chronological order as far as possible, given the overlapping nature of

---

9 Fuller (1971, pp. 325–26; 1978, p. 356) and Menkel-Meadow (2000, pp. 1, 4, 14–15, 26).

some of the events described. Chapters two and three provide background and context to the cases studied. Shedding light on lawyers' and plaintiffs' comprehensions of what these cases and their mediations were about, chapter two examines the disparate understandings of why plaintiffs sued and what they sought from litigation in the first place. These comprehensions provide a critical backdrop to actors' perspectives and behavior during case processing and mediation. Specifically, I look at differences in understandings between all three legal actor groups (physician defense lawyers, hospital defense lawyers, and plaintiff lawyers) compared with plaintiffs' own explications of why they sued and what they sought from the civil justice system. Finally, the chapter examines disparities in discourse within all actor groups on the basis of gender. Chapter three provides further contextual information by comparing legal actors' and lay disputants' understandings and attitudes toward court-mandated versus voluntary mediations, as the dataset provides examples of both. Defense and plaintiff lawyers' attitudes and expectations for mandatory mediations are examined, together with their reasoning for their particular views. This is followed by a look at disputants' attitudes and expectations in the same cases. Finally, the chapter's findings are analyzed, resulting in some unexpected conclusions.

Moving forward to pre-mediation decisions, chapter four analyzes the issue of defendants' attendance at mediation. Attitudes toward this issue shed important light on the diverse meanings ascribed to mediation and conflict resolution, more generally by the actors involved. First, focusing on lawyers' discourse, the chapter explores the mechanics of how attendance decisions are made, together with an examination of lawyers' past experiences with defendants present at mediations. This is followed by an analysis of each legal actor group's views and reasoning behind their views, comparing them with those of mediators. The second part of chapter four compares plaintiffs' and defendants' understandings and reasoning on the same issue of defendants' attendance in cases that mediated both with and without defendants present. The findings illustrate starkly diverse meanings ascribed to case mediation by lay disputants as compared with legal actors. Lastly, gender influences on actors' views are examined for both professionals and disputants, adding further support to the gender findings seen in chapter two.

A final pre-mediation issue is explored in chapter five, which offers a comparative analysis of mediation actors' specific objectives for the process. First, I examine each legal actor group's mediation aims, subsequently highlighting gender divisions within their discourse. This is followed by an exploration of both plaintiffs' and defendants' mediation objectives, also examining differences in males' and females' articulated aims. Finally, the chapter looks at actors' comprehensions and attitudes toward mediation's confidentiality as a way of possibly explaining some of the findings on what legal and lay actors planned to do in order to resolve these disputes.

Actual mediation experiences are then examined in chapters six and seven. Chapter six compares actors' perceptions of "what went on" during mediations.

Chapter seven then focuses on views of mediators and the styles they employed. Chapter six commences with an overview of the unspoken contextual elements occurring throughout mediations, including confrontations between legal actors as well as more subliminal issues between lawyers and litigants, such as the representations or posturing inherent within mediations. The first section ends with an examination of "surface findings" relating to issues not unlike those found in other mediation research, such as actors' perceptions of the fairness of the process and satisfaction with mediation experiences and results. However, the remaining sections of the chapter delve deeper, examining legal actors' versus lay disputants' favored and disfavored elements during their mediations. This radically alters the picture of "what goes on." Finally, the chapter explores gender disparities in the discourse of both legal actors and parties, coming to further conclusions supportive of earlier gender findings in the research.

Chapter seven first examines a number of contextual realities and surface findings relating to judges, lawyer and non-lawyer-mediators, and mediation styles. This is followed by an exploration of attorneys' views on the importance of mediators' backgrounds and the techniques they employ, including lawyers' preferences for evaluative, rights-based mediation. Lawyers' reasoning behind their views is also analyzed, offering further evidence of the different meaning of case processing and mediation for legal actors as compared with parties. Next, the data relating to facilitative style preferences (predominantly deriving from mediators and litigants) are examined. In the final section, two gender findings are discussed, one relating to how mediators' conduct was interpreted by plaintiffs of different sexes, and the other relating to mediators' own genders. The gender findings provide final support to the gender themes present throughout the book.

In terms of how mediators are used and described in the chapter, it is pertinent to note that for many actors – both lawyers and disputants – the mediator "was" the mediation experience, often being perceived as the core element within mediations. Yet, although most were pleased with their mediators, discourse analysis indicated that legal and lay actors viewed mediators through entirely different lenses, marking a pronounced disparity in mediator wants and how mediators were perceived and judged. This affected not only subjective perceptions but also objective realities during mediation processes. Mediators' representations to both litigants and lawyers are also examined, highlighting the competitive realities between mediators in terms of settlement rates, client bases, the number of cases they mediated, and the unspoken awareness of the possibility of mediators precipitating future work from lawyers involved in these mediations. The chapter also elaborates on the issues of mediators representing a new information source for litigants and thus a new interest, potentially affecting lawyer–client relationships. Unspoken power struggles between mediators and attorneys are also evidenced. Yet, lawyers' willingness to devolve power to mediators ultimately affected much of what went on during mediations – something that also directly affected litigants' experiences and case results.

Lastly, chapter eight, the conclusion chapter, summarizes the key findings, making the argument about the differentially experienced parallel worlds of those involved in case processing and mediation of legal disputes.[10]

1.2 Findings and recurrent themes

The data presented here shed new light on how lawyers and disputants think and speak about the meaning of their cases as well as their expectations and aims on how to resolve them. The findings, which will be elaborated on throughout the book, support three recurrent themes that organize each chapter, linking them and maintaining a sense of continuity throughout the book. The first theme relates to the parallel worlds of understanding and meaning inhabited by legal actors versus lay disputants, reflecting materially divergent interpretations and functions ascribed to case processing and dispute resolution. As such, the parallel worlds' findings reveal inherent problems with the core workings of the civil justice system. I suspected sharp divides. But how disparate were lawyers' and parties' understandings? How do lawyers think? Are there different modes of reasoning distinctive of the law or is legal reasoning just like reasoning in any other sphere of human activity? I use the term "parallel worlds" on two levels: First, the parallel worlds' thesis is used to support my argument that legal versus lay actors largely have "dissimilar and separate" understandings, expectations, objectives, and experiences during case processing and mediation. At the same time, highlighting unlikely conceptual alignments, the parallel worlds' theme underscores the "similarity" of comprehensions, goals, and behavior of legal actors (irrespective of their allegiances) on the one hand, and plaintiffs and defendants, on the other. This is manifested in the marked discontinuity of interests, language, and agenda of legal versus extralegal actors involved in these cases. Thus, notwithstanding being comprised of members on opposite sides of the dispute continuum, each "new" conceptual group – that is, (1) lawyers on the offense and defense, and (2) disputing plaintiffs and defendants – wants similar things. However, these "new" groups do not want the same things, nor do they speak the same language. Thus, I argue that actors involved in case processing create competing meanings.[11] As such, the parallel worlds' findings challenge dominant understandings of how dispute resolution linked to the law works in

---

10 Versions of chapters two and four have been published in the *Pittsburgh Law Review* (Relis 2007), the *Harvard Negotiation Law Review* (Relis 2007a), and the *Sociology of Law JASL Series* (Relis 2004).
11 My conceptualization of "parallel worlds" differs from the "parallel seminars" described by Carol Leibman in mediating a dispute between Columbia University and some of its students over the inclusion of "ethnic studies" in the curriculum. There, Liebman describes mediation as a process that normally involves a series of "parallel seminars" in which each sides' participants as well as mediators learn and teach others (including mediators) about their realities, goals, interests, and priorities (Liebman 2000, pp. 157, 163–64, 176).

practice and circumscribe the unfettered praise of mediation,[12] opportunities for empowerment, and disputant self-determination.[13] More generally, the parallel worlds' thesis implicitly argues that the concept of law must be broadened to include litigants' extralegal needs and objectives and that conceptions of the meaning of civil justice must evolve.[14]

The second theme, present in most chapters, has been termed lawyers' "reconceptualization." This notion pertains to the role of mediation experience in transforming legal discourse reflecting lawyers' understandings of their cases and their roles within them. Is there evidence of change in how legal actors speak of their roles and their cases subsequent to mediation? How do lawyer-mediators' understandings of cases compare with their lawyer-practitioner counterparts? Finally, the third theme that runs throughout the book relates to the different gendered understandings of disputes and their resolution within both legal actors' groups and disputants' groups. The gender theme represents a further type of parallelism, as the findings provide evidence to suggest that women lawyers and female disputants comprehend and experience the processing of their cases differently from their male counterparts. Feminist legal theory makes the claim that even at its most neutral, there are gender relations that always affect the way law works (Gilligan 1982, pp. 25–29). Indeed, gender provided a crucial lens for comparing visions of disputes and understandings of resolution. But how did gender affect the way conflict and mediation were perceived and experienced? The following three sections elaborate on the findings supporting each of the three themes and discuss their contributions to the literature debates.

Parallel worlds' theme findings

Much of the data support the parallel worlds' theme, highlighting the discontinuity between the legal world of lawyers and the extralegal world of disputants during case processing. First, while attorneys' conduct in case processing is premised on basic understandings of what those who commenced these suits want, chapter two reveals fundamental misconceptions or incomplete understandings by lawyers about plaintiffs' aims – something that goes to the core practice of law and approaches to the resolution of disputes. Overall, legal actors, regardless of whom they represented, understood that plaintiffs sued solely or predominantly for money. Yet, highlighting

---

12 For example, Meschievitz (1991, p. 198), Reeves (1994, p. 17), Brown and Simanowitz (1995, p. 153), Christiansen (1997, p. 72), Dauer and Marcus (1997, p. 199), Polywka (1997, p. 81), Gitchell and Plattner (1999, p. 459), and Saravia (1999, p. 139).
13 Goldberg et al. (1992, pp. 154–55), Baruch Bush and Folger (1994, pp. 2–3, 81), Baruch Bush (1997, pp. 29–30), Kovach (2001, pp. 935, 939, 942–43, 952), and Welsh (2001b, pp. 15–18).
14 This argument draws on Menkel-Meadow's call for a re-examination of the legal and adversarial system's attributes, objectives, and methods utilized in attaining those objectives. She additionally advocates a "cultural change" for legal actors "as human disputes have not only legal implications, but often a host of other concerns e.g. emotional, interpersonal and moral" (Menkel-Meadow 1996b, pp. 5, 7, 42).

the first facet of the parallel worlds' thesis, plaintiffs' discourse rarely correlated with lawyers' understandings of this basic premise. Indeed, notwithstanding lawyers conditioning plaintiffs on "legal system realities," plaintiffs vehemently stressed they sued not for money, but for a whole host of extralegal aims of principle. Yet, these issues remained invisible to most lawyers throughout case processing. Next, in chapter three comparing voluntary with mandatory court-linked mediations, I reveal gross disparities in expectations, attitudes, and intentions between lay disputants and legal actors – often resulting in dissonant situations. Lawyers had low expectations and negative attitudes toward mandatory mediations, while plaintiffs and defendants present at the same mediations expressed the same needs, intentions, positive attitudes, and high expectations for both mandatory and voluntary mediations.

Similarly, the findings in chapter four on defendants' attendance at mediation reveal materially divergent perceptions of the function of mediation as well as different meanings ascribed to the process by lay disputants versus legal actors, each having different needs. For lawyers on the whole, mediation was a vehicle for monetary settlement or case abandonment, where strategy, negotiation, and money talk played out. Yet, far from a forum of tactical strategies, for disputants mediation was a place to treat human needs and preserve human dignity. It was a place for both verbal and nonverbal communication, information sharing, human interchange, and most importantly "feeling better about their situations." These understandings were evident in the discourse of both plaintiffs and defendants, all being in favor of defendants' attendance at mediation, with no mention being made of monetary settlement or the obvious fact that any settlement monies would not come from physicians themselves. However, unbeknownst to most plaintiffs, enraged at defendants' regular mediation absences and often believing that defendants did not want to face them, the findings indicate that lawyers on both sides were regularly agreeing "not to invite" defendants to mediation. To lawyers, defendants' presence was "unnecessary" or "risky" to their tactical agendas for the process. Although the issue of mediation attendance has not been examined in depth in the literature, the present findings on the consistent absences of defendants at mediation support other similar findings for various case types (Meschievitz 1990, p. 17; Metzloff et al. 1997, p. 124; Gatter 2004, pp. 204–6).

Likewise, in chapter five, legal actors' versus lay disputants' descriptions of their mediation aims evince significantly diverse, often conflicting, objectives and agendas – with each group often being unaware of the other's intentions. Moreover, these disparities generally included clients and their own lawyers. Both plaintiffs and defendants focus almost entirely on emotional, psychological, and extralegal objectives for mediation (e.g., obtaining understanding, apology, and acceptance). Yet, these issues were absent from most lawyers' discourse, which was replete with tactics, strategy, and pecuniary aspirations for mediation. Lack of trust in the confidentiality of the process also pervaded the talk of most lawyers, suggesting that this was a material factor circumscribing what legal actors were prepared to do during mediations in terms of addressing disputants' extralegal needs.

A culmination of actors' parallel realities of understanding and meaning occurs in chapter six, which examines perceptions of "what went on" during mediations including participants' favored and disfavored elements. Mediation is seen to be host to the confluence of the conflicting worlds of tactics and strategy versus that of human needs and desires, as evidenced through actors' different and incongruous perceptions of what took place. In contrast to lawyers' highly strategic accounts, disputants depict the same mediations as very personal encounters, providing emotional and psychological descriptions of what went on. Thus, I argue that dual communication – almost antithetical in nature – occurs between legal and extralegal actors during mediation, being transmitted and received on different planes. This results in very different insight obtained from actors within the same cases. Although participants interact together during the process, they perceive things in completely different ways, often not really communicating at all.

For legal actors, regardless of allegiances, mediation is seen to be a key vehicle for direct tactical communication to opponent lawyers and especially to parties for the purpose of highlighting weaknesses in their cases, litigation risks and realities, and/or how certain numbers were reached – overall, to lower disputants' expectations. Mediation also offered opportunities for strategic insight, for example, through assessing how parties would fare as trial witnesses and viewing the internal dynamics between co-litigants as well as between litigants and their lawyers. In sharp contrast, nearly all disputants discussed the psychological importance of being able to express themselves, being heard, and offering extralegal communication resulting in emotional relief. What was disfavored by parties were elements of hierarchy in terms of being surrounded by lawyers at mediations, the dearth of information received, and importantly, what litigants saw through mediation's window into the legal world. Through verbal and nonverbal communication transmitted by legal actors during mediations, litigants perceived many lawyers as "playing a game" or impersonally handling their tragedies. This was despite the vast majority (87%) not recognizing what I term "the red riding hood syndrome" relating to plaintiffs' strong emotional and psychological needs to tell their stories, express themselves, and be heard simultaneously feeding into legal actors' needs to evaluate them tactically. Thus, there were diverse perceptions of lawyers' presence and power, the unequal flow of information, tactical versus extralegal goings-on, nonverbal communication, learning of positive/negative "truths," healing, and disappointments. Consequently, mediation is seen to frequently fail to address parties' extralegal needs, aims, and plans for the process.[15]

---

15 The study potentially reveals the implausibility of Habermas' theory, both descriptively and prescriptively (as it has both components). No speech situation, however ideal, can be free of power dynamics, different agendas, strategic speech, contrasting perspectives, systematic misunderstandings, and so forth, all of which the chapters' findings point out. Habermas' theory privileges those (like philosophers and lawyers) who are capable speakers, not intimidated, willing to be forceful,

A further finding relates to the mediators who stand "in between" legal and lay actors, mediating their different perceptions during the process – as they are meant to do. However, in addition, the findings contribute a new angle to what goes on during mediations. The data indicate that mediators not only mediate "between" sides but also mediate actors' different senses of reality, practices, and representations – those of lawyers who want to take control and equally those of parties who seek relief, satisfaction, catharsis, and so on (Menkel-Meadow 2006).

Chapter seven presents a final facet to the parallel worlds' theme: an analysis of lawyers' and litigants' perceptions of mediators (being retired judges, legal counsel, and non-lawyer-mediators) and the styles they employed. Actors' discourse on why each style was favored illustrates different understandings of what mediation "is" and adds another facet to the parallel worlds' thesis. Notwithstanding legal actors' strong preferences for particular styles or techniques of mediation – most often evaluative/rights-based as opposed to facilitative/interest-based – for most disputants whatever style their mediator used was perceived as "the best." In fact, in comparing evaluative and facilitative mediation experiences, there was little disparity in parties' discourse. This may be because disputants appeared to judge their mediations very differently from how legal actors judge them. Disputants judged their mediations according to the opportunity they had to express themselves and to communicate with opponents and mediators, regardless of the style in which it was conducted. In effect, this meant that at times essentially different processes yielded the same evaluations from disputants. Still, interestingly, pro-facilitative reasoning included all of plaintiffs' articulated desires and objectives for both litigation (*chapter two*) and mediation (*chapter five*) of their cases.

Furthermore, when comparing what legal and lay actors liked about their mediators, they also spoke on two different planes – highlighting gross disparities in how diverse actors within the same cases conceived, perceived, and assessed their mediators. What attorneys found favorable was described almost wholly in terms of the advice and tactical assistance they provided to lawyers. This included the persuasion of opponents and deflation of opponents' expectations as well as those of the lawyers' own clients. Yet, distant from the lenses through which lawyers judged mediators, when disputants described what they liked they spoke largely of mediators' human attributes, including warmth, caring, and protectiveness – rarely mentioning strategic or tactical issues. In fact, for most disputants almost anything mediators did was perceived positively. This was notwithstanding the fact that litigants had virtually no say in choice of either mediator or style, most acquiescing to lawyers' decisions.

---

and more interested in persuasion, than perhaps in true communication that reaches an emotionally satisfying process as well as resolution (email: B. Tamanaha, May 26, 2008, on file with author; Habermas 1981).

Contribution to the literature debates

In examining the "microbehavioral processes" occurring within case processing and mediation (Menkel-Meadow 2002a, p. 950), the parallel worlds' findings both draw on and provide empirical insight to a number of debates within the literature. These include lawyering theory, formal justice versus informalism, why plaintiffs sue, and the dispute transformation debates.

Lawyering theory and the formal versus informal justice debates

The findings contribute to the literature on lawyering theory, answering questions such as, How do attorneys understand what a particular client's "problem" is? What "facts" do lawyers perceive and what "facts" escape them? Does the legal system ignore persons in favor of rules (Noonan 1993, pp. 9–14)? Does it undervalue the human element? Is the law adequately serving clients' needs? Are there serious disparities between the public's and the profession's sense of what constitutes conflict "resolution" (Sherwin 1992a, pp. 9, 42–43, 48, 51)? Providing in-depth examples of how law and legal processes construct meaning, on the one hand, and the inextricability of litigants' legal and extralegal needs and objectives, on the other, the parallel worlds' findings underscore the fact that disputants' requirements and sense of reality are not being adequately translated into the discourse of law. With litigation-linked processes such as mediation regularly resulting in things being offered to parties in ways that do not deal with their needs as they perceive them, the data contribute to the broader debates on whether the goals of lawyers and clients inevitably diverge as well as whether lawyers intensify or moderate legal conflict (Abel 1995, p. 6).

The findings also add to the dearth of empirical knowledge on how lawyers actually negotiate (Menkel-Meadow 1984, p. 762, n. 24) as well as on legal actors' roles in representing disputants during nonadversarial, litigation-linked mediation – a material transformation in the practice of law (Sternlight 1999, p. 275; Kovach 2003, pp. 400, 403–4). Yet, in so doing, the data suggest that it is lawyers' rather than disputants' values that are primarily served within the system. The findings portray lawyers as the primary gatekeepers for conflicts, largely determining what interests are addressed during case processing leading up to and including mediation (Menkel-Meadow 1991, p. 5; 1997a, p. 408; Reich 2002, p. 188). Attorneys' tendencies to take control of the mediation process correlate with various U.S. findings of lawyers' domination of mediation.[16] Additionally, legal actors' disregard of litigants' empowerment and underlying needs during the process, instead offering their own perceptions of litigation and court realities, can be viewed as distorting

---

16 Meschievitz (1990, pp. 17, 135), Metzloff et al. (1997, pp. 119, 123–25), Gordon (1999, pp. 227–28; 2000, p. 383), and Wissler (2002, p. 658).

informalism and mediation's original ideals.[17] As such, the findings question certain widely entertained premises about mediation – for instance, assertions about disputants' levels of process control and the unqualified praise of the communication that occurs during mediations.[18] Hence, far from the view of ADR being part of a communitarian vision of justice and social unity (Morris 1999, p. 272), the data on legal actors' understandings and needs dominating case processing including mediation highlight lawyers' power as focal, with legal actors exercising hegemonic elements of control.[19]

Additionally, there is a paucity of in-depth empirical data on disputants' perceptions of the negotiating elements inherent within case processing, be they within bilateral lawyers' negotiations or mediations (Relis 2002, pp. 174–77). In injecting parties' perceptions into the analysis of what occurs during mediations – including the effects of mediation's transparent window into the reality of legal processes and settlement negotiations – the present research offers insight into how disputants perceive lawyers' negotiations as well as information provided to them during mediations. The findings provide evidence that litigants view negotiations that concentrate on money alone as trivializing issues of importance to them. They also support claims that the predominant focus on monetary issues and settlements can negatively affect perceptions of procedural justice (Welsh 2001a, p. 860), which are instead positively influenced by disputants' perceptions of having "voice," participating and enjoying interpersonal respect during legal processes.[20]

Finally, the parallel worlds' findings overall show the critiques of informalism by Abel, Fiss, and Auerbach to be fully justified (Fiss 1964, pp. 1075–78, 1085, 1089; Abel 1982, pp. 294, 308; Auerbach 1983, pp. 16, 120). Although delivered from very different ideological standpoints, the critiques amount to an endorsement of superior court adjudication (Palmer and Roberts 1998, p. 29). However, the data here add an important rider to the critiques, particularly to the Fiss criticism: We must not lead our critique of informalism to end in glorification of the formal justice system, as that too is shown to be just as defective. Indeed, Menkel-Meadow notes the phenomenon of "litigation romanticism" (Menkel-Meadow 1995a, p. 1173; 1995b, p. 2669), arguing that "litigation is no more likely than alternatives... to produce complete fairness" (Menkel-Meadow 2004, p. 23). The parallel worlds' findings support this view, indicating that during both formal and informal justice processes with all the benefits legal representation can offer[21] litigants are throughout

---

17 Thornton (1989, p. 756), Currie (1998, p. 220), Welsh (2001a, pp. 788–89, 791–92), and Welsh (2004, pp. 137, 139).
18 Reeves (1994, p. 18), Brown and Simanowitz (1995, p. 153), Baruch Bush (1997, p. 17), Dauer and Marcus (1997, pp. 199, 205, 218), and Forehand (1999, pp. 907, 926).
19 This differs from Laura Nader's argument that it is court-sponsored mediation that represents hegemonic elements of control (Nader 2002, p. 141).
20 Thibaut and Walker (1975, 1978), Casper (1978, 1988), Barrett-Howard and Tyler (1986), Lind and Tyler (1988), Tyler (1988; 1997, pp. 887, 889), and Lind et al. (1990, pp. 965–67).
21 For example, protection against opponents' extreme demands and settlement pressure (McEwen et al. 1995, pp. 1320, 1373, 1394), stronger bargaining power, enhancement of settlement chances,

dominated by lawyers and dependent on their expertise and paternalistic constructions of what is best (Rifkin 1984, p. 30; Rack 1999, p. 295). Yet, this is often incongruous with disputants' own understandings and needs during case processing.

Why plaintiffs sue and dispute transformation debates

Adding to the scant and somewhat dated knowledge on litigants' perceptions of their disputes and their motivations for claiming (Vidmar 1984, p. 515; Genn 1999, p. 11), the findings here resuscitate the importance of litigants' "hidden agendas" for litigation and highlight failures by legal actors to deal with the inextricability of disputants' legal and extralegal needs. Yet, stressing the importance, if not the preeminence, of noneconomic factors for litigants in the context of small claims cases, Conley and O'Barr note that "the discontinuity between litigant agendas and the operating assumptions of the system may be a fundamental source of dissatisfaction with the law.... The law should not leave unexamined the assumptions about rational economic goals that permeate the civil justice system.... It is essential to comprehend litigants' hidden agendas for any evaluation or ... procedural reform" (Conley and O'Barr 1988, pp. 182–84, 196–97). Indeed, notwithstanding arguments that the vast majority of cases are predominantly for monetary stakes (Kritzer 1990, pp. 28–34), the findings here correlate with other research into plaintiffs' extralegal litigation aims in different case types[22] and provide additional evidence to suggest that plaintiffs have a whole host of nonfiscal objectives for litigation that are not recognized by many legal actors in their cases.

Thus, the findings support those who have previously urged lawyers to integrate clients' legal and nonlegal interests,[23] as well as others who advocate a general "ethic of care" to be part of lawyers' practices.[24] The data also resonate with the interdisciplinary literature and approach to lawyering of "therapeutic jurisprudence" whose tenets are argued to be akin to the philosophy of ADR (Kovach 2001, p. 971). That literature posits that lawyers' actions should strive to achieve and maintain the psychological or physical well-being of the individual (Stolle et al. 1997, pp. 50–51; Winick 1997, p. 192) and that lawyers should employ a broader social welfare approach in their work to determine what underlying conflicts may be at issue in disputes (Menkel-Meadow 2004, pp. 19–20). As Tyler notes, "Lay individuals desire

---

higher monetary results (Bingham et al. 2002, pp. 342, 372; McDermott and Obar 2004, pp. 77, 102, 105), and protection of clients' legal rights (McEwen et al. 1994, pp. 171–72).
22 For example, community disputes (Merry and Silbey 1984, pp. 153–54, 160) and sexual violence cases (Des Rosiers et al. 1998, pp. 433, 435, 438). Similarly, other studies of medical disputes, though predominantly utilizing questionnaire data, have found similar extralegal litigation aims, with claimants' desires for pecuniary recompense never found to be a predominant litigation motivation.
23 Binder and Price (1977, pp. 22, 185–86), Lehman (1978, pp. 1079–80), Margulies (1990, p. 213), Pepper (1995, pp. 1602–4), Riskin and Westbrook (1997, pp. 86–95), Nolan-Haley (1998, p. 1386), and Mnookin et al. (2000, p. 169).
24 Gilligan (1982, pp. 8, 33), Shalleck (1992, p. 1078), Ellman (1993, p. 2667), Kovach (2001, pp. 966–67), and Kovach (2003, p. 418).

different things from the legal system than they are typically given. What they want reflects a psychological paradigm. Yet, this is fundamentally different from the paradigm of legal decision-making that legal actors are socialized into in law school, and which dictates discussions in the legal field" (Tyler 1997, pp. 872–84).

Linked to this issue, the data additionally inform the literature on dispute transformation, which remains largely unchallenged within legal scholarship (Felstiner et al. 1980–81, pp. 631–32, 634–47, 650–51). I present the dispute transformation phenomenon as a twofold process: First, notwithstanding plaintiffs' dispute descriptions and initial expressed desires, lawyers condition clients on "legal system realities" and persuade them to aim for what they view as legally realistic. Attorneys then reframe litigants' dispute experiences, feelings, and extralegal aims to fit into legally cognizable compartments suitable for processing within the legal system.

Dispute transformation has been found to occur for various case types in different jurisdictions. These include divorce, poverty law, consumer, general injury, small claims, and harassment cases.[25] Thus, the present findings add medical disputes to the list. However, current debates have failed to address two important issues within the phenomenon of dispute transformation: First, as with many aspects of litigants' perspectives, there has been little investigation from plaintiffs' viewpoints into how, if at all, dispute transformation affects their understandings of their cases and what they seek from the justice system, how they perceive what they hear from their lawyers, and whether their objectives change throughout the litigation process. Second, there is little knowledge of defense lawyers' understandings of plaintiffs' aims and of whether dispute transformation plays any part in their comprehensions. This is significant, as attorneys' approaches to their cases and their conduct during litigation and litigation-linked processes such as mediation are premised on their basic understandings of what plaintiffs want. Likewise, for plaintiffs, their motivations to sue and consequent litigation aims have a marked impact on their experiences during litigation and litigation-track mediations.

The data here illustrate that dispute transformation does affect defense lawyers' understandings of opposing plaintiffs' objectives, yet it does little to extinguish plaintiffs' own extralegal litigation aspirations. I show how plaintiffs interpret their lawyers' explanations of the "monetary realities of the legal system." I also provide evidence of some plaintiffs' intermeshing "principles" with pecuniary recompense. Thus, there may be a degree of transformation in plaintiffs' goals, particularly on the surface. However, challenging a central tenet of transformation theory, that a transformed dispute can actually become the dispute (Felstiner et al. 1980–81, p. 650), the findings here (*chapters two, four, five, and six*) demonstrate that plaintiffs' extralegal aims of principle do not dissipate after dispute transformation

---

25 Hosticka (1979, pp. 600–604), Sarat and Felstiner (1986, pp. 116–17), Conley and O'Barr (1990), White (1990, pp. 20–21, 260–61, 269), Alfieri (1991, p. 2111), Cunningham (1992, pp. 1339–57, 1367–85), and Gilkerson (1992, p. 883).

by their lawyers, nor with the passage of time. The *original* meaning of disputes for disputants as well as their extralegal resolution objectives are not dislodged, even at later stages of case processing. Thus, these findings modify one conclusion noted by Felstiner, Abel, and Sarat that "with a significant portion of any dispute existing only in the minds of disputants... transformations both result from and are responsible for... the revision of perceptions about dispute content, process and institutions" (Felstiner et al. 1980–81, pp. 631–32, 651). In terms of the effects on lawyers, the data suggest practical consequences of dispute transformation, something questioned in the literature. Indeed, it has been argued that transformed legal descriptions of conflicts commonly alter the nature of disputes and may hold little meaning for litigants, resulting in remedies that do not deal with their needs as they perceive them (Conley and O'Barr 1990; Hosticka 1979, pp. 600–604). The findings here shed further light on this issue, which has generally been neglected.

Lawyers' reconceptualization theme findings

Notwithstanding the coexisting parallel worlds of legal and lay actors during case processing, the chapters repeatedly provide evidence of mediation experiences resulting in many practicing lawyers reconceptualizing both their cases and their roles within them, with extralegal considerations becoming inherent within lawyers' thinking. Moreover, in looking at the discourse of most practicing attorneys versus that of lawyers who had become mediators, the data indicate that something had changed within lawyer-mediators' understandings or ways of looking at disputes. This finding was strengthened when comparing the discourse of lawyer-mediators with non-lawyer-mediators, where frequently no discernable differences could be found. It was as if in conceiving disputes and their resolution human beings who studied and practiced law entered a "legal world" premised on rules, norms, and strategies. Yet, these same individuals who later studied, practiced, or even simply experienced mediation seemed to gradually return to the "human world" in terms of their conceptions and understandings of "what these disputes were about" and how to resolve them.

I argue that this is a consequence of mediation's extralegal attributes being thrust upon the legal world, resulting in legal actors viewing their cases on a more extralegal, human, or holistic basis. In this way, mediation experience plays a role in transforming legal discourse, representing part of a shift in what lawyers "are," and how they present themselves. It has been argued that the advent of ADR has resulted in a decline in rights discourse within the legal domain and a move toward an emphasis on human needs and interests to instead evaluate conflict and resolution.[26] The reconceptualization findings empirically support this view. In fact, in the present study talk of "rights" was almost wholly absent from respondents' discourse about their cases and their mediations.

26 Roberts (2002, pp. 25–27), Rifkin (1984, p. 27), Silbey and Sarat (1989, pp. 483, 491), Cobb (1997, pp. 413, 436–37), Alberstein (2002, p. 322), Silbey (2002, p. 177), and Hensler (2003, pp. 195–96).

The first hint of lawyers' reconceptualization is seen when lawyers discuss defendants' attendance in chapter four. Despite non-attendance norms, the talk of most lawyers in each camp was peppered with extralegal pro-attendance reasons on why defendant physicians' attendance could be beneficial to disputants. A few lawyers even spoke wholly within an extralegal paradigm. In chapter five, when examining mediation objectives there is further evidence of the legal world undergoing a process of change, notwithstanding the diversity of mediation aims between legal and lay actors. Conventional legal practice appears to be in a process of expansion to increasingly include psychological and emotional extralegal considerations relating to parties. For instance, plaintiffs' lawyers instructed their clients to "tell their stories" for reasons not limited to law and strategy, marking some recognition of the indivisibility of plaintiffs' legal and extralegal needs. Some plaintiff lawyers' own mediation objectives included extralegal elements. There was additionally some evidence of defense lawyers rethinking their cases once having directly heard plaintiffs' extralegal realities at mediation. Indeed, for legal practitioners overall, notwithstanding their experiencing mediation predominantly tactically, there was some evidence that hearing plaintiffs' recount their life situations subsequent to the injuries or tragedies they had endured sensitized lawyers to the human realities of these disputes. New relationships were also formed at mediations between defense counsel and plaintiffs, relationships that were nonexistent prior to the advent of mediation. This may have contributed to the reconceptualization of legal actors on the defense. Finally, in chapter seven, a number of plaintiff lawyers specifically noted mediators' "warmth" and "compassion" toward plaintiffs as attributes that pleased them. Again, these attributes did nothing for the legal issues in their cases. Likewise, the discourse of those lawyers who were in favor of facilitative mediation styles provides further evidence of their gradual move away from conventional legal thought and practice.

Additional support for the reconceptualization theme relates to the differences in how practicing attorneys spoke about the issues as compared with lawyers who had become mediators. For instance, lawyer-mediators' discourse on defendants' attendance in chapter four included far greater extralegal considerations relating to disputants than practicing lawyers. In fact, all spoke with an extralegal focus – a world away from what legal practitioners were saying. Moreover, no differences were found when comparing lawyer-mediators' views on defendants' attendance with those of non-lawyer-mediators, who consisted in part of social workers. Likewise, in chapter six, further evidence of a move away from traditional legal thinking is seen when examining what lawyer-mediators versus lawyer-practitioners viewed as favorable and objectionable within their mediation experiences. Finally, in chapter seven, lawyer-mediators' pro-facilitative and anti-evaluative mediation style preferences evidence yet a further element of their reconceptualization. Those lawyer-mediators who favored facilitative, interest-based styles spoke a completely different language to lawyer-practitioners. These findings highlight the increasing gap in understandings and meanings between lawyers who remain practitioners and those who become mediators, the latter gradually moving to the "extralegal world" in terms of how they view disputes and their resolution. Consequently, I argue that with mediation increasingly becoming the norm within litigation, the parallel legal and extralegal worlds existing during case processing may converge or at least move closer to one another.

Contribution to the ADR debates

The study's "reconceptualization" theme both draws on and adds new empirical insight to the debates on the role of ADR in the transformation of legal thinking and lawyers' practices.[27] There has been a fair amount of discourse in the literature on both sides of the Atlantic about the expansion of ADR slowly transforming and expanding the practice of law, the values inherent within it, and thus the traditional model of the lawyer.[28] As Roberts notes, "Lawyers have conceptualized virtually their entire role in dispute settlement as 'litigation,' using the framework provided by civil procedure as the primary arena for their attempts to settle." Yet, in speaking of lawyers now offering mediation services, Roberts aptly remarks, "The very identity of the lawyer is placed in question." (Roberts 2002, pp. 21, 25–27, 29). Likewise, although some are skeptical of ADR's ability to transform legal actors (Hensler 2003, p. 193), several commentators have speculated that mediation's incorporation into the formal litigation system will materially alter attorneys' representational roles and reduce adversarial behavior (Lande 1997, pp. 841, 879–80) to allow for the necessary nonadversarial (or less adversarial) roles of lawyers involved in mediation (Kovach 2003, pp. 403–4). Although concerned about adversarial co-option of the mediation process, Menkel-Meadow too notes this transformation in positing that growing numbers of U.S. lawyers are looking to new forms of lawyering, some quite alien to the traditional conception of the lawyer's role. However, very little empirical evidence has been available on the issue of lawyers' transformations (Menkel-Meadow 1999, p. 802). In fact, only four studies were found that alluded to this issue peripherally, with very little data provided from actors themselves.[29] Thus, the present findings add important new insight into this developing area.

27 Rifkin (1984, p. 27), Cobb (1997, pp. 413, 436–37), Menkel-Meadow (1999, p. 802), Alberstein (2002, p. 322), Silbey (2002, p. 177), Hensler (2003, pp. 195–96), and Kovach (2003, pp. 403–4).
28 Nolan-Haley (1998, pp. 1372–73), Macfarlane (2001, p. 191), Nolan-Haley (2002, pp. 237, 299), and Roberts (2002, pp. 25–27).
29 In Metzloff et al.'s research into court-ordered medical malpractice mediation in North Carolina, it was found that lawyers were enthusiastic about mediation notwithstanding low success rates. Metzloff et al. explain this by the fact that numerous attorneys felt that mediation provided the potential for a "better" resolution of disputes (Metzloff et al. 1997, p. 142). Likewise, McEwen et al.'s findings on Maine divorce lawyers, although admittedly not definitive, suggest that involvement in mediation may change lawyers' attitudes outside mediation as well, as subsequent to the introduction of mandatory mediation, lawyers perceived their own practices as having become less adversarial (McEwen et al. 1994, pp. 149, 151, 177–79, 181; McEwen 1995, pp. 1367–68). Similarly, in Macfarlane's interviews with Canadian commercial litigators, some lawyers who had participated in at least ten mediations gave markedly greater importance to emotional and psychological dimensions of disputes than those who had not (Macfarlane 2002, pp. 244, 252, 264, 297–99, 320). Finally, the transformation of lawyers who had become mediators is also reminiscent of findings from the San Francisco Community Board mediations, where mediation training and experience were often found to be more transformative for mediators than for disputants (Merry

More generally, the findings here overall inform several other ADR debates. First, the data inject both lay and professional actors' input into the debate on the mandating of mediation (Grillo 1991, pp. 1551, 1581; Nader 2002, p. 141; Wissler 2002, p. 689, n. 227). Grillo argues that mandatory mediation effaces the virtues of mediation and that it disproportionately harms subordinated individuals in society (Grillo 1991, p. 1610). Contra Grillo, others have argued that mandation dangers have been exaggerated and that mandatory mediation is generally of assistance to all disputants (Rosenberg 1991, pp. 467, 492–93; Duryee 1992a, p. 509). In terms of voluntary versus mandatory mediation, the present findings suggest that disparities between types may be exaggerated as no material differences were found in disputants' experiences, mediation aims, or understandings of mediation's purpose (*chapters three to six*). For lawyers, notwithstanding their negative attitudes toward mandatory mediations' early timing, their articulated mediation aims were also the same irrespective of whether mediations were mandatory or voluntary. Likewise, there was a strong common thread running through all actors' discourse on perceptions of "what went on" during mediations regardless of mediation type (*chapters five to seven*). These findings accord with the one survey found comparing lay, legal, and gendered participants' voluntary and mandatory mediation experiences in different U.S. courts involving various dispute types. There too, few differences were found in terms of how mediations were experienced or assessed (Wissler 1997, pp. 565–66, 577–79, 583–85, 595–96, 598, 601). The present research adds to this theme, not only by providing data from another country, but also because it derives from interview data from all actors involved.

Second, the findings on mediation aims (*chapter five*) serve to question writings premised on actors' unqualified faith in mediation's confidentiality (Johnson 1997, p. 48; Gitchell and Plattner 1999, p. 443). Yet, they also add to the dearth of extant knowledge on participants' objectives for the process. In fact, as no studies were found comparing lay and legal actors' mediation aims, the findings here are particularly important in highlighting fundamental disparities in what mediation players aim to achieve. Third, the data on actors' perceptions of "what went on" during mediations inject disputants' perspectives into the analysis in terms of how they perceive information provided to them during mediations – something little spoken of in the literature. The findings also serve to limit the unqualified praise

and Milner 1993). However, the circumstances in those mediations were somewhat different to the ones in the present study, making the present findings in relation to lawyers perhaps even more striking. The San Francisco mediations covered neighborhood disputes, with mediators being non-lawyer volunteers who joined the program largely for their own personal development. Unlike lawyer-mediators in the present study, the mediator volunteers were predominantly female (60%) and under the age of 45 (83%). Moreover, the training and mediations in San Francisco – and thus measurements of mediators' success – focused primarily upon the degree to which party communication was established, feelings were expressed and relationships built, and only secondarily upon the resolution of disputes (Dubow, F. and C. McEwen, 1993, 125, 127, 139, 149–50, 157–59, 163–64).

of the communication that occurs at mediation.[30] With lawyers being seen to have so much control over what transpires, the findings correlate with various U.S. studies indicating lawyers' domination of mediations.[31] As such, assertions about disputants' levels of process control (Baruch Bush 1997, p. 17) are questioned. The findings also somewhat support Menkel-Meadow's argument that U.S. lawyers as advocates try to manipulate mediation processes to achieve conventional party maximization goals (Menkel-Meadow 1991, p. 5; 1997a, p. 408). Lawyers' tendency to take control, disregarding litigants' empowerment and underlying needs (Currie 1998, p. 220) and instead offering their own perceptions of litigation and court realities (Welsh 2004b, pp. 137, 139), can be viewed as distorting informalism (Thornton 1989, p. 756) and mediation's original ideals (Welsh 2001a, pp. 788–89, 791–92).

Additionally, voluminous procedural justice studies have confirmed that for disputants, assessments of legal procedures' fairness are at least as important as views on substantive issues or outcomes.[32] However, a paucity of in-depth empirical data exist on disputants' perceptions of the negotiating elements inherent within dispute processing, be it bilateral lawyers' negotiations or mediations (Relis 2002, pp. 174–77). Therefore, the findings on the effects of mediation's transparency for litigants, allowing more visible settlement procedures, are particularly important to suggest in adding to the knowledge in this area. The current findings provide evidence to suggest that litigants view negotiations that concentrate on money alone as trivializing issues of importance to them. They also support claims that the focus on monetary settlements can negatively affect perceptions of procedural justice (Welsh 2001a, p. 860).

Fourth, in terms of views on mediators, legal actors' perceptions of mediators have been studied to some extent, overall correlating with the findings here. For instance, Macfarlane's study based on interviews with commercial litigators in Ottawa and Toronto, Canada, likewise found preferences for evaluative mediators to be strong, particularly due to the impact on disputants of hearing evaluative opinions (Macfarlane 2002, p. 285). Other U.S. commentators have similarly noted legal actors' general preferences for lawyer-mediators, particularly those with substantive expertise to value cases and lower disputant expectations.[33] However, little is known about those mediator attributes that are important to litigants. Indeed, the only study that was found related to non-litigated U.S. school mediations. Correlating with the findings in the present research, it was similarly found that

---

30 Reeves (1994, p. 18), Brown and Simanowitz (1995, p. 153), Dauer and Marcus (1997, pp. 199, 205, 218), and Forehand (1999, pp. 907, 926).
31 Meschievitz (1990, pp. 17, 135), Metzloff et al. (1997, pp. 119, 123–25), Gordon (1999, pp. 227–28; 2000, p. 383), and Wissler (2002, p. 658).
32 For example, Thibaut and Walker (1975, 1978), Casper (1978, 1988), Barrett-Howard and Tyler (1986), Lind and Tyler (1988), and Tyler (1988).
33 Gordon (1999, p. 228), McAdoo (2002, pp. 429–30), McAdoo and Hinshaw (2002, p. 524), and Welsh (2004, p. 137).

disputants particularly viewed as important mediators' understanding and sensitivity as part of other procedural fairness criteria (Welsh 2004a, pp. 595, 619). Thus, the parallel worlds' findings are useful in providing a snapshot of the wider picture, juxtaposing legal actors' views opposite those of disputants, thereby highlighting the discontinuity of preferences.

Finally, the mediation style findings speak to the debate on facilitative (Stulberg 1997, p. 985; Kovach and Love 1998, p. 109, n. 4) versus evaluative mediation styles (Weckstein 1997, p. 502), including analyses of distinctions between them (Stempel 2000a, p. 371; 2000b, p. 247). The findings here are particularly useful as the evaluative–facilitative debate has lacked empirical evidence (McDermott and Obar 2004, p. 78), with few studies examining disputants' views.[34] Hence, by examining the issues from actors' perspectives the present study's approach differs from other literature on this topic, extending the limits of previous studies and offering an innovative way at looking at the issues by comparing and contrasting actors' views.

Gender theme findings

Gender was found to play an important role within the various facets of case processing leading up to and including mediation. The data suggest that gender influences the way actors understood and experience conflict and its resolution. The gender theme has two strands: female legal actors' extralegal sensitivity and female disputant disempowerment.

In terms of legal actors, female attorneys' discourse in virtually all chapters generally evinced greater sensitivity than males to disputants' extralegal needs within the diverse elements of mediation and related litigation. This was particularly evident in female defense lawyers' discussions of plaintiffs' litigation aims, needs, and realities (*chapter two*). Female attorneys also generally spoke of greater extralegal considerations than male lawyers when deciding whether defendants should attend mediation (*chapter four*), in their articulated mediation aims and in their awareness of plaintiffs' extralegal, nonmonetary mediation aspirations (*chapter five*). This suggests greater extralegal meaning ascribed to mediation as a process, with female professionals more likely to view mediation not simply as a tactical forum, but also as one to resolve extralegal issues. Additionally, female versus male

---

34 (Waldman 1998, p. 169; Levin 2001, p. 295, n. 143). If the ambit were to be more specific looking solely at medical disputes, the research is significant as in much of the literature worldwide medmal mediation is vehemently debated by proponents and opponents, focusing on advantages and disadvantages but supported by critically little in-depth empirical evidence (Currie 1998, pp. 219–20; Forehand 1999, pp. 921–22) – particularly from the perspectives of those who are by far the most affected by these mediations: the plaintiffs and defendant physicians involved. All too often their views are considered only superficially. Indeed, the few empirical studies with any kind of plaintiff or defendant input predominantly discuss whether parties were "satisfied" with mediation, often relating to time and costs savings. Yet, as Abel notes, "evidence that grievants are 'satisfied' hardly proves they are benefited by informal processes, as when satisfaction is measured disputants' expectations are already deflated and their wishes so shaped that any outcome will be satisfactory" (Abel 1982, pp. 298–99).

defense lawyers provided very different visions of what occurred at mediations, suggesting that females experience mediation more "extralegally" than males, who described what transpired more tactically. Moreover, plaintiffs more often perceived female defense lawyers more positively than males, remarking on their compassion and understanding (*chapter six*). There was also some evidence of female defendants themselves deriving greater psychological benefit from mediation than male defendants, as well as being better equipped to address plaintiffs' psychological needs during mediations (*chapter four*).

The second strand of the gender findings relates to disputants, where the potential for female plaintiff disempowerment could be discerned in a number of respects: First, female plaintiffs regularly exhibited unease in discussing the compensatory element within their claims, something absent from male plaintiffs' discourse (*chapter two*). Females were also initially less inclined than males to face perceived wrongdoers at mediation, more often discussing feelings of emotional difficulty than their male counterparts (*chapter four*). Yet, regardless of mediation results, defendants' presence was something found to be of great psychological benefit to all disputants, including females, most of whom recanted later during interviews acknowledging they had missed out on an important opportunity for closure. Certainly, without defendants present, plaintiffs' articulated litigation and mediation aims could not be fully realized. It was further found that female disputants sought greater emotional recompense at mediation than males, yet suffered greater emotional hardship undergoing mediation. Women plaintiffs were more concerned than males as to how their aims and reactions at mediation would be perceived by others (*chapters four and five*), with evidence of some females partaking or speaking less than male plaintiffs during the process (*chapter six*). In chapter six, an examination of actors' descriptions of mediation experiences suggests that conflict resolution is also perceived and experienced differently by female versus male plaintiffs. This highlights further potential vulnerabilities for females as they tended to be more influenced than males by information conveyed by mediators and opponents' lawyers during mediation (including nonverbal communication). Yet at the same time females were both less aware than males of mediation's tactical goings-on and were far more accepting of whatever transpired during mediations. Equally, females tended to be more accepting and less critical of mediators' behavior, whereas male plaintiffs tended to be less accepting and more critical of mediators.

Contribution to the gender debates

By examining case processing leading up to and including mediation through the discourse of participating actors, the gender findings inform various strands of the extant literature. On a general level, only limited empirical data exist on how males and females actually practice law and whether females contribute to an emphasis on needs versus rights (Menkel-Meadow 1994a, pp. 89, 91, 95). Moreover, no systematic empirical studies have examined gender-based differences in lawyers and parties (Stempel 2003, p. 312). Of course, disparities within gender groups cannot be ignored, nor can the fact that the influence of gender in negotiation and mediation settings varies in diverse situations and may interact differently with power and status as well as diverse personal and demographic attributes. Yet, it is generally accepted that gender may shape the processing of cases that ultimately mediate.[35] Thus, the gender findings inform the conflicting and often inconclusive research and debates in the critical feminist literature, in general, and in conflict resolution and negotiation theory, in particular, on whether males and females have different understandings, objectives, perceptions, and behavior in litigation and litigation-linked contexts including mediation.[36]

In relation to mediation in particular, notwithstanding the fact that "disputing may be influenced by the...gender of those involved" and that "gender-based differences may affect the dynamics of mediation sessions" (Goldberg et al. 1992, p. 139), there is a dearth of empirical knowledge on female versus male legal actors in actual mediation settings.[37] Research indicates that gender may have a significant impact on negotiation and mediation processes.[38] Yet, most of the empirical work to date from various disciplines does not actually study negotiations relating to ongoing litigation, as is the case here.[39] Scholars have speculated that women may be temperamentally better suited to mediation than males as they may be more sensitive to disputants' relationships and relational facets of disputes (Kolb 2000, p. 348; Stempel 2003, pp. 310–11; Subrin 2003, pp. 207–8). Drawing on both Gilligan's and Tannen's research, Menkel-Meadow posits that females' different moral reasoning to males, tending to be motivated by an ethic of care rather than a more hierarchical, independent, rights-based stance, may result in women lawyers having a greater natural inclination for mediation and a greater sense of empathy with the opposing side. Additionally, women who use emotional language and articulate needs with ease might actually be better at "mediation talk" than some men.[40] The present findings tend to support these views as well as those of others who suggest that female attorneys have different perspectives to males in terms of interpreting conflicts differently. Therefore, in attempting to resolve disputes, in

---

35 Kolb and Coolidge (1988, pp. 1, 4), Watson (1994, pp. 191, 203, 205–6), Craver and Barnes (1999, pp. 300–301, 312), Kolb (2000, p. 350), Kolb and Williams (2000, pp. 11, 20–21, 31), Menkel-Meadow (2000a, pp. 357–60, 362–65; 2001, pp. 261, 271), and Evans (2001, pp. 157, 166).
36 Kolb and Coolidge (1988, pp. 10, 18–19), Stamato (1992, pp. 378, 380), Menkel-Meadow (2000a, pp. 358, 360–61, 364), and Kolb (2003, pp. 101–2).
37 Menkel-Meadow (1997b, p. 1427), Stempel (2003, pp. 310–11), Subrin (2003, pp. 207–8), and Klein (2005, p. 792).
38 Stamato (1992, p. 377), Walters et al. (1998, p. 1), Stuhlmacher and Walters (1999, pp. 653, 673), Kolb (2000, p. 348), Evans (2001, pp. 166, 180), Riley and McGinn (2002, p. 7), and Babcock and Laschever (2003, pp. 62–64, 86, 102–4, 106–7, 120). Drawing on empirical research, Kolb and Coolidge similarly argue that there are material differences in how males and females negotiate and the techniques they employ in attempting to reach agreements (Kolb and Coolidge 1988, pp. 1–2, 6).
39 Kolb and Coolidge (1988, pp. 2, 10–11, 18–19), Menkel-Meadow (2000a, pp. 358, 360–61, 364), and Kolb (2003, pp. 101–2).
40 Gilligan (1982, pp. 25–29, 62–63, 173), Tannen (1990, pp. 13, 38, 42, 77), and Menkel-Meadow (1997b, p. 1427; 1985, pp. 43, 52–53).

addition to the legal substance of cases females tend to focus more on the context and individuals involved, generally being more empathetic to parties.[41] This is notwithstanding the fact that this often conflicts with their professional education and adversarial training.[42]

In terms of the findings on female plaintiffs, the data inform and resuscitate the significance of the discourse on the values and limits of the feminist critiques of mediation, which have generally been more concerned with broader structural features. There has been much theoretical debate on the issue of female disputant disempowerment in informal justice processes.[43] Grillo's work has been among the most cited in this regard. Although accepting that formal processes are no better for women, Grillo and others argue that mediation, which stresses compromise over rights, is dangerous for women or those who operate in the female mode as their relational sense to others may result in them being more acquiescing, resulting in agreements that do not serve their needs. Yet, this is masked by informal processes.[44] However, few empirical studies have tested whether females are actually disadvantaged at mediation or whether gender differences hinder women's abilities to mediate successfully (Brinig 1995, p. 33; LaFree and Rack 1996, p. 769). In injecting actors' meanings and understandings into the debate, the present findings support the view that women do not perceive they are disadvantaged (Roberts 1997, p. 157). Yet they also tend to suggest that gender differences may hinder some females' abilities to mediate, as well as the potential for female disadvantage during mediation without adequate legal or other representation.

Moreover, parties' discourse offers a more nuanced understanding of the opportunities provided by mediation as compared with formal adversarial processes in terms of allowing all disputants to tell their stories. In finding that females tended to speak and advocate their positions less than males, the data question unqualified claims that mediation environments accord with women's strengths, empowering them and allowing them to speak on their own terms (McCabe 2001, pp. 459–60, 471). Similar results were found in divorce mediation research (Pearson and Thoennes 1988, pp. 440–41, 449). The findings likewise correlate with research suggesting that females tend to speak and advocate their positions less than males in group settings including negotiation contexts, which may be perceived as "foreign"

---

41 Menkel-Meadow (1985, pp. 39, 43, 46, 49; 1989, pp. 312–13; 1994, p. 75), Kolb and Coolidge (1988, pp. 7, 11), Hill (1990, p. 342), Maslow Cohen (1990, p. 664), Kolb (2000, p. 348), Neumann (2000, pp. 353–57), McCabe (2001, p. 459), and Maute (2002, p. 161). It should be noted, however, that as the research did not examine mediation outcomes or attorneys' negotiating skills, the present findings make no comment on the negotiating acumen of female lawyers.
42 Menkel-Meadow (1987, p. 45; 1994a, p. 639), Stempel (2003, pp. 310–11), and Klein (2005, pp. 772, 777, 792).
43 Rifkin (1984, p. 22), Delgado et al. (1985, pp. 1360–61), Rosenberg (1991, pp. 492–93), Nader (1993, p. 4), Brinig (1995, p. 4), Cobb (1997, p. 397), Palmer and Roberts (1998, p. 139), Rack (1999, pp. 217, 224), and McCabe (2001, pp. 478, 481).
44 Gilligan (1982, pp. 62–63), Grillo (1991, pp. 1549–51, 1561–62, 1583–86, 1602–4, 1610), Bryan (1992, p. 523), Menkel-Meadow (1997b, p. 1420; 2000, p. 13), and McCabe (2001, p. 476).

by many women, making them feel uncomfortable and affecting their "sense of place" (Kolb and Coolidge 1988, pp. 6–8, 10).

Consequently, in utilizing actors' discourse as the primary source of data, the gender findings highlight both female attorneys' strengths and the potential vulnerabilities of female plaintiffs during case processing. In this way, the findings offer insight into the paradox noted by Menkel-Meadow that females are claimed to be disempowered in negotiations and mediations while at the same time are said to be better than men at communicating, expressing their feelings, and collaborative problem solving (Menkel-Meadow 1995c, p. 234; 2000a, p. 365). Others too have commented on this issue (Kolb and Coolidge 1988, p. 2). The data here show both assertions to be correct, with the former relating to female plaintiffs and the latter relating to female lawyers.

1.3 Methodology

The research methodology is based predominantly on a qualitative paradigm, using a multiple case study design. Yet, the work is multidimensional as the primary data derive from 131 semi-structured depth interviews, questionnaires, and observation files of plaintiffs, defendants, lawyers, and mediators involved in 64 mediations of the same or similar medical injury disputes, frequently involving fatalities or serious injuries (18 voluntary, 24 mandatory, 18 College, and 4 where the venue is unclear). Interviews were undertaken and questionnaires administered as soon as possible after each mediation, with all topic guides covering the same issues for all actors.[45] Although the nature of the sample precluded the possibility of meaningful regression or multivariate analysis, a small amount of quantitative analysis was also undertaken. Descriptive statistics were utilized to assess percentages and proportions of particular responses and to evaluate, as far as the data permitted, the strength of any associations between certain variables such as individuals' views/perceptions and their genders or actor positions.

Specifically, the dataset includes seventeen plaintiff interviews, thirteen defendant physician interviews (one physician discussed two separate mediations – one voluntary and one mandatory), and twenty-seven plaintiff lawyer case interviews. The plaintiff lawyer case interviews comprise views of seven general practitioners and eleven specialist medical lawyers, being those who worked on ten or more medical cases per annum and among the top specialist lawyers in the region (nine discussed more than one mediation). Additionally, there are seventeen defense physician lawyer case interviews with views from eight physician lawyers (four discussed more than one mediation), twenty-three defense hospital lawyer case interviews comprising views of seven hospital lawyers (five discussed more than

---

45 Observation data were used solely to support or contradict interview and questionnaire data due to the small number of directly observed mediations (seven) as a result of access difficulties (Bales, R. 1951, 1–29), (Fassnacht, G, 1982).

Table 1. *Breakdown of dataset (interview/questionnaire) files*

Plaintiffs	17
Defendant physicians	13
Plaintiff lawyers	27
Defense physician lawyers	17
Defense hospital lawyers	23
Mediators	29

one mediation), two hospital representative/insurer interviews, twenty-nine mediator case interviews with views from seventeen mediators, ten being lawyers and seven being non-lawyers (seven discussed more than one mediation), and three interviews with program administrators. All physician lawyers and hospital lawyers in the dataset were specialist lawyers; thus, this is not specifically noted throughout the chapters. A number of lawyers and mediators provided data on more than one case as these individuals were repeatedly listed on the court and mediation institutions' files as acting in the various medical disputes. Nonetheless, I obtained a wide range of exposure to different lawyers, parties, and mediators. Accordingly, I am not aware of any bias resulting from the cases included in the study. As views differed for different cases, all charts (apart from those in *chapter four*) are based on the number of cases rather than the number of individuals interviewed. Table 1 sets out the breakdown of dataset files collected.

Analysis of participants' discourse was facilitated by the ATLAS.ti qualitative analysis computer program, enabling grounded theory. To enhance the internal validity and reliability of the data, all interviews were recorded, with narrative descriptions of interview quality, nonverbal issues, and impressions of respondents noted (Patton 1990, pp. 352–53). In cases that comprised two or more plaintiffs, each was interviewed separately. Additionally, the research was conducted over three sites and triangulation of methods (interviews, questionnaires, and observations) was undertaken (Flick 1992, pp. 175–76).[46]

---

46 It is widely accepted that combining data sources acts as a check on the accuracy and reliability of information and findings. Additionally, adding different perspectives assists in the interpretation of results. Although, inevitably, certain disparities existed between the three mediation venues, one must bear in mind the distinction that exists between what may be called "dynamics" of mediation as a process as compared with specific aspects of different types of mediation, for example, legal outcomes. Thus, certain matters are present in any mediation, transcending any differences between venues. Furthermore, the aim of the research was not to evaluate a mediation system per se. The study's focus is on actors' views about the dynamics of case processing and mediation. This relates to all those involved in any mediation, regardless of institutional framework. Moreover, from the human perspective of the parties involved all issues were the same in that all disputes related to conflicts between patients (or their relatives) and physicians/health care providers, someone was injured, breach of trust was involved, redress was sought, and so on.

As to external validity, sampling was done on the basis of natural groupings representing social segmentation. This method is widely employed in qualitative research and has been utilized extensively in similar projects (Metzloff et al. 1997; Gaskell and Bauer 2000; Mulcahy et al. 2000). As is common in qualitative legal research, the sample size is relatively small and it was not possible to obtain a random probability sample for this type of study, limiting the generalizations that can be made from the findings across populations (Metzloff et al. 1997, p. 114). Nevertheless, as people in natural groups share some aspects of identity, a common past experience, or a common project or purpose (plaintiffs, defendant physicians, lawyers for each group, or mediators), in researching the few one can generalize thematic conclusions to others who share these common identities (Gaskell and Bauer 2000). Moreover, by systematically approaching all litigation-linked medical mediations occurring in the research sites during the Fieldwork Period, as well as all defending physicians that had undergone the College's traditional mediation program, a form of census was conducted.[47] The number of individuals approached who consented to partake in the research was over 70%, a response rate considered reasonable in terms of generalizing to outside populations.

Of course, there are inherent risks in extrapolating without qualification from one location to another. However, in view of the consistency of responses and in support of what the findings can say to general legal and mediation practices, although I looked at particular respondents in particular institutions, there is no a priori reason to think that these findings would be different from other cases in other culturally similar jurisdictions. Thus, this research, even if viewed as exploratory and descriptive, should speak to a number of issues raised by the phenomena of case processing and mediation, as well as by the broader theoretical literature on formal and informal justice.

Respondent demographics

In qualitative research, it is not entirely clear that age, sex, education, and so on are relevant. This is why it is often argued that it is best to do segmentation on the basis of natural groups (Gaskell and Bauer 2000). However, for completeness, Tables 2 and 3 delineate age and gender distributions, education levels, and prior mediation experience details of respondents. It should be noted that although the sample comprises a total of thirty females and fifty males, as some of the lawyers and mediators provided information relating to a number of mediations, the dataset consists of data relating to fifty mediation experiences of women and sixty-five mediation experiences of men.

---

47 The three fieldwork sites constituted the core of all medical mediations with legal or possible legal or disciplinary implications, occurring in the Toronto region. The ADR Chambers and the court office (from their "Sustain" database) provided me with weekly updates on impending medical mediations and participants.

Table 2. *Respondents' genders and ages*

Respondents	Gender Males	Gender Females	Age (years) ≤29	30–39	40–49	50–59	60+
Plaintiffs	6	11	2	4	5	4	2
Physicians	10	2	0	1	2	8	1
Plaintiff lawyers	15	2	0	4	11	2	0
Physician lawyers	6	2	0	2	3	3	0
Hospital lawyers	3	6	3	0	4	0	0
Mediators	10 (7 lawyers; 3 non-lawyers)	7 (3 lawyers; 4 non-lawyers)	0	1	6	6	4
Totals	50	30	5	12	31	23	7

Table 3. *Disputants' education and previous mediation experience*

Disputants	Up to secondary school	Secondary school	College	University	Higher level university	Prior mediation experience General	Medical
Plaintiffs	2	3	5	6	1	1	0
Physicians					12	1	4

With regard to prior mediation experience of any kind, only one of the seventeen plaintiffs had general mediation experience, though relating to commercial disputes. Of the twelve physicians, the majority had no prior mediation experience: four had medical mediation experience and one had other mediation experience.

Table 4 displays the levels of lawyers' prior experience in medical dispute mediations. As mediation was common in the jurisdiction and virtually all lawyers had experience in mediation generally, lawyers were asked solely about their experiences in medical dispute mediation. Of the twenty-seven lawyers who provided this information, the majority (74%) had prior experience in at least five medical mediations.

Research sites

The mediations studied include three institutional frameworks: voluntary (ADR Chambers), court-linked mandatory (Mandatory Mediation Program, "MMP"), and those where no financial recompense was sought, though possible precursors

Table 4. *Lawyers' medical mediation experience (not mediation experience generally)*

Lawyers	Medical mediation experience				
	First	2–4	5–9	10–19	20+
Plaintiff lawyers	3	3	2	5	0
Physician lawyers	0	1	0	2	3
Hospital lawyers	0	0	1	4	3
Totals	3	4	3	11	6

to litigation (College of Physicians and Surgeons).[48] Their institutional differences allowed for a broad vision of the mediations occurring during the Fieldwork Period.[49] The ADR Chambers was the largest private voluntary mediation provider in Canada, with sites in Toronto, Vancouver, Quebec, Calgary, and New Brunswick as well as in Europe, Asia, and the Caribbean. The mediators at ADR Chambers, Toronto, included senior counsel as well as sixteen retired Supreme Court and Ontario Court of Appeal judges (ADR-Chambers 1998a, pp. 1, 3; Wheatley, Interview, October 16, 1998). ADR Chambers mediations occurred only when lawyers wanted to mediate, being generally late in the litigation process after discoveries. (All cases were already on trial lists.) The mediations at ADR Chambers usually lasted up to one day and cost Can$3,000 on average (ADR-Chambers 1998b, pp. 1, 3; Lees 1998, pp. 23, 25, 28).

Court-linked mediations under the Ontario "MMP" were similar to many U.S. court–connected programs. In an effort to reform the civil justice system, the MMP was designed to get cases moving more swiftly and efficiently, simultaneously helping litigating parties reduce high costs and delay in litigation and promoting early settlements before cases reached trial (Charendoff, Interview, May 11, 1999) (Harnick 1997, pp. 3, 5; Cameron 1999; Ontario Ministry of the Attorney General 1999, p. 1). The MMP was the result of Rule 24.1 of the Ontario Rules of Civil Procedure, implemented on January 4, 1999 (Macleod et al. 1998, pp. 389–91, 393).

---

48 Having been significantly affected by the use of mediation at the time of the research, Toronto, Ontario, was considered an exemplary "test case" for the analysis. The popularity and growth of ADR had been exponential in Canada, with a substantial number of the larger law firms creating ADR departments in response to market forces (Crawford 1996, p. 8; Lees 1998, pp. 25–26). Mediation in its various forms was the most thriving ADR technique, being utilized in most kinds of disputes. Indeed, in 1996 the Law Society of Upper Canada, which governs Ontario, amended Rule 10 of the Rules of Professional Conduct, requiring lawyers to consider ADR's suitability for every case and to tell clients about ADR possibilities (Law Society 1996, p. 35; Pepper 1996, p. 2).

49 Stringent confidentiality protections in legal practice and mediation necessitated obtaining consent from each participant involved in each dispute on a case-by-case basis (plaintiffs, plaintiff lawyers, physicians, physician lawyers, hospital lawyers, hospital representatives, and insurers). Having obtained consent from virtually all actors in a case, if only one individual objected to partaking in the research, interviews with willing participants could not be included in the study. Unfortunately, this was not a rare occurrence. Thus, the difficulties inherent in obtaining access to these cases and their mediation participants cannot be overstated.

The mandatory court-linked mediations occurred in a variety of locations, predominantly in lawyers' offices. Although adjournments were not uncommon, mandatory mediations generally had to occur within ninety days after the first defense had been filed, unless the court ordered otherwise (Ont. R. Civ. P., January 24, 2009). Therefore, mediations generally occurred prior to discoveries, as opposed to afterward as in many U.S. states (Macfarlane 2002, pp. 244–45). Parties could choose a non-roster mediator (with court leave) or one from the court's roster. Court roster mediators consisted of private-sector lawyers (65%) or non-lawyers (35%) chosen on the basis of educational background, experience and training, familiarity with the civil justice system, and references (Charendoff, Interview, December 16, 1999). If parties failed to agree on a mediator, the local mediation coordinator appointed one. Mediators on the court roster were bound by the Canadian Bar Association – Ontario Model Code of Conduct (Ontario Ministry of the Attorney General 1999, p. 3). The "user-pays" fee for court-roster mediators was $300.00 per party for a three-hour mediation, which could be extended. Non-roster mediators' fees were not regulated. Fees could be waived or reduced where disputants held legal aid certificates or met the Ministry of the Attorney General's financial eligibility test (Dispute-Resolution 1999, p. 1). Disputes that did not settle at mandatory mediation continued down normal litigation routes (Ministry-of-the-Attorney-General 1999; Ontario Ministry of the Attorney General 1999).

Finally, as actors' perspectives and understandings of the mediation process and its dynamics were the focal issues in the research and due to difficulties in accessing defendant physicians through their representing law firms, data were also collected (predominantly from physicians) from the College of Physicians and Surgeons mediations – the self-regulating body of the medical profession. Of the thirteen defendant physician interviews, nine related to College mediation experiences. Subsequent to these mediations, complainants either dropped their cases or filed lawsuits (CPSO 1999a, p. 2). Although unable to order financial compensation, College mediations were similar to litigation-track mediations in many respects: College mediations were viewed by many complainants as precursors to litigation, indicating similar mindsets to litigating plaintiffs. Likewise, physicians at these mediations did not know whether complainants would take further legal action. Thus, defending physicians underwent the same experiences in that they were subject to a complaint with legal repercussions or the threat of legal or other serious professional and personal repercussions. Complaints could remain on physicians' records throughout their careers, affecting their future work opportunities and forcing some to relocate. Attendance was pseudo-mandatory in that physicians opting not to attend had their disputes decided in a discipline committee hearing, likened by some to a trial. Physicians predominantly attended with lawyers, and complainants also generally had legal advice. Some of the mediators were lawyers, with mediations sometimes conducted in lawyers' offices. Finally, a number of the non-lawyer-mediators also mediated in litigation-track mediations (CPSO 1999b).

The next chapter commences the exploration into actors' perspectives by examining a key contextual issue affecting all participants' experiences throughout case processing and mediation: understandings of why plaintiffs sued and what precisely they sought from the civil justice system, that is, understandings of "what these cases were about." Throughout the book, words that have been changed or added for clarity or to protect anonymity are printed in italics.

CHAPTER TWO

Great misconceptions or disparate perceptions of plaintiffs' litigation aims?

This chapter explores and attempts to make sense of an issue fundamental to litigation in general as well as mediation in particular: What do plaintiffs want? Why plaintiffs sue, and their consequent litigation aims should have a marked impact on their objectives and experiences in litigation and litigation-linked mediations.[1] Likewise, as a precursor to evaluating all actors' mediation experiences one must first comprehend others' perceptions of claimants' aims, as attorneys' objectives, approaches to their cases and conduct throughout litigation, and litigation-linked mediation are affected by their basic understandings of what those who commenced these suits want; that is, what these cases were about. Moreover, understanding plaintiffs' aims is particularly important if civil justice evaluations or reforms are to be responsive to their needs. Thus, in this chapter I examine how all litigation players viewed plaintiffs' objectives as well as claimants' own discourse on what they wished to achieve.

Little is known about what litigants really want from the civil justice system and what they aim to achieve. Consequently, we have little knowledge of whether litigants' real objectives are met by the realities of civil litigation (Genn 1999, p. 11) including litigation-linked processes such as mediation. In adding to the scant body of detailed data available on litigants' dispute perceptions and their motivations for claiming, this chapter offers new insight into the area of litigants' noneconomic goals for litigation.[2] Conley and O'Barr's ethnographic research deriving from small claims litigant interviews and trial observations in three U.S. states provides extensive linguistic evidence of the significance of litigants' hidden extralegal, noneconomic agendas. Stressing the "importance, if not the pre-eminence of

---

1 Psychological aspects of legal disputes are curiously under-researched (Lacey 2002). Yet, procedural justice studies and ethnographic legal research suggest that the manner in which litigation processes are subjectively perceived is affected by litigants' expectations, which are linked to their aims (O'Barr and Conley 1988, p. 137; Tyler et al. 1989, p. 629).
2 Vidmar (1984, p. 515), Vincent et al. (1994, pp. 1609–13), Genn (1995, p. 11), and (Guthrie 2001, pp. 165–166). The data here shed light on how lawyers and disputants think and speak about the meaning of cases. They also represent talk about motives, which I hope will be regarded as revealing and useful. I do not claim that this answers the ultimate psychological question of why people do things. This is one of several windows on motivations, adding to the scant depth research on the needs of plaintiffs and why they sue.

non-economic factors for litigants," they conclude, "the discontinuity between litigant agendas and the operating assumptions of the system may be a fundamental source of dissatisfaction with the law.... The law should not leave unexamined the assumptions about rational economic goals that permeate the civil justice system.... It is essential to comprehend litigants' hidden agendas for any evaluation or ... procedural reform" (Conley and O'Barr 1988, pp. 181, 182–84, 196–97).

In juxtaposing the views of all sides within the same or similar cases, this chapter presents a picture of discontinuity, providing disconcerting evidence of the surprising degree to which disparate perceptions of plaintiffs' litigation aims exist as between plaintiffs and attorneys in their cases – at times even between lawyers and their own clients on the elemental issue of what these cases were about. Irrespective of allegiances, the bulk of lawyers understand that plaintiffs sue solely or predominantly for money. Even many plaintiff lawyers, who are more aware of their clients' extralegal aspirations, swiftly translate these objectives into finance alone, as "that is all the legal system can provide." Yet, concurrently, I show how notwithstanding any needs or desires for pecuniary recompense, virtually all plaintiffs vehemently insist, "It is not about the money!" Instead, their explanations of why they sued and what they were seeking from the legal system are thickly composed of extralegal aims of principle, regardless of whether their cases had been litigating for three months or five years.[3] Yet, plaintiffs' objectives of obtaining admissions of fault, acknowledgments of harm, retribution for defendant conduct, prevention of reoccurrences, answers, and apologies remain invisible to most lawyers throughout the duration of litigation and mediation.[4]

In shedding light on how lawyers and disputants speak about the meaning of cases and their expectations and aims on how to resolve them, the data inform the literature on lawyering theory, answering questions such as "how do attorneys understand what a particular client's problem is?" and "what 'facts' do attorneys perceive versus those that escape them? Are there serious disparities between the public's and the profession's sense of what constitutes conflict 'resolution'? Is the law adequately serving clients' needs?" (Sherwin 1992a, pp. 42–43, 48, 51). The chapter's findings additionally inform the literature on dispute transformation (Felstiner et al.

---

3 I have termed nonmonetary objectives "extralegal" as only monetary damages are discussed within legal rules and the traditional world of legal practice. Some of the literature on legal policy, victims' rights, mediation, and legal consciousness refers to a number of nonmonetary litigation aims I have termed "extralegal" as "legal," for example, plaintiffs' desires to obtain acknowledgment of error (Engel 1984; Ewick and Silbey 1998). However, I have used this term to highlight an important recurrent theme within the book and to reflect the views and perceptions of the lawyers within my sample. To them, these aims were not within the province of the law or legal practice and were thus "extralegal."

4 Of all the plaintiffs involved in the study, perhaps only one, if any, might be viewed as "wealthy" in terms of being non-representative of plaintiffs generally. This conclusion is based on information obtained during the research process, for example, from what plaintiffs said during interviews and observed mediations including private caucuses, respondents' questionnaire responses about their homes, their job descriptions, and information on the principal financial providers in each household.

1980–81, pp. 631–32, 650–51). Dispute transformation, formulated now long ago, is generally accepted and remains largely unchallenged within legal scholarship. It may be understood as a twofold process. First, notwithstanding plaintiffs' dispute descriptions and initial expressed desires, lawyers condition clients on "legal system realities" and persuade them to aim for what they view as legally realistic. Attorneys then reframe litigants' dispute experiences, feelings, and extralegal aims to fit into legally cognizable compartments suitable for processing within the legal system.[5]

However, there has been little investigation from plaintiffs' viewpoints during case processing how, if at all, dispute transformation affects their understandings of their cases and what they seek from the justice system, how they perceive what they hear from their lawyers, and whether their objectives change throughout the litigation process including mediation.[6] Additionally, there is little knowledge of defense lawyers' understandings of plaintiffs' aims and of whether dispute transformation plays any part in their comprehensions (Relis 2002, p. 193). The findings here suggest that dispute transformation does affect defense lawyers' understanding of plaintiffs' objectives, yet it does little to extinguish plaintiffs' own extralegal litigation aspirations. I show how plaintiffs interpret their lawyers' explanations of the "monetary realities of the legal system." I also provide evidence of plaintiffs' intermeshing "principles" with pecuniary recompense. Thus, there may be some transformation in plaintiffs' goals, particularly on the surface. However, challenging a central tenet of transformation theory, that a transformed dispute can actually become the dispute (Felstiner et al. 1980–81, pp. 649–50), the chapter demonstrates that plaintiffs' extralegal aims of principle do not dissipate after dispute transformation by their lawyers, nor with the passage of time.

---

5 Although dispute transformation in medical malpractice cases has not been examined in depth, it has been found in various other case types. These include divorce, poverty law, consumer, general injury, small claims, and harassment cases (Hosticka 1979, pp. 600–604; White 1990, pp. 20–21, 260–61, 269; Alfieri 1991, p. 2111; Cunningham 1992, pp. 1339–57, 1367–85; Gilkerson 1992, p. 883). Relying on observations of conversations between divorce lawyers and clients in two U.S. states, Sarat and Felstiner found that divorce clients repeatedly attempt to broaden the dialogue with their lawyers. However, lawyers' dispute interpretations reflecting their own sense of legal reality generally prevail (Sarat and Felstiner 1995a, pp. 106–7; 1995b, p. 406), (Sarat and Felstiner 1986, pp. 116–17; 1988, pp. 741–42, 766–67). Yet, little is known from clients themselves as to whether they internalize what they hear from their lawyers (Cunningham 1992, pp. 1339–57, 1367–85).

Legal transformation has also been found in various jurisdictions. In discussing the Kenyan legal system, Abel notes that lawyers have "elaborated highly sophisticated techniques for explaining disputes in terms of the norms involved... diverg*ing* from that employed by society at large" (Abel 1974, pp. 234, 271). Likewise, utilizing case studies from both Western and non-Western settings (e.g., Tanzania), Mather and Yngvesson found that "disputes altered as they were processed in response to the interests of various participants...," with "narrowing being the most common process of dispute transformation" (Mather and Yngvesson 1980–81, pp. 775, 778, 780, 789, 796). The legal narrowing of disputes "determined by the needs and purposes of the legal process" was also noted by Boaventura de Sousa Santos in the context of Pasargada (Santos 1977, p. 18).

6 It has been argued that litigants' understandings of their disputes, their goals, or their perceived needs may change during litigation due to contact with their lawyers, obtaining new information, delay, and/or despair (Sarat 1976, pp. 342, 342, n. 7; Felstiner et al. 1980–81, pp. 637, 642–43; Sarat and Felstiner 1995, p. 53; Genn 1999, p. 11).

First, differences in understandings of claimants' aims between physician, hospital, and plaintiff lawyers are explored. This is followed by an examination of plaintiffs' own, quite divergent, litigation objectives articulated within many of the same cases. Several case studies juxtaposing all sides' views then provide disconcerting evidence of the degree to which perceptions of plaintiffs' objectives are not only diverse but frequently contradictory, highlighting the first phase of the parallel worlds of understanding existing within these disputes. In an attempt to deconstruct this phenomenon, lawyers' conditioning of claimants on the monetary realities of the system is evidenced, followed by the consequent fusion of principles and money within some claimants' discourse on their aims. Gender differences within groups are subsequently explored. Finally, in the chapter conclusion, I present a theory that argues that these parallel worlds of understanding occur largely due to the institutional framework of the civil justice system, coupled with the practical and economic realities of legal practice that result in dispute transformation.

2.1 Lawyers' comprehensions of plaintiffs' litigation aims – group differences

The following subsections on lawyers for physicians, hospitals, and plaintiffs evidence their particular understandings of plaintiffs' litigation aims. Despite overall similarities, there were some differences of opinion between groups.

Physician lawyers: It's only about money

Virtually all physician lawyers were of the strong belief that plaintiffs had sued for financial compensation alone. Even the two who mentioned that nonfiscal objectives might also have been involved put much emphasis on claimants' primary monetary aims. The following excerpts are typical of defense physician lawyers in answering the global question, "WHAT IN YOUR VIEW WERE THE PLAINTIFF'S AIMS IN LITIGATING?"

> "My view is the issue was money, to compensate for the pain associated with the deterioration, and to compensate for lost income associated with the surgery that was necessary. SO IT WAS MONEY ALONE? I believe so." **Male – in fifties – prescription alleged to have destroyed bone tissue, resulting in forty-year-old plaintiff undergoing hip replacement surgery – litigating several months**

> "To settle it. Their assumption was that this would never go to trial; that they would get money out of this beforehand. SO, YOU FEEL IT IS SOLELY AN ISSUE OF OBTAINING FINANCIAL COMPENSATION? Yes, but I also think that they are of the view that if they obtain financial compensation it will make . . . them feel better. I think they're misguided on that." **Female – in thirties – abdomen not left intact after surgery – litigating several months**

> "I think in virtually all cases it's directly driven by their desire for compensation. . . . The sole aim, you know, in most of the cases it is to be financially compensated for the

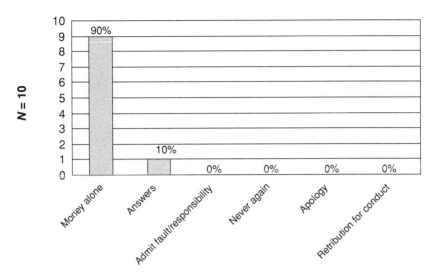

Figure 1. Physician lawyers' understandings of plaintiffs' litigation aims. The vast majority of defense physician attorneys felt that litigating plaintiffs sued for money alone.

wrong. And I would say that's in 99% of the cases I do, that's what plaintiffs want."
Male – in thirties – child fatality case – litigating four years

Figure 1 summarizes the responses of physician lawyers.

To understand the stance of physician lawyers it may be relevant to bear in mind that these lawyers were part of a group of defense firms working on generally high-paying cases that generate large legal fees. Like most attorneys, they were judged by their peers and superiors, at least to a material degree, by the amount of money they brought to their firms in terms of billable hours, and particularly the amount of money they were able to save their paying client, the Canadian Medical Protection Association ("CMPA"), which underwrites the vast majority of trial judgments and settlements in these cases (CMPA, 1999). Defense lawyers for doctors and hospitals in these cases each represent two clients: the individual physician or the hospital (and/or its employees) and the insurer or insurer-type body, which is the attorneys' paying client. Thus, these lawyers' own personal achievement and career trajectories had much to do with finances as well as "getting rid of cases... *and* settling them."

Yet, as one prominent female physician lawyer put it,

> I've heard many people say, "I never wanted to go to a lawyer. I only went because the hospital or the doctor wouldn't answer my questions." They say, "I only commenced an action because I want*ed* to be very sure this never happens to anybody else;" or they say "I wanted to hear the doctor say 'I messed up' or 'I'm sorry'." And they always say "It isn't about the money." I'm not so sure I always buy that. But I guess it's possible that it's also about something else.

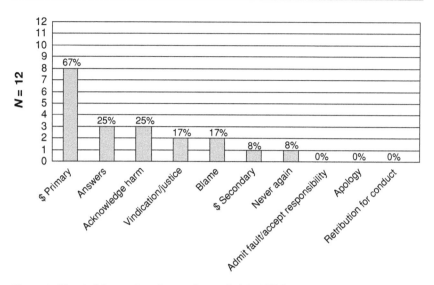

Figure 2. Hospital lawyers' understandings of plaintiffs' litigation aims. (*Note:* "$ Primary" indicates those people who felt that money was plaintiffs' primary litigation aim; "$ Secondary" indicates those people who felt that money was plaintiffs' secondary litigation aim.) As with physicians' lawyers, most hospital lawyers viewed monetary recompense as the primary driver for plaintiffs. However, other secondary objectives were recognized by some.

This "something else" was somewhat more prevalent within the views of hospital lawyers, who were often co-defendants in the same actions.

Hospital lawyers: It's mostly about money

Similar to physician lawyers, the widespread view of hospital lawyers was that plaintiffs sued primarily, though not solely, to obtain financial compensation. Yet, only two individuals (17%) felt the issue was money alone. Thus, in contrast to physician lawyers, hospital attorneys' discourse about claimants' primary fiscal aims was regularly coupled with talk of other nonpecuniary, nonlegal motivations, albeit on a secondary level. Figure 2 highlights the views of hospital lawyers.

The following interview excerpts are illustrative of the responses of hospital attorneys to the question: WHAT DO YOU THINK THE PLAINTIFFS' AIMS WERE IN SUING?

> "To recover money. I think that was one of the big things. But *also* to gain a sense of control over what happened. I think there's just a lot of bitterness. And I think it's finding someone to blame for a lot of things that happened in *the plaintiff's* life."
> **Female attorney – in thirties – plaintiff's abdomen not left intact after surgery – litigating approximately one year**

> "Well *the plaintiffs are* definitely very angry. And they also want a lot of money.... I think there's [*sic*] a lot of other issues going on. But I also have the sense that money was a primary driver." **Female attorney – in twenties – dispute over failed vasectomy and consequent abortion where plaintiffs were practicing Catholics unable to support a further child – litigating just under one year**
>
> "Partially *financial compensation.* I think clearly they're a struggling family.... Even though it could be said that these cases aren't worth very much, they're probably worth a great deal to them. And I think also there's the ... element of, you know, truth, getting at the truth and the matter of principle." **Female attorney – in forties – death of infant subsequent to labor and delivery – litigating five months**

Although both defense lawyer groups overall held similar views, the disparity between the views of hospital attorneys and physician lawyers may have been due to the identity of their clients. For physicians' attorneys, claims may have been viewed more as personal attacks against their individual clients. Admissions of error can be personally devastating for doctors. Whereas hospital lawyers represented large entities where claims may have been perceived as less personal, as for hospitals responsibility is collective. This, in turn, may have created a less defensive environment, allowing for greater openness to plaintiffs' extralegal aims. Moreover, if it was clear that there was going to be financial liability, there would likely be little personal cost to admitting error (Abel 2005). However, another possible cause for the disparity in responses could be attributed to the gender composition of the two groups. The hospital lawyers' group was predominantly female (67%), whereas 80% of the physicians' lawyers group were male. Gender differences are discussed in Section 2.5.

Plaintiff lawyers: It's mostly about money, but also other issues

> "Horrible, gruesome, plaintiffs open up their life.... Things get very emotional but defendants treat it as a liability, a debt to be minimized. The defense houses are running a business, 'How much do we have to pay to get rid of it'?" **Plaintiff lawyer – specialist, male – in forties**

Plaintiffs' lawyers are clearly in a different position to defense lawyers in terms of knowing plaintiffs' objectives. Yet, it was interesting that as with defense lawyers, most plaintiff lawyers felt that money was plaintiffs' primary litigation aim. Still, the bulk of plaintiffs' counsel viewed claimants' nonpecuniary litigation objectives as being more important to plaintiffs than their defense lawyer counterparts. These nonmonetary factors, illustrated in the chart shown in Figure 3, included obtaining answers about what happened, acknowledgements of harm, apologies, defendants accepting responsibility, and retribution for insulting physician conduct.

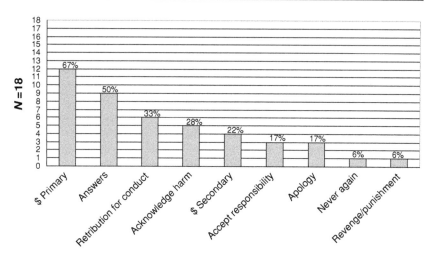

Figure 3. Plaintiff lawyers' understandings of plaintiffs' litigation aims. (*Note:* "$ Primary" indicates those people who felt that money was plaintiffs' primary litigation aim; "$ Secondary" indicates those people who felt that money was plaintiffs' secondary litigation aim.) The bulk of plaintiffs' lawyers viewed monetary recompense as their clients' primary aim. Yet, they were more aware of extralegal litigation objectives as compared with defense lawyers.

Nonetheless, claimants' monetary aims were prominent in most plaintiff lawyers' parlance. As one female generalist lawyer noted in a case that had been litigating for several months,

> I think always, when a client proceeds with a lawsuit, including a medmal lawsuit, money is one factor. But I think that's because that's the only thing our courts can compensate an individual with. But often the individual wants to understand what happened to them and why it happened. So I think that for the individual is very important... as compared with the money involved.... So the plaintiff's aim would be... information and understanding.... And I guess there's always the monetary consideration. I don't think people ever launch a lawsuit unless at some level there's a monetary consideration.

Similarly, an experienced male specialist lawyer in his fifties stressed,

> "*My aims are* to restore to my clients some kind of dignity as their lives have been shattered. I feel a responsibility to financially restore to them some kind of security."

In fact, a significant minority of both specialist and generalist plaintiff lawyers viewed financial compensation as their clients' only aim. Yet, in comparison with most defense lawyers, they generally explained this on a less legal, more "human" level. Plaintiffs' lawyers would generally be most likely to acknowledge other motives, as plaintiffs express their emotions directly to their legal counsel. Perhaps some plaintiffs' lawyers may also want to see themselves as champions, not just hired guns. At the same time, the only remedy plaintiffs' lawyers can get for their clients through the formal civil justice system is money. Therefore, plaintiffs' attorneys seek to monetize other client motives (Abel 2005).

The monetization of legal claims argument was first made in the dispute resolution context by Menkel-Meadow in 1984 in setting out a problem-solving framework for lawyers as negotiators to more closely meet parties' underlying needs and aims (Menkel-Meadow 1984, pp. 759, 764, 794–95). Similarly, Lande later posited that "money is often a symbol of other things such as finding a fair and honorable result, validation of injury, vindication of justice, 'winning'... attribution of fault, perception of (not) being 'taken'." (Lande 2000, p. 328). Although translating disputes over other issues into being about money alone allows the legal system to resolve many cases utilizing a common denominator (Shapiro 1981, p. 10), Menkel-Meadow argues that focusing solely on financial issues in disputes – although perhaps easiest – may result in dissatisfying resolutions for disputants, as disputants generally have underlying needs or aims in relation to their disputes, with monetary damages simply acting as a proxy for these other objectives (Menkel-Meadow 1984, p. 771, n. 72, pp. 767–68, 795). As will be seen later, this very much correlates with the plaintiffs' findings in the present study.

Yet, interestingly, Menkel-Meadow's argument on the monetization of legal claims was challenged by Kritzer in asking that "if more than money is sought for personal injury cases, how are lawyers to be paid in contingency fee situations?" In discussing the business dimension of the lawyer–client relationship, Kritzer emphasizes that attorneys are not selfless actors, but work to earn a living, relying on clients for their income (Kritzer 1984, p. 413). Indeed, contingency fee arrangements between plaintiffs' lawyers and their clients existed de facto for almost all of the cases studied. Contingency fee lawyers accept cases only if they see the opportunity for an economic return: if the cases look like sound investments. As such, regardless of clients' motives, contingency fee systems drive lawyers to evaluate their cases initially as investments and to constantly reevaluate them in the same way. Moreover, as with defense counsel, plaintiffs' lawyers, other than sole practitioners, are also judged by their peers and superiors based on fiscal considerations such as how much money they bring into the firm in legal fees and the amounts of settlements they are able to achieve. Judgments based on these considerations have a significant impact on lawyers' own career trajectories, including election to partnership within their firms. Thus, economic realities of legal practice may have played a role in how the various legal actors in the study talked about plaintiffs' motivations and litigation aims.

Further interview excerpts from attorneys are included in the case studies below. Notwithstanding the economic realities of legal practice, it was startling that not a single plaintiffs' lawyer suggested that money had little to do with what their clients wanted from litigation. Yet, this, in fact, was something that most plaintiffs vehemently stressed.

2.2 Plaintiffs: "It's not about the money! It's about principles"

Of all respondents, plaintiffs' views are arguably the most important in answering the question of what motivated them to sue and what precisely they wanted. Surely, they must have known best? Interestingly, plaintiffs' articulations of their litigation objectives rarely correlated with legal actors' perceptions. In fact, a regular and conspicuous occurrence was the failure to mention financial compensation as an objective at all unless probed (occurring in 65% of interviews). Instead, what plaintiffs recurrently repeated was a lexicon of nonfiscal, extralegal objectives for litigation. The issue of "principle" was prominent for plaintiffs as revealed in the various objectives they passionately spoke about. "It's not about the money" was a recurrent theme throughout. Many of the comments concerned dignity and respect after the injury, inability to be heard, refusal to listen, dismissal, and victim blaming. All of this added insult to injury (Abel 2005).

The plaintiffs' group was overall uniform in terms of the litigation aims discussed. There were no material differences in plaintiffs' articulated objectives between claimants of different genders or education levels. Moreover, plaintiffs' extralegal objectives did not appear to be affected by the passage of time,[7] as there were no marked disparities in the way plaintiffs spoke of why they sued and what they wanted from the civil justice system as between plaintiffs who had commenced litigation three to four months earlier (interviewed subsequent to court-linked mandatory mediations) and claimants who had been litigating for several years (interviewed after voluntary mediations of cases already on trial lists).[8] Nor were opinions different based on whether claimants had complained to the College of Physicians and Surgeons as well as having sued. Only nine plaintiffs (53%) sued as well as filed College complaints, whereas all but one plaintiff discussed extralegal objectives in litigating. Figure 4 illustrates the spectrum of objectives iterated by plaintiffs.

One might argue that plaintiffs may have felt that money is a culturally inappropriate goal and thus offered other motives as rationalizations to the interviewer.[9]

---

[7] Cf. Felstiner et al. (1980–81, p. 638), arguing that disputants' feelings and objectives change over time and complicate disputes.

[8] Interviews were conducted with ten plaintiffs subsequent to voluntary mediations and seven plaintiffs subsequent to court-linked mandatory mediations. Plaintiffs would have commenced litigation within one year of the disputed incidents as per Ontario's limitation period for medical malpractice cases (Limitation of Actions Act, R. S. A., ch. L-15, §§ 55(a), 56 (1980)). College mediations, which were pre-litigation, were not included in the analysis of plaintiffs' litigation aims.

[9] In relation to the present findings, Kritzer makes the point that a distinction should be made between plaintiffs' goals in litigation and their goals in the underlying dispute, as few litigants would choose to invest their own money in litigation if there were not a prospect of a significant recovery (e-mail: Kritzer, November 7, 2006, on file with author). This is a valid point in some circumstances. However, in the present study, some of the claims were for relatively low damages (e.g., infant death case, child operation case, and vasectomy case). Moreover, besides the contingency fee clients, some litigants were paying their lawyers on an hourly rate basis, being told there was no guarantee of financial recovery. Additionally, plaintiffs in the present study were asked specifically about why they instituted legal proceedings and their goals for litigation itself, not simply about

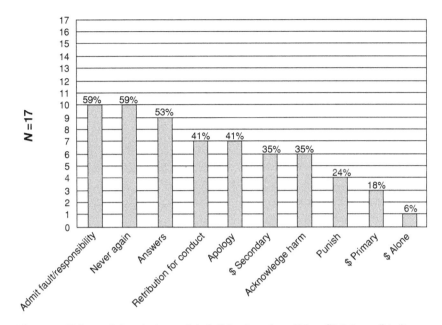

Figure 4. Claimants' descriptions of their litigation aims. (*Note:* "$ Primary" indicates those people who said that money was a primary litigation aim; "$ Secondary" indicates those people who said that money was a secondary litigation aim; "$ Alone" indicates those people who said that money was their only litigation aim.) Plaintiffs' articulated litigation aims were thickly composed of extralegal objectives of principle, with 41% not mentioning monetary compensation at all, 35% viewing it as being of secondary importance, 18% describing money as their primary objective in suing, and 6% (i.e., only one person) saying it was money alone.

However, findings in several studies on medical injury plaintiffs in various jurisdictions (predominantly using survey data) lend credence to those in the present research. In these studies, desires for monetary compensation were never found to be of primary importance to most plaintiffs. Instead, extralegal litigation aims similar to those noted by plaintiffs in the present research were found.

In Britain, Genn's questionnaire data revealed that less than half of medical plaintiffs viewed obtaining financial compensation as a "very important" objective. Prevention of similar occurrences, physician acknowledgment, admissions that something had gone wrong, and answers were objectives most often rated as "very important" (Genn 1995, pp. 393–412). Likewise, another British survey deriving from 227 medical negligence plaintiffs' questionnaires suggested that legal action

their underlying dispute objectives (although, arguably, these would be intertwined once litigation commenced). Finally, I do not make the claim that plaintiffs' aims for litigation never include monetary objectives, but simply that plaintiffs have a whole host of nonfiscal objectives for litigation that are not recognized by many legal actors involved in their cases.

was taken to prevent reoccurrences, for explanations and apologies, accountability, and admissions of negligence. Only 17% described compensation as a reason for suing. Thus, the authors argue that "if litigation is viewed solely as a legal and financial problem, many fundamental issues will not be addressed or resolved" (Vincent et al. 1994, pp. 1609–13). Similarly, a Florida study of 127 perinatal injury plaintiffs (utilizing telephone-administered questionnaires) found that litigation goals included not only requiring money (24%) but also wanting to uncover coverups and wanting to protect others in future (Hickson et al. 1992, pp. 1359, 1361). Other research in the United States and Australia note similar findings (Meschievitz 1991, pp. 200–201; Dauer and Marcus 1997, pp. 185–86, 218; Daniel et al. 1999, pp. 598–601; Nisselle 1999, pp. 576–77). In view of these multinational findings, although possibly different for plaintiffs in non-Western contexts where money might more often represent core needs for survival, I would argue that the issue of money being of secondary importance to many plaintiffs should not be regarded as an instance of North American exceptionalism.

It might further be argued that plaintiffs in medical malpractice cases may be more invested in acceptance of responsibility than other tort plaintiffs because doctors are so invested in seeing themselves as motivated only by patients' wellbeing. In comparison, the stranger defendant in automobile accidents or product liability cases rarely pretends to be interested in victims' well-being (Abel 2005). Yet, in various contexts, scholars have argued that extralegal concerns are often the most important issues for plaintiffs far outweighing legal worries. Thus, plaintiffs may sue for psychological reasons, to express feelings, anger, or to achieve moral vindication.[10] Moreover, plaintiffs' nonmonetary or extralegal litigation objectives have also been found for other case types. Survey data deriving from thirty plaintiffs in sexual assault cases who sought legal compensation similarly indicated that most of those who sued wanted more than money from civil litigation. Most claimants discussed therapeutic as opposed to monetary goals. They frequently wanted to be heard; they wanted validations of their experiences, public declarations of the wrong, closure, retribution, apology, and to deter similar events. Thus, the authors advocate a rethinking of civil justice assumptions and how monetary damages are regarded (Des Rosiers et al. 1998, pp. 433, 435, 438, 442).

Likewise, studies in tort, divorce, injury, and small claims cases have shown that plaintiffs frequently have material hidden aims involving more than just money, which may be their cardinal goals. Divorce litigants have been found to often seek emotional vindication or acknowledgment that they have been treated unjustly as evidenced by the fact that they commonly seek apologies (Sarat and Felstiner 1995a, p. 93). Similarly, research into small claims cases has demonstrated that litigation may be used to express feelings, to let off steam, or for moral vindication, and may have symbolic or psychological value (Sarat 1976, p. 346; Conley and O'Barr 1990, p. 181). In the British National Consumer Council survey, covering diverse dispute

---

10 Binder and Price (1977, pp. 22, 185–86), Engel (1984, pp. 558–562), Galanter (1986, p. 191), Binder et al. (1991, p. 33), and Shalleck (1993, p. 1743).

types, only one-third of respondents said monetary compensation was the most important thing they wanted to achieve, with apologies and prevention of similar occurrences also being frequently noted primary goals (NCC 1995).

In analyzing observations of 156 small claims court hearings as well as interviews with twenty-nine litigants, Conley and O'Barr similarly present evidence of the "invalidity of the law's operating assumptions that civil litigants come to court to pursue discrete economic objectives and that people define their problems in financial terms, and are thus prepared to accept monetary solutions." They additionally remark on the "striking divergence between approaches to cases between legal professionals and lay disputants who, in effect, speak different languages" (Conley and O'Barr 1990, pp. ix, xi, 126–31, 141–49, 173).

Merry's ethnographic, in-depth research in *Getting Justice and Getting Even* produced similar findings. In examining family and neighborhood cases in Massachusetts' lower courts and court-linked mediations, Merry found that plaintiffs turned to the courts to establish the truth, when they viewed important principles at stake and when they sought authoritative determinations on who was right and who was wrong. Plaintiffs were also found to seek therapeutic forms of assistance through the legal system (Merry 1990b, pp. 2, 4, 17, 172, 179).[11] Providing an example of a professional female making a $30 claim against a repairman for allegedly using her kitchen tools and causing damage in her house, Merry notes that plaintiffs seek more than simply financial compensation from the justice system (Merry 1990b, p. 98).

Likewise, in Merry and Silbey's *What Do Plaintiffs Want?* research, they found that plaintiffs in small claims, family, and neighborhood disputes pursued cases not only for material interests, but also for integrity, self-respect, conceptions of right and moral reasons. In fact, similar to the present findings, disputants frequently described their cases as conflicts of principles and values. In turning to the legal system, plaintiffs sought vindication and for the 'truth' to be ascertained, and viewed their disputes as "principled grievances." Therefore, in questioning the theories underlying the dispute-processing paradigm, Merry and Silbey argue that it is misguided to assume that plaintiffs choose various paths on the basis of rational calculation of stakes, costs, and probable results alone, as to this must be added the noneconomic reasons for litigating, which include respectability, responsibility, and being a good individual (Merry and Silbey 1984, pp. 151–58, 160, 171, 176).[12]

The fact that the formal justice system does not deal with litigants' perceived requirements and real objectives, including their nonmonetary agendas, has been found to be a major reason for litigants' dissatisfaction in small claims and injury

---

11 Merry's study included observations of mediations and court proceedings in criminal, juvenile, and small claims cases, interviews with disputants and professionals, quantitative analysis of caseloads, and an ethnographic study of three neighborhoods (Merry 1990a, pp. 13, 17–18).
12 Merry and Silbey's article was based on data from observations of 125 cases in court and two mediation programs covering small claims and minor criminal cases in family and neighborhood disputes, 73 interviews with disputants, and an ethnography of 3 neighborhoods (Merry and Silbey 1984, pp. 153–54, 160).

cases.[13] Indeed, what was particularly remarkable in the present research was that in comparing legal actors' understandings with those of plaintiffs in the same or similar cases, very few lawyers noted either of plaintiffs' most recurrent stated objectives. Out of forty lawyers interviewed, not a single physician lawyer or hospital lawyer and only three plaintiff lawyers (17%) mentioned that plaintiffs wanted defendants to admit fault or accept responsibility. Likewise, not a single physician lawyer and only one hospital lawyer (8% of that group) and one plaintiff lawyer (6% of that group) noted that plaintiffs wanted to "ensure it never happened again." Similarly, "obtaining answers or explanations" about what happened was plaintiffs' second most repeated litigation objective. All plaintiffs stated that they had either not received any explanation or had received an unsatisfactory one after the incident, regardless of the severity of their injuries. Although discussed by 50% of plaintiff lawyers, a mere 25% of hospital lawyers and only a single physician lawyer (10% of that group) mentioned that plaintiffs wanted answers or explanations. Likewise, the third most repeated plaintiff litigation objective was to obtain an apology and retribution for insulting physician conduct. Not a single physician or hospital lawyer ever mentioned the issue of apology or physician conduct, and only three plaintiff lawyers (17% of that group) did.

The following four case studies illustrate actors' perceptions of plaintiffs' litigation aims, making quickly apparent the parallel worlds of understanding and perception existing within these cases on the elemental issue of what these cases were about.

2.3 Case studies: Parallel worlds of understanding the meaning of litigated cases

Child operation case

This case, which had been litigating for less than one year, involved an operation on a four-year-old child, in which only one of the two parts necessary had been completed. As a result, the child had to undergo three operations, having to be sedated three times. He had had other medical procedures and had developed a fear of doctors. Therefore, as far as the plaintiff parents were concerned, the dispute involved much more than simply undergoing another operation. As the father noted during mediation, "I said everything would be okay after the first operation and then it wasn't. I lost credibility with my four year old." Yet, as the following excerpts illustrate, understandings of the case were disparate among the actors involved.

Male attorney for defendant surgeon – in fifties

> WHAT DO YOU THINK THE PLAINTIFFS' AIMS WERE WHEN THEY SUED? Money. DO YOU THINK THAT'S THE SOLE AIM? Yes. ANY UNDERLYING ISSUES? No.

---

13 Conley and O'Barr (1988, pp. 182–84, 196–97), O'Barr and Conley (1988, pp. 159–60), and Merry (1990, pp. 134–37, 142–46, 170–70).

Female hospital attorney – in twenties

> They sued obviously to recover some money for their ... pain and suffering. ... I think that in any lawsuit there's an aim to get some money for pain and suffering. ANY OTHER KIND OF UNDERLYING OBJECTIVES? I don't think so.

Male plaintiffs' attorney – in thirties

> I think there was as much hurt on an emotional level, as there was, you know, a desire for compensation. ... First of all he didn't apologize for what he did. ... He offered no words of condolence. ... So I think there was an element of personal scorn there ... and I think also recognition that there was a wrong that there was going to be compensation for. So their goals were twofold I think: to get him to acknowledge the error of his ways and also to ensure some compensation for their son.

Co-plaintiff – father – in thirties

> WHAT WAS YOUR REASON ... FOR STARTING A LEGAL ACTION? I think mostly because of the lack of concern. The surgeon didn't seem to be concerned about the mistake that he made. If we really got a sincere apology and they said, "Oh, we'll do anything we can to make your family, your son, more comfortable". ... But there was no apology. It was like they tried to smooth us over with some free parking passes. It was just the principle of it. They really affected somebody's life. So, I wanted them to know that. ... Because we really didn't want, like I don't need the money. My son doesn't need the money. It was the fact that we wanted somebody to notice. We didn't want it to happen to anybody else. ... It's about somebody being accountable for their actions and what they've done. ... I mentioned in the mediation ... that's why we get fined when we speed down the highway because it deters us from speeding again. If you dip into somebody's pocket ... then obviously somebody is held responsible for that. ... Then maybe next time ... they'll ... double check ... and make sure the procedure he's doing is right.

Fatality case relating to a disputed "do not resuscitate ('DNR') order"

The next case had been litigating for approximately one year. It involved a dispute over a "do not resuscitate" order and the consequent death of the plaintiffs' husband and father.

Physician lawyer – male – in fifties

> I think it was motivated by emotional factors, and also money.

Hospital lawyer – female – in thirties

> I think their aim was that they just wanted to be heard. I think ... they wanted to be compensated *financially* for what they viewed as a wrong.

Plaintiffs' lawyer – specialist, male – in forties

> They sought compensation for the loss of the family member who made a contribution to a ... business, and to the spouse who ... depended upon him much more than might be expected ... and she felt that loss very acutely. SO WOULD YOU SAY THEN THAT

IT'S A MIX OF FINANCIAL COMPENSATION AS WELL AS OTHER ELEMENTS? Um, by definition, a civil action is there for financial compensation. Whether that also represented a symbolic suing for hurt feelings is hard to say.

Co-plaintiff – widow of deceased – in seventies

WHY DID YOU SUE? My husband was neglected in hospital the last six days until he died, and I blame doctor.... You know the doctor told my son, "You dropped your father in the hospital because you wanted to get rid of him".... Those were hard words. SO YOU FELT ANGRY ABOUT HOW THE DOCTOR SPOKE TO YOU? I know that it is such negligence.... But our main point, we think that many old people, sick people are neglected, and we say we have to teach them. We suffered, but so many others are suffering from this. SO THAT WAS YOUR GOAL WHEN YOU DECIDED TO SUE? Yes ... we wanted to stop this.... We want to open the whole system, and what's going on in the hospitals.

SO THE REASON THAT YOU WENT TO A LAWYER WAS NOT ONLY BECAUSE YOU WANTED TO HAVE FINANCIAL COMPENSATION? No, no! Absolutely not. Court, you know, it's lots of headaches, lots of worries and lots of financial.... We feel very hurt.... I told the doctor, "why did you tell my son that we dropped my husband in the hospital because we want to get rid of him?" This was "very" hard for me and for him. Big insult. I think it pushed us to go to legal proceedings.... All this situation pushed us to go ask for legal help.

Co-plaintiff son of deceased – in forties

WHAT WAS YOUR GOAL IN SUING? Primarily I wanted to ... bring to light ... any other malpractices ... until he admits he made an awful mistake.... I'm not fighting for my father, but for whoever else he's erred as well.... The physician was totally arrogant. He didn't say "Listen, I'm really sorry about the loss of your father. I made a mistake".... He could have ... and I think I would have felt good about that. We're all human. We make mistakes ... We're not seeking anything. We wanted answers.... It was his arrogance that pushed us to sue him.... When we spoke initially ... he made implications we're only here to hunt him for money.

This is not about money. This is about the respect and dignity of my father.... We didn't get an apology.... This could have been done so civilly, before legal proceedings. You push us into a corner. SO THE REASON YOU WENT TO A LAWYER WAS NOT ONLY BECAUSE YOU WANTED FINANCIAL COMPENSATION? Well you can tell by where we live and everything, the money is not part of it. AND FINANCIAL LOSS? Yeah, well, okay. They could have said ... "Let's pick up the tab for the funeral expenses...." Or even, you know, do something. It's not a matter of the money now. It's just, "here's a gesture," you know. You made a mistake. And I think we would have probably gone away a lot quieter.... We even waited right to the last month until we said we're going to commence a claim. This is what we want to do because in our hearts Dad unjustly died.

Loss-of-sight case

This case, which had been litigating for three years, involved a woman who had glaucoma. She subsequently lost all vision in her right eye and 60% of her vision in her left eye, which was expected to diminish. The dispute related to the issue of failure to diagnose the disease in its early stages, which was argued could have prevented or arrested the loss of sight. She had been going to the same optometrist, the defendant in the suit, for sixteen years.

Optometrist's lawyer – male – in fifties

> APART FROM FINANCIAL COMPENSATION, ANY UNDERLYING REASONS FOR WHY THEY SUED? Purely financial.

Plaintiffs' general-practice lawyer – male – in forties

> Compensation FINANCIAL COMPENSATION? Ya. ANY UNDERLYING ISSUES? ... from when my involvement started, what I gathered was mostly a motivation for compensation.

The plaintiff explained that she had asked the optometrist to do a glaucoma test because her father had been inflicted with the disease, and she felt film on her eye. She said, "He told me he'd already done the test and I was negative.... I then went to another clinic and tested positive for glaucoma and was told that the right eye was at an advanced stage and could not be repaired – and that it should have been detected many years ago."

Female plaintiff – in forties

> WHEN YOU INSTITUTED LEGAL PROCEEDINGS, WHAT DID YOU WANT TO ACHIEVE? ... My objective was more or less to see that this man is either punished for what he did, or he's kicked out ... stopped from practicing. I don't know how many people he has overlooked. If he continues to practice, there's going be a lot of people like me *who will lose their sight*. ... SO THAT WAS YOUR MAIN AIM? Oh, yes. I take this very seriously. This punishment is a very serious thing. ... We also lodged a complaint at the College of Optometrists.
>
> DO YOU FEEL YOU SHOULD BE COMPENSATED ALSO? Oh, definitely. Presently I am taking drops every day ... eighty bucks every three weeks. This is something that's coming out of our pockets ... and this will be for life. Now, I have to have the money at least for the drops. SO IS IT A MIXTURE OF YOU NEEDING FINANCIAL COMPENSATION BUT THERE ARE OTHER REASONS, THE MAIN REASON BEING THAT YOU FEEL THAT IT SHOULDN'T HAPPEN TO SOMEBODY ELSE? That's right. And that was the truth. That was very important to me; and my lawyer knew that.

Co-plaintiff – husband – in fifties

> Wrong diagnosis ... no explanation. ... She lost the right eye's vision and sixty percent of the left eye. ... I think one of the reasons for the dispute is to "cover." It's not accepting

blame. It's obvious that the doctor is wrong. So it's like "let us not admit fault, sweep it under the carpet" that sort of attitude. THE REASONS YOU SUED, WAS IT FOR FINANCIAL COMPENSATION? The principle. Also the principle. I don't want that my wife loses her eye, and nothing is done. Somebody has to take responsibility for it. And I believe that the doctor and the insurance company need to be responsible for it... although you can never compensate.

A case involving a bladder operation, which had been in litigation for several months, provides a final example of the discontinuity between legal and lay understandings of plaintiffs' aims. The case involved a man who had a severe bladder problem, resulting in urination eight to ten times daily, headaches, vomiting, and strong belly pain. The defendant urologist performed an operation to attempt to alleviate the problem. Subsequent to the operation, the plaintiff felt his problem had materially worsened, having to urinate approximately twenty to twenty-five times a day and still suffering persistent headaches and belly pain. Consequently, the plaintiff could not keep his job as a carpenter. However, other issues were involved as well. The plaintiff's lawyer suggested that the initial diagnosis and operation may not have been correct and may have worsened the problem. The following excerpts from separate discussions with both the plaintiff and his attorney illustrate the discontinuity in their respective understandings of the case.

Bladder operation case

Male general-practice plaintiffs' attorney – in forties

WHY DID HE SUE? Money SOLELY? Yeah. I think the guy is simply looking for compensation for what he feels has been done to him and worsened his quality of life. There isn't a lot of anger, there isn't a desire to make the doctor accountable, as far as I can tell.... He did start a complaints process.... So maybe he's got a desire to see the doctor brought to account.

Male plaintiff – in forties

WHY DID YOU SUE? After the surgery, I said to *the* doctor... "Everything's getting worse," and he replied, "Oh, you complain too much. I have no idea what the problem is,"... and he was shouting at me. Then he walked away and took some other guy's file.... He didn't have time for me. He just ignored me like that.... He must see what he did; and he must pay for what he did.... I believe he's just not sorry... to bring me back... to my normal position.... I want the truth.... I don't know what he did. IS THAT WHY YOU SUED? Yeah. I want to get to the bottom of this, what he did.... He didn't care about his patients. He cares for his professional career.

WAS YOUR MAIN AIM NOT FINANCIAL COMPENSATION? Financial compensation is not so important.... Compensation is not really the problem or the solution.... After they didn't cooperate with me after complaining at the hospital and the College, I went to a lawyer.... My situation is very bad.... I am in a lot of pain.... If he tried to fix the problem, or the hospital tried to help me, I would not go to my lawyer. But they tried to brush me off.

In sum, it appeared that the vast majority of plaintiffs wanted other things or at least more than simply financial compensation for their harm. Yet, what was particularly remarkable was that out of the numerous recurrent litigation aims vehemently stressed by plaintiffs as being of greatest importance to them, few, if any, were mentioned by the legal actors in their cases – sometimes not even by their own lawyers. Yet, these lawyers generally worked on these cases on a regular basis for several years. These findings correlate with procedural justice studies, which argue that "lay disputants want disparate things from the justice system than what is routinely delivered to them. What they desire reflects a psychological paradigm. Yet this is inherently different from the paradigm of legal discourse and decision-making that attorneys and judges are socialized into in law school, and which dominates discussions by legal actors" (Tyler 1997, pp. 872–84, 894).

This discontinuity of understandings may have related to the fact that these aims were not within the norms of traditional legal practice. Still, apart from suggesting that academic knowledge of plaintiffs' litigation objectives is not filtering through into the field of lawyers' operations, it appeared that critical needs of claimants who had generally suffered traumatic injuries or family fatalities were not being recognized. As will be seen in the chapters to come, lawyers' misconceptions or incomplete understandings of plaintiffs' aims had a marked impact on how they approached these cases and how they behaved toward plaintiffs during litigation-track mediations in attempting to resolve these disputes. For instance, in chapters five and six, a recurrent theme for plaintiffs is their astonishment, anger, and incomprehension of why defendants or their lawyers generally did not provide any explanations, acknowledgements of their harm, or apologies during mediations, not even in a qualified manner that would not increase defendants' vulnerability during lawsuits.

In delving deeper, I sought to comprehend how claimants' stated aims were so misconstrued or overlooked when they were given such importance in the discourse of virtually all plaintiffs. This paradox may have been a result of lawyers' "system conditioning" and the phenomenon of dispute transformation.

2.4 System conditioning, dispute transformation, and principles intermeshed with money

This section examines evidence of "system conditioning" as part of dispute transformation – both as a phenomenon in itself and as a means of comprehending how plaintiffs' extralegal aims of principle were overlooked by most attorneys in their cases. Dispute transformation has been discussed by various scholars who note that narrative constructions of reality are ubiquitous in legal procedure via lawyering processes (Bruner 1992, p. 177; Sherwin 1992b, p. 2). Yet, as Merry aptly notes, dispute transformation should not presume that disputes alter in a unidirectional fashion, but must encompass the fact that various interpretations of disputes can exist simultaneously, although they may be disputed by some actors.[14] Moreover, disputes themselves do not change per se; it is simply that different actors understand them differently, illustrating the malleability as well as the constancy of disputes (Merry 1990b, pp. 92–93). This perspective draws on Comaroff and Roberts' work, who postulate that disputing can be viewed in terms of competing ways of construing events and selves within particular normative frameworks (Comaroff and Roberts 1981, p. 238). Some have argued that "what a dispute is in terms of its relevant facts is contingent upon whether it will be litigated or mediated" (Rubinson 2004, p. 834). The present findings cast doubt on this assertion and suggest that the meaning of disputes is contingent on whom one asks, the lawyer or the disputant, as each creates competing meanings regardless of mode of resolution.

Research has highlighted sharp distinctions between litigants' dispute descriptions, expectations, goals, and views of justice and lawyers' far narrower objectives and explanations of law's capabilities. Consequently, the phenomenon of lawyers treating plaintiffs' articulated aims as something ephemeral, regularly urging clients not to pursue goals such as emotional or moral vindication, has been well documented for a variety of case types.[15] Attorneys have been found to sidestep, be reluctant to deal with or not to respond to "nonlegal" or legally irrelevant issues or to engage clients' more personal concerns – often of prime importance to litigants.[16] Instead, by relying on their knowledge and experience, lawyers condition clients on civil justice system realities and direct them to aim for what they view as legally realistic.[17] System conditioning by lawyers in the present study was done to steer clients away from their extralegal litigation aspirations and to train them to view their cases as relating to money alone – as "that is all the system can provide." The following excerpts from interviews with lawyers in response to my question WHY DO YOU THINK THE PLAINTIFF SUED? provide evidence of system conditioning in the cases covered.

---

14 Compare Felstiner et al., who put forward a framework for analyzing perceived or unperceived injurious events (naming), those that do or do not result in grievances (blaming), and those that develop into disputes (claiming) as well as subsequent dispute transformations. They argue that at each stage of development disputes, being social constructs, are subjective, reactive, partial, and unstable (Felstiner et al. 1980–81, pp. 630, 632, 637).
15 Macaulay (1979, pp. 115, 136–40, consumer cases), Griffiths (1986, pp. 135, 146–49, divorce cases), Hosticka (1979, pp. 600–604, poverty law cases), Alfieri (1991, pp. 620–28, poverty law cases), and Mather et al. (2001, pp. 68–69, 91–92, divorce cases).
16 Rosenthal (1974, pp. 63, 65, injury cases), Sarat and Felstiner (1986, pp. 93, 116, matrimonial cases; 1989, pp. 1672–76, matrimonial cases; 1995, pp. 85, 106–7, matrimonial cases), Conley and O'Barr (1990, small-claims cases), Kritzer (1998, pp. 803–5, contingency fee lawyers), and Mather et al. (2001, pp. 68–69, 91–92, divorce).
17 Alfieri (1991, pp. 2118–25, poverty lawyers) and Sarat and Felstiner (1986, p. 116, divorce cases; 1989, pp. 1663, 1664, 1671–76; 1995, pp. 85, 106–7). Sarat and Felstiner's research was based on observations and interviews with matrimonial clients in forty cases in two American towns. They found that in response to their questions, clients were given "law talk" by their lawyers. Lawyers described legal processes and actors in critical, cynical, and negative ways, stressing limitations while at the same time attempting to be sympathetic to clients' situations and emphasizing their insider knowledge, connections, positions, and reputations.

"That's a little hard to say. I think ultimately... they do get the message that... the object of the exercise... is trying to resolve their case based on a reasonable compromise of the prospects of the case.... I do believe, by and large, that they understand when it's explained to them that this is about compensation. So therefore it is about money." **Male, specialist plaintiff and physician lawyer – twenty years' experience – over one hundred cases – in forties**

"I've worked on about 150 medical malpractice cases. Their aims once it gets to litigation are primarily financial because they listen to the lawyer, and lawyers can only quantify these things in dollar terms.... Yes, they would have to say that it's finances; but the undercurrent for them is an explanation and an apology... which they never got... the doctor never showed up to even explain anything." **Male, specialist plaintiff and hospital lawyer – infant death case – in forties**

"Day in and day out people say to me 'We've got to go forward, even if it's only to make sure nobody else has to go through what I've gone through'. So there's an altruistic aspect to people's motives... or money doesn't matter, you know 'I just need enough to do this ...' or getting back at the doctor. Although once they begin to understand the financial implications of getting into litigation I think they find they can't afford litigation on principle. There has to be the prospect of an economic recovery to make it worthwhile.... Then the focus later on does become money. Perhaps because I continually remind people that's all a lawsuit is about. It doesn't make the world a better place.... It provides compensation, and as such it has to be looked at in a business-like way.... Whether it's a change that would happen regardless of what I say to my clients and what I try and train them to do.... I don't know. But I tell clients that investing in a malpractice case is no different from investing in the stock market. It's all about money, and you should look at it that way." **Male, specialist plaintiff lawyer – twenty-five years' practice – in fifties**

Thus, in assisting disputants to understand their cases and what can be done about them, lawyers as gatekeepers to legal institutions virtually always transform disputes. Subsequent to system conditioning, injurious incidents and litigants' experiences and extralegal aims are translated, reconstituted, and coerced by lawyers to fit into legal and monetary compartments, ignoring aspects deemed irrelevant in law and ultimately translating them into money.[18]

Yet, dispute rephrasing, which occurs early on, entails a struggle of dispute paradigms as each interpretation has consequences for the way cases are dealt with (Mather and Yngvesson 1980–81, pp. 106, 777, 780–81). Viewing cases as competitions over how they are to be interpreted sheds light on the relative power of those involved, as the ability to frame the terms of a dispute using a particular discourse demarcates the nature of a problem and what should be done about it,

---

18 Campbell (1976, pp. 195, 208–10) Hosticka (1979, pp. 600–604), Sarat and Felstiner (1986, pp. 116–17), Cunningham (1989, p. 2474; 1992, pp. 1339–57, 1367–85), White (1990, pp. 20–21, 260–61, 269), Alfieri (1991, p. 2111), Bruner (1992, p. 182), and Gilkerson (1992, p. 883).

shaping its outcome.[19] Thus, as Merry argues, naming, categorizing, and labeling is a form of subtle power domination by third parties over disputants as only a few issues are "crystallized out of the wider matrix of the problem." Portraying this as a paradox of legal entitlement, Merry asserts that in using the legal system for empowerment, plaintiffs are inevitably disempowered by the state in that they are confined to present their requests for help in the language of the legal system, affecting how their cases are understood (Merry 1990b, pp. 92–93, 98, 108, 111, 131–32, 181–82).

Sarat and Felstiner found that the way divorce lawyers spoke about clients' stories reflected their own sense of legal reality (Sarat and Felstiner 1986, pp. 116–17). Moreover, Felstiner et al. posit that in assisting disputants comprehend their grievances and modes of redress, lawyers (among others) frequently transform the issues, "shaping disputes to fit their own interests rather than those of disputants." Yet, relatively little is known about what difference attorneys interacting with clients make (Felstiner et al. 1980–81, pp. 634–37, 645). After some negotiation between lawyers and clients, system conditioning has been found to result in claimants not demanding social justice or anything overly different from what they are told courts would provide.[20] Indeed, in the present study, having experienced system conditioning during contacts with their attorneys, plaintiffs often appeared to have simply ceased to discuss their extralegal objectives with their lawyers. It has therefore been argued that most litigants' expectations are consequently deflated or reshaped, as they are persuaded not to expect too much from the legal process.[21] However, although some studies include data from litigant interviews, much research relies on observational data and interviews with lawyers alone. Challenging some of the arguments in the extant literature,[22] the data here from litigant interviews suggest that simply because plaintiffs may cease to overtly demand things from their lawyers does not mean that system conditioning diverts plaintiffs' focus from their extralegal aims of principle throughout their litigation and subsequent mediations (*see further chapters five and six*).

That being said, lawyers' efforts to condition plaintiffs on the monetary realities of the civil justice system appeared to play a role in causing some plaintiffs to intertwine their extralegal aims of principle with talk of financial recompense or to express these extralegal aims through monetary compensation in their articulations

---

19 Silbey and Merry (1986, pp. 25–27), Merry (1990a, pp. 2–5, 34; 1990b, pp. 10–11, 92–93, 98; 1992, pp. 215, 218), and O'Barr and Conley (1990, pp. 98–99).
20 Felstiner et al. (1980–81, pp. 634–37, 645), Sarat and Felstiner (1986, pp. 116–17, 125–28; 1995, p. 406, divorce), Alfieri (1991, p. 211, poverty lawyers), and Cunningham (1992, pp. 1339–57, 1367–85, consumer cases).
21 Rosenthal (1974, pp. 76–77, personal injury cases), Maiman et al. (1992, p. 50, divorce cases), Sarat and Felstiner (1995, pp. 85, 106–7, divorce cases), and Kritzer (1998, pp. 803–5, personal injury cases).
22 This finding challenges arguments that plaintiffs alter their goals (Macaulay 1979, pp. 115, 136–40; Felstiner et al. 1980–81, pp. 631–32, 650–51; Mather and Yngvesson 1980–81, pp. 775, 778, 780, 789, 796; Griffiths 1986, pp. 135, 146–49; Sarat and Felstiner 1989, pp. 1664, 1671–76; 1990, pp. 139–48; 1995, pp. 106–7; Felstiner and Sarat 1992, pp. 1451–59).

on what they sought from litigation. Consequently, all aims including pecuniary ones became bound up together. Thus, notwithstanding case differences in relation to claimants' needs for finances, plaintiffs' litigation aims were far less straightforward than was often presumed.

A good example of claimants' perceptions of "system conditioning" and its effects was provided by a female plaintiff in her fifties in describing the inherent financial part of her legal action that had been ongoing for three years. However, as the following interview excerpt illustrates, financial compensation was not driving her claim following the death of her son.

> WAS ANY PART OF THE REASON TO SUE TO GET COMPENSATION... I wanted the truth about this. And they said they couldn't promise me the truth; they could just promise me dollars.... All along you're told "civil equals dollars" even though dollars mean nothing.... Dollars weren't going to bring my son back.... The dollars feel really bad when you compare them to a life. They hurt.... So then you move that you'd like X number of dollars to do something. Like I'd like to give a million dollars to *this* hospital.... So then it didn't make me angry that this is about dollars. AND YOU WERE ABLE TO DO THAT? Early up.
>
> *My ultimate goal was* "never again"... to get that particular drug that killed my son off the market.... If they were accountable early up, we wouldn't be here today.... *But,* if the doctor's going to be that remote, eventually you've got to get him to the table. I mean I went into the whole civil case saying "I want the truth. I don't want dollars, I want the truth".... And then I was told "well, the truth isn't going to be; that isn't part of what a civil case is about".... It's just dollars.... So I'm not going in with a price tag. But unfortunately you come out with a price tag, even though you didn't go in with that mindset.

It was interesting to note that while this legal claim was not about money, after system conditioning this plaintiff in some way accepted that her case had been transformed on some level into being about dollars. Thus, system conditioning appeared to have an effect on some plaintiffs' understandings of their litigation aims. Likewise, the discourse of the following male plaintiff in his forties who sued subsequent to the death of his father further illustrates how clients' perceptions and aims are affected by system conditioning. Nevertheless, the plaintiffs' extralegal objectives did not disappear, but instead became intermeshed with the pecuniary aspects of their claim. The case had been litigating for nearly one year.

> WOULD YOU SAY YOUR PRIMARY AIM WHEN DECIDING TO START LEGAL PROCEEDINGS WAS TO OBTAIN FINANCIAL COMPENSATION FOR YOUR LOSS? Unfortunately through lawsuits it's only financial compensation you can achieve.... In the mediation... their lawyer made an offer saying "We'll pay $5,000 or $7,000." *But* it's not a matter of the price.... SO IN THAT CASE, I'M GOING TO ASK YOU AGAIN, WHEN YOU SUED, WHAT WAS YOUR AIM? Well, when we went to see the first lawyer, he said "Look, *litigation* has nothing to do with what you want. This

is only about money" ... That's ... the way we were explained it ... The legal system, all it can give you is only financial ... *not answers or an apology.*

I don't want money out of this personally ... All I want is the funeral paid for and my mom's out of pocket expenses ... *The doctor's lawyer said at the mediation,* "Well, if you're struggling and hurting for money ... " He doesn't know about our financial situation ... *He's* thinking maybe we're trying only to get money out of the doctor for financial benefit. But no ... this is our family, and there's not a dollar value to it.... I'm doing it for my father, it's my passion, my heart.... And I want everyone to know ... senior citizens should not be disgraced ... They should have dignity in their lives ... I'm selling my factory, I'm devoting my life to *this.*

One lawyer provided insight into the phenomenon of the concretization of principles expressed as monetary aims.

"WHAT IN YOUR VIEW WERE THE PLAINTIFFS' LITIGATION AIMS? ... Money was not the issue. I think there was a desire for some revenge ... along with a desire to see the wrongdoer punished ... and a desire to find the truth ... and ultimately making the defense pay an amount.... BUT FOR NON-FINANCIAL REASONS? Yeah, that's right." **Male, specialist plaintiff lawyer – fatality case – in fifties**

In comparison, the issue was expounded from a different perspective by an experienced female non-lawyer-mediator,

DO THESE CASES RELATE TO MONETARY COMPENSATION ... ? No, not even usually relating to money. There are many other issues. I mean money is the way it often gets described as a problem.... I'm not saying there aren't legitimate monetary issues, but there are many other factors at play ... Sometimes I think lawyers in particular make it a substantive issue when it's really more than that.... In the mediations I mediated at the College, in every single case they withdrew their complaint ... even fatality cases.... In one case a woman's ... husband had been misdiagnosed and died.... She said to me ... "This is my doctor for 25 years.... I had all my children with him ... And when my husband died, he never called me...." It's a conduct issue. So how can conduct be reconciled by money *alone*?

On the court-mandatory cases I've mediated, I think the focus is "get my clients $500,000 and I will walk away." I've known cases where they got the $500,000 and they haven't walked away. So why did this process fall short for them? It's because there are other issues that are going on that were never addressed.... People only know that the way to get recognition is to do legal proceedings. When they call a lawyer, they're not told "Gee maybe you should mediate this *without starting legal proceedings."*

A hospital accident case that had been litigating for five years provides a final example of this phenomenon. The case involved a nurse's failure to assist the plaintiffs' mother, a hospitalized patient, who repeatedly asked for her help but did not receive it. The patient subsequently fell in the hospital, resulting in her having to wear large casts on her leg continuously for three years, rendering her immobile for what were to be the last years of her life. Although subsequent care for the woman necessitated money, the expressed objectives of the plaintiffs, her surviving children, clearly demonstrated that it was principles they sought from litigation: acknowledgment, apology, acceptance of responsibility, and the prevention of recurrences. The issue was not about money. However, again, financial compensation became entangled with the principles plaintiffs sought.

Co-plaintiff – daughter of victim – in fifties

> What this dispute has always been about... there was no acknowledgment of the fact that she fell, nothing... That nurse was so rude to my mother... And then... trying to get them to say "We're sorry your mother fell." You know, nothing.... The whole reason for all of this, as we said to our lawyer was "My mother needed an apology." "That" is what this is about: the mistakes and no apology, nothing.... What's so difficult about acknowledging that this was a mistake, and saying we're sorry? That's all we wanted. SO THAT WAS THE REASON YOU DECIDED TO SUE? Yeah. And my mother's care. What was going to happen to her?... It wasn't as if they had all this money stored away for a time like this, because they didn't have it. So what are you supposed to do? You know, somebody had to be responsible for this. Because if this happened to my mother, how many other people was it going to happen to?

Co-plaintiff – daughter of victim – in forties

> WHY DID YOU DECIDE TO TAKE LEGAL PROCEEDINGS? We had become so frustrated. The hospital weren't even acknowledging it to start with. It was unbelievable... They just kept sweeping it under the rug, that this accident had even happened... It's important they should admit to such things, and take care of it properly; and promptly. Otherwise, you know what, there wouldn't have been any lawsuit... Part of it was that I felt the hospital should be accountable... We were looking at my mother losing her leg... as a result of the fall... That's what we had basically been told... How was she going to be able to cope with all of this? We told our lawyer, "We want an apology... and some acknowledgement of this"... It wasn't about a dollar amount to be compensated, it was about so they could know what damage was done to the family.

Plaintiffs' lengthy accounts of their motives and objectives for litigation demonstrated that their extralegal aims of principle remained important objects of plaintiffs' desires throughout the processing of their cases. This was notwithstanding their lawyers' delineations of what the litigation system could provide, the legal reformulation of plaintiffs' cases, or the passage of time. Thus, although the intermeshing of principles and money added complexity to the issue, it was clear that notwithstanding any needs or desires for pecuniary recompense to continue life in their newfound situations, plaintiffs were intensely seeking extralegal principles from the civil justice system. Plaintiffs sought "truth" as they had suffered harm and deserved answers. They wanted perceived wrongdoers to "do right" in recognizing their wrongs, admitting fault, accepting responsibility, and apologizing.

Some plaintiffs may have sought compensation as a signal of being heard and acknowledged or as a deterrent to future conduct. Yet, through litigation, these principles were ultimately manifested in money alone, in a system that was repeatedly described to them as one which could only provide financial compensation for their harm. Consequently, plaintiffs who also mentioned pecuniary recompense when speaking of their litigation aims at the same time vehemently stressed, "It's not about the money!"

Some plaintiffs may have initially pursued solely extralegal aims of principle through litigation, with lawyers subsequently persuading them to substitute money. Others may have had multiple objectives from the outset, seeking from litigation both extralegal issues of principle and financial compensation for their harm. In these cases, plaintiffs' lawyers may have then simply translated all of plaintiffs' aims into monetary ones. Regardless of which of these versions was most common, the fact remains that many of the things that plaintiffs uniformly indicated they sought from the civil justice system were not mentioned by most defense lawyers or by many plaintiff lawyers in their cases.

The next section explores another angle of the parallel understandings of plaintiffs' aims existing within actor groups – those on gender lines.

2.5 Gender differentiations

Discourse analysis was also conducted within groups in order to ascertain whether gender affected the degree to which lawyers discussed claimants' extralegal litigation objectives (i.e., those not relating to financial compensation) and whether gender impacted on plaintiffs' articulations of their aims.

Female lawyers' extralegal sensitivity

In exploring gender differences among legal actors, plaintiff lawyers were omitted from the inquiry as there were only two females within that group, precluding meaningful gender analysis. This was similarly the case with physician lawyers, who also comprised only two females. However, when analyzing hospital lawyers' discourse (eight females, four males), interestingly only one of four male respondents discussed plaintiffs' extralegal aims (25%), whereas seven of the eight female respondents did (88%). Moreover, when aggregating the views of all twenty-two defense lawyers (for hospitals and physicians – ten female and twelve male), it became even clearer that awareness of plaintiffs' extralegal litigation aims was more commonly associated with female defense lawyers than with their male counterparts. Eighty percent of females mentioned plaintiffs' extralegal objectives when discussing litigation aims as compared with only 25% of males. Figures 5 and 6 illustrate this point.

Although these gender findings must be regarded as tentative due to the small number of individuals studied, the data suggest that defense lawyers' awareness of

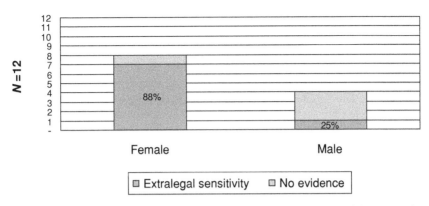

Figure 5. Instances of hospital lawyers mentioning plaintiffs' extralegal litigation objectives. Awareness of plaintiffs' extralegal litigation aims was predominantly seen among female hospital lawyers as compared with males.

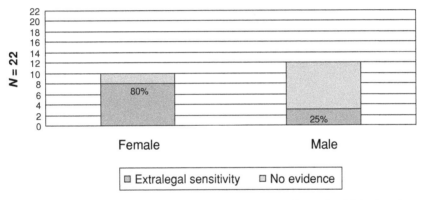

Figure 6. Instances of all defense lawyers mentioning plaintiffs' extralegal litigation aims. In aggregating all twenty-two defense lawyers' interviews, eight out of ten female responses as compared with only three out of twelve male responses mentioned plaintiffs' extralegal objectives when discussing litigation aims.

plaintiffs' extralegal litigation aims was affected by gender. This finding therefore adds another facet to the parallel worlds of perception and understanding within these disputes. It additionally suggests that women have different interpretations of events than men, lending support to writings in feminist legal theory claiming that even at its most neutral, there are gender relations that continuously affect the way law works (Gilligan 1982, pp. 25–29, 62–63, 173). Thus, it may be that female professionals have the potential to offer greater assistance in addressing disputants' extralegal needs during litigation-linked processes, as has been suggested by some (Stempel 2003, pp. 311–12; Subrin 2003, pp. 207–8). This is further explored in chapters five and six.

Female plaintiffs' compensatory unease

Although no substantive differences in litigation aims were found within the plaintiffs' group in terms of gender, a further tentative finding relates to evidence of a degree of unease among female plaintiffs in discussing the financial objectives inherent in their claims. This was noted in 73% of female plaintiffs' interviews (eleven individuals), yet in 0% of male plaintiffs' interviews (six individuals). Even in cases where a mistake was admitted and/or an apology given and a settlement agreed on, female plaintiffs often appeared less comfortable in speaking about pecuniary issues. This was evident even in cases comprising the most serious harm. Seeming more concerned than males about how others perceived their litigation aims, only female plaintiffs stressed that they were not the sorts of people who sued for money. The following are excerpts from interviews with female plaintiffs whose cases had been ongoing for three to five years.

> "From day one I said, 'I'm all about truth here. I have to feel good within me'. And that's the reason why I said, 'I'm not the type who would get a slight hit on the *car* bumper and, in all this neck brace and what have you'. I am not that." **Female – in fifties**

> "We're not like that. We don't want money." **Female – in forties**

> "As . . . it got progressively worse, we weren't able to cope with it financially. . . . Also starting a law suit, because you know, we don't sue people. We never have. . . . My parents never sued anybody. We don't do that kind of thing. And that car accident . . . We don't do that." **Female – in forties**

> "To me, suing . . . That's your only recourse . . . She would have needed money for these things. So we 'had' no choice. But, it was that sense too, thinking 'Well what do they think? That we're after money'?" **Female – in forties**

If we are to accept that financial compensation is a legitimate objective of injured litigants, why then do some plaintiffs seem uncomfortable to discuss the compensatory aims inherent in their claims? What underlies these feelings? Is it that desiring financial compensation represents individuals of lesser integrity or greed, regardless of how meritorious their claims are or the degree to which they have suffered?

This finding resonates with British survey results, which suggest that women are less likely than men to make legal claims (NCC 1995, p. 21). It is also consistent with Babcock and Laschever's research on salary differentials and negotiations of men and women. Babcock and Laschever's detailed empirical research review in Europe and the United States reveals that women are more hesitant than men to ask for higher compensation for their jobs, tend to expect less than men, and tend to undervalue their real worth (Babcock and Laschever 2003, pp. 1–3, 33, 41–61, 64). This is found to be due to women feeling less comfortable in negotiating situations than males, with men believing that they must act to obtain what they deserve and females thinking more that they will ultimately obtain what they deserve. Women are also less likely to believe that they can modify their personal situations (Babcock and Laschever 2003, pp. 19–20, 23, nn. 10, 33). Explaining these findings, Babcock and Laschever note studies examining different societal gender-based expectations. "Men are thought to be assertive, dominant, decisive, ambitious, and self-oriented, whereas women are viewed as warm, nurturing, emotional, and friendly." Thus, due to their other-oriented upbringings, females find it more difficult to ask for things for themselves or make demands that relate to bargaining processes than males who are more self-oriented (Babcock and Laschever 2003, pp. 62–63, 102–3, 106–7, 114, 116–20).

The gender findings in the present study are particularly intriguing and will be focused on throughout the chapters in an attempt to elucidate a further facet of actors' parallel perceptions of conflict and its resolution during legal disputes.

2.6 Chapter conclusion

This chapter presents a picture of discontinuity relating to basic understandings of what these cases were about in terms of comprehensions of plaintiffs' litigation aims. This discontinuity appears to be due, in part, to failed communication. Yet, instead of viewing this simply as conflicting perceptions at a single moment, I argue that it can be understood as part of a system that acts on those perceptions and channels behavior in ways that reinforce those perceptions. So the structures of roles and expectations outlined here might be seen as creating some of the problems and the perceptions. More specifically, I explain this discontinuity as a product of a system that forces legal action for dollars partly because it is structured that way and partly because lawyers and insurance representatives understand disputes in those narrow terms. These understandings are reinforced by the behavior of plaintiffs who have had their disputes transformed by both their own lawyers and the nonresponsiveness that a defense posture focused on money creates.

In recovering actors' understandings of plaintiffs' aims within the structure of litigation, these findings add to the scant depth research on why plaintiffs sue and highlight the degree to which disparate perceptions exist as between claimants and legal actors – at times even between lawyers and their own clients. This represents the first facet of the parallel worlds of perception, understanding and meaning prevalent within these cases. A second aspect relates to differences in female legal actors and female plaintiffs' discourse as compared with their male counterparts. Female lawyers tended to display greater awareness of claimants' extralegal litigation ambitions than did male lawyers. Female plaintiffs (unlike males) tended to display elements of unease when discussing any monetary aspirations within their claims. Moreover, they appeared to be more concerned than males with how others perceived them in this regard.

Interestingly, the disparate lawyer groups, regardless of allegiances, overall tended to hold the same view: that plaintiffs sued mostly or wholly for money. Physician lawyers tended to view claimants as solely questing for financial compensation, whereas hospital and plaintiff lawyers generally viewed money as litigants' primary aim to compensate for harm. Yet, even for those plaintiff lawyers who mentioned clients' extralegal objectives, these were swiftly translated into monetary compensation alone – as "that was all the legal system could offer."

At the same time, virtually all plaintiffs vehemently stressed they sued not for money, but for principles. Plaintiffs' aims of principle did not appear to dissipate over time, as their descriptions of what they sought were the same in cases that had been litigating for three months or for several years. This was also notwithstanding the fact that they may have been conditioned by their lawyers on the "realities of the justice system," resulting in their own increased perceptions of litigation being all about money. Yet, although financial recompense was involved at some level, intertwined within some claimants' descriptions of their objectives, plaintiffs' articulations of what they sought from the civil justice system were thickly composed of extralegal aims of principle – even when speaking of the monetary part of their claims. However, remarkably, the things plaintiffs repeatedly described as being of greatest importance to them were omitted by virtually all physician lawyers, most hospital lawyers, and sometimes even by plaintiffs' own lawyers. It may be that gender had a role to play in lawyers' sensitivity to plaintiffs' extralegal aspirations. Nevertheless, plaintiffs' expressed motivations and litigation aims rarely correlated with legal actors' understandings of this basic premise.

Why were perceptions of plaintiffs' litigation desires so divergent as between the camps involved? I offer a four-stage institutional theory as to how this may have occurred. This should arguably describe both cases where plaintiffs approach lawyers seeking solely extralegal aims of principle through litigation and those where plaintiffs seek principles as well as financial compensation for their harm.

First, consistent with legal system norms, lawyers are trained to operate according to rights and rules, applying law to facts and placing people and occurrences into legal categories including damages. Thus, lawyers often emphasize money issues in contrast to disputants' tendencies to be more emotional about their cases.[23] Moreover, litigants in diverse case types have been found to largely talk past their lawyers who interpret their descriptions without there ever being a shared comprehension of events.[24]

Second, as a result of the civil justice system's denial of certain human needs and desires, deeming them legally irrelevant, lawyers condition plaintiffs on legal system realities, preparing them to expect only money as "that is all the system can provide." Thus, system conditioning was seen to contribute to some plaintiffs eventually articulating that very same interest in economic recompense despite having other strong extralegal objectives for litigation. During litigation, lawyers then inevitably redefine plaintiffs' perceptions and transform the reality litigants

---

23 Felstiner and Sarat (1992, p. 1456), Sternlight (1999, pp. 323–24, 326, 342), and Relis (2002, pp. 162–63, 166).
24 Hosticka (1979, poverty lawyers), Macaulay (1979, consumer cases), Alfieri (1991, poverty lawyers), and Sarat and Felstiner (1995, p. 406, divorce cases).

describe (Cunningham 1992, pp. 1339–57, 1367–85). This involves narrowing the scope of the issues and reformulating all of plaintiffs' objectives to fit into legally cognizable categories – ultimately relating to monetary compensation alone and regularly altering the very nature of litigants' disputes.[25] This commonly results in litigants being effectively silenced, while lawyers purport to recount their stories (Alfieri 1991, p. 2119). As Merry notes, legal words and practices powerfully assert some meanings while silencing others (Merry 1990b, pp. 8–9). The effects of dispute translation should not be underestimated, as the linguistic definitions of conflicts are critical aspects of disputes, affecting understandings and solutions (Merry 1990a, pp. 2–5, 34; Mather and Yngvesson 1980–81, pp. 780–81). Indeed, psychological research has demonstrated how language and words influence the perceptions and views of listeners and readers (Kay and Kempton 1984, p. 65).

Third, plaintiff lawyers' dispute translations and transformations must also serve to cement their own convictions that financial compensation is either entirely or primarily what their clients seek, as plaintiffs were consequently found to cease or reduce the extent to which they discussed their extralegal aspirations with their counsel over the years in which litigation ensued. This too was found in Sarat and Felstner's observations of divorce lawyers and clients (Felstiner and Sarat 1992, pp. 1460, 1463–64). Thus, during the years of litigation, plaintiff lawyers' own convictions as to their clients' fiscal aims may have been strengthened.

Fourth, this, in turn, may have furthered the compensatory slant in how plaintiffs' aims were described by their lawyers to other actors involved in their cases. Thus, the translated fiscal manifestations of plaintiffs' extralegal objectives of principle may have been transmitted by plaintiffs' lawyers to defense lawyers in their subsequent bilateral communications and monetary negotiations that continued throughout the months or years of case processing. Hence, opposing lawyers' communications may have served to further each other's beliefs that the issues were solely or predominantly about money. Defense attorneys interviewed had little contact with plaintiffs themselves. Yet, they regularly mentioned their communications with plaintiff lawyers. This, coupled with the economic realities of legal practice for plaintiff lawyers, such as contingency fee arrangements, and for defense attorneys – who generally act for insurance-type entities that view cases solely monetarily – must have further reinforced lawyers' misunderstandings or incomplete understandings of what plaintiffs want. In fact, it may be that these understandings are subsequently passed down from defense lawyers to their defendant clients. So the cycle of at least partial misconception of plaintiffs' aims continues throughout litigation processes, including litigation-track mediations.

Were plaintiffs' extralegal aims unreasonable or too much to ask from the system? Are these goals not well suited to the traditional legal system (Genn 1999, p. 11)? Perhaps conceptions of the meaning of litigation must evolve. Perhaps the ubiquitous view about "all that the system can provide" must be reassessed in light

---

25 Hosticka (1979, pp. 600–604), Sarat and Felstiner (1986, pp. 116–17), Alfieri (1991, p. 2111), and Cobb (1997, pp. 397, 400–401, 436–37).

of changes to legal processes such as mediation – as behind this understanding lies the belief that this is right. As Menkel-Meadow notes, the adversarial paradigm is premised on the fact that money is the only issue within personal injury disputes. Yet, by assuming that money is the only factor in negotiations, parties' other concerns may be masked and thus remain unresolved (Menkel-Meadow 1984, pp. 783, 788–89, 793). Thus, a paradox of legal entitlement is that plaintiffs who engage the power of the legal system lose control of their disputes to that same power as their cases are reformulated, reinterpreted, and renamed, altering meaning and also consequences (Merry 1990b, pp. 2–3, 111). Are plaintiffs' objectives more fully recognized and achieved in mediation linked to the formal civil justice system? This will be explored in the coming chapters. Providing further background analysis into the mediations covered within the present study and presenting another facet of the parallel worlds' thesis, chapter three examines actors' disparate understandings and meanings ascribed to mandatory versus voluntary mediations.

CHAPTER THREE

The voluntary versus mandatory mediation divide

"I guess the difference is in the culture or the mindset of the parties. I think in a perfect world we would have a voluntary system. But I don't think our society, our culture, is there yet where we can look at the benefits beyond a settlement outcome." **Senior female – lawyer-mediator – in forties**

As court-linked mandatory mediations ("MMP") made up a material part of the dataset (twenty-three mediations), it was important to obtain a sense of actors' attitudes toward these mediations, as compared with voluntary mediations so as to more fully understand actors' mediation agendas and consequent experiences. By comparing lawyers', parties', and mediators' discourse in both mediation types, this chapter highlights the disparities in perception prevalent particularly within mandatory mediation case processing. Moreover, in offering frequently elusive data from litigants as compared with lawyers (Wissler 2002, p. 697), the findings expand on other studies that focus on evaluating particular mandatory programs or settlement rates (Macfarlane 1995; Metzloff et al. 1997, p. 115, n. 34).

Mandatory mediation is used in various jurisdictions for different case types due to low take-up rates of voluntary mediation, notwithstanding participant satisfaction (Pearson and Thoennes 1988, p. 448; Wissler 1997, pp. 565–66; Menkel-Meadow et al. 2006, p. 287). Critics of mandatory mediation have argued that it contradicts the consensual nature of mediation and mediation ideology that advocates disputants' self-determination. It has also been posited that without equal bargaining power, weaker parties are vulnerable to coercion to accept unfair agreements (Pearson and Thoennes 1988, pp. 431–32, 440; Thoennes et al. 1991, pp. 2–3; Wissler 1997, p. 565). For instance, Grillo asserts that mandatory mediation effaces the virtues of mediation and that it disproportionately harms subordinated individuals in society (Grillo 1991, pp. 1549–50, 1610).

However, others have argued that dangers have been exaggerated and that mandatory mediation is generally of assistance to all disputants (Rosenberg 1991, pp. 467, 492–93; Duryee 1992a, p. 509). In fact, no consistent research suggests that mandatory mediation harms disputants. For instance, studies of mandatory divorce mediation, including that of Thoennes et al., tend not to lend credence to concerns about harm to parties, additional disadvantage to vulnerable parties, or pressures to agree to unfair settlements. Nor was mandatory mediation found to negatively affect parties' mediation experiences (Thoennes et al. 1991, pp. 7, 168; Wissler 2000, p. 36; Menkel-Meadow et al. 2006, pp. 286–87). Likewise, Pearson and Thoennes found that making mediation mandatory does not necessarily affect participation in mediation, the voluntariness of mediated agreements, or satisfaction with the process. Moreover, parties were just as likely to recommend mediation as parties in voluntary mediation cases.[1] Similarly, in Wissler's study of voluntary and mandatory mediation involving various dispute types, few differences overall were found in terms of how mediations were experienced or assessed by male and female parties and lawyers, countering concerns that mandatory mediation produces coerced settlements. There were no differences in parties' descriptions of mediation sessions and opportunities to present their views, efforts to understand opponents, feelings of control over the process, whether disputes were truly resolved, or views on mediators (Wissler 1997, pp. 565–66, 577–79, 583–85, 595–96, 598, 601–2).[2]

Likewise, in Wissler's later work on court-connected general civil case–mandatory mediation in nine Ohio common pleas courts, the vast majority of litigants were very pleased with both the mediations and the mediators in terms of fairness, being able to tell their stories and affecting outcomes. Lawyers also held positive views (Wissler 2002, pp. 661–63).[3] Overall satisfaction by parties in mandatory mediation was also found in Macfarlane and Keet's research relating to civil court–connected mediation for various case types.[4]

In terms of "weaker" parties' views, in various divorce studies women have been found to be either similar or more positive about mandatory versus voluntary mediation experiences in terms of fairness and feeling their rights were safeguarded (Bethel and Singer 1982, pp. 27–29; Kelly 1989, pp. 81–86; Duryee 1992b, p. 265; Clement and Schwebel 1993, pp. 98–99). Despite one study where females felt more pressure to settle than males (Pearson and Thoennes 1988, pp. 440–41), various other studies of divorce mediation found not only that women were not disadvantaged (Wissler 1997, pp. 570–72), but that men more often reported feeling

---

[1] Pearson and Thoennes conducted two studies of court-linked mediation involving divorce and custody cases in Denver, Los Angeles, Connecticut, and Hennepin. The Denver study of voluntary mediation involved a quasi-experimental design. The remaining research related to mandatory mediation and utilized 530 questionnaires, observations, and interviews with parties at three stages (Pearson and Thoennes 1988, pp. 429–32).

[2] Wissler's study derives from phone interviews with Boston small claims parties (171 plaintiffs and defendants in 124 cases, 30% undergoing mandatory mediation, where mediators were students and community members, and 70% undergoing voluntary mediation) and questionnaire data in 610 cases from mediators, lawyers, and disputants in three Ohio common pleas courts' mandatory and voluntary mediations (Wissler 1997, pp. 577–80, 588, 590, 592).

[3] Wissler's findings derive primarily from questionnaire data in over 1,200 cases from lawyers, parties, and lawyer-mediators in various case types (including 69% personal injury cases) where generally some discovery had been completed (Wissler 2002, pp. 642, 644–46, 648–50, 652–53, 655).

[4] Their research was done via focus groups and interviews with over sixty lawyers, thirty-one litigants, thirteen mediators, and a small sample of judges in Saskachewan (Macfarlane and Keet 2004–5, pp. 677, 686–87).

disadvantaged in mediation (Kelly 1989, p. 81). For instance, in Thoennes et al.'s study of mandatory divorce mediation in Indiana deriving from interviews with parties, lawyers, and mediators, it was found that men were almost twice as likely as women to report feelings of disadvantage during mediation in terms of their bargaining power and control over outcomes. However, most of those who reported feelings of lack of power ended the sessions. Therefore, the issue of power in mediation is more complex than is often assumed and does not always align with financial resources. Power imbalances can result from various factors including unequal knowledge and communication abilities (Thoennes et al. 1991, pp. i–iii, 7–9, 65, 73–74, 82, 151–52, 161, 168).

Addressing the mandatory–voluntary mediation debate from actors' perspectives, the present findings similarly suggest that differences between mediation types may be exaggerated, as no material differences were found in disputants' perceptions of mandatory versus voluntary mediations in terms of their experiences, mediation aims, or understandings of mediation's purpose (*chapters three to six*). Similarly, for lawyers, notwithstanding their negative attitudes toward mandatory mediations' early timing, their articulated mediation aims were the same irrespective of whether mediations were mandatory or voluntary. Likewise, as will be seen in the chapters to come, there was a strong common thread running through attorneys' discourse on perceptions of "what went on" during mediations regardless of mediation type (*chapters six and seven*).

In the present study, three principal disparities existed between mandatory and voluntary mediations: timing, defendants' attendance, and mediators. Chapter four analyzes views on defendants' attendance and chapter seven examines perceptions of mediators, encompassing those on the MMP. In this chapter, I consider the most profusely discussed topic relating to mandatory mediations, being their court-imposed timing as compared with voluntary mediations (which occurred solely at the behest of lawyers, far closer to trial). Mandatory mediations had to take place within ninety days after the first statement of defense had been filed, unless the court ordered otherwise (Ontario R.Civ.P. 24.1.09). Thus, they were generally pre-discovery.

The following sections construct the "big picture" from the views of all groups, attempting to gain a greater understanding of the "voluntary versus mandatory divide" as perceived by mediations' actors. In examining attitudes and perceptions as well as the underlying meaning of the various realities depicted, something unexpected occurs. Critical pieces of the puzzle are seen to be omitted by the powerful groups, consequently transforming the big picture into one where opposing camps become unexpectedly aligned, making strange bedfellows. This adds another facet to the parallel worlds of understanding existing within these legal disputes, as yet again disputants and lawyers are seen to have completely different expectations and use different language to describe mandatory and voluntary mediation. Implications of this are discussed in the chapter conclusion.

3.1 Lawyers' world – mandatory versus voluntary mediation divide

Conceptually, there was virtually no difference between voluntary and mandatory mediations for lawyers. Notwithstanding their critiques of the MMP's mechanics, attorneys' complaints had little to do with the fact that mediations were mandatory. Only a small minority viewed the concept of court-linked compulsory mediation per se as problematic. This may have been because the mandatory mediation program had been operative for eighteen months at data collection. Therefore, lawyers may already have become accustomed to the idea of mandatory mediation as part of the norms of courts' case management. In the vast majority of questionnaire responses relating to both mandatory and voluntary mediations, lawyers either "agreed," "strongly agreed," or "very strongly agreed" that "mediation provided an important settlement opportunity." Moreover, when lawyers recounted what transpired at various mediations, they frequently spoke of voluntary and mandatory mediations interchangeably without differentiating them conceptually.

Virtually all attorneys spoke particularly positively about voluntary mediations. However, for mandatory mediations it was basically universal among lawyers (all but one in each group) as well as most mediators that for medical disputes, they generally occurred too early within the litigation process. These findings are not unique to medical cases or to the respondents within the present study. In Macfarlane's research based on forty interviews with commercial litigators in Ottawa and Toronto who had undergone at least ten mandatory mediations, many similarly complained about the early (pre-discovery) timing of mandatory mediations stating that it sometimes rendered mediations useless for settlement purposes or "a waste of time" due to inadequate information to assess cases or damages (Macfarlane 2002, pp. 244, 251–52, 263, 280–81).

Similarly, in the Wisconsin medmal mandatory panel mediations, both plaintiff and defense lawyers strongly felt that mediations (also being pre-discovery) occurred too early, prior to adequate information being available for informed settlements (Meschievitz 1991, p. 210). Likewise, Metzloff's survey of seventy-two defense and forty-five plaintiff lawyers in North Carolina's court-ordered medical mediations found that although 75% of lawyers were in favor of mandatory mediation, some lawyers felt that mediations would only be beneficial if they occurred after discovery. Many noted that realistic appraisals of cases' strengths were not possible (Metzloff et al. 1997, pp. 140–41, 143). In Britain too, research on early mandatory mediation was viewed negatively by lawyers who felt mediations should not occur before damages were known (Polywka 1997, p. 81). However, these studies include little or no mention of plaintiffs' or defendants' views on the matter. This is explored in Section 3.3.

The issue of mediations' timing is a professional one. However, in view of the historic shape of settlement processes through litigation, lawyers' views as to timing were not surprising. Attorneys are not culturally accustomed to settling early. Thus, they would obviously not feel comfortable with early mediation, as this disrupts their preferred timing of "late" settlement and all that entails. Legal actors' discourse on mandatory versus voluntary mediations' timing is later examined in greater depth, additionally revealing something about the meaning lawyers ascribe to mediation itself.

Defense lawyers – Although not all of the fifteen case interviews with physician lawyers related to mandatory mediations, all lawyers (but one) had experience in mandatory mediation. Most were positive about mandatory mediation in general; all were very positive about voluntary mediation. Similarly, in the fourteen case interviews with hospital lawyers, all had only good things to say about voluntary mediations, and the majority were positive about mandatory mediations overall.[5] The big issue of concern was "timing." One senior female defense attorney encapsulated some of the key issues as follows: "DO YOU SEE THE VOLUNTARY AND MANDATORY MEDIATIONS AS TWO DIFFERENT EXPERIENCES No, arguably they shouldn't be. DO YOU SEE DIFFERENCES BETWEEN EARLY AND LATER MEDIATIONS Very much so ... I think in the earlier pre-discovery ones ... it's less clear who's going to win and who's going to lose except in the very clearest of cases. So there may be better opportunities to resolve it on some other basis.... The later ones tend to be more like a rights-based kind of pre-trial thing."

Indeed, although never articulated as such in discussing the voluntary versus mandatory divide, defense lawyers' discourse evinced the fact that they were predominantly interested in rights-based mediations that occurred later on. No mention was made of disputants' desires or extralegal needs. In speaking of mediations' timing, what defense lawyers required was sufficient time before mediations to obtain information deriving from experts' reports and oral discovery of parties (who provided answers in person to opposing lawyers' questions, simultaneously demonstrating the "type of witnesses" they would make at trial). This information enabled defense lawyers to make their own assessments and decisions about (1) whether there was liability and (2) if so, how much they wanted to pay. This information affected how defense lawyers were going to play it strategically at mediation in light of what they thought would happen at trial. Indeed, doctors' lawyers noted,

> "The difference I've seen between them I don't know so much derives from the mandatory versus voluntary so much as it's driven by the mandatory timeframes ... If this case had gone to mandatory mediation within the court timeframes, it never would have resolved in mediation. It's just far too soon. We wouldn't have had experts review the files; we wouldn't have had discoveries ... we wouldn't have known ... As long as it's post-discovery far enough that I've had a chance to assess the case ... " **Male – in thirties**

"If plaintiffs' counsel ... recognizes this is a potential winner for them, or there are some real issues, we're going to need discovery evidence to go to experts, to figure

---

5 This topic was discussed in fifteen case interviews involving nine physician lawyers, fourteen case interviews involving nine hospital lawyers, and sixteen case interviews involving fourteen plaintiff lawyers.

out our cases and our perspective; because it's a waste of time before that." **Male – in fifties**

"Timing is often skewed, which makes the mediation useless." **Male – in fifties**

The same types of concern were reiterated by virtually all hospital lawyers. For example,

"I think in the medmal, they're too early. So I don't find them that helpful... The discovery process is your fat gathering. And then you have to get your expert opinions... because I've had cases I've defended on paper that looked great. And you get in there to the discovery, and the nurse or physician is a terrible witness, or whatever. So by the time you leave discoveries, you have a very different view of the case." **Female – in forties**

"I think mandatory mediation is a good thing, but... for this area of law, unless liability is 100% and the parties have exchanged the totality of their records... and they've obtained expert reports, we're not going to settle... because there's too much unknown still." **Female – in twenties**

"Once I've have the opportunity to develop a solid position of what my case is, and I've got either opinions or whatever. Everyone has had the opportunity to really investigate and determine where they're at... But frequently... you don't have enough information." **Female – in twenties**

Yet, at the same time a serendipitous tactical benefit of early mediation noted by defense lawyers (particularly hospital lawyers) was that they offered the opportunity to get out of actions early in cases where they felt they should not have been involved to begin with. For instance,

"I have partners who are madly in favor of early mandatory mediation... Even though it's a piece of crap case, it's an early opportunity to go in, hit the plaintiff with the realities of the situation... your 'one and only' chance to speak directly to the plaintiff and tell them just how bad their case is... We're not there to play cosy with them, to make them feel better, and do all those things that we would do in a case where we're actually feeling very exposed and do not want to put our people through a trial." **Hospital lawyer – male – in forties**

"It's more productive towards settlement to have the mediation after discovery. *But* when I don't think the hospital should be there, I like the early opportunity to try and get out of the action *early*, and to give that pitch." **Hospital lawyer – female – in twenties**

"It's only potential value *pre-discovery* is that it might persuade a plaintiff who is not hearing his or her lawyer that there's no case, to hear it in a neutral kind of setting. The doctor would come across persuasively in why there's no negligence; and that might help plaintiff's counsel say 'Stop wasting your money and let's not go forward'." **Physician lawyer – male – in fifties**

This was also noted by one plaintiff lawyer, foreshadowing a different meaning of mandatory mediation for plaintiffs.

> "In some ways it's very positive in that it may be the face to face meeting they want, to talk to somebody about what they've caused; and maybe they'll be satisfied with explanations provided there... I think there's a greater likelihood that the litigation would be abandoned.... If you've got a general litigation practice... you might go home with your client and say 'Listen, they had a lot of important things to say and it's probably best we found out now rather than having to pay an extra $3,000 to do that'."
> **Plaintiff lawyer – specialist, male – in thirties**

Plaintiff lawyers – In the sixteen case interviews with plaintiff lawyers, their views on timing issues effectively repeated those of defense attorneys – essentially tactics related. There was no differentiation between specialist and generalist lawyers. The following quotes are illustrative of plaintiff lawyers' views.

> "Mandatory mediation is fine. It's got to be late in the day and it's got to be when the parties can truly evaluate the case." **Male, specialist – in fifties**

> "In this case, if we'd had everybody hand in their experts reports... then we could say 'Okay, we know pretty much the kind of facts that are going to come out at trial' and you can assess the odds, which is what you have to deal with." **Male, generalist – in forties**

> "My experience in mandatory mediations is that... nobody wants to commit at this early stage. I think it's atrocious *my clients are* having to incur these expenses and you're not getting anything at the end of the day... They should take place after discovery."
> **Male, specialist – in forties**

Whether, in fact, disputants perceived they were going "to get anything" out of mandatory mediation is dealt with in Section 3.3. Yet, in discussing timing preferences for mediations, most lawyers made little reference to either parties' perspectives, the ostensible protagonists in these disputes.

Interestingly, in Wissler's study of mandatory mediation in Ohio where 69% of cases were for personal injury, although there were mixed views on discovery status and mediation timing, no overall relationship was found between the timing of the mediation in terms of proximity to trial and the chances of settlement. Lawyers' views on whether mediation was too early seemed to be affected more by their own expectations as to timing than by the actual timing of mediation. In fact, Wissler found that cases were more likely to settle if mediation occurred earlier rather than later, with the likelihood of settlement not being linked to discovery (Wissler 2002, pp. 677, 698). In Wissler's 1997 work on various case types including personal injury, she also notes that settlement was more likely if cases were mediated earlier rather than later (Wissler 1997, pp. 588, 594).

Negative lawyer attitudes

When looking deeper into lawyers' complaints about mandatory mediation, it appeared that most important was whether documentary evidence had been exchanged by opposing sides – particularly by plaintiff lawyers on whom the onus lay to prove their cases. Certainly, mediation preparation is critical. Yet, a minority of lawyers in each group and most mandatory mediators felt that plaintiff (and in some cases defense) lawyers were inadequately preparing for mandatory as compared with voluntary mediations. These views derived from both pre-discovery and post-discovery mandatory mediations, including those that had been postponed several times. This suggested a problem of lawyer attitude. The following quotes illustrate this phenomenon:

> "Some plaintiff lawyers tend to treat it just as another step, not ready to do what they should be doing." **Physician lawyer – female – in fifties**

> "The plaintiff's side was much less prepared for the mediation... It was the plaintiff's side who said 'Don't waste your time because there's not going to be a settlement'... The plaintiff's lawyer was reminded what medical reports he should be providing... and he hadn't done that. I was really shocked." **Mandatory – lawyer-mediator – female – in fifties – bladder operation case**

> "We prepared; *the defense* didn't prepare. THAT'S YOUR GENERAL EXPERIENCE? Ya, they hold the cards for a long time." **Specialist plaintiff lawyer – male – in forties**

> "If you go into a voluntary mediation, it's because you want to really give it a chance to resolve and you'll prepare differently... You'll make sure all your documents are in order." **Hospital lawyer – female – in twenties**

In Macfarlane and Keet's study of a mandatory mediation program for various case types that had been running for ten years, lawyers generally had positive views on early pre-discovery mandatory mediation, not viewing it as problematic (although there were some criticisms about flawed timing). Yet, reasons given for mediation failures included failure of other lawyers to sufficiently prepare for mediation, not taking the process seriously or lacking "good faith." Lack of preparation as a result of negative views of mediation's early timing was also noted in Macfarlane's study of commercial lawyers. Attorneys' preparation for mediation is vital in legitimizing the process, directly affecting its usefulness. Thus, as Macfarlane notes, lawyers' lack of preparedness may mask the fact that lawyers still view mediation as simply an obstacle to get through and not a meaningful settlement opportunity (Macfarlane 2002, pp. 261, 279–80; Macfarlane and Keet 2004–5, pp. 688–90).

General negative lawyer attitude to mandatory mediations as compared with voluntary mediations was also noted by all mediators who conducted mandatory mediations.

"YOU DO BOTH VOLUNTARY AND MANDATORY MEDIATIONS? Yes. DO YOU SEE A DIFFERENCE... for these cases the mandatory's are totally perfunctory. It's just 'What's the process we've got to do? Let's get out of here'. WHO FEELS THAT WAY? All the lawyers. If you're going on a voluntary mediation, you're going with the goal of settling it. In mandatory, many times they have no real interest in settling." **Popular non-lawyer-mediator – male – in forties**

"The mandatory mediations don't work that well... They're not really here to be serious." **Lawyer-mediator – male – in forties**

"They kept saying 'What are we going to accomplish here today'? BOTH LAWYERS? Yes, in terms of 'how can we get through this quickly'. WHAT ABOUT YOUR PREVIOUS MEDIATION? They wanted to *settle*. It was a voluntary mediation." **Non-lawyer-mediator – female – in thirties – vasectomy case**

Negative attitudes were likewise conveyed by most lawyers regardless of allegiances. For instance, physician lawyers said,

"Generally when we go to voluntary mediations, it's because we recognize there's some liability issues... whereas quite often I'm at mandatory mediations and the initial view is that the case is completely defensible. So really, not much is going to be accomplished... unless the plaintiff... can be convinced to go away... I'm not going to be convinced to pay money at a mandatory mediation that happens that early. So I think it affects the way the mediation goes, because I go in with a completely different attitude." **Male – in thirties**

Similarly, hospital lawyers commented,

"The process is the same. I think what's different is the substance behind it.... Frequently... in a voluntary mediation... a lot of meaty things can be discussed in detail.... You typically put together a whole package of stuff and you present your entire case.... When it's mandatory, it's sort of like 'Okay, we all have to go. So, throw something together and let's go'. In mandatory... nine out of ten *mediations* you go to each party makes their pitch. No one wants to hear what the other person has to say yet because it's too early and everyone goes home. And they would say 'that was a really big waste of time'. It's rare that anyone is really talking about settlement." **Female – in twenties**

"I think frequently at a voluntary mediation... everyone's there to really try and talk about settlement... A lot of counsel treat mandatory mediation differently. So that infuses the process. If all counsel agree that mediation will be useful and volunteer to engage in it, then... the right people will be there and the right things will be said. When it's mandatory, some counsel resist it or they say 'This is a waste of time'." **Male – in forties**

Likewise, most plaintiff lawyers had negative attitudes.

> "We're only doing this because the court is telling us we have to... In voluntary mediation... the ones that work take place close to trial... They are voluntary, so that tells you about the motivations." **Male – in forties**

> "Mandatory mediations or any early mediation doesn't get anything done... We know nothing can be resolved... nobody's ready, nobody has the information they need, nobody understands the case well enough... It's looked upon as a bit of a time-waster... Let us pick the time." **Male – in fifties**

There were, of course, a few positive views proffered by lawyers about the mandatory mediations. For instance,

> "There was some kind of exploration of the issues in the presence of both parties... There was something positive... an interest in trying to address the issues from all sides... an airing of the issues... that the doctors' side was also there somewhere in the process." **Physician lawyer – male – in fifties**

> "I think any of these dialogues are good... because I can use it as an opportunity to have a face to face discussion with the plaintiff's lawyer, to talk about what they think their strengths are... their weaknesses... I learn more things about the case." **Physician lawyer – male – in thirties**

Additionally, a number of female hospital lawyers stressed the positive communication element inherent in mandatory mediation.

> "It's always of some benefit just to meet the human beings behind the paper, both lawyers and litigants. Apart from that, no *benefit*." **Female – in forties**

> "I like mandatory mediation for all cases. I just think it's a really good idea to get parties face to face." **Female – in twenties**

> "Most times it's rare you walk away and say 'That was a total waste of time,' even on the mandatory ones... There's value in everyone getting together and talking about it." **Female – in twenties**

Similarly, one female plaintiff lawyer noted,

> "It was helpful. We didn't resolve anything necessarily. I don't think it's ever bad in any litigation... for counsel to sit down and talk and meet each other." **Female – in thirties**

To combat lawyers not meaningfully participating in mandatory mediation, "good-faith" requirements have been advocated and added to some U.S. statutes and court rules on mandatory mediation (Kovach 1997, p. 620; Boettger 2004, pp. 1–4, 11, 15). Notwithstanding debates on the meaning of "good faith," "bad faith" would generally include failure to prepare and exchange information for mediation. However, the issue of mandating good-faith rules in mediation is highly controversial, not least because it may adversely affect parties' self-determination, mediators' roles, and neutrality and mediation confidentiality. It may also encourage adversarial conduct and satellite litigation.[6] Therefore, court encouragement of parties to mediate in good faith has been suggested instead, together with further education for attorneys (Boettger 2004, pp. 2–4, 12, 14, 25, 39, 41, 44).

In the present study, it was clear that for lawyers, attitudes, agendas, and tactics were quite different in mandatory versus voluntary mediations. But what else could be discerned from attorneys' concerns?

Underlying meaning of lawyers' mandatory – voluntary mediation preferences

Although rarely mentioned outright, perhaps the most salient issue implicit in legal actors' discourse on mandatory versus voluntary mediations, and in particular on the problem of early timing, was that lawyers wanted to decide about liability themselves prior to mediations and objected to discussing issues relating to liability or fault during mediations. This implied that most lawyers viewed mediation solely as a forum for negotiating about money in cases where they thought there may be liability. This was something attorneys did prior to the advent of mediation and continued to do during bilateral lawyer negotiations. Indeed, as candidly noted by some in relation to voluntary mediations, unless the defense perceived possible issues of liability (whereby the focus at mediation then became quantum), they would not propose, or agree to, voluntary mediation. The following excerpts highlight this point:

> "I think it's probably understood in the mediation business that if the *defense* shows up at a voluntary mediation, they're in a mood to pay money." **Specialist plaintiff lawyer – male – in fifties**

> "If we were of the view that the case was defensible, we wouldn't agree to go to a *voluntary* mediation. We don't go to mediation to simply say we won't pay any money. It's a waste of everybody's time." **Physician lawyer – male – in thirties**

> "Typical in mandatory mediation is you don't get the documents, just a brief statement of issues. So therefore you can't really have a discussion about damages." **Hospital lawyer – female – in twenties**

> "The plaintiffs' counsel was only interested in sitting down with defendants' counsel and flogging numbers, because they'd gone through discoveries." **Mandatory lawyer-mediator – male – in fifties**

---

6 U.S. courts have had difficulties with the tension between good-faith requirements and mediation confidentiality. In Foxgate v. Bramalea, the California Supreme Court overruled the Court of Appeal, holding that there are no exceptions to mediations' statutory confidentiality and thus mediators cannot report bad-faith conduct (25 P.3d 117 (Cal. 2001)). Likewise, in Decker v. Lindsay, Texas, the Court of Appeal held that unlike mediation attendance, good faith could not be mandated (824.S.W.2d247 (Tex. Ct. App. 1992)), (Lande 2002, pp. 70, 127; Macfarlane and Keet 2004–5, p. 689; Menkel-Meadow et al. 2006, pp. 301, 308–9).

Indeed, as one severely harmed voluntary mediation plaintiff noted,

> "They were really interested in what I was expecting financially. What were the things I needed to make my life as good as possible. Monetary. No, they weren't going into, you know. They'd heard it all. That's not why they were there... They weren't interested in listening to me, you know." **Plaintiff – female – in sixties**

This conclusion was additionally supported by legal actors in speaking of perceived "productive" mandatory mediations. Cases where it was felt not to be too early to mediate, irrelevant of pre- or post-discovery status, was where liability was clear and plaintiffs' lawyers had produced all necessary documentary evidence. Again, these amounted to cases where defense lawyers had already decided their standpoint on liability prior to mediation. Hence, what was discussed and negotiated was solely "how much money for the injury." For instance,

> "If the only focus is damages, then provided there's full disclosure of documents... mediation is fine early on." **Hospital lawyer – female – in twenties**

> "Because liability was not in issue, we had tried to focus on what the damages would be... This was a perfect case for mediation... It was a matter of coming up with a figure that's reasonable to both sides." **Hospital lawyer – female in twenties – discussing "successful" mandatory mediation**

> "If it's the kind of case where liability is clear, then that's different; when it becomes a matter really of quantum only." **Plaintiff lawyer – generalist, male – in forties**

> "This was a mandatory mediation. And in fact, it was a case that was suitable to have an early mediation because it looked like liability wasn't in issue. And the isssue was, 'could we come to some reasonable figure on damages'?" **Physician lawyer – male – in fifties**

Having explored legal actors' stance on the mandatory versus voluntary mediation divide, I then examined disputants' views on the issue and whether they were of different mindsets when undergoing mandatory versus voluntary mediations. Although mainly referring to plaintiffs (as defendants were often absent from litigation-linked mediations – *see chapter four*), in discussing voluntary versus mandatory mediations only a few defense lawyers and fewer than half of plaintiff lawyers alluded to plaintiffs' perspectives in any way. Virtually no mention was made of defendant physicians' perspectives. This appeared to indicate that legal actors generally perceived mediation to be their forum first and foremost. Yet, as will be seen, lawyers' understandings of what should occur at mediations and their implicit objections to discussing liability or fault at mediations, be they mandatory or voluntary, were in sharp contrast to parties' desires to discuss issues of fault in all mediations, including obtaining answers, explanations, and apologies. This is examined later and in chapter five, illustrating the next facet of the parallel worlds of understanding within case processing.

3.2 Parties' world – no mandatory versus voluntary divide

Upon entering the world of disputants, remarkably all tactics talk and negative attitudes relating to mandatory versus voluntary mediation were absent. There was no mention of problematic early timing, insufficient information, lack of expert reports, or inadequate lawyer preparation. Indeed, for the vast majority of disputants, undergoing mandatory or voluntary mediation was overall the same in terms of their attitudes and expectations – equally, as will be seen further in chapter five, so were their mediation aims.

Just a stage in the litigation process

First, it appeared that all plaintiffs viewed their mediations, regardless of whether they were mandatory or voluntary, simply as a stage in the litigation or court process. This was confirmed by various lawyers in response to the question, "HOW DID YOUR CLIENTS FEEL ABOUT MEDIATION BEING COMPULSORY?"

> "I don't think that they necessarily understood it was compulsory... I think they just saw it as part of the process." **Plaintiff lawyer – specialist, male – in thirties**

> "I don't think that they had a feeling about that... *They* don't know how the whole process works... They go through mediation as a stage in the lawsuit." **Plaintiff lawyer – generalist, male – in forties**

> "They all seem to be happy that there's some action in their case... WHAT ABOUT THAT IT'S COMPULSORY? He didn't really distinguish between this as anything more than just another step in the legal proceeding." **Plaintiff lawyer – generalist, male – in forties**

Defendant physicians appeared to have the same perceptions.

> "Neither doctor had any experience with the legal system, so everything is mandatory to them... They didn't take it as anything other than one of the rules that guides how the lawsuit proceeds." **Male – defense physician lawyer in fifties – speaking of two different mandatory mediations**

> "Well, they set it up as part of the court process. So it's one of the steps you have to go through." **Defendant surgeon – male – in fifties**

Second, not only was timing not mentioned by plaintiffs, but it appeared that defendant physicians were keen to have mediations early on.

> "My view is that it should happen as soon as possible. Because the wait is dreadful. I suppose it allows the family a cooling off time but for me it was awful. It was a terrible thing to have that kind of a time... IF YOU WOULD HAVE NEEDED CERTAIN EXPERT REPORTS. Ya, but you can get these things in three months." **Female physician in College mediation of fatality case that may have litigated – in fifties**

"A reasonable time for obtaining expert opinion, no longer than eight weeks... I have given a lot of expert opinions for both plaintiffs and defendants, and when I get a request... I try my absolute best to get something out within two to three weeks... because there is not a lot of evidence that you've got to get." **Male surgeon in court-linked mandatory mediation – fatality – in fifties**

Although only a few defendant respondents underwent court-linked mandatory mediation, their perspectives were important – particularly as the literature suggests they accorded with the feelings of many similar defendants who were in favor of having their disputes mediated or resolved as soon as possible.[7]

Same positive attitudes – same eagerness

Third, although difficult for some emotionally, in sharp contrast to attorneys' negative attitudes to mandatory mediation, positive attitudes and eagerness to undergo both mandatory and voluntary mediations were the reality for virtually all plaintiffs who viewed both forms of mediation as their "day in court."

"SOME PEOPLE SAY THEY WANT TO HAVE THEIR DAY IN COURT Oh, my day was there. YOUR DAY WAS THERE? Yes... My day was at the mediation. I didn't need to go to court for my day. It was already there." **Female – plaintiff – in fifties – voluntary mediation – no settlement – loss-of-sight case**

"They wanted a day of reckoning or their day in court... In some ways it's a day of reckoning at mediation where somebody can say 'I'm sorry this has happened to you. We all felt terrible about it'." **Plaintiff lawyer – specialist, male – in thirties – mandatory mediation – settled – child operation case**

"Any time you're going to what they would generically think of as court, it's like your day. Someone's going to tell you 'Yeah you suffered and you're entitled to be compensated'. So you have to kind of ratchet down their expectations... But to them it's an event in the lawsuit, an important day." **Plaintiff lawyer – generalist, male – in forties – mandatory mediation – no settlement – vasectomy case**

Moreover, in direct contrast to most lawyers, plaintiffs' discourse in both voluntary and mandatory mediations displayed the same eagerness to partake in mediation. This eagerness was reiterated by virtually all plaintiff lawyers discussing their clients' attitudes.

"I *felt* so happy to go into the mediation, to reach the doctor." **Male plaintiff – in thirties – pre-discovery mandatory mediation – no settlement – bladder operation case**

"HOW DID YOU FEEL ABOUT HAVING TO GO THROUGH MEDIATION? I felt good... I was looking forward to it, to getting up, everything open. I thought we're

---

7 Teff (1994, pp. 13, 57), Johnson (1997, p. 45), Hobbs and Gable (1998, pp. 1–2), Simanowitz (1998, p. 63), and Forehand (1999, p. 910).

all going to just hash it out... HOW DID YOU FEEL ABOUT MEDIATION BEING COMPULSORY? I thought it was great thing. I've never been to mediation before and I thought it's something before we get into formalities of courts; something where total laymen could understand, without getting into a legal, without saying anything you're not supposed to say, just free form. I think it was a great thing to have." **Male plaintiff – in forties – post-discovery mandatory mediation – fatality case – no settlement**

Same overall understandings, expectations, intentions, and needs

Fourth, analysis of plaintiffs' discourse revealed that in sharp contrast to lawyers, expectations for voluntary and mandatory mediations were overall the same. This was notwithstanding any differences in "expectation management" from their attorneys prior to mediations (as in voluntary mediations lawyers may have suggested that the defense might be more acquiescing). Although generally uncertain about what would transpire at mediation, virtually all plaintiffs appeared equally certain about defendants' liability in both mandatory and voluntary mediations. Thus, although voluntary mediation plaintiffs would have undergone more protracted waiting periods, virtually all claimants regardless of mediation type attended mediations with the same aims and expectations of reaching settlement. The following interview excerpts illustrate this point:

"WHAT WERE YOUR GOALS FOR MEDIATION? Just resolving the issue... WHAT DID YOU EXPECT WAS GOING TO OCCUR? Before mediation I thought we were going to have a conversation, totally open forum with questions and answers... and that we would have a heart to heart, the two of us. *The doctor*... would have said 'Listen, I made an honest mistake. I hope you... somehow forgive me... That's all I can offer you here at this time; and I'll see what I can do to offer you some damages. And let's carry on with our lives'. That's what I was sort of thinking." **Male plaintiff – in forties – post-discovery mandatory mediation – fatality DNR case – no settlement**

"DID YOU THINK YOU WERE GOING TO MAYBE SETTLE THERE? I think so. Because our lawyer and this mediator told me *many* cases are settled in mediation. I *thought* there would be some settlement." **Female plaintiff – in seventies – post-discovery mandatory mediation – no settlement – fatality DNR case**

Voluntary mediation plaintiffs' discourse on the issue was similar to mandatory plaintiffs overall.

"WHAT DID YOU EXPECT? I thought that would be the end of it.... That it was going to be over at that point. I didn't know it was going to extend after that." **Female plaintiff – in fifties – voluntary mediation – no settlement at mediation, but subsequently – loss-of-limb case**

"I went with the expectation of settling this." **Female plaintiff – in forties – voluntary mediation – no settlement – loss-of-sight case**

"DID YOU HAVE ANY EXPECTATIONS? Well I thought there would be some sort of negotiation... and also acceptance of guilt... You know, they come in and say 'Well, we screwed up and we just want to settle. We know that money can't bring back... But just to show that we understand, we're going to give you X amount. I thought more or less they were there to apologize because *my lawyer* told me that the mere fact that they are having this session, it appears that they are going to settle. And I thought apart from settlement was also acceptance of guilt and apology and so forth. So I was upbeat, hoping that would take place'." **Male co-plaintiff – in fifties – voluntary mediation – no settlement – loss-of-sight case**

Similar to plaintiffs and in sharp contrast to lawyers, the few defendant physicians who underwent mandatory mediation were far less certain that their mandatory mediations would not end in settlement. For instance,

"I knew that the mediation was not going to get to anything except maybe... something would come out of it to satisfy their request... for a number (money)." **Mandatory mediation – defendant physician – male in fifties – no settlement – fatality case**

A final indication of the absence of the mandatory versus voluntary divide for plaintiffs lay in the fact that notwithstanding gross disparities in their charges ($600 mandatory versus $3,000 voluntary) plaintiffs undergoing both mediation types were generally unaware of how much their mediations had cost.

The following case study illustrates the overall picture for many of the mandatory mediations. It related to a dispute involving a claim for a failed vasectomy and a consequent pregnancy and abortion for a practicing Catholic family financially unable to support a further child. The case had been litigating for just under one year. The mediation was pre-discovery and did not end in settlement. Yet, unaware of the realities occurring for legal actors, the plaintiffs described their understandings and expectations for mediation as follows:

"I was a little bit eager to be there, to tell him my side and ask them for answers like 'why', and just to see what he would say... YOU EXPECTED... that we were going to go to the mediation and see if we can get this resolved so that it wouldn't have to go to court, and whether or not a settlement could be reached... *My lawyer* told me that's why you had mediation... and I guess if there was a lot of evidence... then their lawyer will try to push figures at you or whatever IS THAT WHAT YOU EXPECTED. Ya... DID YOU THINK THAT IT MIGHT HAVE SETTLED THEN? Ya." **Male plaintiff – in thirties**

"I thought maybe there would be some kind of... maybe they were willing to give a little bit. You know, the doctor's lawyer maybe would own up to, maybe that it 'was' a mistake. That's what I thought. But I thought at least his lawyer would come, at least... understanding that 'of course' there was something wrong." **Female plaintiff – in thirties**

The female non-lawyer-mediator (in thirties) described the mediation as follows:

> "There was a lot of emotion and tension for the plaintiffs but no motivation to mediate by the lawyers... This was the mini-court that was going to solve the issue WHAT GAVE YOU THAT IMPRESSION Because I asked them.
>
> The plaintiffs' lawyer, to my surprise, didn't even have all the information they needed to proceed during the mediation... *Both lawyers* kept saying "What are we going to accomplish here today?... in terms of "how can we get through this quickly."

Indeed, the male defense lawyer (in forties) said in a telephone interview prior to the mediation,

> "Waste of time as no expert reports yet.... I expect to be there for five minutes."

Finally, the male plaintiffs' lawyer (in forties) described the mediation as follows:

> "This particular mediation didn't last all that long, in part because we were, I think, too early in the process.... It was just the doctor's lawyer there... saying "Well no, the doctor did everything he was supposed to do. You haven't proved your case. We're not offering you any money. We're not offering you an explanation for what happened."

Notwithstanding the dissonant situation of disputants' (particularly plaintiffs) similar expectations in voluntary and mandatory mediations in stark contrast to those of lawyers', interestingly only a small minority of attorneys remarked on this. For example,

> "If the intention was never to settle because you're not at that stage then people, particularly plaintiffs, go away feeling like they've been slapped in the face... I think they were furious with the mediation. And I felt sorry for them because I think they had unrealistic expectations... I think they had an idea of what was going to happen, thought they would walk home with a check. And as a result were hugely disappointed."
> **Female – physician lawyer – in thirties – mandatory mediation**

> "It's probably very frustrating for them to have me come to a mediation and say 'I have no instructions to settle this case because it's way too early... unless you're going to abandon your action'... Because they're very much of the view that, 'What are you talking about? This is obvious. Look at me' or 'My child is dead. What do you mean you don't have to pay, there's no liability?' They just don't have the training. They don't understand it." **Male physician lawyer – in thirties**

> "I think plaintiffs come in with expectations that are often totally ridiculous and their expectations are not what ours are. Frequently in a mandatory mediation, I don't go in expecting to settle. I find the plaintiffs often do come in and think 'today's the day I might get money or I might get this'... So when that doesn't happen, while during the process there might be some benefit, at the end of the day they're often quite frustrated." **Female hospital lawyer – in twenties**

Thus, the dissonant realities prevalent within mandatory mediations very often resulted in plaintiffs being set up in advance for disappointment. Similarly, in Macfarlane and Keet's research of a mandatory mediation program in Saskatchewan, litigants viewed the mediations positively, but also expressed disappointment and frustration in relation to attorneys' affects on the process, shaping litigants' experiences. Lawyers were regularly described as being adversarial, working against open information exchange or being reluctant to negotiate (Macfarlane and Keet 2004–5, pp. 690–92). Implications of these findings are discussed next.

3.3 Chapter conclusion

In exploring legal actors' understandings, perceptions, and attitudes toward mandatory and voluntary mediation, lawyers' strong support for voluntary mediation and their lack of resistance overall to the compulsory nature of mandatory mediation highlighted the fact that similar to findings in other research in North America, lawyers in the present study were at an advanced stage of acceptance of mediation per se during formal legal processes (Metzloff et al. 1997, pp. 140–41; Macfarlane 2002, p. 279). This was an important finding for this case type in light of empirical data throughout numerous jurisdictions persistently demonstrating that take-up rates in voluntary mediation programs are consistently low, regardless of lawyer or party satisfaction. For instance, in the United States, the dearth of information on voluntary medmal mediation in the literature has been blamed on lawyers not mediating these cases voluntarily (Johnson 1997, p. 46). Likewise, in England, subsequent to the National Health Service Medical Mediation Pilot it was noted that mandating mediation was the only way most medical disputes would mediate (Easterbrook 1996, p. 411; Polywka 1997, p. 84).

Yet, in comparing how parties and lawyers described voluntary and mandatory mediation settings, their completely different expectations, attitudes, and language illustrate another facet of the discontinuity in understandings and meanings between the legal, tactical world and the parallel, extralegal world inhabited by disputants during case processing. Legal actors, irrespective of camp, emphasized the significant tactical disparities of the two mediation types – something that parties appeared to be unaware of. In fact, plaintiffs' and defendants' perceptions and expectations for mandatory and voluntary mediations were very similar.

In relation to the timing of mandatory mediations, in sharp contrast to lawyers' complaints about mandatory mediations being too early, neither claimants nor defendants mentioned any difficulties with this. For disputants, and particularly defendants, the general consensus was "the earlier the better." Notwithstanding the legitimate need to obtain the necessary information prior to mediations, lawyers' interests may have been in delaying mediation. Delay is often in the strategic interests of defense lawyers. It also generally results in increases in legal fees. Thus, historically lawyers have been culturally accustomed to late settlement of cases on the litigation track. This is not to suggest that lawyers consciously attempted to delay mediations for this reason. Still, as one respected mediator noted, "I did one where the lawyer said 'I am a problem to you because I don't care if this case settles. I'll get paid more money if the case doesn't settle'."

Second, dissonant expectations existed between lawyers and parties about what could transpire during mandatory mediations. Unbeknownst to claimants, lawyers' discourse frequently exhibited negative attitudes and low expectations. This was not only due to timing problems, but at times also due to perceived inadequate preparation by opponents. Moreover, in contrast to voluntary mediations, defense lawyers were frequently not prepared to explore settlement at mandatory mediations.[8] Yet, parties made no mention of lawyers' negative attitudes or expectations, any lack of lawyer preparation, or the issue of requiring discovery in order to make mandatory (or voluntary) mediations "worthwhile." Consequently, hope and high expectations for resolution and other extralegal aspirations pervaded plaintiffs' discourse equally in mandatory and voluntary mediations.[9]

Finally, the chapter's findings highlight disparate interests of legal and lay actors relating to the issue of lawyer control at mediations. Mandatory mediations' early timing resulted in lawyers having less legal and tactical information and thus less influence over the substance of discussions at mediations – something undesirable to them. As one hospital lawyer noted, "I'm a firm believer in mediation ... but counsel should have greater input.... It should take place according to the will of counsel." This highlights on one level what, in fact, the whole mandatory versus voluntary divide came down to. The findings implicitly suggest that the bulk of lawyers wanted to keep mediation discussions focused on legal and monetary lines once they themselves had decided liability and quantum issues prior to mediation. The vast majority were not interested in meeting at any type of mediation to discuss the parties' views on fault or extralegal issues. They were there to talk about money or no money, related to the likelihood of legal liability in court. If this was impossible because of insufficient time to obtain information relating to liability and quantum, then lawyers generally perceived mediations as a "waste of time." Defense lawyers viewed early mediations as helpful only when they could "get out early," that is, convince claimants that they should not pay any money for their injuries because their cases were unmeritorious on legal lines. Although the absence of liability would have to be explained in order to achieve this goal, the goal itself related to money alone.[10]

Lawyers may also have felt more comfortable in later (generally voluntary) "quantum-only" mediations as they would primarily be the protagonists, with parties often more in the background than in earlier mandatory mediations. As

---

8 This has been similarly found in other research (Metzloff et al. 1997, p. 115, n. 34).
9 As will be seen further in chapter five, this included closure, emotional and psychological vindication, fault admissions, and acknowledgments of harm.
10 This conclusion is supported by the data on legal actors' mediation aims (*chapter five*), views on defendants' attendance at mediation (*chapter four*), as well as how they later assessed their mediations (*chapter six*).

noted by one senior male hospital lawyer, "I think the ones towards the beginning tend to be less money focused. The ones... close to trial, it's pretty well down to money by that time. Often... the patient is kind of in the background at that point and the lawyer is basically saying 'Here's what we're prepared to settle for in the face of an impending trial'." But as was seen in Section 3.3 and as will be seen further in the chapters to come, this was opposed to disputants' interests in additionally having a measure of control during mediations in terms of having discussions about what happened and in seeking answers, explanations, apologies, acknowledgments of harm, and so on. These issues had nothing to do with calculating damages.

These conclusions are consistent with Metzloff's U.S. findings. Despite the majority of lawyers being in favor of mandatory court-ordered mediation, numerous lawyers surveyed similarly restricted their endorsement of mandatory mediation to cases where the amount of damages was the main issue in dispute as opposed to those where liability was in dispute (Metzloff et al. 1997, p. 142). These conclusions also correlate with chapter two's findings on understandings of plaintiffs' litigation aims. Lawyers' mediation understandings and agendas as discerned from their discourse on the mandatory versus voluntary mediation divide appeared to be premised on the fact that the issues in these disputes were all or primarily about money, disregarding or unaware of any extralegal issues pervading these disputes for the parties involved. Yet, this ignored the indivisibility of plaintiffs' legal and extralegal needs, the latter frequently being of prime importance to them. This chapter therefore highlights a further aspect of the diverse legal versus lay worlds existing in mediation. Indeed, of all the defense lawyers discussing the mandatory versus voluntary divide, only one female hospital lawyer referred to claimants' extralegal needs, saying, "In mandatory mediation, defendants have an opportunity to speak their views with the plaintiffs present. I think that's important; and offer apologies or do whatever."

The very diverse expectations and language used by parties and lawyers to describe voluntary and mandatory mediations have a number of implications: First, it is clear that in most such mandatory mediations, without any change in lawyers' "culture" there is little chance of plaintiffs' expectations for, or understandings of, mediation being realized. This, of course, remains unknown to litigants. Second, in terms of implications for lawyers, the early timing of mandatory mediation means that lawyers' work ethos and ways of thinking about cases need to change. Early mediation necessitates research and case assessment to be done much sooner in the life of a case. This requires a material change in lawyers' time management and billing practices. Moreover, a transformation in legal culture is necessary as early mediation alters lawyers' influence vis-à-vis clients, with litigants having much more of a substantial role and involvement in the process in terms of guiding lawyers on case appraisals and knowing what to expect (Macfarlane 2002, pp. 261–62, 271).

The findings in this chapter additionally underscore a further reality inherent in mediation: lawyers' influence on the mediation process itself. Attitudes toward mediation and any preparation or lack thereof by lawyers directly affected not only what transpired at mediations in relation to settlement, but also what occurred at mediations generally. This, in turn, affected the perceptions and experiences of all those present – particularly disputants. In exploring realities and views on who should attend mediations, chapter four makes plain another aspect of legal actors' influence on what occurs during mediation processes. In doing so, a further facet of the parallel worlds' thesis emerges, as sharp distinctions between lawyers' and parties' views on the issue further challenge the basic premise that litigants and their lawyers broadly understand and desire similar things from case processing leading up to and including litigation-track mediations. In examining views on defendants' attendance at mediation, further differences in lawyers' versus disputants' perceptions, desires, and meanings ascribed to the process and how they wish to resolve their cases there short of trial become clear. Yet, due to disparities in knowledge, power, and interests between litigants and attorneys, plaintiffs and defendants are seen to be regularly not afforded communication opportunities to address issues of prime importance to them during the processing of their cases.

CHAPTER FOUR

Consequences of power: Legal actors versus disputants on defendants' attendance at mediation

"A lot of times the defense will not bring the defendant. Now, this is against the case law. There have been rulings by the ADR Masters that everyone has to be there. So what happens is... I get the consent of all parties... that if someone's not there everyone consents to proceed; which is really the poor way." **Male lawyer-mediator – mandatory mediation – in fifties**

"I have had but one *physician attend* out of in excess of 100 *voluntary mediations*... as a plaintiffs' counsel. So they just don't show up." **Male, specialist plaintiff lawyer – in forties**

"The court-linked mediations... are not party-oriented. They're solution-oriented." **Female non-lawyer-mediator – voluntary and mandatory mediations – in forties**

What was the real nature of these serious disputes that were proceeding down the litigation–mediation route? To whom did these cases belong? What did litigation-linked mediation mean to the lawyers, parties, and mediators involved? These questions emerge upon examining the issue of defendants' attendance at mediation. In exploring the views of legal actors and mediators, followed by a comparison of disputants' perspectives certain important realities become apparent. Yet, in looking deeper, the findings represent much more than simply a matter of mediation participation. Through the conduit of analysis on the attendance issue, the data additionally provide insight into the diverse purposes and meanings ascribed to mediation itself by each of its actor groups.

In so doing, this chapter further challenges the basic premise that litigants and their attorneys broadly understand and desire similar things from case processing leading up to and including mediation that might end their litigation. Instead, the findings here offer disconcerting evidence of the surprising degree to which perceptions, needs, and meanings actors ascribe to mediation are not only diverse, but frequently contradictory. I demonstrate that notwithstanding their different allegiances, lawyers on all sides of cases have similar understandings of the meaning and purpose of litigation-track mediation. I further present evidence of attorneys' regular decisions and reasoning against having defendants present regardless of court rules to the contrary and unbeknownst to most litigants. At the same time, I show that plaintiffs and defendants have strikingly similar needs and comprehensions of what mediation "is" and how they wish to resolve their cases there, short of trial. Yet disputants' understandings and agendas for the process are frequently opposed to those of legal actors, often including their own lawyers. Moreover, due to disparities in knowledge, power, and interests between litigants and attorneys, plaintiffs and defendants, are regularly not afforded communication opportunities to address issues of prime importance to them. In light of contingency fee realities, these mediations may represent disputants' only chance for communication within litigation.

Thus, the attendance issue provides another window to the differentially experienced worlds of parties locked involuntarily in disputes, with lawyers controlling the orchestration of who attends mediation and thus what can be said there. Consequently, mediation is unable to express its higher aspirations and instead itself becomes a further object of lawyer control.[1] The original vision and fundamental basis of mediation involve disputants' self-determination and empowerment, with parties being the main actors directly participating, communicating, and controlling the process.[2] However, with court institutionalization, scholars have noted that the original vision of mediation is giving way to one where parties are not the main players. Instead, lawyers are the central participants and controllers of mediation, infusing the process with traditional legal practices including settlement norms (Welsh 2001a, pp. 838–39; 2001b, pp. 4–5, 8, 16).

Physician defendants did not attend most litigation-linked mediations within the present study, be they voluntary or mandatory. This was evident from the discourse of virtually all legal actors. Under Rule 24.1 of the Ontario Rules of Civil Procedure, all litigants and their lawyers are obliged to attend court-ordered mandatory mediations or face penalties, unless a court order to the contrary is made.[3] This clearly includes named defendants. Yet, instead, defendant lawyers attended alone (sometimes accompanied by insurance and/or hospital representatives). Prior agreement between the "parties" generally provided a way out of the court rule.

---

1 Fuller (1971), Folberg and Taylor (1984, p. xii), Menkel-Meadow (1996b; 1997a, p. 452; 2006), Welsh (2001b, pp. 3, 15–19), Moore (2003), and Folberg et al. (2005).
2 Bush and Folger (1994, pp. 2–3, 81), Baruch-Bush (1997, pp. 29–30), Goldberg et al. (1999, pp. 154–55), Kovach (2001, pp. 935, 939, 942–43, 952), and Welsh (2001b, pp. 15–18).
3 Ont. R. Civ. P. 24.1.11(1). At the time of data collection, costs penalties were the sanction for noncompliance with attendance rules. However, at the time of writing although no case law on the issue was found, Rule 24.1 notes the following: If any party is absent, mediators should cancel mediations and file certificates of non-compliance. Parties are subsequently required to appear before case management judges or masters who may establish timetables for actions, strike out any documents filed, dismiss actions, order non-complying parties to pay costs, and/or make other orders that are deemed just (Rules 24.1.12/13; O. Reg. 453/98, s. 1). Insurer representatives are also mandated to attend unless the court orders otherwise, as well as those with settlement authority who must at least be available by telephone. http://www.attorneygeneral.jus.gov.on.ca/english/courts/manmed/notice.asp, http://www.attorneygeneral.jus.gov.on.ca/english/courts/manmed/factsheet.asp, http://www.travel-net.com/~billr/Rules/mainW.html, http://www.e-laws.gov.on.ca/DBLaws/Regs/English/900194a_e.htm#Sched75.1.01 (last visited June 7, 2007).

Defendants' absence at medical dispute mediations has been reported in the scant empirical research in this specific area. For instance, notwithstanding North Carolina's courts requiring the presence of all parties (unless all lawyers and mediators involved agree otherwise),[4] in Metzloff et al.'s study, defendant physicians were frequently absent from mediations (Metzloff et al. 1997, pp. 112–13, 123–25). Likewise, in the Wisconsin panel mediation program, defendant doctors were absent 35% of the time.[5] Other scholars have also noted that in the United States for various case types, including personal and medical injury cases, defendants are rarely present in court-linked mediations and even when they do attend, their attorneys do much, if not all, of the talking (Kovach and Love 1998, p. 99; Welsh 2001a, pp. 801–2, 838–39; 2001b, pp. 4–5, 25–27; Menkel-Meadow et al. 2006, p. 580). Thus, "face-to-face communication between defendant physicians and plaintiffs is the exception rather than the rule in medical mediation, just as it is in other forms of mediation" (Gatter 2004, pp. 204–6). However, no literature was found discussing the issue of mediation attendance in depth or comparing the meaning of mediation for disputants with that of their legal representatives.

Yet, interestingly, upon analysis of the attendance issue in the present research, the second most utilized code in the entire dataset was "physician should attend." Consequently, I sought to delve deeper into the attendance issue to better comprehend why it was that a party to a dispute, generally extremely serious in nature, was regularly not participating in the mediation of that same dispute. The results were surprising.

The preliminary issue of how attendance decisions were made and by whom is examined next. This is followed by attorneys' descriptions of their mediation experiences with defendants present as well as what lay beneath lawyers' and mediators' views on physicians' attendance. The chapter subsequently presents data on the different, but surprisingly uniform, understandings and needs of defendants and plaintiffs on the issue of who should partake in their cases' mediations. Finally, the gendered views of lawyers and litigants are analyzed.

4.1　The attendance arbiters

In exploring the existing allocation of power in terms of the behind-the-scenes decisions on who attended mediation, views from the bulk of legal actors in all groups clearly indicated that in the vast majority of instances, defendant lawyers, plaintiff lawyers, or both were responsible for whether or not defendants (and in some cases plaintiffs) attended mediations, be they mandatory or voluntary.

"Normally I don't take my doctors to my mediations... I never had one there. DO THEY WANT TO GO? Um, no. NO? I've never really canvassed it with them to tell you

---

4　N.C.R. Implementing Mediated Settlement Conferences in Super. Ct. Actions Rule 4 (1991) (amended 1995).
5　Meschievitz (1990, p. 7; 1994, p. 135), Wis Stat A (pp. 655–56) (Act 340) (WSA 655.42–455.68).

the truth. Most of them don't. I mean, if they're busy, um, it's stressful, uh, because it's just dollars and cents. It's really in the hands of the lawyers... I don't think they can play a significant role." **Male physician lawyer – in forties**

"The more logical and rational and less emotional the physicians are, the more likely it is that I'm going to say to them 'Why don't you come'?" **Female physician lawyer – in thirties**

"I consented to the physician not attending... I would still not want the doctor to be there.... My instinct is 'no.' And then I got the call in this case... and I got the call recently in another case." **Male, specialist plaintiff lawyer – in forties**

The situation appeared to be the same with hospital attorneys representing other named defendants.

"I haven't seen too many where we wanted to have the nurse there." **Female hospital lawyer – in forties**

In view of lawyers being "attendance arbiters," coupled with the fact that defendants generally did not attend litigation-linked mediations, I paid particular attention to lawyers' descriptions of their mediation experiences with defendants present. Given that lawyers most commonly decided against defendants' participation, one would have expected their experiences with defendants at mediation to have been negative. Interestingly, not a single one was.

Lawyers' experiences with defendants at mediation

First, it was notable that lawyers had few or no mediation experiences with defendant physicians present. Of those with experience, it was striking that no lawyer stated that it would have been better if the defendant had not attended. In fact, all experiences were depicted positively. For example,

"In a very large, tragic case... the doctor was there. And I was quite surprised. He was very helpful. Whenever the judge-*mediator* would say 'I wonder about this', he would stand up and offer 'Well, let me explain that to you'. And his counsel would say 'Sit down, sit down'. He was just being very good about it." **Female, specialist plaintiff and hospital lawyer – in forties**

"YOU HAVE BEEN TO ONE VOLUNTARY MEDIATION WITH THE PHYSICIAN THERE. HOW DID THAT GO? It was fine. I mean, because there was a credibility issue of who said what. It was somewhat important for the mediator to listen to both people. So it was okay. But it was okay primarily because that was the purpose; and the *plaintiff and defendant* involved both went about it in a businesslike way." **Male, specialist plaintiff lawyer – in fifties**

"HAVE YOU EVER ATTENDED WITH PHYSICIANS PRESENT? Yes. Only once. HOW DID THAT GO? From what I recall, it was very helpful. But in that case there was absolutely no chance for settling unless the plaintiff was walking away. And it was helpful because the plaintiff came to that realisation... But for the most part, I don't think the presence of the physician is critical." **Female physician lawyer – in thirties**

Moreover, some descriptions of mediation experiences with defendants present included references to the fact that both plaintiffs and defendants themselves benefited from these encounters. For instance,

> "A woman complained of chest pains, was taken to the hospital and released. She had a heart attack and died the next day. So we sued the doctor who examined her. And he was able to go through all of the extra tests he went through... and it became obvious in a way that it hadn't been before that the guy really spent time... to satisfy himself that she was okay... I learned this *at mediation*... The clients also realized that their mother hadn't been mistreated... I think it was important for our client to hear that this doctor tried, cared... I think it helped the plaintiffs accept that we're going to drop our case against the doctor but it's not like he's getting away with murder." **Male, generalist plaintiff lawyer – in forties**

> "DO YOU FEEL THERE WAS ANY BENEFIT TO THE DEFENDANTS... In the two cases *I've had with physicians there*... yes. But it would be very difficult to articulate what the benefit was... There was something positive in... trying to address the issues from all sides in the presence of both parties... The doctors' side was there... They wanted their point of view put forward... to have it understood that this is their explanation. They didn't do anything wrong, or they didn't mean to do anything wrong. They were able to sit in a room with the people on the other side in this lawsuit and actually talk about it. And people didn't scream and do terrible things to each other." **Male physician lawyer – in forties**

Still, most lawyers were inclined not to have defendants present at mediations. Some attorneys surmised that physician lawyers did not want doctors at mediation because of fears that they may divulge too much information, equating mediation with an "informal" or "free" discovery process where opponents would "get to hear what happened." Another reason may have been lawyers' own comfort levels. As one lawyer noted,

> "I only had one occasion when the physician was there. Um, I don't think it interfered with the process; may even have been conducive to the process. Oddly enough, just because maybe it's what you're used to, I, um, actually felt a little uncomfortable myself. I was the plaintiff's counsel. I had to change my way of expressing myself. My sense is that there could be a lot of cases where, from a plaintiff's counsel point of view, I think it might not at all be a good idea. That particular case... went pretty good. It went much better than I anticipated. I don't know whether... all physicians could benefit from being at these things. But it's just so foreign to have the physician there." **Male, specialist plaintiff and physician lawyer – in forties**

Lawyers being "attendance arbiters" has much to do with appropriate ethical and professional allocation of decision-making authority in litigation, which differs in different jurisdictions (Menkel-Meadow 2006). It is widely believed that all parties' attendance at mediation is critical (Lande 2002, p. 133; Wise 2006, p. 859). Thus, in U.S. jurisdictions with good-faith requirements for mandatory court-ordered mediation, notwithstanding definitional difficulties and arguments relating to the utility of "good-faith" requirements, objectively determined "bad faith" has generally included failure to attend mediation.[6] Consequently, legal sanctions have been invoked against attorneys and/or litigants when a party to a case is required to attend mediation by statute or court rules but does not. Sanctions have included awards of opponents' mediation costs, including legal fees, mediators' fees, default judgments, dismissals, or contempt orders.[7]

Accordingly, I looked to see what lay behind the views of lawyers and mediators to more fully comprehend the phenomenon of defendants' absences from litigation-track mediation.

4.2 Professionals' reasoning on defendants' attendance

Each lawyer group was asked about their views on defendants' attendance at mediation. Mediators' views were additionally sought in order to provide greater insight into this issue from the non-disputant standpoint. To better comprehend the issue of defendants' absences from mediations, first all reasoning "for" and "against" defendants' attendance was segregated within each non-disputant actor group.[8]

---

6 Kovach (1997, pp. 622–23), Lande (2002, pp. 72–76, 84–85, 87, 139–40), and Menkel-Meadow et al. (2006, pp. 301–3, 309–10).
7 Anderson (2003, pp. 202, 208), Menkel-Meadow et al. (2006, p. 301), Scott (2006, p. 351), and Wise (2006, pp. 861–62). For example, Triad Mack V. Clement Bros. 438 S.E.2d 485 (N.C. Ct. App. 1994) (default judgment for defendant's absence without good cause); Schulz v Nienhuis, 448 N.W.2d 655 (Wis 1989) (case dismissed due to plaintiff's mediation absence) (Menkel-Meadow et al. 2006, p. 312); Tobin v. Marriott Hotels, Inc., 683 A.2d 784 (Md. App. 1996) (failure to attend); Lucas Auto. Eng'g v. Bridgestone/Firestone, 275 F.3d 762, 769 (9th Cir. 2001) (sanctions against plaintiff for failing to attend); Bulkmatic Transp. Co. v. Pappas, No. 99Civ.12070(RMB)(JCF), 2002 WL 975625, at 1 (S. D. N. Y. May 9, 2002) (mem.) (monetary sanctions against party for mediation absence). Parties or attorneys who fail to attend mediations in Texas can also be sanctioned severely under courts' inherent powers, for example, Luxenberg v. Marshall, 835 S.W.2d 136, 141 (Tex. App.) (striking parties pleadings for failure to attend mediation); Raad, 1998 WL 272879, at 4–8 (monetary sanctions against party who failed to attend mediation); Ky. Farm Bureau Mut. Ins. Co., 136 S.W.3d at 459–60 (affirming dismissal of suit for failure to attend mediation); Seidel v. Bradberry, No. 3:94-CV-0147-G, 1998 WL 386161, at 1–3 (N.D. Tex. July 7, 1998) (sanctions on party for failure to attend); Roberts v. Rose, 37 S.W.3d 31 (Tex. App. 2000) (attorney sanctioned for client failure to attend mediation); Garcia v. Mireles, 14 S.W.3d 839, 842–43 (Tex. App. 2000) (dismissal of suit for failure to attend mediation). In South Carolina, courts may impose sanctions for mediation absence ranging from attorney's and mediators' fees to any other sanction authorized by South Carolina Rule of Civil Procedure 37(b), including contempt of court, default judgments, strike outs. S. C. Cir. Ct. Alt. Disp. Resol. R. 5(a) and R. 11(b)–(c) (2004); S.C. R. Civ. P. 37(b) (2003).
8 The data breakdown for this topic was as follows: fifteen mediation interviews with nine physician lawyers; fourteen mediation interviews with nine hospital lawyers; twenty-three mediation interviews with sixteen plaintiff lawyers; and twenty-five mediation interviews with fifteen mediators. Because the attendance issue hinged on individuals' opinions regardless of case details, percentages in the charts within this chapter alone have been based on the number of individuals interviewed who discussed attendance and not on the larger number of interviews I may have had with them (as some lawyers were involved in more than one mediation). In all other chapters, all charts are

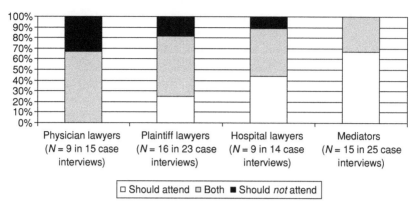

Figure 7. Non-disputants' views on defendant physicians' attendance at mediation. A substantial proportion of lawyers in all groups spoke of reasons both for and against defendants' attendance. Yet, it was only in the mediator group (including lawyer-mediators) where the majority spoke only of reasons why defendants should attend – with no members speaking solely against defendants' presence.

Interestingly, despite defendants' non-attendance norms, a similar and material proportion of actors in each lawyer group discussed reasons both for and against physicians' attendance, with only a minority speaking solely against defendants' presence. Still, no physician lawyers and only a minority of plaintiff lawyers solely proffered reasons in favor of defendants' attendance at mediation. In sharp contrast, the majority of mediators (including lawyer-mediators) spoke only of reasons why defendants should attend. Figure 7 illustrates the dispersal of views.

The data were then further subdivided into the particular explanations proffered by actors on this issue. Figure 8 illustrates non-disputants' expressed reasoning, highlighting the overall similarities in thinking of legal actors regardless of camp.

The fact that lawyers in all groups offered similar reasoning against defendants' attendance compared with the mediator group was interesting. The two most frequently cited reasons against doctors' presence – that it raises emotions and that physicians do not instruct about money – offer significant insight into the stance of legal actors, as will be seen later. The majority view of physician lawyers that defendant doctors did not want to attend mediations is further examined from doctors' perspectives in Section 4.3.

Other studies have reported similar reasoning for defendants' absence at mediation. For instance, in the North Carolina study, reasons included busy schedules, travel difficulties, and decisions made by defense lawyers and insurers that physicians' attendance would be counterproductive due to disputants' anger or animosity

based on the number of cases rather than the number of individuals interviewed (as views differed for different cases).

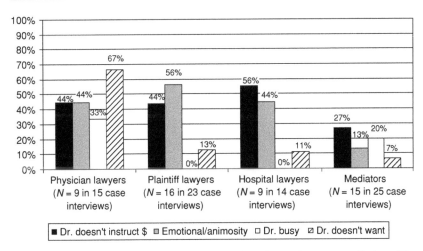

Figure 8. Non-disputants' reasons against defendants' attendance at mediation. (*Note:* "$" stands for money.) Reasons against defendants' attendance were relatively similar across lawyer groups as compared with the mediator group. Lawyers most often noted that doctors did not instruct on how much money to pay and that physicians' presence would raise emotions or animosity in mediation.

obstructing settlements (Metzloff et al. 1997, p. 125). Similarly, in an Ontario study of various dispute types, there were differing opinions on the appropriateness of mediation for emotion-laden cases, with some lawyers of the view that settlements would be far more elusive in mediations where emotions ran high (Macfarlane 1995).

Reasons in favor of defendants' mediation attendance included "for the plaintiff's benefit," "for the physician's benefit," and "to encourage settlement." The first two reasons demonstrated – at least in part – extralegal considerations (including psychological, emotional, or learning issues) not critical for fiscal or legal settlement of particular disputes. Figure 9 illustrates these findings.

Interesting points emerged. First, most actors in each non-disputant group did not mention physicians' learning as a reason why they should attend mediation. A disparate picture emerged when speaking to physicians themselves, as will be seen later. Second, in contrast to the majority of plaintiff and physician lawyers who did not feel that defendants' attendance could assist settlement, the bulk of mediators did feel this way. This suggested a paradoxical situation. On the one hand, lawyers wanted settlement but chose not to bring defendants to mediation for various reasons. On the other hand, mediators, chosen and judged by lawyers based on their settlement rates, were mostly of the view that defendants' absences adversely affected their abilities to facilitate settlements.

Third, it was intriguing that a greater proportion of hospital lawyers felt plaintiffs could benefit by seeing physicians at mediation than did plaintiffs' own lawyers.

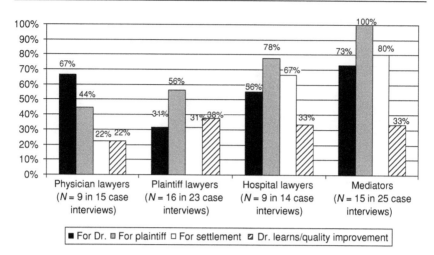

Figure 9. Non-disputants' reasons in favor of defendants' attendance at mediation. Notwithstanding physician and plaintiff lawyers regularly deciding against having defendants at mediation, the majority in each group noted that attendance could help their clients personally. The fact that only a minority of legal actors (versus the majority of mediators) felt that defendants' presence could assist settlement chances may provide an explanation.

This may have been a function of the different tactical position hospitals were in vis-à-vis the other lawyer groups. It may also have related to the gender makeup of the actor groups. Claimants' lawyers were 88% male and 12% female, whereas hospital lawyers were 33% male and 67% female. These issues as well as what may have been underlying each actor group's stated reasons for their attendance views are explored in greater depth below.

Physician lawyers

"DO YOU THINK IT HELPS PLAINTIFFS TO HAVE DEFENDANTS THERE OR NOT? Oh, I have no idea what goes through the minds of plaintiffs." **Male physician lawyer – in fifties**

All physician lawyers offered reasons why doctors should not attend mediations. It was particularly noteworthy that 44% acknowledged that physicians' attendance could assist plaintiffs, although only one lawyer said that plaintiffs actually wanted physicians at mediation. This tied in with the findings in chapter two, that virtually all physician lawyers were of the view that these disputes were solely about money for plaintiffs. These lawyers' often-stated reason against attendance – that doctors did not instruct them on monetary issues – further built on this theme.

Yet, what was particularly intriguing from the overall views of physician lawyers was that despite non-attendance norms and reasons for decisions against doctors' presence at mediation, most physician counsel (67%) said that attendance could benefit defendant doctors personally (e.g., hearing their side put forward, facing plaintiffs, hearing plaintiffs' perspectives), and virtually all noted in their questionnaires that underlying issues were "much more important" or "about as important" to their clients as compared with financial compensation. Yet, these lawyers did not seek to ensure that their physician clients attended mediations so as to provide them with the opportunity to address these underlying issues. The fact that only 22% felt doctors' presence could assist settlement chances seemed to explain this dissonance. The following quotes elucidate physician lawyers' views.

On doctors not instructing about money,

"First of all, the doctor's not the decision-maker on what's going to make the plaintiff happy, which is money. Plaintiffs are looking in the vast majority of cases for compensation for their injuries, financial compensation. Doctors don't decide that. So I don't see a purpose, a role for them at mediation... I've never gone to one of these mediations where plaintiffs' counsel said 'My client wants your client here'.... I've never seen that as being a stumbling block... *Doctors* don't give us instructions *on* how much money to pay. So the doctor sitting there is not going to make a difference. *Plaintiffs* don't want an apology from the doctor." **Male – in thirties**

DOCTORS DON'T ATTEND... There's really no point. They don't make the decisions *on numbers*... If you're number crunching, it's not a place for emotion... I suppose there could be cases where there are mixed issues... both emotional information gathering and quantum. **Female – in fifties**

On emotions and animosity,

"I don't like the emotional component. I think there are other places for it. YOU DON'T SEE ANY BENEFIT FOR EITHER SIDE BY PHYSICIANS ATTENDING? No. I don't think *doctors* need to have that, eh, thing. And I'm not sure it's productive... Because this isn't an opportunity for *doctors* to feel better... For the most part, I don't think that the presence of the physician is critical... It just raises the emotions up, without any resolution." **Female – in thirties**

"Quite frankly I think it might be a detractor to it, to have them all sitting in the room... because there's... a lot of animosity that they don't have towards us... and a lot of physicians are quite upset about being sued... I think *the animosity* could be a deterrent to it... So I don't see a role for *physicians*; I don't see a benefit." **Male – in thirties**

Others made similar comments. Yet, at the same time it was generally accepted that physicians themselves could benefit by attending mediations.

"I see no need to have the client there... Very often, I think they pose a greater risk of being a stumbling block... I've never found the defendant to be particularly helpful. And very often uh, simply get in the way at mediation in terms of getting a resolution... ANY BENEFIT TO PHYSICIANS THEMSELVES... Sure, I mean clients are always interested in how these things are resolved... But I don't think they add to the environment in terms of a 'successful' mediation. It's insurers' call... *Defendants would* have to be persuasive in terms of what they can add, and if they can't add anything my practice is simply not to have them there." **Male – in fifties – never mediated with physicians, only with clients in commercial cases**

"They're very interested in knowing the process, and knowing what's going to go on. But... experts, peers are going to decide *liability*, not them... And because it's one-dimensional, it's just compensation and liability, I don't think they can play a significant role." **Male – in forties**

"I've never seen a reason at mediations, where I said 'Gee I wish the doctor was here. We could have settled that case if he'd been here'... Plaintiffs are... not there to help educate the doctor on his misdeeds. The doctors by that point aren't in a position where they want this opportunity to vent. And if that's what they want, it's probably not going to help settle the case. It might make him feel better. I don't know... The physician I took to *mandatory mediation*... I think it helped *him* further understand *how* this person was feeling and what she suffered... *and her way of thinking*... but it didn't make him... reassess the care." **Male – in thirties – attended twenty-five to forty mediations – only one with physicians**

Thus, notwithstanding the few physician lawyers commenting on the benefits of defendants' attendance, overall these attorneys were firmly situated in the anti-attendance camp. Few mentioned whether plaintiffs could benefit from seeing physicians at mediations without probing by the interviewer. When asked, they often stated that they did not know what plaintiffs felt, sometimes were not sure what their physician clients felt, and frequently were of the view that doctors had little to gain legally by attending mediation. These attorneys may not have wanted their clients at mediation because it could shift the discussion from money to responsibility, making it more difficult to settle. Thus, overall, physician lawyers' discourse suggested that they perceived mediation as their forum first and disputants' only secondarily. Hence, unsurprisingly, physicians were usually absent from mediations.

Hospital lawyers

Hospital lawyers were generally not involved in defendant physicians' attendance decisions. Therefore their views are not elaborated on here. Suffice to say that most (89%) spoke of positive reasons why defendant physicians should attend mediation, with the most cited reason being extralegal benefit "for the plaintiff" (78%). For instance,

"Plaintiffs... need to be able to tell their side of the story. Sometimes if the doctor is there it helps, because *plaintiffs* want them to hear it." **Female – in twenties**

Interestingly, the majority of hospital lawyers with these views were female. Gender is further examined later. Yet, hospital lawyers were in a different position tactically on doctors' attendance. They may have wanted physicians present to shift responsibility from the hospital to the doctors, who were sued separately.

> "I thought it was helpful because there were a lot of allegations being shoved to the hospital, which clearly the doctor was responsible for. And he was there accepting responsibility for things. So he was able to say 'No, you're wrong. I did that. I did this. The nurse does this.' So it was very helpful... And it was a lot more credibility than me saying exactly the same thing... *to* plaintiffs' counsel." **Female – in twenties**

At the same time, 57% of hospital lawyers gave reasons similar to those of physician lawyers as to why their own defendants, for example, nurses, should not attend mediations. The most common reasons were that nurses did not instruct on money and that their presence resulted in raised emotions.

> "It's helpful in cases where there's a misunderstanding as to what was done. It's not helpful in cases where there's a lot of bitterness... It just won't add... because they don't provide us with instructions in terms of settlement." **Female – in twenties**

> "We kind of treat the process, so it was a little bit more palatable for everybody... WITH DEFENDANTS NOT ATTENDING? Yup... I don't have a need to have my client there to assist me... in order to bring things to settlement... I'm not convinced that their personal presence would necessarily be helpful to the process... I'm able to remain a little bit more detached... and save them the agony of going through something that is not pleasant for them and that they really don't have a whole lot to contribute to anyway." **Female – in forties**

> "A nurse... severed a nerve... So he was quite disabled. I would not have brought that nurse to the mediation because the plaintiff, years later, was still so angry." **Female – in forties**

Thus, defendant attorneys' views on mediation attendance formed an intrinsic part of their litigation and mediation strategies, which focused solely on monetary settlement or abandonment of claims. Plainly, these views resulted from lawyers' conceptions of what litigation-track mediation "was." Interestingly, like physician lawyers, hospital lawyers' discourse impliedly suggested that they viewed mediation as their forum first and disputants' only secondarily. This phenomenon was similarly found within the discourse of plaintiff lawyers.

Plaintiff lawyers

The views of most plaintiff lawyers were strangely reminiscent of those on the defense, explaining why more plaintiff attorneys were not demanding defendants' attendance at mediation. This suggested that shared professional roles were more important than partisanship (Abel 2005). Most (81%) discussed reasons in favor of defendants attending mediations. At the same time the majority (75%) also gave reasons against attendance (Figure 7). As with the other legal actor groups, plaintiff lawyers' cognizance of extralegal issues important to disputants appeared to conflict with their own tactical understandings of mediation's purpose, that is, "getting a settlement." Similar to the findings on physician lawyers, this conclusion was supported by the fact that only a minority of plaintiff lawyers (31%) felt that defendants' presence could assist in reaching settlements (Figure 9). Although few disputed that physicians' attendance could benefit plaintiffs, claimant attorneys' reasons against defendants' mediation attendance were also redolent of those proffered by defense lawyers: doctors did not instruct on money (44%) and defendants' presence would raise emotions and animosity, impeding settlement chances (56%) (Figure 8). The following quotes are illustrative of the views of most plaintiff lawyers:

> "ANY BENEFITS OF DEFENDANT ATTENDANCE... There may be something therapeutic for my clients... But the worry I always have is that we get derailed by emotional issues that will get in the way of getting the legal issues solved. So, um, perhaps I can be accused of lacking compassion and the psychological expertise to know what my clients need on a mediation... A mediation is supposed to be to get a case settled. So I do have a narrow focus... to get as much money as I legitimately can for the client... In most cases, *doctors* would just get in the way. Typically the doctor doesn't make the decision to settle the cases. But invariably they seem to have a lot of say on the subject if they're given the opportunity. And I would think it would be an impediment to efficient mediation. Now, that's a bit of guesswork... but... it might create another layer of emotion and conflict at mediation. Very rarely do people care about how sorry the doctor is by the time they get to mediation... The only time I think the presence of a doctor is necessary or helpful is where there is some issue on liability that involves a question of who said what to whom." **Male, specialist – in fifties**

> "In a lot of cases... plaintiffs are very angry. There may be some cathartic benefit in having face to face... to see the human side of the doctor. But I don't know if it's going to make cases go away... It's not like... it's a way of, sort of, helping the lawyer get rid of a case that's just driven by emotion and letting the client see the light." **Male, generalist – in forties**

Moreover, similar to other legal actors, most plaintiff lawyers' discourse (58%) demonstrated that their attendance decisions were reached utilizing considerations within the framework of their own strategic agendas. For example,

> "I've seen some cases where defendant attendance was useful in terms of the overall strategy of what we're going to do with our case, proceed or not.... I suppose *it's useful* because with a doctor being there, able to apologize, perhaps cut through some of the anger, you can perhaps lower the expectation a little for settlement purposes." **Male, generalist – in forties**

In comparison, the minority of plaintiff attorneys who discussed solely pro-attendance reasons (25%) stressed plaintiffs' extralegal needs. For instance,

"It could be a good thing... For plaintiffs in some cases it would be useful just to have that emotional confrontation, for the feelings that they have about this person whom they trusted who had done something in their mind wrong, even in cases where liability is in issue... There are lots of cases where they want some kind of explanation from the doctor himself... about what might have happened... as opposed to from a lawyer... It's really plaintiffs talking to lawyers. That's not really what plaintiffs want to do... But yeah, I think in one sense or another we're back in this non-legal way to approach a case." **Male, generalist – in forties**

However, among plaintiff lawyers who discussed both reasons for and against defendants' attendance, only 56% mentioned that defendants should attend "for the plaintiff" and only 25% specifically said that plaintiffs generally wanted physicians to be present at mediation. In light of plaintiffs' views given next, this was surprising.

Analysis of lawyers' views

In sum, although attorneys discussed reasons both for and against defendants' attendance at mediation, the vast majority – regardless of allegiances – decided or acquiesced in decisions to exclude defendant physicians, proffering similar reasoning. Of the few with experience of mediation with physicians present, none recounted a single instance of doctors' attendance raising emotions or behaving arrogantly and thereby reducing settlement chances.[9] Nevertheless, this was one of the two primary reasons proffered by lawyers. Similar reasoning was found in Metzloff's research (Metzloff et al. 1997, p. 142).

However, the premise for this reasoning is weakened by the fact that the physician attendance issue predominantly pertained to mandatory court-linked mediations, where – as seen in chapter three – for a whole host of reasons unrelated to physicians' attendance (e.g., mediation timing being far too early) most lawyers generally viewed settlement as unlikely in any event. This attitude undermines the basis of the "emotions" argument, which seems to largely rest on conjecture about what may occur with defendants present. In fact, at that early stage, one might argue that from lawyers' perspectives doctor attendance could only assist, in attempting to get at least some plaintiffs to abandon their claims.

Another articulated reason against physicians' attendance was that many physician lawyers said that doctors did not want to participate. Yet, lawyers' overall negative attitudes toward early mandatory mediation made it unlikely that mediation was described to physicians as any form of opportunity for them, legal or extralegal. For example, several physician's lawyers described mandatory mediations as a "waste of time," or that "nothing is going to happen." Hence, apart from

---

9 One might argue that it was only congenial physicians who were invited by their lawyers to attend mediation, explaining why experiences were depicted positively. However, this argument is weakened by the fact that in some cases physicians attended mediations solely because plaintiff lawyers (who knew little of their dispositions) insisted they be there.

the obvious difficulties in facing such situations, it would be logical that physicians would not want to engage in such a process. Lawyers also noted doctors' busy work schedules. Yet, as will be seen later, not a single doctor mentioned this when interviewed directly. Furthermore, legal actors discussed conflicting circumstances as to when physicians should not attend mediations. These included "if mediation was early on" and "if mediation was later on after expert evidence was obtained," not in "mandatory mediations" and not in "voluntary mediations," not "if liability was disputed," and not "if liability was accepted and the focus would be on getting to a number." Arguably, the inconsistency of the individual reasons further serves to weaken the arguments against physicians' attendance at mediations.

Consequently, the only other primary reason proffered by attorneys against defendants' attendance remains the fact that doctors are not responsible for whether or how much money to settle for. The importance of this reason for legal actors was underscored in their describing physicians' presence as "not critical," "an interference," or "disturbing." This must highlight a simple truth: overall, legal actors did not need physicians at mediation. Why would they when mediation was perceived predominantly as a venue for monetary settlement or case abandonment resulting from outside expert opinion? Why would they when another player, the insurer, was now involved in the dispute, altering its dynamics if not its perceived nature? Indeed, throughout the attorney interviews there was a duality constantly present about the very nature of these disputes. On the one hand, all lawyers clearly acknowledged that these disputes were between doctors and patients or surviving relatives. Yet, at the same time, their discourse on the attendance issue reflected something different: that these disputes were between insurers and plaintiffs arguing about whether their losses warranted monetary compensation and, if so, how much?

Attorneys' discourse surrounding defendants' attendance was linked almost exclusively to issues of settlement and the effect of defendants' presence on lawyers' strategic agendas. For most legal actors, mediation was a place where strategy, negotiation, and settlement or money talk played out. Lawyers on all sides generally perceived parties' attendance as an assistance or hindrance to this end. Moreover, legal actors' discourse repeatedly suggested that lawyers perceive mediation as "their" forum first and foremost, a tool to assist their tactical and legal missions. Therefore, any talk of mediation being a venue for disputants' extralegal communication and psychological healing was discussed only secondarily or as a serendipitous effect. Lawyers are not assessed by their peers or employers on extralegal assistance they confer on disputants at mediation. So it follows that such assistance would generally not form part of the mediation equation for them. Although most acknowledged the possibility of treating disputants' extralegal needs through defendants' attendance, the majority of lawyers were ultimately against having doctors present, most believing defendants' presence would be risky or unnecessary to assist them in reaching settlement. Thus, the discourse on defendants' attendance reveals unspoken understandings of mediation's purpose and meaning.

Decisions against having defendants present at mediation may also have been a function of what lawyers were used to in terms of their own comfort levels, as some attorneys described feeling restricted in what they could say at mediation if doctors were there, utilizing words such as "foreign" and "uncomfortable" to describe their experiences. Even in relation to claimants, one male defense lawyer remarked, "There wouldn't necessarily be the kind of honesty with the plaintiffs sitting there.... *But I'd be comfortable to say that to their counsel.*"

Nevertheless, notwithstanding practicing attorneys' focus on tactics and monetary issues, in speaking of defendants' attendance at mediation the bulk of lawyers' discourse in every legal actor group was peppered with extralegal references in the form of pro-attendance reasons "for the plaintiff" or "for the physician." This appeared to denote extralegal considerations now inherent in attorneys' thinking about their cases, something essentially absent in the days when bilateral lawyer negotiations ruled.

This may be a consequence of mediation's extralegal world being thrust upon the legal world, gradually resulting in lawyers reconceptualizing their roles and thinking about their cases on a more holistic, human basis. Some lawyers even spoke about the defendant attendance issue not within a legal paradigm, but predominantly within an extralegal one, discussing at length the benefits derived by their clients from mediation in cases where no settlements had been reached. These issues were not normally within the province of the law or the legal world.

Still, defendants were not present at most mediations predominantly because of legal actors' needs and tactical decisions. Repeating one physician lawyer's words, "My job's not, you know, primarily to help the doctor feel better about stuff. My job is to achieve a resolution to this dispute between the parties." However, this begged the question: In line with their needs to resolve their disputes what did disputants, the protagonists in these cases, perceive as the meaning and purpose of mediation? Mediators' comprehensions were closer to what I heard from disputants themselves.

Mediators

In view of the fact that the mediator group consisted of practicing lawyers who had become mediators (ten lawyer-mediators; seven non-lawyer-mediators), it was fascinating that in discussing reasons in favor of defendants' attendance, 100% of mediators offered reasons "for plaintiffs" and 73% said "for physicians." This indicated greater acknowledgment of extralegal elements within disputes as compared with practicing lawyers. Furthermore, there were few differences in the discourse of lawyer-mediators and non-lawyer-mediators. Could this mean that once an attorney trains as a mediator and experiences numerous mediations a type of metamorphosis occurs, resulting in the same individual reconceptualizing their perception of disputes in more holistic, less tactical ways? The degree of "extralegal talk" by mediators on the defendants' attendance issue was almost a world away from practicing attorneys, highlighting divergent understandings of these cases and their resolution. The following quotes are from practicing lawyers who became mediators:[10]

For disputants

"If a doctor's there it's more humane, and there can be interaction... I would have brought out how bad *the doctor* would have felt. How difficult it is to face something like that. I think it's 'very' important for plaintiffs... It would be so helpful for doctors too. It'll give them a chance to vent... It may not settle, but I still think... both parties would benefit in most cases." **Male lawyer-mediator – mandatory – in fifties**

"It's different when a lawyer talks about what their client doctor or what the plaintiff has been through versus having them express that themselves to each other, face to face... It's critical doctors attend because firstly there's a great need for plaintiffs to see the doctor. The fact that they even show up shows... plaintiffs... that they care enough to be there. So there's great benefit... Physicians have an opportunity to say in their own words what they believe happened, and to express their emotional and psychological interests; and for plaintiffs to hear how the suit has affected the doctor... That can change the whole dynamic." **Female lawyer-mediator – mandatory and voluntary – in forties**

"They can find out why their patient is distraught... And if there is a problem, the doctor will say 'Did I handle it properly at the time? Maybe I should've said I'm sorry at the time....' The doctor may not have thought of any of these issues... Minor things to him, which he might not recognize, which the patient felt was very important... It's a learning process... Because *people* are in stressful situations. They go into distress, and they end up with lawyers." **Male lawyer-mediator – voluntary and mandatory – in fifties**

It was also striking that lawyer-mediators' discourse on this topic was often more similar to that of non-lawyer-mediators (e.g., of social work backgrounds) than to practicing attorneys. For example,

"When parties get a chance to speak to doctors and have it facilitated... It makes a tremendous difference... in terms of moving the thing forward to real closure... You're going to get a lot of emotion... But if they work through that... Physicians' views change because they are face-to-face with the real people, and they realize it's not about whether they're gonna be found guilty or innocent. It's about much more of a process of healing, and resolving this on a much deeper level... I think we've

---

10 Mediators' views are introduced in this chapter for a number of reasons. As mediators only worked on cases briefly and not from their inception, I did not ask mediators specifically about why they thought plaintiffs had sued – only about what they understood mediated disputes to be about. Therefore, their views were not included in chapter two. Likewise, mediators were not included in chapter three as most were either court-linked mandatory mediators or voluntary mediators, and they did not mix. Therefore mediators generally had little knowledge about the other type of mediation and could not provide comparative views. However, as mediators knew much about the issue of defendants' attendance at mediation, their views are introduced in chapter four.

lost sight of what mediation is... It's meant to offer a process, to explore with people what their interests and needs are." **Female non-lawyer voluntary/mandatory/College mediator – in forties**

Moreover, when speaking of settlement in the context of defendants' mediation presence, mediators' and practicing lawyers' differing understandings became even more apparent. The following are views of practicing attorneys who became mediators:

For settlement

"Unless the emotional aspects are addressed, it's very difficult to get a resolution. The emotional aspects are key to either resolving the case or to moving it forward... There's all sorts of other benefits that happen from parties attending." **Female lawyer-mediator – mandatory and voluntary – in forties**

"The only way you can work is if you have the two parties who are... directly involved... So *they* can talk to each other, share information... If the doctor doesn't come... he is not going to hear what the plaintiff says and understand what's going on... Isn't that the whole point of mediation – to get the parties together so that they can discuss their mutual differences? That may be a philosophical bend, but that's what I think works... You may have somebody else who's paying the bill... PEOPLE SAY EMOTIONAL IS NOT CONDUCIVE TO SETTLING... Then what's the point of mediation?... Plaintiffs get to vent their spleen from an emotional point of view, and advise the physician of what they felt was wrong. They may be totally off the wall, but at least they get that feeling out. Once they get that out things tend to move along quicker towards 'Now, what's the legal obligation they had'?" **Male lawyer-mediator – mandatory and voluntary – in fifties**

"Especially if liability is disputed, they want to be able to tell their version of it. They may or may not be able to express some catharsis in the plaintiffs' direction. And if they can, that can sometimes help... Any kind of expression of regret or acknowledgment of whatever the plaintiff's gone through can help move towards settlement. It can soften the plaintiff a little." **Male lawyer-mediator – voluntary and mandatory – in forties**

These insights not only underscored differing understandings and interests on the "defendants' attendance" issue between mediators and lawyers, but also suggested a move by lawyer-mediators away from traditional legal thought and into the extralegal realm of thinking about cases and their resolution. Indeed, the vocabulary of lawyers who had become mediators was noticeably different to practicing attorneys, frequently focusing on extralegal concerns. Yet, these were individuals with similar education and training to practitioner-lawyers, many having spent years as practicing attorneys themselves, most probably perceiving disputes at that time predominantly on legal and tactical lines. Moreover, the fact that there was little difference between lawyer-mediators' and non-lawyer-mediators' discourse on the attendance issue was significant. It was as if experiencing mediations with

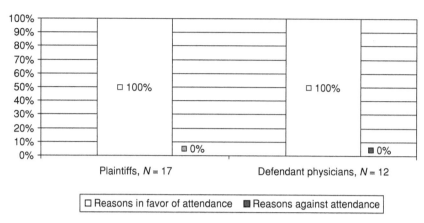

Figure 10. Disputants' views on defendants' mediation attendance. In stark contrast to legal actors, all plaintiffs and defendant physicians felt doctors should attend mediation, with none offering any reasons why they should not be present.

disputants present sensitized lawyers-mediators to the human realities of cases and perhaps changed their way of perceiving disputes. This change seemed to be more than mediation training alone could achieve.

Nevertheless, defendants' absence at mediation was a recurrent reality in these cases, with non-attendance decisions of legal actors at times resulting in profound consequences for disputants. Section 4.3 now explores how disputants, the protagonists in these cases, perceived the attendance issue as well as the meaning and purpose of mediation for their cases on the litigation track.

4.3 Facing opponents: Disputants ascribe common meaning to case resolution

In exploring lay disputants' perspectives on the same issue of defendants' attendance at mediation, I entered a different world, one almost anathema to the one seen previously. It was a world bereft of tactical or monetary settlement considerations, where the concept of mediation presaged not only human, psychological interchanges, but ones of significance in the lives of many disputants. Surprisingly, the views of opposing disputants on the issue were very much the same, even though in most cases plaintiffs and defendants had no relationship prior to the disputed incidents. Even on the surface, the charts in Figures 10 and 11 affirm unexpected similarities between the views of plaintiffs and defendants, being materially different to the general stance of lawyers, including their own attorneys. First, disputants' discourse overall was examined. In stark contrast to the findings on legal actors, all plaintiff and defendant physicians felt that defendants should be present at mediation, with none offering any reasons why they should not attend.

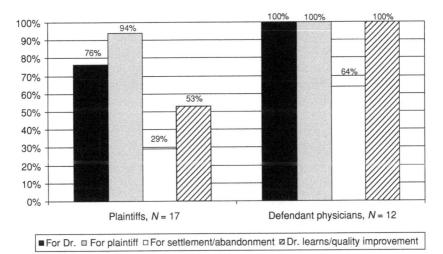

Figure 11. Disputants' reasoning on why defendants should attend mediation. Claimants' and physician defendants' reasoning in favor of defendants' mediation attendance was similar.

Second, when looking more closely at the specific reasoning behind disputants' attendance views, plaintiffs' and defendants' discourse was also quite similar.

Yet it is only on hearing disputants' own voices that the coexistence of two almost entirely discordant worlds of disputes and their resolution becomes evident, making plain that attorneys' attendance decisions impacted many disputants profoundly. Moreover, a further layer of meaning also emerges through the discourse of female disputants. These issues will be explored by first considering the views of doctors followed by those of plaintiffs, which are examined in five case studies (two with defendants present and three with defendants absent). Gender disparities in professional and lay actor groups are examined in Section 4.4.

Defending doctors' views on attending mediation

"IN CIVIL CASES THE MONEY COMES FROM *INSURERS*, SO REALLY IT'S BETWEEN THEM? No. That is ridiculous... The dispute is initiated by the plaintiffs, and defended by doctors, defending *their* actions. That is the focus... What happens is you get egos and other issues, which take away the focus... Mediation is *to*... convince plaintiffs there is really nothing that has gone on. There has been no maliciousness... That is the objective of mediation... What you're talking about is a settlement, which is quite different than mediation. That is not mediation of the dispute. That is mediation to a settlement. And they are different objectives... What you have got there is a confused issue. I am not sure the system they have set out is wise enough for that." **Male surgeon – College and mandatory court-linked mediations – in fifties**

For physicians, mediations were part of disputes that were often extremely stressful and very upsetting, particularly if connected with lawsuits. Their professional reputations, livelihoods, and what they strived to do could be at stake. Still, notwithstanding the difficult nature of the mediation exercise for doctors, all were willing to attend, perceiving mediation as an opportunity to explain their side. In the thirteen cases discussed, not a single physician mentioned their busy practices as a deterrent to their attendance. For instance,

> "I welcomed the opportunity to defend myself. AT MEDIATION? Oh yeah... For me, it was an opportunity to speak to them." **male surgeon – in fifties – fatality – College**

> "I think anybody would welcome the opportunity... to explain why they did what they did. They can explain... why they thought it was a reasonable approach to the problem." **OBGYN physician – College – male – in sixties**

> "I've been sued before, 20 years ago. I had made a mistake; and it took a long time for me to admit *it* to myself. I think this is because basically you don't want to do anything wrong. I mean we were trained to do good stuff. So when you do bad stuff *it's* like 'ochh'... AND COMPULSORY MEDIATION ATTENDANCE? I don't have a problem with that. I mean, as long as the frivolous stuff gets sorted out beforehand." **Male ENT surgeon – in sixties – mandatory court-linked mediation**

These findings contribute to the scant body of knowledge on mediation objectives of defending physicians. In view of the predominantly positive feedback received by defending physicians, it should be noted that doctors were invited to voice their views with the possibility of precipitating change in the context of a new court-linked mandatory mediation program that effectively forced them to attend mediations. Thus, doctors who felt negatively about mediation should have been equally willing to offer their views as doctors who felt positively. On the issue of willingness to attend, however, it should be noted that most physicians interviewed had already undergone mediation. Doctors whom physician lawyers had referred to as "not wanting to attend" most probably had not experienced mediation. Therefore the views here may offer greater understanding of how, if at all, defendants' mediation perceptions may have changed with mediation experience. What dominated defendants' discourse most significantly was the very different meaning they ascribed to the resolution of these disputes as compared with legal actors. This meaning emerged not only in discussing the importance of their attendance, but also in describing personal benefits they derived through mediation.

"Real" mediation could not occur without defendants

For defendant physicians, mediation was about disputants communicating with each other. Therefore, "real" mediation could not occur without them.

"IF YOUR LAWYER ATTENDED ALONE? Oh no, that process could not have taken place without my being there. It would have been a 'very' different thing... A lawyer would never have done *what I did*... My lawyer wouldn't have sat there with the family commiserating with them about... her death... I was able to say that to them... I think that may have been the best thing that happened there for them... To me, the whole process, the whole notion of a mediation, is that it's a personal process. If the doctor is not present, what's the point? You know, it's a legalistic exercise, a hypothetical exercise. AND WHERE THERE'S A CIVIL ACTION... I would probably always attend. That would be my choice." **Female emergency specialist – fatality – College – but litigation anticipated – in fifties**

"WHY DIDN'T YOU GO TO THE MANDATORY MEDIATION? Because I wasn't asked. That might have been my counsel's advice, or it may have been the standard procedure. I'm not sure... I would have loved to be there... The first *mediation of this dispute* I had to attend *with my lawyer at the College*. That was genuine mediation... because I was there with the family and we discussed the issues; and then we came to an understanding.

This is supposed to be primary interaction between physician and patient. Mediation is not between lawyers. That is the whole point of this... *Mediation* is an opportunity... to sit down and have a less excitable environment in which to discuss *what happened*... to communicate with the patients, get our point across... When you have all this cacophony going on behind you of experts disputing, it takes away the physician's and the patients' ability to communicate themselves." **Male surgeon – court-linked mandatory and College mediation – fatality – in fifties**

"I think trying to resolve it between lawyers is cumbersome, misguided, and nonproductive... With lawyers representing doctors at mediations you cannot make people feel better about things." **Male, specialist surgeon – in forties**

Defendants' perception of mediation as a forum for "human communication" and "feeling better" further emerged when physicians described the benefits they derived from mediation.

Mediation is "human communication" and "feeling better"

Regardless of mediation venue or whether settlement or abandonment ensued, all physicians described how they benefited personally by attending mediation. Similarly, all doctors felt their presence benefited plaintiffs, and most (64%) were of the view that it could assist in resolving disputes. In discussing these benefits, physicians' discourse repeatedly reflected their understandings of mediation as a forum for various types of human communication, learning, and addressing psychological needs, for example, the need to explain their perspectives and intentions (in response to upsetting complaints or litigation documentation). This was equally the case for defendants who initially were not eager to attend mediation. It may have been that through mediation participation they felt they regained some control over their disputes. For instance,

> "I went to the mediation because... *it was pseudo-mandatory*... At the end *of the mediation*... there was a positive feeling between the family and myself... We all understood that my intervention... wouldn't have changed *the fatality*... They said they wanted to make clear they weren't after my head... they weren't out to denounce me... They wanted to feel she had not died in vain... DID YOU KNOW THAT PRIOR TO MEDIATION? I don't think I knew that prior to mediation." **Female emergency physician – in fifties – College mediation – with litigation anticipated**

> "They wanted answers... as to why the fatality had occurred... and just didn't know how to go about getting them... They were caught up in the process... *Mediation was* an opportunity... to be able to sit down and actually... discuss it... ANY EMOTIONAL OR PSYCHOLOGICAL RELIEF? Absolutely. Oh ya. WHAT MADE YOU FEEL THAT... That they had listened; that I was able to put my points across; and that they saw I really cared... I was there and able to express. That is the key... *Mediation* becomes your forum... I think they were surprised that... I cared that much... I can still see them looking at me... When people see how you react and there are nonverbal cues that you do care, that makes a significant difference... FOR COURT-LINKED MEDIATIONS SHOULD YOU BE THERE? Absolutely." **Male surgeon – in fifties – College and court-linked mandatory mediations**

> "If *plaintiffs*' questions are left unanswered often they leave with a misunderstanding and angry feeling as though you in some way have caused this... and in fact, it is completely wrong... So there is definitely benefit for the physician." **Female physician – College – in fifties**

It was also noteworthy that views of plaintiffs after College mediations were not negative, despite subsequent litigation. For instance,

> "*Going into mediation*... you are always worried... AFTER SPEAKING I felt better... I benefited... *closure*... The mediation was really just... a conversation between *me and the son at the lawyers' office*... I wanted them to understand my perspective... hear his side... show I cared... My perception of the son changed at mediation... better... Actually, he was quite reasonable... Their main feeling was just to help prevent this from happening again... We shook hands at the end... They did go on to do the legal action. But even that was resolved very quickly and simply." **Male emergency physician – College and litigation – fatality case – in forties**

Conversely, the discourse of defendant physicians who mediated without complainants present evinced their own lack of closure and need for communication. For instance,

> "The complainant was not there... In spite of the mediation... I *need* some closure to the situation... because I feel like I have never had closure brought to this." **Male OBGYN – specialist – College – in fifties**

"It would have been better for me that the other party attend the mediation... The patient may have had a different perspective if she would have heard my point of view. I think she had a biased viewpoint; that I did not provide proper care, that I did not care about her... those sorts of things." **Female physician – College – in fifties**

Regardless of mediation venue or their particular mediation experiences, in discussing their attendance defendant physicians spoke of diverse personal needs and human benefits. This was far removed from most lawyers' tactical perceptions and surprisingly more akin to plaintiffs' discourse, as will be seen later. In fact, notwithstanding the tragedies and potential animosity between them, on the mediation plane a conceptual alignment of plaintiffs and defendants emerged through their discourse on disputants' joint attendance at mediation, regrouping them in opposition to mediation's legal actors, including their own representatives. For instance, regardless of mediation timing, most physicians spoke of mediation as a chance to satisfy their need to put forward their side. This correlated with claimants' needs to do the same as well as to hear physicians' explanations. In fact, in looking at Figure 11, defendants were even more uniform than plaintiffs in their reasoning as to why they should attend mediation. This was significant as some physicians were initially not eager to mediate, had negative experiences with mediation institutions, and in some cases, subsequent to College mediations plaintiffs sued.

It therefore appeared that something unexpected took place at mediation. This may have been linked to the fact that despite most legal actors' views to the contrary, all defendant physicians discussed learning things they would not have known otherwise than through mediation. By attending mediation and hearing claimants directly, physicians acquired insight into plaintiffs' perspectives. They learned the meaning of these disputes and their consequences for plaintiffs as well as intangible issues like plaintiffs' perceptions of defendants' conduct or their perceptions of how incidents unfolded. In speaking of defendants' attendance at mediation, many of the same issues were discussed by plaintiffs. The only difference was that they spoke from opposite ends of disputes.

Plaintiffs on defendants' mediation attendance

For claimants who had suffered serious injury or loss of loved ones, it was psychologically and emotionally difficult to undergo mediation involving those perceived to be responsible. Yet like physicians, every plaintiff provided reasons why defendants should attend, the vast majority wanting defendants to see and hear them directly. Interestingly, most plaintiffs (76%) felt that defendants' attendance would also benefit physicians themselves. This was regardless of age, injury type, whether physicians attended their mediations, or whether mediations induced settlement. In fact, claimants discussing defendants' attendance at mediation did not – in contrast to legal actors – generally mention "settlement" unless probed. As with defendants, mediation for plaintiffs predominantly meant communication between disputants and treating their psychological needs. Thus, plaintiffs' discourse provided evidence to strengthen their conceptual alignment with defendants in terms of the common meaning they ascribed to mediation and how their cases should be resolved. The following five case studies – two where defendants were present, followed by three where defendants were absent – illustrate these points, highlighting the starkly different understandings and views of legal versus lay actors as well as the harm involved when plaintiffs attend mediations alone.

Mediations with defendants present

Whatever occurred at mediation, physicians' presence clearly altered mediation's dynamics and experiences for disputants.

Case 1: Fatality "DNR" case – post-discovery mandatory mediation – no settlement

This case involved a dispute over a "do not resuscitate" order and the fatality of the plaintiffs' husband and father. Notwithstanding the deceased's age of 86, the mediator noted, "it came out in mediation that this man was looking forward to living and had a lot to live for."

The physician's lawyer did acknowledge during his interview that there was something positive in having the defendant there who wanted his perspective put forward (evidencing some reconceptualization as to how he viewed the case). However, in his questionnaire responses he "agreed" that mediation was a total waste of time, "very strongly agreed" that mediation was inappropriate for this type of case, and "strongly disagreed" that mediation was successful in clarifying or narrowing the issues. The plaintiff lawyer's questionnaire responses were also notable. He "disagreed" that mediation revealed facts that helped move the parties toward settlement and "disagreed" that mediation clarified or narrowed the issues. Yet he also "disagreed" that mediation was inappropriate or a waste of time and "agreed" that his clients were satisfied. This suggested some reconceptualization of his role or case perceptions in taking greater account of extralegal issues for disputants – knowingly or not. He described the mediation as follows:

> "The physician was very quiet and seemed to participate very little... I am not at all sure why he was there because he made no statement, and his position was basically ignored by his counsel... I don't think there was anything valuable to having him there. When you think of what's being asked for, the person who's really making the decision for *the lawyer, the insurer*, is not there at all... DO YOU THINK THE DOCTOR BENEFITTED AT ALL? I don't think so... I think he feels badly... not medically... I think he's genuine. I think he's sincere about the fact that he did not have that communication he should have." **Plaintiff lawyer – specialist, male – in forties**

What was not mentioned was that this understanding resulted from the defendant being present at mediation. Yet, in comparing plaintiffs' and defendants' discourse in the same case, one begins to see the legal versus lay actor alignment on the attendance issue emerge.

Male plaintiff – son – in forties

> HOW DID YOU FEEL ABOUT MEDIATION WITH THE DOCTOR? I felt really good, because we are the two parties directly involved with each other. That's important, because I don't want to have some faceless person... lawyer... This is between you and I... I'm taking time out of my life and I think you should be there. If you did your job right in the first place, all of us would not be there... So this way the doctor and I are there face to face. I know what happened in my heart. You know the truth... you look me eye to eye, and I'll tell you. And you can question me back. That's the best thing... It's important the doctor is always, always there. Even though there's a lack of doctors. Give me at least that respect.

Later he said,

> The most important thing to me in the mediation was to see Dr... a very aggressive person, very vocal, loud, *now* primarily defensive. He was just a very meek man... quiet at mediation... He was so quiet because he knows he's wrong... I could barely hear him... DID YOU GET ANY EXPLANATION? No, nothing... *But* I know he felt guilty, otherwise he would have... looked at you... But for two hours... he had his head down... Nobody can tell me he didn't feel... his conscience... He heard my mom. He heard me... He knows the truth... But unfortunately it's the law as his lawyer's saying "Don't look into the light ..." *But* I feel good. This is what I got out of mediation... *seeing doctor*... That is the most important thing to me... I would have never known that *without* mediation.... That's a benefit to me, because I know at night-time he's not living with himself too well... Dr... knows in his heart he did wrong, but he can't admit to it. YOU LEARNED THAT AT MEDIATION? I saw that in his face. That told me everything... ANYTHING ELSE YOU THOUGHT WAS GOOD AT MEDIATION? No, not really.

Female plaintiff – widow – in seventies

> I *am* 100% sure I wanted *him* there. I even told my lawyer, if he will not *attend* we should postpone mediation... I am very happy that I explained everything... and I noticed when I *said* "Dr... you admitted in your office... His lawyer didn't know about that. I noticed they whispered during my speech... DID HE ANSWER YOU? No... Dr... was little bit shaky... [she chuckles] He didn't even look at me... All those people, I told my story *to*, and Dr... never looked at me... WHERE WAS HE LOOKING? Down; all the time down... He felt he is guilty... uncomfortable.

The descriptions of the physician's body language matched observation data on other defendant physicians during court-linked mediations. However, looks may have been deceiving. Nonetheless, it was equally evident in the defendant's explanation that mediation for him was about human communication and dealing with psychological needs.

Defendant physician – male – in fifties

> I was told I *had* to attend... *Without having had the prior meeting*... I would be curious to know what their arguments are, what they are looking for, and just to see their point of view would have been helpful... I think mediation is good if no contact has been

made. It has a lot of positive things, because it allows people to talk... express... and then see the point of view of the other person.

At mediation... I had feelings of apprehension initially... with time I felt more at ease... just getting to face them and becoming more familiar and knowing what I'm dealing with, what I'm facing... I tried to avoid eye contact. I didn't feel I would have anything to gain... Questions were addressed to me... I didn't mind... actually, because I expressed again my point of view... *because they really conceived things totally differently*... *After I spoke* I was pleased... I thought I had a very professional attitude and I really said what needed to be said... I was happy the way things happened... AFTER MEDIATION... I felt that I'm dealing with people that weren't worth any sympathy from me... and I should not have any regret about it at all.

In describing defendants' mediation attendance each disputant recounted verbal and nonverbal extralegal communication and psychological benefit, perceiving these as inherent to mediation. This was despite the emotionally charged atmosphere, the fact that no settlement ensued and regardless of the intended meanings of those who were communicating. Although disputants' views of each other remained negative, having gone through mediation each felt less disturbed about the other as well as about their own situations. Parallel to these understandings, perceptions of the legal actors on opposing sides of the case were similar to each other but markedly different to those of the parties involved, illustrating the very different meaning they ascribed to the process.

Case 2: Bladder operation case – pre-discovery mandatory mediation – no settlement

Although the next dispute had different case facts, the same disparate perceptions of mediation were evident in comparing lay versus legal actors' discourse on defendants' attendance. As with the previous case, the plaintiff's lawyer did not think much of the mediation. However, his discourse on defendants' attendance also revealed another side to his thought processes, providing evidence of reconceptualization of his role to include consideration of his client's extralegal needs within the case.

Plaintiff lawyer – generalist, male – in forties

We all felt we're wasting our time *at mediation* and wished we didn't have to be there. The defense side as well... There was no way were going to discuss a settlement... EXCEPT FOR THE EMOTIONAL ELEMENT? Ya, and who knows how important that is, ultimately. But in terms of the more narrow focus of "will it assist me in winning or losing a case?" No; waste of time.

Yet, he spoke differently when I asked about his client.

WAS IT IMPORTANT FOR YOUR CLIENT... *Clients* very much want a chance to confront the person they feel has harmed them. I think that's true in most kinds of legal disputes. And it's an important part of it... Once you've done that, it's easier to then consider settlement positions... The doctor... stared implacably... There was no communication between physician and plaintiff.

I came there, somewhat irritated at what I perceived to be an unnecessary expense for my client... It actually amazed me to see *my client* rise up and take charge verbally... It was a different person I'd never seen... I couldn't have shut him up if I'd wanted to. He went on and on, outlining his complaints and his feelings in a way that I'd never heard him express. I mean, it was an important moment for him, irrelevant to the case itself, the legal procedure, the issues, the likelihood of settlement. But it was important for him because it may be the only chance he gets.

He doesn't have any money, as many people in his situation don't. So when plaintiffs' lawyers take on cases without retainers, without money, if we don't have a damn strong sense that there's going to be money at the end, we're not going to waste months of our lives on it... After discovery you might have to say "Sorry, I'm not going to do this without money." It's certainly an issue in all cases. And so that may be the one chance they have to confront their perceived assailant.

As in all cases, the plaintiff spoke from a "parallel world" about the mediation and the attendance issue.

Male plaintiff – in thirties

Oh, I *felt* so happy to go into the mediation, to reach the doctor face to face... to talk to him... because I want*ed* to let him know *and* let him *tell* to me what surgery he *did* to me... or what he didn't do... I *felt* so happy because I just want*ed* to explain and let Dr... know how I *felt* because he always *kept* ignoring me... I want*ed* to hear his side. But Dr... didn't say much at mediation. SO WHAT MADE YOU FEEL HAPPY? Because to have *the doctor* there... to let him face the guy who he *did* the surgery to... *You* become a victim and *doctors* should know about how they affected you... It's *important for* the doctor to hear for his future career... He could learn... how to treat somebody else.

He didn't say the truth *at mediation*... I didn't believe *him*... He didn't give no explanation... He *was* just bending his head down... I was thinking he believes he *did* some things that he's not supposed to do. So, he feel*s* shame... *Mediation* helped me a lot because by... fac*ing* the doctor... I gained... I *got* to know the doctor a little more than what I kn*ew* before... from his behavior at mediation... I learned he's not a good guy. He just thinks about... his career... *I learned* right now maybe his professional *life is* going down... *Others* will not trust him... I was thinking about it before, but I learned a little more at mediation.

Thus similar to the previous case, despite being costly for the plaintiff ("more than his weekly pay check"), no resulting settlement and his lawyer viewing the mediation as a waste of time, the plaintiff felt mediation "was worth it" and "helped him out a lot" predominantly due to the defendant's presence and the consequent communication that ensued. As in other cases, much occurred beneath the surface during mediation. This was notwithstanding the doctor speaking little and the plaintiff not believing what he did say. Yet, by thinking worse of the physician, the plaintiff appeared to feel better about his own situation.

By defendants simply being present, even without uttering a word, disputants saw, heard, and learned things, both tangible and visceral. This was regardless of the correctness of individuals' perceptions or whether disputants' views changed about their opponents. Plaintiffs wanted defendants "to hear" what they had been through and "to see" what had happened to them. Thus, even when doctors said little or nothing at mediation, their perceived nonverbal communication resulted in plaintiffs feeling better about their situations. This was the same with physicians, regardless of the level of their mediation participation. Therefore, whatever transpired, including whether or not settlement resulted, defendants and plaintiffs who mediated together repeatedly discussed material psychological benefits – even when viewing each other in a worse light after mediation.

Yet, as the next three case studies illustrate, this interchange was effectively taken away from parties in mediations where lawyers decided against physicians' attendance for reasons far removed from the understandings and needs of disputants themselves. Disputants who did not mediate together lacked closure. Furthermore, defendants' absence from mediation harmed plaintiffs' perceptions of them and likewise did not improve physicians' perceptions of plaintiffs. Nevertheless, it was striking that even without defendants present – consequently being surrounded at mediations solely by lawyers and/or representatives – the meaning plaintiffs ascribed to court-linked mediations was the same as for disputants who mediated together.

Mediations without defendants

"Even if she just sat in the corner and didn't say a word. But she had to listen to us. She had to see our tears. She had to see my mother in those pictures and see what it was like three years later... She needed to come to hear what her actions caused... What she could have learned from it may have benefited her patients... I don't have a sense of closure because she was not there... She didn't have to sit there and look at me and say 'I am sorry' or 'This is what happened to me. I've had repercussions ...' I'm very interested to know; and I have no sense of that." **Female plaintiff – in forties – settlement at mediation**

"Clients inevitably follow advice given by their lawyer. If their lawyer says 'This is the deal... This is the figure; settle it', it doesn't matter whether the *defendant* has been there to hear the whole story or not. The case settles, because the family are usually unsophisticated litigants... It's very rare that they will say 'no'." **Male hospital lawyer – in forties**

When defendants were absent from mediation, most plaintiffs either did not know why or believed that it was the doctors themselves who chose not to attend. As one mediator noted, "Plaintiffs are thinking the doctor just doesn't want to face them." Only a minority of claimants (24%) appeared to be aware that lawyers decided whether defendants attended. Interestingly, all seemed quite accepting of this, with few exhibiting negative feelings toward their attorneys. This may have been because virtually all were first-time litigants.

Case 3: Loss-of-sight case – post-discovery voluntary mediation – no settlement

Having lost most of her vision as a result of undetected glaucoma, the plaintiff never received an explanation or any form of apology from the defendant optometrist, whom she had visited for sixteen years. There had been no contact since the incident in dispute.

Male defendant lawyer – in fifties

> The optometrist did not attend. He was advised early on that despite his feelings to the contrary, he would lose in a courtroom. So his involvement after that became rather peripheral... He was advised of the mediation, but not invited to attend, given that liability was not in issue. *It was* just quantum.

Male plaintiff lawyer – generalist – in forties

> I'm not sure how I feel about whether defendants should show up. DID YOUR CLIENTS WANT THE DEFENDANT THERE? I'm not sure. I never discussed it with them. I'd be curious to see what they say about that.

The plaintiffs discussed the attendance issue without even being asked about it.

Female plaintiff – in forties

> DID MEDIATION BENEFIT YOU AT ALL [pause]. Well, I didn't see *the doctor*. I didn't get to tell him how I felt... You messed up. You should be there... His time is not any more precious than mine... I refuse to feel inferior to anybody... He should jolly well be there... Money does not equate closure... If I had gotten the check, the open wound would still be there. I would still be... marking blind on the same spot. If the doctor had been there that would definitely have brought me closure to all this madness.

Husband – co-plaintiff – in fifties

> I wish I had the opportunity to say to the doctor instead of them... *psychological relief*... He should have been there. I still want an apology from the doctor... It's the doctor that caused it, and having the opportunity to address him directly... would help... Why should plaintiffs miss work to be there and they don't make that sacrifice? They should be the first person to be at mediation... They... messed up the plaintiff's life... That made me more resentful towards him... because there was absolutely no apology, no remorse... Maybe the reason he was not there is he felt as if he has deceived us, an embarrassment... Why did he not make it? He just didn't want to face us... CAN DOCTORS BENEFIT BY MEDIATION? Oh yes... They'll see the blind eyes... and that will enable them to be more careful. These are real people... But when you don't see them, you don't deal with them. It's like out of sight out of mind.

This scenario was repeated throughout virtually all of the case studies.

Case 4: Vasectomy case – pre-discovery mandatory mediation – no settlement

In the vasectomy dispute, upon the wife's subsequent pregnancy and abortion, the only explanation the couple said they received from the surgeon was "it must be an act of God... maybe one in one hundred thousand cases this might happen." No form of apology was given. As the female non-lawyer-mediator explained,

> I think more than any kind of compensation, the *plaintiffs* are looking for an acknowledgement that something went wrong... There was never an acknowledgement to them that "What a horrible thing, wanting this baby, but not being able to keep it, due to economic conditions"... The defendant *lawyer* was focused on "No. This isn't malpractice." Can't pass that. I think this happened because the doctor wasn't there... I think if they heard from the doctor "I'm sorry you went through all this... But, let me amplify for you again ..." eventually they would listen... He was *also* very upset about the comment the doctor made... If the doctor was there to explain his comment, it would have been very different... His lawyer wasn't even aware... I think it's in doctors' best interests to defend themselves and put a human face to this versus a legal face.

Male plaintiff – in thirties

> HE WASN'T THERE... No. It was bad. I would have liked to have seen him there so I could tell him my side of the story... Because I wanted him to know. Hear it coming from my mouth... Because of this operation we went through a lot of grief... DO YOU KNOW WHY HE WASN'T THERE? No I don't, no... I assumed he would be there... I was eager to... tell him my side and ask for answers like "why," and just to see what he would say... I don't want to hurt this doctor. I just want him to own up for what he's done, the mistake. But he wasn't even there to listen to it. So what the heck, you know? He wasn't even there, like why should he care? If he's not even going to be there to listen... He's done his job and like "leave me alone"... He's done me wrong, and he's not owing up to it.

Female plaintiff – in thirties

> I was angry, because I would like to see who put me through all this... My dispute wasn't with the doctor's lawyer. My dispute is with the doctor. He's the one that did the damage. He should be the one that's there... ANY EXPLANATION? I got a lot of mumbo jumbo! But nothing that would give me an understanding of why this happened... *If the doctor was there*, I would have asked a lot of questions... I didn't get the answers I was looking for; not just with the settlement. I'm just angry that my questions will never be answered about why things happened.

Again, the defense lawyer's understanding of this mediation was quite different to that of the plaintiffs. Yet, the plaintiff lawyer – although not demanding that the defendant attend – did seem to view matters somewhat extralegally.

Physician lawyer – male – in forties

> The mediation will be a waste of time as there are no expert reports yet. No physician will be there and I expect to be there for 5 minutes.

Plaintiff lawyer – generalist, male – in forties

> I didn't know for sure whether the doctor would be there... They probably would have liked him to be there... to hear from him what he says went wrong... to have him try to explain how this happened... They'd get a sense of what has happened to *the doctor*... The doctor would get a better appreciation of what they've gone through, was sorry for what they had gone through... and maybe an understanding as well that what the plaintiff is looking for is not... just money.

Finally, the last case study represents a classic case of the phenomenon of "mediation for a settlement without mediation of the dispute."

Case 5: Child operation case – pre-discovery mandatory mediation – settled

Defendant surgeon – male – in sixties

> WHY DID THEY SUE? I have no idea... I would like to have been at the mediation... WHY DIDN'T YOU ATTEND? I wasn't asked. My lawyer sort of said to me... "I don't think you need to be there"... If I would have said "Oh, I'd like to be there" I probably could have. But the way it was put to me "I'll let you know if you need to be there."
>
> It troubles me... the mistake was made because we were trying to make things happen sooner for this family. So... I would like to have been there... to make sure that information came forward... My concern was to simply have the parents appreciate the sequence of events... We apologized right up front. I said "Look, there's been a mistake made here"... I probably would have benefited *by attending* because I might not feel as strongly that these parents took advantage of a clerical error.

Plaintiff – father – in thirties

> When he was first told about the mistake... He didn't look too concerned... No apology, nothing like that... His tone of voice, very monotone... no sincerity... like "Oh, I'm really sorry. Let me look into it"... But *instead* "Here's the form I read." Then he just walked away.
>
> I would have liked him to be there and to say, "I'm sorry" at least... Even if he had just walked in and showed his presence, at least to show he was concerned, that he was sincerely sorry for what happened... But my lawyer asked him not to be there for some reason, and I never got an explanation to that. But I trusted my lawyer's judgement... YOU KNEW HE WAS NOT GOING TO ATTEND? No, not till the *mediation* morning... If I was some... millionaire... maybe the surgeon would have been there.

Plaintiff – mother – in thirties

> DO YOU KNOW WHY THE DOCTOR DIDN'T SHOW UP? I have no idea... He should have been there... to apologize... He didn't give us any apology when the

whole incident happened... DID MEDIATION AFFECT YOUR UNDERSTANDING OF DOCTOR... SIDE? No, not at all... because nothing was really explained.

For these plaintiffs, notwithstanding the defendant's absence, the meaning of mediation still entailed communication between disputants to fulfill their psychological needs. Despite settling, the plaintiffs did not feel better about their situations, describing a far less satisfying mediation experience than that of plaintiffs who mediated with physicians in cases that did not settle and involved more serious harm. A substantial reason for this involved the lack of communication by plaintiffs and defendants. Why did this occur?

Male, specialist plaintiff lawyer – in thirties

> It was my recommendation that we not insist the doctor be there... It would make it an uncomfortable three hours... a more uncomfortable atmosphere for everybody because they had this animosity... The defense lawyers had advised me that for settlement purposes... liability wouldn't be an issue. So because we were only dealing with quantum, I didn't think it would be necessary or helpful to have the doctor there. It would ratchet up the tension level, and it wasn't like we were going to need an apology from him to get it settled because my clients were only talking about quantum... The doctor doesn't make the decision about how much to pay... So I didn't think there was much to be gained by having him there.

Male physician lawyer – in fifties

> Could we come to some reasonable figure on damages? That was the issue *at mediation*... Although the doctor was available and willing to attend, I felt it was unnecessary, given that liability wasn't going to be a focus. It was entirely an issue of money, and really he had no role or interest in that... Then when *the plaintiffs' lawyer* said... I thought "well that's great... everybody's in sync. We don't need to have him attend..." Given they had some animosity... his absence probably assisted in the resolution. They might have been more intransigent... But I don't know. That's pure speculation.

This mediation, as others, underscored the alignment of legal versus lay actors' interests in the attendance issue. By exemplifying missed opportunities for disputants to communicate, understand, and "feel better" about their own situations, it highlighted another facet of a system where disputes are no longer completely owned by disputants, with decisions sometimes resulting in material consequences for them being taken out of their hands. Although the case settled, neither side ever came to understand the other's perspective or the reasoning that led to their conduct. Still, regardless of defendants' attendance, for all plaintiffs, mediation meant communication with defendants and treating their psychological needs. These issues, as well as resentment toward defendants for mediation absences – although it appeared often not to be their fault – were recurrent in virtually all cases. Moreover, irrelevant of mediation venue, the issues in dispute, or whether settlement ensued, material issues remained unaddressed for disputants without defendants there.

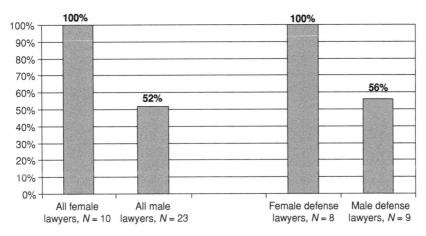

Figure 12. Extralegal reasons for defendants' mediation attendance by gender. Among lawyers overall as well as solely defense lawyers, females spoke more often of disputants' extralegal needs (psychological, emotional, understanding, learning, etc.) when considering whether defendant physicians should attend mediations.

4.4 Gender disparities

Further analysis was undertaken on professionals' and disputants' groups to examine whether any differences existed in their discourse on the attendance issue based on the independent gender variable.

Professionals' gender disparities

Due to small numbers resulting from subdivisions, legal actor groups were combined. Views in favor of physicians' attendance "for the plaintiff" or "for the physician" (as opposed to "for settlement") included psychological, emotional, learning, and understanding issues. These were termed "extralegal reasons" for attendance.

The data suggested that gender was a factor affecting how non-disputants viewed the attendance issue and/or their decisions about it. Whether looking at all lawyers combined (ten females; twenty-three males) or solely those on the defense (eight females; nine males), the discourse of females as compared with males more often included extralegal considerations when speaking about whether defendants should attend mediations. This was consonant with the gender findings in chapter two on understandings of plaintiffs' extralegal litigation aims. Figure 12 sets out these findings.

To further test this finding and in light of the fact that material numbers of lawyers discussed reasons both for and against defendants' attendance, views against attendance were also examined. These related solely to tactical reasons against having doctors present at mediations. Here too, the findings were similar as illustrated in Figure 13. When looking at all lawyers combined, 83% of males but only 60%

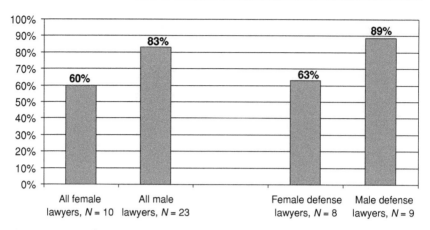

Figure 13. Tactical reasons against defendants' mediation attendance by gender. Male lawyers, both overall and when looking solely at defense lawyer groups, more often proffered tactical reasons against defendants attending mediations than did their female counterparts.

of females discussed reasons against physicians' presence at mediations. Likewise, when considering solely defense lawyers, 89% of males but only 63% of females discussed tactical reasons against attendance.

Similar to the lawyer findings, it was interesting to note that although all mediators offered reasons in favor of defendants' attendance at mediation, 0% of females (0/6) as compared with 44% of males (4/9) also discussed reasons against having defendant physicians attend mediations. Hence, in this sense the data overall suggested that gender was a factor affecting non-disputant actors' understandings of conflict and its resolution as well as the meaning of mediation itself.

Parties' gender disparities

Disputants' discourse on defendants' attendance at mediation revealed two notable gender trends: one relating to female plaintiffs, and the other to female defendants.

Female plaintiffs

In mediations where defendants were absent, although all disputants proffered reasons in favor of defendants' attendance, only male plaintiffs wanted physicians there without hesitation. In comparison, most females (73%) discussed emotional difficulties in facing defendants. For a small minority, this resulted in them feeling unable to face their perceived wrongdoers. Some female claimants also expressed concern about how their reactions to defendants at mediation might be perceived by others. This too was absent from males' discourse.

Consequently, unlike male plaintiffs, a material number of female plaintiffs initially discussed relief at physicians' absence from mediation. However, on reflection all recanted and noted how they had lost out without defendants there.

Furthermore, females regularly discussed how defendants themselves lost the opportunity for understanding and learning for their own closure. In fact, several females expressed a need to know how, if at all, their perceived wrongdoers had been affected by the disputes. This too was not seen in male plaintiffs' discourse. The following interview excerpts from female plaintiffs illustrate this trend:

Loss-of-limb case – voluntary mediation – settled subsequently

This case involved a woman who went for knee replacement surgery. She explained that during the course of the surgery, the surgeon must have severed an artery. Despite her complaining of severe pain to the surgeon during the following weeks, the problem was not detected. As a result, she was forced to undergo limb amputation. This wholly transformed her life, both physically and psychologically. In discussing the mediation she said,

> He was not there. YOU DIDN'T WANT HIM THERE? I didn't think I had a choice. They just said he wasn't going to be there... I was relieved he wasn't there... If he was going to be there, I was going to have a problem... because I didn't know how I was going to handle him, if I saw him face to face... I didn't know how I was going to react to seeing him again.

However, later she noted,

> I felt it was important for them to hear my side. I wanted to be treated as an individual... whoever was there. [pause] It would have been – and here I am changing my mind mid-stream – it would have been good for him to be there. Yes. I really think it would have, because he had to put a face to a deed. I'm a human being, just like him. And he can't take his work lightly. Yes, yes. I do think it would have been... important... a good thing if he had been there.
>
> No matter how hard it was for me... It puts closure on his case too... I think it's important that they realise... what follows... where people's lives go... after surgical mistake... amputation... From his act my life had changed. His life hadn't changed. Maybe it had. I don't know... I truly hoped... all this hadn't gone on for nought, that he would listen to other patients a little closer... He always asks *my colleagues* about me. So, I have the feeling he needs closure too... I wasn't out to get him... I could have told him that *at mediation.*

Loss-of-sight case – voluntary mediation – no settlement

> I was sorry he wasn't there, but at the same time happy, because I don't know what my reactions would have been.... It's good I did not vent my anger, because I think I would probably say things that I would later regret... So that's why it was good he wasn't there... It was a more pleasant atmosphere not having him there.

But later she said,

> I wanted him to see who Mrs... is. I wanted him to see what is left of me... *It would have been* much better... It would have been good for him to be there to see the

person that has lost the eye. I am not a file case, but it's me; it's real. What you did was real... That fellow should be there.

Fatality of fourteen-year-old – voluntary mediation – settled

This case involved a dispute relating to physician conduct and the effects of medication prescribed to a fourteen-year-old boy who consequently developed liver failure. Despite two attempted transplants, the boy died.

Plaintiff – mother – in fifties

DID YOU WANT HIM THERE? It was going to make it more difficult for me. I needed to prepare for that. It was going to change things for me... It would have been a lot harder emotionally... I didn't want his behavior, his answers to control me, to affect me... He had the power, perhaps, to do that. So it made it a whole lot easier for me to have him not there.

But she too later discussed what could have been.

UNDER MANDATORY MEDIATION... DOCTORS ARE ESSENTIALLY FORCED TO ATTEND. Definitely good. WHAT MAKES YOU FEEL THAT? I think it will force the doctor to consider what he's done. To face it... It's going to force people such as myself hopefully to begin to forgive him, to be across the table. Eventually they need to forgive each other and move on with their lives. Though this hasn't happened in our process... If *he'd been* there, that's the higher ground than what happened. I would respect him more... Would have been better for him... He could see we got our lives back on track... He could feel good about that... It would have been more challenging, but it would have raised it all to higher ground... Maybe it would have been a very difficult process. But difficult can get better... HOW DO YOU FEEL ABOUT HIM NOW? It hasn't changed... because he wasn't there... He's still small... But he had the chance to be bigger, right?

This female trend may be significant in mediations where plaintiffs have real input into defendants' attendance. Without specifically being made to consider all aspects of defendants' attendance by their representatives – something unlikely in view of lawyers' interests in the issue – the data suggest that females are more likely than males to initially refuse or more readily acquiesce in decisions against mediating with defendants present. Consequently, female plaintiffs and the defendants involved in their disputes may be disadvantaged by missing opportunities for material benefits described by disputants who mediated together. Moreover, plaintiffs' articulated litigation goals (*chapter two*) and mediation aims (*chapter five*) cannot be fully realized without defendants present.

This finding supports feminist critiques of mediation, but with the twist in that female claimants may be contributing to their own disadvantage at mediations in this respect. As such, the data inform the strand of feminist critiques relating to the internalization of disempowerment (Ricci 1985, p. 49; Kandel 1994, p. 882). Interestingly, similar findings were reached in a Canadian survey study on victims of sexual violence who sought legal compensation (ten female litigating plaintiffs and thirty who sought government compensation from the criminal injuries compensation board ["CICB"]). There too, it was found that plaintiffs sought from litigation more than money. They frequently wanted public declarations of the wrong and sought to "be heard." Yet, interestingly, it was also found that many females chose the CICB program instead of litigation because they did not want to face the alleged perpetrators as it was too difficult for them emotionally and psychologically (Des Rosiers et al. 1998, pp. 433, 435, 438). Tannen's sociolingual research similarly found that most women prefer to settle disputes without direct confrontation, whereas many males view confrontation positively, as necessary in order to negotiate their status (Tannen 1990, pp. 75, 94, 150).

Female defendants

The second gender finding for disputants suggests that female defendants more often than males derive greater psychological benefit from mediation and may also generally be better equipped to offer plaintiffs greater psychological assistance at mediation. This view is tentative due to very limited numbers of female physician respondents. However, mediators' discourse about other cases also supported this finding. For instance, one experienced mediator recounted,

> "Most of the *defendant* doctors who were the most helpful were women... incredibly sympathetic and helpful... In one case, a voluntary mediation... A baby had been dropped after birth, days later died... There were three counsel for the parents, one for the doctors... One of the three doctors, a woman, was able to express to the mother her incredible concern and sadness. And was even able to say things like 'I have two daughters, and I can't imagine how I would feel in your position... I can't bring your baby back *but* is there anything I can do to help you'? And the mother physically changed before my eyes... The other two male doctors were relatively useless... But when the female doctor started to relate to the mother it was a 'major' shift in the process." **Female – court-linked mandatory/voluntary/College non-lawyer-mediator – in forties**

This conclusion was borne out to a certain degree by some defendants' discourse when they recounted their mediation experiences. For example, in three mediations – all involving fatalities and emergency physicians – a marked qualitative difference was evident in defendants' descriptions of their own and plaintiffs' needs and benefits at mediation. Two were College mediations that either subsequently sued or were planning to; one was a court-linked mandatory mediation. The female physician (in fifties) described the mediation as follows:

> The mediation was three years after the death. That was so hard for me... because I was devastated... I wanted to have some kind of resolution. I wanted a chance to sit down with the family. I was willing to meet at any point... There were all these letters... terribly offensive... I saw it as a real mark against my professionalism, and I

wanted a chance to clear my name. DID YOU FEEL YOU HAD THAT AT MEDIATION? To some extent, ya . . . I was there because the family was bereft and they wanted to be heard.

Lawyers on both sides attended . . . I was very sympathetic with what they had gone through . . . I said I was devastated to hear she had died, that I was very disturbed and distressed . . . DID THEY KNOW THIS BEFORE? I don't know how they would have . . . The things the family were concerned about . . . I was able to clarify easily . . . *They* were based on . . . assumptions and misinformation.

ANY PSYCHOLOGICAL RELIEF . . . I tell you, we hugged each other . . . It was very nice to have the family hug me . . . You haven't met these people. They are on paper . . . It was nice for me to express my sympathy to the family, to let them know how I felt . . . It was probably more beneficial to me than to the family . . . There was some closure for me in terms of feeling like the family saw me as some sort of criminal or someone complicit in killing their sister or daughter . . . They were really trying to make it very clear that they weren't a kind of lynch mob . . . I ended up with positive feelings about the family.

The female physician described mediation in terms of almost therapeutic benefit. In contrast, despite also being in favor of attending, neither male physician discussed next articulated the same type of needs or benefits.

"There was a lot of emotional thing . . . *AT MEDIATION* . . . one has to be very careful because sometimes things could be said by plaintiffs which probably are not relevant, maybe create some irritation. If the *doctor* is not cool enough to hold himself maybe *it* can create some issues and problems . . . It could make *mediation* even worse. There were instances where I could have reacted differently . . . Because I didn't feel *the plaintiffs* were really objective in the way they were putting things to me *about the death*. I think that could have been avoided one way or another. THE EMOTIONAL ELEMENT YOU MEAN? That's right, ya. They were trying not to be, but they couldn't escape it. In a sense maybe it's good because they got their frustration out." **Male court-linked mandatory mediation – in fifties**

Likewise, another male defendant in a fatality case explained,

Mediation was at a lawyer's office, with a lawyer-mediator . . . The son just presented the facts ANYTHING NEW? Nothing at all. DID YOU UNDERSTAND THINGS BETTER FROM HIS VIEWPOINT? No, because it already had been presented *on paper* . . . You don't . . . give an apology . . . You just discuss basically what happened . . . DO YOU THINK HE OBTAINED ANY BENEFIT FROM MEDIATION? It's hard to tell . . . but there was no ranting, no raving, no shouting, no accusations.

Thus, though differences in physicians' characters and feelings of responsibility would have been factors in their perceptions of mediation, there was some indication that female defendants both contributed and derived greater psychological or emotional benefit from mediation than did males.

4.5 Chapter conclusion

> Without both accuser and accused retelling their stories... there can be no real understanding of the conflict, nor of its roots. Genuine resolution cannot occur. Mere settlement will be the closest parties come to achieving closure (Christiansen 1997, pp. 70, 72).

In examining the trajectory of professional and lay actors' views on defendants' attendance at mediation, this chapter has provided further insights into the book's three themes: the parallel worlds of understanding and meaning of legal actors and lay disputants, evidencing the discontinuity between legal and extralegal interests in case processing; changes occurring in lawyers conceptualizing their cases and their roles in resolution – particularly consequent to some becoming mediators; and gendered worlds of perceptions of conflict and its resolution in professional and lay groups.

First, evidence was proffered as to defense and plaintiff lawyers' regular agreements "not to invite" defendants to mediations. Although legal actors discussed reasons both for and against defendants' attendance – and despite most attorneys' scant experience with defendants present – the vast majority decided or acquiesced in decisions to exclude defendant physicians, proffering similar reasons. Talk of defendants' attendance was linked directly to issues of settlement and the effect of defendants' presence on lawyers' strategic agendas. Most lawyers viewed defendants' presence as risky (by causing "raised emotions") or unnecessary (as any settlement monies would not come from physicians themselves).

Thus, despite evidence of some lawyers' (particularly lawyer-mediators) reconceptualization of their cases and roles, in speaking about defendants' attendance, extralegal communication and psychological healing were not at the forefront of most legal actors' understandings of what mediation "was." Thus, any talk of mediation being a venue for disputants' extralegal enterprises was discussed only secondarily or as a serendipitous effect. Hence, although most acknowledged the possibility of treating disputants' extralegal needs through defendants' attendance, the majority of lawyers were ultimately against having doctors present. As such, the discourse on defendants' attendance reveals unspoken understandings of mediation's purpose and meaning. For most legal actors, mediation was a vehicle for monetary settlement or case abandonment, not a forum for fault talk or extralegal discourse. This ignores the indivisibility of disputants' legal and extralegal needs – something made plain by parties' discourse on defendants' attendance. Yet, in the words of one plaintiff attorney, "Catharsis... is not going to help lawyers get rid of cases." These findings are in line with those discussed in chapter two in terms of attorneys' reluctance to deal with "nonlegal" issues their clients spoke about – often of significant importance to litigants.

Second, the largely uniform discourse of both plaintiffs and defendants on who should attend mediation evidenced the fact that disputants inhabit a world informed by disparate comprehensions and requirements in case processing to those found within the world of legal actors – including their own representatives. Instead of strategic considerations and regardless of venue, the disputed issues, or whether settlement ensued, all plaintiffs and defendants spoke of psychological, therapeutic, and/or educational reasons for mediating together. Thus, far from a forum where tactics played out, for disputants mediation was a place to treat human needs and preserve human dignity. It was a place for both verbal and nonverbal communication, information sharing, human interchange, and most importantly "feeling better about their situations." Mediation was an environment where material psychological, therapeutic, and learning benefits were in reach. In speaking of defendants' attendance, no mention was made of monetary settlement or the obvious fact that any settlement monies would not come from physicians themselves. This was consonant with plaintiffs' descriptions of their litigation aims not being about money (*chapter two*). Indeed, why would virtually all plaintiffs want defendants to personally attend mediation if all they were after was monetary compensation paid by an insurer? Notwithstanding any emotional difficulties in attending, both plaintiffs and defendants emphasized the importance of defendants' presence and the lack of empowerment and closure when defendants were absent. Even for disputants who did not mediate together, their discourse on "what could have been" revealed identical conceptions of this litigation-track process.

Plaintiffs' needs to have defendants at mediation may also have been related to desires to level the playing field. Without defendants present, mediating plaintiffs were surrounded by professionals in a room where no one – apart from plaintiffs themselves – had anything to lose personally. This psychological leveling of the playing field also appeared to serve physicians' interests. Although being put into a forum with plaintiffs introduced a form of lay scrutiny of defendants' actions, it may have been that by attending mediations defendants felt they regained some control over their disputes.

Yet, third, primarily due to the unequal knowledge and power relations inherent in lawyer–client relationships, lawyers' interests in the attendance issue were seen to trump those of disputants. However, by shutting defendants out of a fundamental part of their own disputes, legal actors caused mediations to represent missed opportunities for disputant communication and psychological healing – leaving material issues for parties unaddressed. In view of contingency fee realities, mediation may be the only opportunity disputants have for face-to-face interaction during litigation. With doctors – the central participants – absent, mediations cannot address the core issue of responsibility. Instead, mediations are transformed into venues for bargaining over money, depriving plaintiffs of any other remedy such as acceptance of responsibility or acknowledgment of harm (Abel 2005). Additionally, defendant doctors were blamed for their absences by most plaintiffs who perceived defendants as refusing to face them and acknowledge their tragedies or pain. Yet, this was a fact unknown to most defendants whose absences frequently appeared not to be their fault.

The attendance issue is also of deeper significance in terms of mediation theories and philosophies. Lawyers' interventions, influencing who attends and thus controlling the dynamics and what can be "said" during mediations, prevent mediation from expressing its higher aspirations, including its most important attributes of party empowerment and self-determination.[11] Parties' self-determination is viewed as "the fundamental principle of all mediation" (Welsh 2001b, p. 3), "empowering parties to have voice in all discussions of their dispute, to be heard by opponents and mediators, to decide themselves about the 'right' resolution without undue emphasis on a legally rights-based determination, and to encourage parties to understand others' perspectives even if disagreeing. Settlement though important, should not be sufficient."[12] Thus, the absence of key parties is a major threat to the justification of mediation in its opportunities for disputants' direct participation, face-to-face communication, and party-determined solutions. In this way, the findings here provide examples of how lawyers and legal strategy are harming disputants and deforming mediation's aspirations in terms of avoiding, rather than directly dealing with pain and emotional issues, needs for apologies, human understanding, and meaningful communication (Welsh 2001b, pp. 18–19; Menkel-Meadow 2006).

Looking at mediation within a bargaining paradigm as reflected in lawyers' traditional practices, its goal is settlement, not disputants' perceptions of just treatment. However, procedural justice research emphasizes that all disputants should attend mediations (Welsh 2001a, pp. 805, 845). Moreover, voluminous social psychological research highlights the fact that disputants seek procedural justice in resolution of their cases (Welsh 2004a, p. 672). Disputants' views on procedurally just processes contribute to parties' perceptions that substantive outcomes are fair, acceptance of results, and beliefs that decision-making institutions are legitimate (Welsh 2001b, pp. 7–8). Criteria used to assess procedural justice include disputants' perceptions of having the chance to fully express their views, evidence, and concerns; tell their stories and be listened to; as well as whether third parties consider what they say and treat them fairly and respectfully.[13] In particular, the procedural justice literature stresses the importance of disputants' opportunities for "voice" and "being heard" in improving procedural justice perceptions. Indeed, disputants have been found to view the opportunity for "voice" as just as important as control over decisions (Lind et al. 1983, p. 339).

Thus, it is clear that exclusion of disputants from mediation is incompatible with procedures that are perceived procedurally just. When defendants are absent, not only are plaintiffs "not heard" by them, but absent parties are unable

---

11 Fuller (1971), Menkel-Meadow (1996b; 2006), Moore (2003), Folberg et al. (2005), Welsh (2001b, pp. 4–5, 25–27), and Menkel-Meadow et al. (2006, p. 580).
12 Folberg and Taylor (1984, p. xii), Menkel-Meadow (1997a, p. 452), Welsh (2001b, pp. 15–18), and McAdoo (2007, p. 426).
13 Lind and Tyler (1988, pp. 66–70, 218, 101–4, 205, 236), McEwen et al. (1995, p. 1384), Welsh (2001a, pp. 817–18, 820–21, 825, 835), and McAdoo (2007, p. 421).

to hear their lawyers express their perspectives or to be treated first-hand with respect. Nor do they know if their story was put forward (Welsh 2001a, pp. 838–39, 845). Thus, parties' perceptions of process fairness will be adversely affected if all parties are not required to attend mediations (Welsh 2001a, pp. 820, 838–39, 845).

Further, by being instrumental in defendants' absences from mediation, lawyers are also appropriating important learning opportunities from plaintiffs and defendants. Dauer's study of voluntarily mediated disputes suggests that quality improvement can result through physician education at mediation (Dauer and Marcus 1997, pp. 186, 211). In cases where defendants did attend and heard plaintiffs directly, each discussed learning things they would not have known otherwise than through mediation – particularly issues relating to plaintiffs' understandings, perceptions, perspectives, and the consequences of their injuries or loss of loved ones. Plaintiffs too learned of repercussions for defendants. Social learning theory holds that learning can occur through observation of others' behavior and its consequences (Bandura and Walter 1963; Merriam and Caffarella 1991, pp. 134–35; Morton and Einesman 2001, p. 269). Indeed, much human behavior is learned through environmental conditioning by observing or modeling the conduct of others (Bandura 1977, pp. 22–54). Thus by orchestrating who will attend mediation and hence the types of communication possible there, attorneys were, in effect, taking away an opportunity for social learning from plaintiffs and defendants.

Finally, on the gender divide, similar to the findings in chapter two, gender differences were evident in lawyers' discourse on defendants' attendance at mediation. This illustrated a further facet of the parallel worlds inherent in these legal disputes. In contrast to males, female lawyers spoke more often of extralegal considerations and reasons for defendants' presence and less often of tactical reasoning against having defendants attend mediations. This suggested a diverse layer of meaning ascribed to conflict and its resolution as well as to the mediation process itself, viewing it also as a forum for resolving extralegal issues. The gender findings for disputants were also notable. Although later recanting, most female plaintiffs were initially less inclined than males to face their perceived wrongdoers at mediation. This finding suggested that where claimants had real input into mediation attendance decisions, females would be more likely to choose or agree to defendants' absences at mediations. Consequently, disputants in their cases would be disadvantaged by not obtaining the psychological and learning benefits resulting from face-to-face interaction as described by plaintiffs and defendants who mediated together. The data also suggested that female defendants may have derived and been able to offer greater psychological assistance at mediation than males.

Linked to actors' conceptions of mediation's purpose and decisions on who will attend, a final pre-mediation issue is examined in chapter five: that of actors' specific aims for the process.

CHAPTER FIVE

Actors' mediation objectives: How lawyers versus parties plan to resolve their cases short of trial

Following chronologically from actors' views on who should attend mediation, this chapter explores the final pre-mediation topic of what actors specifically plan for and aim to achieve during mediations, which may resolve their cases short of trial. To put this chapter in context, although supporting the findings in chapter two on plaintiffs' motivations to sue and their consequent litigation aims, this chapter is distinct. Chapter two deals with plaintiffs' versus lawyers' understandings of plaintiffs' litigation aims alone, which provides context to actors' perspectives during case processing. However, chapter two does not relate to mediation per se – only to litigation. Nor does it examine the aims of any actors other than those of plaintiffs. In contrast, this chapter focuses solely on aims for mediation. Moreover, it examines and compares all actors' articulated objectives for the process, not simply those of plaintiffs.[1]

The findings here are striking, although not completely unexpected. Mediation actors' aims were generally found to be disparate as between legal and lay groups. Significantly, the data also demonstrate that what plaintiffs want from litigation and the civil justice system can be expressed during mediation. Moreover, as plaintiffs' mediation aims are seen to be even more focused on extralegal dispute issues than their articulated litigation aims (*chapter two*), I argue that as with legal actors, mediation acts to reorient parties' attention toward the extralegal aspects of their cases.

These findings add to the dearth of extant knowledge on participants' objectives for mediation. Only two studies were found examining mediation aims (discussed later). However, as no studies compare lay and legal actors' mediation objectives in the same or similar cases, the data here are particularly important in highlighting fundamental disparities in what mediation actors aim to achieve. The findings also serve to question writings premised on actors' unqualified faith in mediation's confidentiality (Johnson 1997, p. 48; Gitchell and Plattner 1999, p. 443). In fact as will

---

1 To avoid conflation of responses, the question on litigation aims was among the first to be asked to respondents, whereas those on mediation objectives were asked midway through the interviews that generally lasted between one and three hours.

be seen, I argue that lawyers' distrust of mediation's confidentiality circumscribes their mediation aims in terms of what they are prepared to say and do during the process.

First, each legal actor group's mediation objectives are examined. This is followed by an exploration of gender divisions within lawyers' discourse. Plaintiffs' and defendants' mediation aims are then considered, also examining gender differences within their discourse. Finally, the chapter looks at lawyers' attitudes toward mediation's confidentiality as a way of possibly explaining what may have been limiting what attorneys were prepared to do during mediations.

Objectives were first explored by means of an open question, "What did you want to achieve at mediation; what were your aims/objectives?" Subsequent to respondents' answers, a series of closed questions were asked, outlining other possible mediation aims; that is, "Did you want mediation to include apology, admission of fault, make them understand your side, to be told what happened, defense to show they care, money, improve quality, to hear the other side, anything else?" "Apology" was explained to include "qualified apologies" where fault admissions were not implied. For instance, "I am really sorry you have suffered."

Due to similarities in mediation aims voiced across sites, all mediations have been analyzed together. It was particularly striking that despite mandatory mediations occurring far earlier within the litigation process than voluntary mediations (sometimes years earlier), no material differences were found in the mediation objectives of any group, disputants or lawyers.[2] This finding questions assertions made by some lawyers that over time the issues for plaintiffs increasingly become related to money alone. All disputants in voluntary and mandatory mediations discussed "settlement" or "resolution" of their disputes among their mediation aims. This was not surprising, and correlated with the disputants' findings in chapter three. What was surprising, however, was that notwithstanding legal actors' low expectations for mandatory mediations (*chapter three*), most lawyers also cited "settlement" as their main objective for both mandatory and voluntary mediations. It was also interesting that within the physician data (75% deriving from College mediations and 25% from court-linked mandatory mediations), no material differences were found between their aims for College mediations as compared with mandatory court-linked mediations.

To begin, Figures 14 and 15 illustrate the distribution of each group's articulated mediation aims.

Each group's articulated mediation aims are then explored separately in greater depth. The findings are interspersed with case studies, illustrating the diversity of actors' objectives within specific disputes.

---

2 Of all the lawyer groups, the only difference in mediation aims was that hospital lawyers less often discussed wanting to hear plaintiffs' sides in voluntary mediations than in mandatory mediations.

Actors' mediation objectives 131

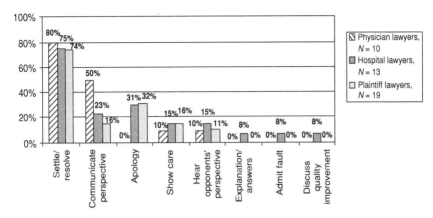

Figure 14. Legal actors' mediation aims. The findings indicate strong similarities in what legal actors did and did not plan to do at mediation, regardless of allegiances. Settle/resolve included discussing legal liability and/or quantum.

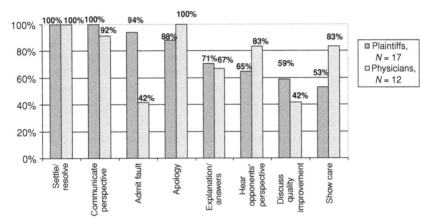

Figure 15. Disputants' mediation aims. Apart from the aim of admitting fault,[3] there were obvious similarities between plaintiffs' and defendants' articulated objectives for mediation, distancing them from legal actors.

5.1 Legal actors' mediation objectives

Plaintiff and defense lawyers' mediation objectives were initially studied separately. However, subsequent analysis revealed strong similarities among all legal actor groups in terms of what they aimed to do and not to do during mediation, as seen in Figure 14. The following subsections examine lawyers' objectives in greater detail.

3 Not all five physicians who wanted to admit fault were involved in serious injury cases.

Physician lawyers

> "The objective was to see if we could get on the same radar screen *for settlement*... The secondary objective was to see for myself is it the plaintiffs or their lawyer who's being difficult in this case." **Mandatory mediation – female – in thirties**

> "YOUR MEDIATION OBJECTIVES to get the case settled... at the most reasonable figure we could get... Also... to see how credible these people are going to be as witnesses... ANYTHING ELSE? No... WAS ONE OF YOUR OBJECTIVES TO HEAR THE PLAINTIFF'S VERSION... no. DID YOU WANT TO SHOW THE PLAINTIFFS YOU CARED ABOUT WHAT HAD HAPPENED? It wasn't a stated objective... DID YOU WANT TO TRY TO MAKE THE PLAINTIFFS UNDERSTAND THINGS FROM THE DOCTOR'S PERSPECTIVE? No." **Fatality case – voluntary mediation – defendant absent – male – in forties**

Of the ten interviews with physician lawyers (all but two being male) in which they discussed mediation objectives, most (80%) mentioned settlement as a mediation aim, often stressing that it was their primary aim regardless of mediation type. Linked to this, they predominantly wanted to relay directly to plaintiffs' legal and tactical information relating to plaintiffs' risks. This included things these attorneys believed plaintiffs' lawyers may not have told their clients, resulting in claimants having unrealistic expectations as to the value of their claims.

Physician lawyers' discourse of tactical mediation objectives contained little of what plaintiffs said they sought at mediation (Figures 14 and 15). For instance, only one physician lawyer (10%) intended to show plaintiffs that "the defendant cared" about what happened. This was in sharp contrast to defendant physicians' aims, where most (83%) aimed to show care. Moreover, regardless of their case assessments, no physician lawyer intended to admit any fault or to provide explanations or answers to plaintiffs about defendant physicians' perspectives on what occurred. This was despite virtually all physician lawyers' questionnaire responses, indicating that underlying issues were more important for their physician clients than was financial compensation. Yet, none discussed relaying this information as a mediation objective.

Likewise, no physician lawyer planned to give any form of apology at mediation. One attorney with past experience as a plaintiffs' counsel noted that he had been to over one hundred mediations and never did a physician's side apologize. It was unclear, however, why qualified apologies – without admitting fault – were not planned. Perhaps this was linked to the meaning lawyers ascribed to mediation (*chapter four*), that is, solely a tactical vehicle for financial settlement or abandonment of cases. Lawyers' trust in mediation's confidentiality may offer another possible explanation. Still, as seen in Figure 16, comparing the mediation aims of defendants and defense lawyers highlights very different experiences for plaintiffs when mediating with and without defendants present.

Actors' mediation objectives 133

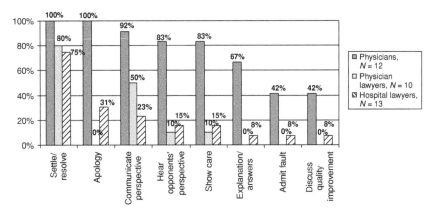

Figure 16. Defendants' versus defense lawyers' mediation aims. Gross disparities in mediation aims were found when comparing the discourse of defendant physicians with defense lawyers, particularly in the areas of apology, explaining their perspectives, listening to plaintiffs' viewpoints, and showing care.

In terms of what physician attorneys thought claimants wanted out of mediation, it was noteworthy that apart from the desire for financial settlement, only one physician lawyer (10%) said plaintiffs wanted acknowledgments of harm, admissions of fault, or apologies. Furthermore, only a minority (40%) – including the two females – noted that apologies would benefit plaintiffs. None mentioned that plaintiffs sought answers at mediation. For instance,

> "Certainly... by voluntary *mediations*... They're looking to be compensated... I don't get the feeling... they want an apology from the doctor or a chance to vent to the doctor, or other non-legals... That's never been an issue." **Male physician – in thirties**

> "WHAT *DO DISPUTANTS* WANT OUT OF MEDIATION? I think... the vast majority of them understand the object *of* mediation... It's about compensation... money." **Male plaintiff and physician lawyer – in forties**

The disparities in mediation aims between legal actors and disputants were particularly clear in the following case. Hearing the defendant's side directly might have somewhat balanced out the playing field for these plaintiffs. However, the balancing never occurred.

Loss-of-sight case – voluntary mediation – defendant absent

Male plaintiff – in fifties

> I wish he or his lawyer would express some remorse... an apology... their acceptance of guilt. We received absolutely nothing like that... *Dr* ... wasn't there... He could express remorse some way.... It was like "I'm here to write a check"... It's much more than dollars... It's my wife's eyes.

> I definitely wanted to hear their side... for some sort of closure... to see if their story has some credibility... DON'T YOU KNOW THEIR STORY FROM THE PAPERS?... Absolutely nothing. We've received nothing, no document from any lawyer we had... We don't know what their story is.

Male physician lawyer – in fifties

> WHAT WERE YOUR MEDIATION OBJECTIVES? Only to get the case settled.

Male, specialist plaintiff lawyer – in forties

> APART FROM SETTLEMENT, DID YOU HAVE ANY OTHER MEDIATION OBJECTIVES? No... If there had been no mediation and just a bilateral settlement between the lawyers, I don't know if the clients would have felt any loss in doing it that way... I'm not sure... because I really haven't asked them about that.

Still, when comparing physician lawyers' views of plaintiffs' litigation aims with what they thought claimants sought in mediation, there was some evidence of lawyers reconceptualizing disputes after having heard and seen plaintiffs' realities at mediation. For instance,

> WHAT DO YOU THINK THE PLAINTIFFS' AIM WAS WHEN THEY SUED? Money. THE SOLE AIM? Yes.... PLAINTIFFS' AIMS IN MEDIATION? There were other issues in the mediation... the issue of feeling that they hadn't received a proper apology, or there hadn't been proper responsibility taken for the error; recognition, the inconvenience, the unfairness and so on. I think they felt that was an issue and in the circumstances of what occurred, I'm sure it was. **Male physician lawyer – in fifties – child operation case – mandatory mediation – defendant absent**

Overall, however, apart from the desire to "get rid of the case" there was little similarity between physician lawyers' mediation aims as compared with their physician clients – even less so with plaintiffs.

Hospital lawyers

Of the thirteen cases discussed by hospital lawyers, most (75%) noted monetary settlement or abandonment as a mediation aim. Similar to physician lawyers, apart from one case where liability was obvious, no hospital lawyer planned to provide explanations or answers to plaintiffs or to admit any fault. In only a minority of cases (31%) did hospital lawyers intend to give any form of apology. As most noted that apologies could benefit the mediation climate (56%) and that plaintiffs wanted apologies during mediations (67%), the question arose again as to why they did not plan more often to give even qualified apologies. This is explored in Section 5.3.

Additionally, as with physician lawyers, there was little awareness of plaintiffs' mediation aims. Only two hospital lawyers (including one who also represented plaintiffs) mentioned that claimants wanted answers/explanations in mediation.

Still, as compared with doctors' lawyers, hospital attorneys' discourse on their mediation objectives generally evinced greater extralegal considerations. This may have been a function of lawyers' experience with mediation, reconceptualizing the meaning of cases. For example,

> "WHAT DID YOU WANT TO GET OUT OF THIS *VOLUNTARY* MEDIATION? Clearly it was to reach a monetary settlement... Whereas I think plaintiffs... feel really strongly that something was done wrong and they want to be able to say their piece. And it's very important for them to have that opportunity, I think." **Male – in forties**

Extralegal awareness may also have related to attorneys' gender. However, despite some gender disparities within lawyers' groups (discussed later) as well as evidence of some dispute reconceptualization, overall defense lawyers' mediation aims were focused on tactics.[4] This too was evident in plaintiff lawyers' explanations of their mediation objectives.

Plaintiff lawyers

Overall plaintiff lawyers' mediation aims were not dissimilar from those on the defense, both inhabiting the tactical world. As with defendant attorneys, in the nineteen plaintiff lawyer interviews most discussed monetary settlement aims for mediation (74%). This included tactical aims relating to achieving settlements, for example, having their clients hear directly from the defense and/or mediators the risks and weaknesses within their cases to deflate expectations. For example,

> "YOUR AIMS... For the defense to see the plaintiffs are well spoken, presentable, make a sympathetic impression... that these people will do well at trial." **Male, specialist plaintiff lawyer – in thirties – child surgery case**

> "WHAT DID YOU WANT TO ACHIEVE IN MEDIATION? Basically I wanted some pre-discovery... to get a better handle on what their defense is going to be... DID YOU HAVE ANY OTHER AIMS? AN APOLOGY OR SHOWING THAT THEY CARED? No." **Male, generalist plaintiff lawyer – in forties – vasectomy case**

Thus, as with defendants and defense lawyers, there were marked disparities when comparing plaintiff lawyers' mediation aims with those of plaintiffs themselves. Figure 17 sets out the findings.

Other than wanting settlement, the mediation objectives of plaintiffs and plaintiffs' lawyers were diverse in all categories. For instance, though some plaintiff

---

4 Macfarlane's research, based on interviews with commercial litigators, found similar tactical mediation aims to those found here. These included obtaining information on opponents' motivations and interests, assessing opponents, and providing "reality checks" for their own clients or opponent litigants (Macfarlane 2002, pp. 265–66).

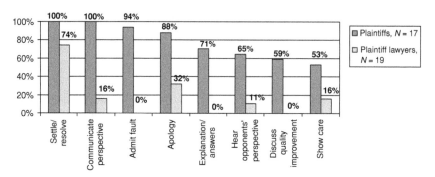

Figure 17. Plaintiffs' versus plaintiff lawyers' mediation aims. As with defendants and defense lawyers, the disparity in mediation aims of plaintiffs and plaintiff lawyers revealed important differences in what each planned for mediation.

lawyers noted that their clients wanted defendants to admit fault (37%), regardless of feasibility not a single one sought this at mediation. In comparison, virtually all plaintiffs (94%) sought fault admissions at mediation. Similarly, plaintiff lawyers never mentioned wanting to hear defendants' explanations of the disputed incidents. Again this was something that most plaintiffs desired (71%). Finally, as compared with the bulk of claimants (88%) who sought apologies at mediation, only a minority (32%) of plaintiff lawyers did (though almost half remarked that apologies were important for their clients). Perhaps plaintiffs' attorneys did not seek fault admissions, explanations, or apologies at mediation because they did not expect they would be forthcoming. A few attorneys noted that apologies would not make their cases "disappear." That being said, mediation scholarship has stressed the role of apology and expressions of remorse in assisting the resolving of disputes.[5] Likewise, experimental study findings suggest that apologies positively influence receivers' inclinations to accept or reject settlement offers, with full apologies accepting responsibility increasing the chances of respondents accepting offers made (Robbennolt 2003, pp. 462, 486).

The disparities in plaintiff lawyers' and clients' mediation aims may have related to their different understandings of the meaning of mediation. The fact that a material number of plaintiff lawyers (33%) felt that claimants were solely seeking monetary recompense may also have been a factor. However, as apologies are generally viewed by lawyers as admissions of responsibility resulting in greater legal liability (Vallance 1990, p. 103; Robbennolt 2003, p. 501), plaintiff lawyers' attitudes toward mediation's confidentiality may also have influenced their mediation aims. Views on confidentiality are examined in Section 5.3.

---

5 Tanick and Ayling (1996, p. 22), Levi (1997, p. 1199), Goldberg et al. (1999, pp. 159–60), Shuman (2000, p. 181), O'Hara and Yarn (2002, p. 1126), Pavlick (2003, pp. 843–46), and Bibas and Bierschbach (2004, p. 119).

Reconceptualization

Nonetheless, despite evident differences in mediation objectives, some plaintiff lawyers' discourse made plain the reconceptualizing of their cases and their roles. For instance, in only a minority of cases (37%) did plaintiff lawyers limit their mediation objectives to financial settlement alone. Plaintiff lawyers were instructing their clients to "tell their stories" at mediation. This must have been at least partly to address plaintiffs' extralegal needs, as all legal issues would have already been elucidated within their written pleadings and other documentation. Likewise, although apology plays no part in the formal justice system, some plaintiff lawyers (32%) did include obtaining an apology as one of their mediation objectives. The following quotes illustrate this trend:

"Before mediation we talked about their goals – being apology – So I became aware of what they wanted... WHAT DID 'YOU' WANT TO ACHIEVE AT MEDIATION?... I wanted the risks pointed out to them by the defense and also by someone in a more objective role... the mediator... But in a larger way... I wanted it to be an emotionally satisfying event for them. I knew for my clients – not as much as I found out on the day – but that the money wasn't a big issue for them... I knew very much that if I was to succeed... at mediation, I would have to satisfy them on a much more than financial level.

I think that generally when plaintiffs' lawyers approach mediation, they're... calculating appropriate settlement values, strategy. That's a single-minded focus... About the human factors... you can structure plaintiffs' involvement and... the defense response in mediation in a way that can see those human and emotional factors satisfied to a better degree... I think there are ways to satisfy disputes in a greater way than just simply getting to the right numbers." **Male, specialist – in thirties – hospital fall case**

"This is unrealistic on their part, but they would like some kind of apology or acknowledgement that they've suffered as a result of something this person has done... It may not lead to a resolution... or to the doctor... admitting they did something wrong and apologising... In a lot of cases I think that's what they're hoping will happen.... They wanted somebody else to hear what... they had gone through... At least someone else would listen." **Male, generalist – in forties – vasectomy case**

"WHAT DID YOU WANT TO ACHIEVE AT MEDIATION? Just to maximize their financial recovery. ANYTHING ELSE? I was hopeful somebody would come and apologize to make them feel better... I expected some sort of admission. But it wasn't part of my game plan. I wouldn't have said "If we don't get this, we won't take your money." AND YOUR CLIENTS' MEDIATION OBJECTIVES? They wanted a day of reckoning... where somebody could say 'I'm sorry this happened to you. We all felt terrible about it', some sort of cathartic process." **Male, specialist – in thirties – child operation case**

In fact, as with some on the defense, when comparing what a number of plaintiff lawyers described as their clients' litigation aims (*chapter two*) with their subsequent discourse on claimants' mediation aims, it appeared that lawyers' comprehension of what plaintiffs wanted was broadened when bringing mediation into the equation. For instance,

> WHAT DO YOU THINK THE PLAINTIFF'S AIM WAS WHEN HE SUED? Money SOLELY? Ya.

Yet, when later asked what he thought the claimant's mediation aims were, the plaintiff lawyer discussed at length numerous extralegal aims, never even mentioning money.

> "I think my client wanted a chance to tell the doctor that he'd been mistreated, not just in the surgery, but in all the follow up... He felt the doctor had been dismissive, downright contemptuous. And this was a chance to talk back... In almost every... case I get, the lack of concern... *afterwards* seems to be as important as the initial incident."
> **Male, generalist plaintiff lawyer – in forties**

Thus, as with defense lawyers, some rethinking and reconceptualizing of cases to include things "nonlegal" was evident in plaintiff lawyers' discourse on their own mediation aims as well as those of their clients. The reconceptualization findings for legal actors overall suggest that through mediation, addressing disputants' extralegal needs during litigation-track processes is incrementally becoming something that lawyers "do." This conclusion was strengthened when examining lawyer-mediators' aims. For example,

> "My objective was to find out firstly and foremost where the plaintiff was at. Was it monetary?... Ninety percent of the time, there's a lot more than what appears to be... on the table... *and* in the pleadings... So I usually concentrate on the plaintiffs... *Second* I wanted to get some consensus on a range of... damages... I find that in mediation... there's a lot of therapeutic... People can walk out of there feeling good, feeling better... This was a golden opportunity for the plaintiff to vent." **Male lawyer-mediator – in fifties – practicing attorney for twenty-five years**

> "WHAT WERE YOUR OBJECTIVES? Well, obviously in any mediation the mediator wants to see people have their ability, their right to speak to each other, and to express 'everything' on how they feel about the case. But also I'm looking to see if I can bring them together to mutually agree upon resolution... So I wanted to see if I could bring them together, where each side has a way of expressing their grief. On the plaintiffs' side, what they're looking for, and from the defense side if they feel they should offer an apology – which they did – *and* in this case say 'This should not have happened. We did our investigation and we've learned from this.' That helps bring people together."
> **Male, senior counsel – lawyer-mediator – in sixties – practicing lawyer all career**

> "My objective is to get it settled. But it's terribly important for the plaintiffs to feel very much involved. So right away at the beginning... I want the plaintiffs to have *their* say in full, get it off their chests... And then counsel for the defense may say 'We're terribly sorry'... It's of tremendous importance... because it makes the plaintiff feel someone's listening... really listening, and being sympathetic and involving them.

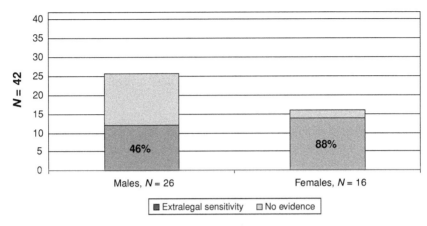

Figure 18. Lawyers' references to extralegal mediation aims. In discussing their own or plaintiffs' mediation agendas, female lawyers more often than males mentioned extralegal aims outside the realm of tactics and monetary settlement.

They're having their say; they're having an effect." **Male, retired judge – mediator – in eighties**

Notwithstanding evidence of lawyers' reconceptualization, as is clear from the aforementioned charts and quotes, legal actors' mediation aims were generally correlative of lawyers' perceptions of mediation as a tactical forum to achieve strategic objectives in their case battles (*chapter four*). Yet there were some differentiations in lawyers' discourse on the basis of gender. These are explored next.

Lawyers' gender divisions

Despite lawyers' mediation aims generally being very different to those of parties, in examining lawyers' discourse more closely, there was some indication that gender had an effect on what lawyers planned to do at mediations. It has been noted that gender as well as other contextual considerations may shape the mediation process as well as the substance of communications there (Evans 2001, p. 157, n. 66). Figure 18 illustrates the gender differences in attorneys' discourse within all case interviews that covered mediation aims. As mediation objectives were similar across all legal actor groups, lawyers' groups were combined and their discourse was analyzed in terms of demonstrating any extralegal sensitivity in speaking of either their own mediation objectives or those of plaintiffs (i.e., mentioning even one issue irrelevant to tactics or monetary settlement negotiations).

In breaking down the data into specific lawyer groups, although the numbers were small, the findings were similar. Of the ten case interviews with physician lawyers where mediation aims were discussed (eight with males and two with females), 100% of females and 13% of males included talk of extralegal mediation aims. Likewise, in the hospital lawyers' group, of the thirteen case interviews with hospital lawyers (ten with females and three with males), 80% of interviews with females versus 67% of those with males included any mention of extralegal mediation objectives. Finally, in the plaintiff lawyers' group, of the nineteen case interviews where mediation aims were discussed (four with females and fifteen with males), 100% of females' interviews but only 60% of those with males included talk of extralegal mediation aims. Male plaintiff lawyers tended to prioritize plaintiffs' monetary mediation objectives whereas females tended to speak of extralegal issues as well as financial settlement.

Thus, the data overall suggest that females more often than male attorneys planned to use mediation as a forum for things other than strategy and monetary negotiations alone. For instance, only female hospital attorneys said they wanted to relay extralegal information and communicate their side to claimants at mediation. Similarly, only females articulated the aim of hearing plaintiffs' viewpoints. Some stressed the importance of mediation in providing the one chance to speak directly to plaintiffs. Indeed, it has been found that dialogue, communication, and interaction with others – as opposed to persuasion, debate, and disputing – are key to females' model of problem solving. Women seek to explore issues with others so that mutual understanding is achieved (Kolb and Coolidge 1988, p. 5). The following quotes illustrate this trend:

> "I think what makes the biggest difference in mediation is compassion being shown to plaintiffs... I mean, this is probably the most important thing in their lives. It's not the biggest thing in our lives. But if you start out by saying, 'We're here because we really want to listen'... I think that... will be important to them." **Female – in twenties**

> "I'm always interested to hear what the plaintiffs have to say." **Female – in twenties**

> "*THROUGH* MEDIATION *Defendants may* understand what the person's gone through... I think it is important for *plaintiffs to hear apologies or explanations.*" **Female – in forties**

> "DID YOU WANT TO SHOW THE DEFENSE CARED? It does come into it, because if the mediation fails the case continues to trial, and it's extremely helpful to have had an opportunity to try to build up trust. The mediation is generally our only opportunity to speak directly to plaintiffs." **Female hospital lawyer – in forties**

This finding of female defense lawyers' mediation aims being somewhat closer to those of disputants was evident in some of the case studies. For instance, in the child operation case,

Male physician lawyer – in fifties

This lawyer's questionnaire response indicated that for his absent physician client, underlying issues were "about as important" as financial compensation. Yet, in discussing his own mediation aims he said,

> WHAT DID YOU WANT TO ACHIEVE AT MEDIATION? A reasonable settlement. ANYTHING ELSE... no. HEAR THEIR SIDE, OR PUT FORWARD YOURS? No... I was hoping *at mediation* that I could indicate to them that *their lawyer's* figures were not

reasonable... and they were going to face significant resistance from me... Therefore be prepared to modify the figures... In that sense, yes, speaking to them that there was another view of this, and there were some risks although... a clear winner on liability. ANYTHING ELSE, TO SHOW THAT YOU CARED, OR... No.

Female hospital lawyer – in twenties

> I think it was necessary for the family to get some kind of apology or explanation from someone at the hospital, as opposed to from lawyers. I think that was very helpful... At the end of *mediation*... when I went to speak to them, they both said that meant the most to them, the most important part of the day – that I was able to apologize to them... That someone had apologized and that they had known I took it seriously, and that we have learned from it.

Male plaintiff – in thirties

> YOUR MEDIATION AIMS ... Just to show that they really affected somebody's life... I wanted them to know that... I wanted somebody to be accountable. I wanted somebody to say "Okay, it was our fault and we're sorry, and we'll do whatever we can... I wanted an apology from both the surgeon and the hospital.

Female co-plaintiff – in thirties

> WHAT DID YOU WANT TO ACHIEVE IN MEDIATION? I wanted them to apologize... and to make sure that stuff like this... shouldn't end up in such a huge ordeal like it was for us... It was definitely important for them to understand our side.

Still, notwithstanding the gender differences among lawyers, disputants' mediation aims were generally markedly different to those in the legal world processing their cases.

5.2 Disputants' mediation aims

> "Many lawyers are looking for the wrong solution *at mediation*. IN WHAT WAY Lawyers are focused on the money... The plaintiffs' lawyer was interested in the money, you know, winning the case meant getting more money. They're going to get a bigger percentage if they settle higher. These people didn't need to get as much money as they needed to get a conclusion and an acknowledgement, apologies. 'Here's what we've done to make sure this doesn't happen again'. They needed that kind of discussion. And all the lawyer was saying was 'more money, more money'... And the money was horrendous. You don't get paid a lot for loss of a baby." **Experienced non-lawyer-mediator – male – in forties**

Plaintiffs' and defendants' discourse on their mediation aims was initially studied separately. However, as with legal actors, notwithstanding being at opposite poles of the dispute spectrum, strong similarities surfaced in their discourse as to what they wished to achieve in mediation in terms of resolving their cases short of trial (Figure 15).

Plaintiffs' mediation aims

Plaintiffs' mediation objectives were quite consonant throughout the claimant group. Plaintiffs agreed that financial settlement was one aim. However, they regularly stressed that they wanted numerous things from mediation apart from settlement. Most aimed to hear defendants' perspectives (65%) and sought answers or explanations of what had occurred (71%).[6] All plaintiffs stressed the need to be seen, heard, and understood by the defense in terms of what they had been through and their present situations. This included obtaining acknowledgments of their suffering. Such objectives contributed to plaintiffs' pervasive desires for catharsis and closure through mediation.

These findings are consonant with the data in chapter four, highlighting plaintiffs' perceptions of mediation as a place for information, human communication, and psychologically "feeling better." Consequently, most plaintiffs also wanted defendants in mediation to show they cared (53%) and to assure them the events would not recur (59%). The data here inform other writings, which stress that often more important than pecuniary recompense, medical plaintiffs frequently desire explanations of what happened, want to have their views heard, ask questions, and have the opportunity to discuss their anxieties.[7]

Wanting defendants to admit fault or accept responsibility pervaded claimants' discourse on their mediation aims (94%).[8] In fact, the code "accept/admit fault in mediation" was among the most commonly used within the entire dataset, highlighting the intensity of this mediation objective. Regardless of the feasibility of this desire or the fact that "blaming" was exogenous to the language of mediation, apart from one case where liability was obvious, no legal actor on any side mentioned this most recurrent of plaintiff aims. Similarly, most claimants wanted apologies (88%) at mediation,[9] with many (41%) saying that even qualified apologies would help them. This finding is consistent with other research, suggesting that victims often put greater value on genuine expressions of sorrow and remorse than on monetary recompense (Strang and Sherman 2003, pp. 17–23). Even in the commercial sphere, interview data of commercial litigators likewise indicate that commercial plaintiffs seek apologies (Macfarlane 2002, p. 306). Interestingly, nearly half (47%) of plaintiffs in the present study equated receiving apologies with acceptance of fault. This could be significant in the case of qualified apologies, where defendants would not legally be accepting liability but may address claimants' needs as well as bolster the resolution environment.

---

6 All those who did not seek answers during mediation explained they already knew what happened.
7 (Meschievitz (1991, pp. 200–1), Phillips (1992, p. 583), Dauer and Marcus (1997, p. 206), Johnson (1997, p. 49), and Simanowitz (1998, p. 63).
8 The only one who did not seek an admission of fault at mediation explained that one had already been made.
9 Claimants wanted apologies from defendants themselves, with almost half (47%) saying apologies would mean less or little coming from lawyers. The only two who did not want apologies explained this was because they did not think they would receive them.

Importantly, plaintiffs' articulated extralegal mediation objectives for closure, catharsis, wanting to be heard, wanting answers, apologies, admissions of fault, and defendants to show they cared were the same or similar regardless of whether mediations were mandatory (occurring within months of the commencement of legal suits) or voluntary (often years later). This suggests that plaintiffs' extralegal needs do not change over time. Moreover, when comparing claimants' discourse on their litigation aims (*chapter two*, figure 4) with their mediation objectives, the findings here reinforce those in chapter two on what plaintiffs said they sought from the justice system through litigation. In fact, although very similar, extralegal, psychological objectives appeared to be even more pervasive among plaintiffs when discussing mediation desires. For instance, 59% noted the litigation aim of defendants admitting fault, whereas 94% wanted defendants to admit fault during mediations; 53% sued to obtain answers, whereas 71% wanted to receive answers at mediation; 41% said they sued to obtain apologies, whereas 88% of plaintiffs said they wanted apologies during mediation. These findings may have been influenced to a degree by the question format. However, they may also suggest that as with legal actors mediation reorients claimants' attention toward the extralegal aspects of their disputes.

The confluence of disputants' and lawyers' mediation aims is best illustrated with reference to particular cases.

Fatality – DNR dispute – mandatory mediation – defendant present

Son plaintiff – in forties

> WHAT DID YOU WANT TO ACHIEVE AT MEDIATION... Just closure, just resolving it... *Mediation* should be an open forum... so it could all come to a close... I was looking for a longer, more in depth explanation... Give me a brief synopsis of it. Tell me "something"... I wanted to know why it took three days to release my father's body. ANY EXPLANATION... No, nothing... I wanted to hear their side... Everyone's burying the truth... people are intelligent people. Don't hide the truth from them... Offer whatever they can to resolve, to carry on. Because all you're doing is paying the lawyers. They're getting paid three hundred bucks an hour... But the parties involved are not resolving the issues.
>
> TO UNDERSTAND YOUR SIDE? Yes, because this way they could learn from it... to see *us*... If they showed they cared *at mediation*... I would have said "... Maybe we're on the wrong track"... Even a limited *apology*... That would have gone a lot further... and I'd say "He's a decent human being; and we're looking for him for unnecessary reasons..." We were hoping we'd make a settlement *at mediation*, something fair... We wanted them to pay for the funeral expenses and our legal expenses.

Widow – plaintiff – in seventies

> WHAT DID YOU WANT AT MEDIATION? An apology... I very much wanted to hear *the* doctor's side... I would like that they explain what happened. I told them

everything... But it was not question and answering. Everybody had... four minutes and no questions... I was hopeful that we would settle.

Male emergency physician – in fifties

My objectives really were quite simple. I just wanted to... hear from them... listening to everything they were saying. And obviously tried to see again their point of view and to see what are the main issues they are raising... the way *they* think things were done... My attempt was to make them understand what happened... trying to explain how things happened and why things happened... that there was no intention of harm in anything that was done.

The legal actors had other mediation objectives in mind.

Male, specialist plaintiff lawyer – in forties

WHAT DID YOU WANT TO ACHIEVE AT MEDIATION? What I always want to achieve as an advocate. I wanted to get in, make my point, and get out as fast as I could... I would have hoped that we'd been done in fifteen minutes, simply in the interest of doing an efficient job, of letting everyone understand. Counsel for the defense is an experienced, sensible person. Hopefully, I am too. We sat down; we've analyzed the issue. There it is. Let's go home.

I don't think there were any underlying issues... By *mediation* time it was an issue of straight compensation for what had happened, and that was it... The plaintiffs know this case is only about financial compensation, period, full stop; and that if they want something else, it's about a complaint to the College... You might consider having the physician *at mediation* for only a brief period of time if only to offer at an entirely human level, an apology.

Male physician lawyer – in forties

We did not expect to settle at mediation. There was an interesting legal issue... and the enthusiasm of the lawyers on the legal issue was picked up by the mediator as much as to say "Maybe what's motivating you to keep this case running is the interests of the lawyers on a neat legal issue that could go to the Supreme Court..." I found that an interesting observation.

Female hospital lawyer – in twenties

I wanted to find out whether or not the plaintiffs really viewed the hospital as a player in this. Because that's not how we see it... ANYTHING ELSE? Not particularly... I was interested in hearing what the plaintiffs had to say.

Similarly,

Vasectomy case – mandatory mediation – defendant absent

In describing his view of the upcoming mediation, the male physician lawyer did not mention any aims, simply saying the mediation would be a waste of time and that he expected it to be very brief. In the same vein, the hospital lawyer noted,

"I wanted the hospital to be dismissed from the action, was number one... I often like to say to people that we are truly sorry for the circumstances they find themselves in... when I think the hospital has no involvement at all and I think we should be let out. So I try and explain that. The second thing that I wanted to achieve if that didn't happen is to get a missing lab report." **Female – in twenties**

Yet, again the plaintiffs had different objectives for mediation.

Male plaintiff – in thirties

I wanted... to tell him my side and ask them for answers... I just wanted answers to tell me why did this happen to me, and just to see what he would say... I wasn't looking *for* a settlement. I was just looking for them to own up to what they did to me... Sure, I wanted an apology... and show care.

Female plaintiff – in thirties

I wanted... to hear their side... You want to find out answers... You don't go to mediation just to get money... Give me an understanding of why this happened... I would have liked more information... I thought I would get some answers... *I thought* the doctor's lawyer maybe would own up... that it "was" a mistake... I wanted a settlement... *but* I would have liked to have an apology... It was important that at least they understood what I had been through, *that* they heard our side.

The discontinuity of mediation objectives of disputants and most legal actors was evident throughout the case studies. There were additionally some gender disparities found within the plaintiffs' group in speaking of their mediation aims.

Plaintiffs' gender differences

Although overall planning the same things for mediation, in examining plaintiffs' discourse on their mediation aims more closely despite numbers being small there were differences in how males and females discussed what they planned to do at mediation (eleven females and six males). For instance, only females evinced concern about how their mediation aims were perceived (82% females versus 0% males). Similarly, females more often than males made comments relating to the integrity of their mediation objectives (91% of females versus 17% males). Likewise, females more often than males mentioned that it was important to be perceived as individuals during mediation, not just case numbers or records (73% females versus 17% males). These differences are illustrated in the chart shown in Figure 19.

The following quotes illustrate the findings on female plaintiffs' greater concerns than males about how their mediation aims would be perceived by other actors, including the integrity of their mediation missions. This was equally seen in cases of the most severe harm, including fatalities, loss of limb, and loss of sight.

"I'm not a whiner. I'm not a gold digger. I wasn't out for blood. All I wanted was a fair settlement. Because I'm a fair person myself... That was my aim. I wasn't out to gouge anybody. I wasn't out to tell lies... All I wanted was fair play." **Female – in sixties**

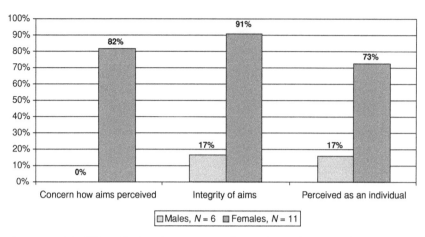

Figure 19. Plaintiffs' mediation aims concerns – by gender. In discussing their mediation agendas, only female plaintiffs discussed concern about how their mediation aims would be perceived, with females more often than males stressing the importance of being perceived as individuals with integrity.

"I said to my lawyer, 'You know what? I'm a very proud person. I don't want to be perceived as some money-grabbing, hungry person. That's not what it's all about'. I said 'I am not one of those... in... a bumper to bumper accident; and you see them wearing a... neck brace... That's not me'. And I think *my lawyer* mentioned that to them." **Female – in forties**

"YOUR MEDIATION OBJECTIVES... You want to listen to what they had to say. Because you know what went on. And, is the truth going to be said?... That was my purpose... Because she was liable and she knew she made an error... So I'm going to say it right here in front of everybody." **Female – in forties**

The next quotes highlight female plaintiffs' desires to be perceived as "individuals" during mediations.

"FOR THEM TO UNDERSTAND WHAT YOU HAD BEEN THROUGH? Yes, it did make a difference... It's a real person... not just your case number." **Female – in forties**

"DID YOU WANT TO MAKE THEM UNDERSTAND WHAT IT HAS BEEN LIKE FOR YOU? Yes, yes I did... It's like, you become a number... I just wanted them to realise that I was an individual." **Female – in sixties**

"I wanted them to understand what my new life is about. It was very important *because* I wanted this doctor to realise that I am not just a number in a case. I am a person." **Female – in sixties**

Actors' mediation objectives   147

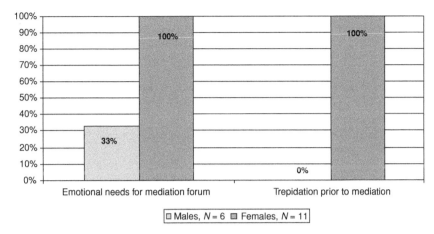

Figure 20. Plaintiffs' mediation needs and fears – by gender. Female plaintiffs more often than males expressed their emotional needs for mediation. Yet at the same time all females, but no males, mentioned trepidation prior to undergoing mediation.

At the same time, female plaintiffs spoke more often than males about their emotional needs for a mediation forum to deal with their disputes (100% females versus 33% males). This was notwithstanding the fact that all females (100%) and no males (0%) also mentioned emotional trepidation prior to undergoing mediation. This latter finding correlates with communication and negotiation studies, which suggest that women may be less eager and less self-confident than men to undergo mediation, possibly due to perceptions of mediation as a "male" process (Walters et al. 1998, p. 20; Evans 2001, p. 166). Babcock and Laschever's research into salary disparities suggests that as boys are raised to have a greater sense of entitlement and of deserving than girls, females develop an "imposter syndrome" whereby they more often question their abilities to perform well in male-dominated arenas (Babcock and Laschever 2003, pp. 51–54, 77–78). The chart in Figure 20 highlights these findings.

The following quotes illustrate the finding that female plaintiffs spoke more often of emotional needs for mediation than did males, who seemed to seek information more at mediations (45% females versus 67% males discussed seeking explanations/answers at mediation).

"I wanted him to realize I am a person with emotions... It was really important *for me* to be there... to have a voice. I wanted his camp to know exactly what I felt and was going through; not from my lawyer... It was important for them to hear my side. Not only hear it, but actually 'see' the person. I wanted to be there for his lawyer to look me in the face and tell me what his thoughts were on my condition... I wanted them to definitely *admit fault*... And I waited. And *his lawyer* talked about that he was here to make an offer. I was hoping he would say you know '*Mrs*... we're not here to restore your eyes. We are sorry that it ever happened'." **Female – in forties**

Similarly,

> "WHAT WERE YOUR MEDIATION OBJECTIVES... I wanted them to be accountable and to apologize... It may be silly, but that was our big thing: somebody has to say sorry for heaven's sake or acknowledge it... It wasn't about a dollar amount... It was more the emotional side why we were there... WERE YOU INTERESTED TO HEAR THEIR SIDE? Yes." **Female – in forties**

> "You want to be there to express yourself and tell them how you felt about things... They needed to know how it affected our family. They had to be aware of the fact that because of this... it isn't all rosy posy... They had to be made aware of what happened... to our lives." **Female – in fifties**

> "I wanted an apology... needed to make them understand... That's why we wrote that *posthumous* statement and read it out. I wanted them to understand how deeply this affected us... *Even* being there as representatives, I felt they should understand what it is they're defending, and the impact that it had on this lady... It was important that they understand how we felt." **Female – in forties**

The loss-of-limb case that settled illustrates well the convergence of mediation aims when female plaintiffs – who often had more emotional needs for the process than any males present – were involved.

Female plaintiff – in sixties

> My objectives were to resolve it... and explain my side of the case... I wanted closure. I was tired... *I wanted* to be understood where I was coming from on a lot of issues. Like where I was emotionally, and what was "really" important to me, like the fact that I had to give up babysitting my grandchildren... I can't walk in the woods anymore... things I missed most since amputation... over and above any dollars issues... WERE YOU LOOKING FOR THE DEFENSE TO SHOW THEY CARED? Oh, of course.

Male plaintiff lawyer – in fifties

> YOUR MEDIATION OBJECTIVES... It was a financial call... So I could say "I believe I've gotten enough money that's within the range of numbers a court is likely to award"... That was my goal going in. ANYTHING ELSE, LIKE APOLOGY? No... INVESTIGATION INTO WHAT HAPPENED? No. TO MAKE THEM UNDERSTAND WHAT IT'S BEEN LIKE FOR HER? No. TO HEAR THEIR SIDE... Sure. She had to understand... why they wanted to pay less money than I wanted them to pay.

Male physician lawyer – in forties

> MEDIATION OBJECTIVES I wanted to settle the case on a basis that I thought was better or equal to what would happen at trial.

Thus, unsurprisingly, in later describing the mediation, where all participating lawyers were male, the plaintiff recounted,

> They were really interested in what my needs were going to be. I think they were trying to figure out financially... That's what it was all about... obviously... They weren't interested in listening to me.

Notwithstanding the gender differences in plaintiffs' discourse on their mediation aims, overall plaintiffs' mediation aspirations were markedly similar to those of defending physicians – both being very different to legal actors.

Defendant physicians' mediation objectives

As seen in Figure 15, what physicians said they planned to do during mediations was remarkably similar to what claimants desired. Virtually all defendants expressed the need to communicate their perspectives at mediation and for claimants to understand their viewpoints (92%).[10] Moreover, as illustrated in Figure 16 in contrast to their lawyers, where few (10%) aimed to hear claimants' perspectives, most physicians did (83%).[11] For example,

> "As far as confidentiality of the environment... I don't trust the system... My primary objective was to dialogue with the family... attempting to get them to understand the specific circumstances... The first thing is that we don't want the results that occurred to have happened in the first place. Therefore... most of us... take several weeks to recover. And that has to be conveyed to the family... In other words, I am sorry with them. I'm not sorry for them... and that I cared... THEM TO UNDERSTAND YOUR PERSPECTIVE? Oh, absolutely... DID YOU WANT TO HEAR THEIR SIDE? Oh yes. What is written down is often, just an indication of what they may have, as far as misapprehension is concerned. So you really want to know what they're talking about. It is the only way you're going to solve it." **Male surgeon – in fifties – fatality – College and court-linked mediation**

> "The lawyers brief*ed me* to not say 'I'm sorry for what I did'... *but* I acknowledged to them what my feelings were about... I was there to say 'This is a terrible thing, this young women died. I feel very badly'... DID YOU PLAN TO EXPLAIN... Oh yes. I told them what happened... and I agreed with them she was not well served by the system... I was very sympathetic with what they had gone through." **Female emergency physician – in fifties – fatality – College mediation – litigation anticipated**

> "ANYTHING SAID IN MEDIATION CANNOT BE USED ELSEWHERE I was told that. I'm not sure I believe that... My wish was to make them... understand we did

---

10 In speaking of mediation aims, no notable gender differences were found in the defendant physicians' group.
11 The only data found on defending physicians' mediation aims related to non-litigated cases. In Dauer's study of the Massachusetts Voluntary Medmal Mediation Pilot, although not empirically rigorous and covering only ten cases, it was similarly found that physicians wanted the chance to apologize, express regret, and provide assurances that occurrences would not recur (Dauer and Marcus 1997, pp. 211, 186).

our best. And in the face of doing the best we thought we could do, there was an unsatisfactory outcome." **Male pediatric surgeon – in fifties – surgery dispute**

"To explain what happened... and state *my* case. So the plaintiff can understand what was done and why, hopefully as a means to diffusing the whole thing... In this case... to explain... and that I didn't do anything wrong. I took her complaint seriously. I treated her appropriately. I did my best to find out why things were going wrong... And I was sorry what happened to her." **Male orthopedic surgeon – in thirties – College**

These findings provide further evidence of plaintiffs' and defendants' perceptions of mediation as a place for extralegal information exchange and "feeling better" (*chapter four*). But the question remained, Why did legal actors not plan to do at mediation most of the things disputants so desired? After all, anything said in mediation is "confidential." This led me to examine the issue of attorneys' trust in the confidentiality of the mediation environment.

5.3 The confidentiality premise

"There's an issue that we as a profession ought to talk about frankly. This business is about winning cases [pause]. And maybe it shouldn't be. Because if we make winning cases the ultimate objective... if I am a defense counsel, I don't want to tell anybody anything for as long as I possibly can. My tactics are to capitalise on the ability to provide as much information in as controlled a fashion as late as possible, in order to catch the other side by surprise – because that will maximise my chances of winning a case. My client will be far happier with me than if I lose. That's the truth. And for plaintiffs it's the same thing." **Male, specialist plaintiff and physician lawyer – in forties**

"*In caucus*... I discovered that the physician's lawyer would have been really fearful of allowing his client to speak more on... where he was coming from or what had happened... I asked the doctor 'What was really important to you'? And he said he would have liked them to understand... And I looked at the physician's lawyer, and he said 'No'.... I have been beating myself over this case because to me it wasn't the $10,000... I think more than any kind of compensation, what they're looking for is an acknowledgement that something went wrong." **Female non-lawyer-mediator – in forties – fatality DNR case**

In an attempt to understand why legal actors (particularly on the defense) were not intent on providing the information or acknowledgments sought by plaintiffs at mediation or offering even qualified apologies, I examined the way lawyers described the confidentiality of the process. Confidentiality, a basic tenet of mediation, has been expressed as "critical" and "integral" to the relationship between the mediator and the parties and... "*to* the free and frank disclosure that is necessary if obstacles to settlement are to be overcome" (Roberts 1997, p. 133).

Some critics have questioned the necessity of confidentiality in mediation.[12] However, many writers stress the significance of actors' reliance on confidentiality and on most mediators operating under this assumption, viewing confidentiality as fundamental to effective mediation as it encourages actors to speak freely (Johnson 1997, p. 51; Lande 2000, p. 332; Deason 2001, p. 80).

Rule 24.1.14 of the Canadian Bar Association's Ontario Model Code of Conduct for Mediators (1999) states that "all communications at a mediation session and the mediator's notes and records shall be deemed to be without prejudice settlement discussions... and mediators shall inform the parties of the confidential nature of mediation."[13] Confidentiality in the present study was also protected by a written contractual agreement, signed by all mediation participants at the commencement of each mediation. This meant that all mediation communications, both verbal and written, were treated as privileged and absolutely confidential and without prejudice. Thus, they could not be used outside the confines of the mediation forum (subject to court subpoena).

Nonetheless, upon analysis of lawyers' discourse on their mediation aims, it emerged that of those who discussed confidentiality, most felt it was partly or completely fallacious.[14] Moreover, perceptions of the "fallacy" of confidentiality seemed to influence lawyers' mediation objectives and subsequent mediation conduct. The following quotes are illustrative of defense lawyers' views:

"If someone goes into a room and sort of bears their soul and everybody signs... they won't use it... how does the lawyer at trial cross-examination later extract that information from his mind? It's like asking an unsustainable question in front of a jury. It's overruled, but the jury's heard it." **Female physician lawyer – in fifties**

"I would never dream of disclosing something at mediation not expecting it to come back at us at trial, even though they couldn't use it technically." **Female hospital lawyer – in forties**

"I don't think in any mediation you let out anything more than you want to let out... Because if it doesn't settle, they are going to come back to haunt you... having seen all those cards." **Male hospital lawyer – in forties**

---

12 Hughes (1998, p. 14), Goldberg et al. (1999, p. 442), and Reich (2001, p. 197). Indeed, certain U.S. programs have operated without confidentiality safeguards. Moreover, U.S. case law as well as statutes and Rules of Civil Procedure in some states have allowed exceptions or qualifications to mediations' confidentiality. For instance, some states require the disclosure of settlements and issues relating to public bodies and public matters such as health and safety (Menkel-Meadow et al. 2006, pp. 317–20, pp. 324–25).
13 Ministry-of-the-Attorney-General (1999, p. 5), Attorney-General-of-Ontario (1999d, p. 6), and http://www.travel-net.com/~billr/Rules/mainW.html (last visited June 5, 2007). This is also noted in Rule 75.1.11 of the Ontario Rules of Civil Procedure (O. Reg. 290/99, s. 2).
14 Seventy-one percent of physician lawyers, 75% of hospital lawyers, and 92% of plaintiff lawyers.

"Even though it's supposed to be confidential... It's naïve to say the moves you make or the discussions in mediation don't set a tone and don't carry through the file... Like if you say in a mediation that you're not disputing liability, then you're not disputing liability ever. You might pretend that you are and write letters that suggest that you are... But everybody knows you've given up on that." **Female hospital lawyer – in twenties**

Plaintiff lawyers spoke similarly.

"Confidentiality's a fallacy in many ways... You all know that whatever information that's communicated... won't be admissible. But they will... assess their strategies based on knowing more about my whole perception... of the case also knowing what my client will be like as a witness. So they don't want their doctor to speak because then I know what kind of witness I'm going to be dealing with. If he says something that is contrary to their position or their theory, then I would hope that I'm going to get the same answer out of that doctor if I ask him that on the witness stand." **Male plaintiff – generalist – lawyer – in forties**

"You can say as much as you want about the issue of confidentiality. But the reality is once the disclosure is made, it's made. *If* plaintiff's counsel uses the process to get a free examination... of the doctor, nine times out of ten if you ask that same question *after mediation*, you're going to get the same answer. Because if you don't, then the plaintiff's counsel is going to say to his client 'Look, this guy is just selling you a bag of goods, and we can tag him'." **Male, specialist plaintiff and physician lawyer – in forties**

"MEDIATION IS CONFIDENTIAL... What does that mean? Once something enters my head, sure I'm going to use it. I'm not going to use 'he said, she said'. But... *mediation confidentiality is* a fallacy... The information that you gain in terms of the insights to the other side's case, sure they're going to be used." **Male, specialist plaintiff lawyer – in forties**

"I think lawyers sometimes caution the client not to *speak* before they go into a joint mediation session because it's not a free shot at discovery. There has to be a controlled flow of information." **Female plaintiff lawyer – generalist – in thirties**

Legal actors' overall lack of faith in mediation's confidentiality was an important finding. It shed further light on the highly tactical way lawyers perceive mediation, and it appeared to have had some impact on lawyers' mediation objectives in terms of what they were prepared to say and do in mediation. With little trust in mediation's confidential environment, acceding to plaintiffs' desires for mediation was regularly viewed by legal actors as a tactical risk. In comparison, it was interesting that although most physicians similarly did not trust mediation's confidentiality, they were far more prepared than lawyers to have real communication during the process, providing information and at least qualified apologies.

5.4 Chapter conclusion

The analysis of legal versus lay actors' mediation aims makes apparent one more facet of the parallel worlds of understanding and meaning prevalent within litigated case processing involving mediation: the legal world of tactics and strategy versus disputants' extralegal world grounded on psychological needs, feelings, and emotions. Indeed, in line with the conclusions in chapters three and four on the different legal and lay visions and meanings ascribed to mediation, this chapter has underscored lawyers' and disputants' very diverse agendas for the process. Legal actors' mediation objectives and lack of faith in mediation's confidentiality were very similar in all camps. Moreover, for most lawyers mediation was not about information flow for the sake of education or the provision of psychological relief. It was about relaying information to the opposing side in order to assist the sender tactically in highlighting the strengths of their own cases and the weaknesses and risks of opponents' cases – similar to traditional advocacy. Yet, there appeared to be little awareness by defense lawyers and even some plaintiff lawyers of disputants' objectives for mediation – which were dramatically different in many respects.

At the same time, plaintiffs and defendants were most similar in their mediation aims, which complemented each other but included little of what was on lawyers' agendas. The similarity of plaintiffs' mediation objectives in both voluntary and mandatory mediations – often occurring years apart – highlight the fact that plaintiffs' extralegal dispute needs do not change over time. The findings also support plaintiffs' assertions that mediation was about much more than money. Thus, although both lawyers and disputants wanted to communicate at mediation, seeking for "the other" to agree, legal and lay actors were in many respects speaking different languages. This was seen even between lawyers and clients. For example, correlating with the findings in chapter four on defendant physicians' conceptions of mediation as an extralegal environment, defendants aimed to explain their side, provide information, show care, offer a form of apology, and hear and understand plaintiffs' perspectives. These objectives were patently distinct from their counsels' mediation aims (who regularly attended mediations without them).

Plaintiffs' articulated mediation objectives were consistent with their accounts of why they sued and their litigation aims, discussed in chapter two. In fact, in comparing the charts on claimants' litigation aims (*chapter two*, figure 4) with their mediation objectives (Figure 15), the only difference appeared to be that in speaking of mediation, plaintiffs spoke even more of extralegal aims. What pervaded disputants' talk on mediation agendas was their wanting to directly communicate their perspectives, be heard, seen, and understood. Thus, as with legal actors, being involved in and thinking about mediation appeared to reorient litigating parties' attentions to focus even further on the extralegal aspects of their disputes. This suggests that what plaintiffs want from the civil justice system in terms of extralegal aspirations can be expressed during litigation-track mediations.

In terms of the gender findings, although lawyers' mediation aims were generally very different to those of parties, in examining attorneys' discourse more closely, the data suggested that gender had an effect on what lawyers planned to do at mediation. In speaking of either their own mediation objectives or awareness of those of plaintiffs, female lawyers more often than males spoke of extralegal mediation aims, planning to use mediation as a forum for things other than solely strategy and monetary negotiations. For instance, the desire for communication with plaintiffs and hearing plaintiffs' perspectives, not only for settlement reasons but also for extralegal purposes, appeared to be associated more with females than with males. These findings lend some support to assertions that female professionals may have the potential to offer greater assistance in addressing disputants' extralegal needs at mediation (Gilligan 1982, pp. 62–63; Stempel 2003, pp. 310–11; Subrin 2003, pp. 310–11). This will be further explored in chapter six.

For plaintiffs, gender differentiations were particularly apparent when speaking about mediation aims. Although planning the same things for mediation as males, only females evinced concern about how their mediation aims were perceived and commented more often than males on both the integrity of their mediation missions and on wanting to be perceived as individuals during mediation, not just case numbers or records. At the same time, female plaintiffs spoke more often than males about their emotional needs for a mediation forum to deal with their disputes. This was notwithstanding the fact that all females and no males mentioned emotional trepidation prior to undergoing mediation.

Finally, this chapter evidenced further indications of lawyers' reconceptualization of their cases and roles through mediation involvement. Despite the generally different mediation agendas of legal and disputant actor groups, lawyers in all camps demonstrated to various degrees a marked consideration of nonlegal issues. For instance, only a minority of plaintiff lawyers (37%) limited their mediation aims to settlement alone. Some (32%) sought apologies for their clients. Moreover, plaintiff lawyers instructed clients to "tell their stories" for reasons that could not have been confined solely to the realms of law or strategy. This marked some recognition of the indivisibility of disputants' legal and extralegal case needs. The reconceptualization findings were strengthened when comparing plaintiff lawyers' discourse on their clients' litigation aims with comprehensions of plaintiffs' mediation aims – the latter reflecting a wider understanding of what plaintiffs wanted in resolving their cases.

Defense lawyers' discourse on mediation objectives also provided some evidence of rethinking cases as a result of hearing plaintiffs at mediation. This was similarly seen in comparing physician lawyers' views of plaintiffs' litigation aims (*chapter two*) with their understandings of plaintiffs' mediation objectives. In addition, hospital lawyers' mediation agendas generally included extralegal objectives outside the realm of traditional legal practice. Thus, it appears that through mediation, with its inclusion of cases' extralegal dimensions, thinking about disputants' extralegal needs is incrementally becoming something that lawyers "do." Indeed, what has been conventionally recognized as within the province of legal practice seems to be expanding to increasingly include disputants' psychological and emotional needs as part of the legitimate fields of lawyers' operations. This conclusion is strengthened when examining lawyer-mediators' mediation aims, which were very much focused on extralegal dispute concerns.

Nevertheless, claimants' pervasive mediation objectives of interpersonal communication coupled with defense attorneys' overall lack of desire to communicate much information other than that pertaining to opponents' tactical risks foreshadowed an imparity in the flow of information at mediation. Thus, unsurprisingly, as will be seen in chapter six, few plaintiffs received all they sought during mediation. However, providing further support for the parallel worlds' theme, the next chapter additionally explores the diverse perceptions of what was positive and negative during the process for each actor group, as well as the jigsaw of views on "what went on" during mediations.

CHAPTER SIX

Perceptions during mediations

Moving forward chronologically in terms of case processing, the chapters thus far have related to contextual and then pre-mediation issues. Therefore, in some respects, this chapter and chapter seven represent the culmination of all earlier chapters' findings, as they examine legal, lay, and gendered actors' actual mediation experiences. In "setting out to make explicit the truth of primary experiences" through actors' discourses on what transpired during mediations, I discover the properties of... actions 'from within' actual settings" (Bourdieu 1977, p. 3; Garfinkel 1984, pp. vii–viii, 1). In this chapter, I examine the disparity of perceptions of "what goes on" during mediations, both in terms of contextual confrontations and representations as well as actors' favored and disfavored mediation elements. Chapter seven covers issues specifically related to mediators during the process.[1]

Participants' "satisfaction" with mediation in numerous jurisdictions has been well documented.[2] Yet, when the premises underlying actors' incongruous discourse on their mediation experiences are examined, mediation emerges as a forum for

---

[1] To ensure meaningfulness of the findings, the analyses in chapters six and seven focus solely on discourse relating to experiences in specific mediations. However, other data from additional cases (discussed during interviews on specific mediations) and general interviews (relating to no particular mediation) were utilized for background knowledge in support of the findings. For completeness, the data for chapters six and seven consist of the following: Physician lawyers' data derive from twelve interview files (ten with males; two with females), seven of which relate to specific mediations (four mandatory, three voluntary; four settled) and five were general interviews or additional cases. Hospital lawyers' data derive from seventeen interview files covering ten specific mediations (with seven female and three male respondents; six mandatory, four voluntary mediations; six settled), six additional mediations, and one general interview. Plaintiff lawyers' data derive from seventeen interview files involving thirteen specific mediations (seven mandatory, six voluntary; five settled), three general interviews, and one additional mediation. Overall, fifteen plaintiff lawyers provided data (thirteen males, two females, being eight specialists, five generalist lawyers). Mediators' data derive from eighteen mediation interview files (eight specific mediations with five male and three female mediators, being six mediator-lawyers, two non-lawyers), six general, and four additional case interviews. All mediators had five to twenty-five years of experience. Plaintiffs' data (six males, nine females) derive from fifteen plaintiff interviews, all relating to specific mediations (seven mandatory, eight voluntary). The physician data on this topic derive primarily from pre-litigation College mediations (seven College and two mandatory court-linked mediations where physicians attended). Therefore, only where the particular issues discussed by physicians related to all mediation types were they included.

[2] Macfarlane (1995), Polywka (1997, p. 84), Wissler (1998, p. 28), and Shack (2003).

dual communication – transmitted and received on different planes. Mediation reflects the confluence of conflicting interests, realities, and worlds: the legal world of tactics and strategy versus the human world of extralegal needs and desires. Lawyers provide highly strategic accounts of what went on, perceiving mediation as a key vehicle for direct tactical communication and strategic insight. In sharp contrast, disputants depict the same mediations as very personal encounters, providing emotional and psychological descriptions of what occurred. Despite plaintiffs' anger at the dearth of information they received as well as what they saw through mediation's window into the legal world (i.e., the focus on money and perceptions of lawyers "playing a game" or impersonally handling their tragedies), disputants describe the therapeutic benefit of having "voice." This is notwithstanding most not recognizing what I term "the red riding hood syndrome" relating to parties' strong emotional and psychological needs to tell their stories, express themselves, and be heard, simultaneously feeding into legal actors' needs to evaluate them tactically.[3] Thus, although participants interact together during the process, they perceive things in completely different ways, often not really communicating at all. In this way, mediation is seen to frequently fail to address many of parties' extralegal needs, aims, and plans for the process.

A key theme within this chapter relates to mediators who stand "in between" legal and lay actors, mediating their different perceptions during the process – as they are meant to do. Yet, in addition, the findings contribute a new angle to what goes on during mediations. The data indicate that mediators not only mediate "between" parties but also mediate actors' different senses of reality, practices, and representations – those of lawyers who want to take control and equally those of parties who seek relief, satisfaction, catharsis, and so on (Menkel-Meadow 2006). On another plane, gender provides a crucial lens for comparing mediation experiences and mapping relationships between actors.

Interestingly, notwithstanding the tactical differences lawyers referred to in chapter three on mandatory versus voluntary mediations, a strong common thread ran through each actor group's discourse on what transpired during the process, regardless of mediation type.[4] Thus, this chapter first explores the contextual "goings-on" during all mediations as well as a number of surface findings relating to actors' views about their experiences. Next, delving deeper into what transpired during the process, legal actors' and then disputants' mediation perceptions and understandings are compared through their discourse on favored and disfavored elements. Finally, some disconcerting gender disparities are highlighted.

3 Conley and O'Barr's research into small claims litigants similarly found that many people, needing to tell their stories, treat the litigation process as a form of therapy (Conley and O'Barr 1990, p. 130). Thus, communication opportunities in court are sometimes of greater importance than results (Conley and O'Barr 1988, pp. 186–87).
4 Similarly, in Wissler's survey research in common pleas courts in Ohio, whether mediations were mandatory or voluntary did not affect parties' assessments of the process or the mediator in terms of fairness and mediator conduct; nor did it influence parties' ratings of their abilities to tell their stories (Wissler 1997, pp. 588, 594, 596).

6.1 Mediation's contextual worlds: Confrontations and representations

> "Every case... depends on the dynamics of how *opposing* lawyers interact, how plaintiffs interact with defense counsel and how plaintiff and plaintiff lawyers interact. These are all part of the dynamics of the mediation process." **Male, retired judge – mediator – in seventies**

Although often not mentioned, a number of concomitant dimensions colored in features of the landscape during mediations. They entailed two types of confrontations and conflicts as well as representations. First, there were the confrontations between legal actors.

Legal actors' confrontations

Far removed from most disputants' understandings and disputes, considerable interview and observation data suggested that during mediations, conflicts on another level were raging on concurrently. These were manifested by confrontations between the lawyers involved – sometimes being veterans of previous encounters against each other. These "confrontations in tandem" were materially affected by attorneys' personalities. Indeed, the second most used code in the dataset was "lawyer personalities/interactions strong effect." Needless to say, this often had material effects on all actors' mediation experiences and results.

> "INTERACTIONS BETWEEN COUNSEL, PERSONALITIES? Ya, ya, just, you never know [she laughs] what you're going to find when you get to mediation. IS THAT PART OF MEDIATION? Oh, huge." **Female hospital lawyer – in twenties – mandatory**

> "I have a lady counsel and I can tell the plaintiffs' counsel doesn't like dealing with young women. He's probably about 60 or so. At one point he was starting to lecture her... So you know, you get the personalities... Mediation should be between the parties. It is not the parties and their entire entourage. And what is happening here is that the entourage takes over from the actual parties." **Male physician defendant – fatality case – in fifties – mandatory**

> "What happens at mediation depends as well on the characters of the lawyers and the particular people. You can't ever control for that." **Male physician lawyer – in fifties**

> "The nurse had given a fellow an injection and severed a nerve in his leg, so he was quite disabled... It was a mistake, there's no question. I didn't make a big issue about liability. But the lawyer fed into that. He was very obnoxious, aggressive. And I had to bite my tongue... really counter-productive to resolution." **Female hospital and plaintiff lawyer – in forties – mandatory**

Within the world of lawyers' confrontations were also hierarchical issues, which similarly could affect disputants' mediation experiences, unbeknownst to most.

"One of the interesting variables is the age and experience of the lawyers and how that affects mediation... the age gap, the gender gap, the prestige gap. Defendants' counsel came from very large firms; *so it affected* the plaintiff counsel's mental state at mediation... In mediations, there's an 'us' and 'them' attitude. If... all the lawyers are from big firms, it's all between us... If... one is a very large firm lawyer and one is a sole practitioner or a small firm, we have the extra chip." **Male lawyer-mediator – in fifties**

"Typically the more severe cases get the more experienced lawyers... You're going to get a very different ball game than when you've got somebody who does general litigation and a couple of malpractice cases." **Female physician lawyer – in fifties**

"So much depends on the calibre of counsel. I think that's sometimes under-rated... If I were opposed by inexperienced counsel... it would do nothing... But if you have competent counsel on the other side who know how to do the case... If there is respect all around the table...." **Male physician lawyer – voluntary – in fifties**

"We had a junior lawyer that attended for the obstetrician and a very seasoned, experienced, competent lawyer that attended for the hospital... The lawyer for the hospital did most of the talking. The rather inexperienced, although competent physician/insurance lawyer sat in the bushes and tried not to say very much." **Male plaintiff lawyer – specialist – in forties – mandatory**

The inequalities inherent in the confrontations between legal actors were magnified in mediations' second type of contextual conflicts: those between lawyers and litigants. Despite much evidence of their existence, these issues were rarely mentioned by the parties involved.

Conflicts between legal and lay actors

First, it was lawyers, not disputants, who subliminally controlled what transpired at mediations. Again, the code "lawyer–client control" was among the most used in the dataset, reflecting the prevalence of this phenomenon.

"It was very much a lawyers' game in terms of what happened there." **Female non-lawyer-mediator of twelve years – mandatory – in thirties**

"I'm constantly working through the lawyers. So I speak to the lawyers and I find out what the lawyers are looking for. I really don't have an understanding what the family members or the doctor want... So I come in looking for the legal angle they're looking for... which in many ways puts the human component right down at the bottom... I'm accustomed to having the human component up here. The other stuff usually works itself out if you... deal with the human component." **Female non-lawyer mandatory mediator – ten years' experience – ran victim-offender and community mediation program – in forties**

"The control of the process is in the hands of the lawyers... I often meet with the lawyer ahead of time to see what he wants to do, excluding the plaintiff. That's because lawyers sometimes want to say 'My client's very difficult. They don't want to do this, that. Here's what I'd like to ask'." **Male, senior lawyer-mediator – voluntary – in sixties**

"The lawyer basically is the person in control because the injured party knows nothing about the process and is somewhat intimidated by going into the room with a bunch of strangers, even though it is quite informal. They tend to rely very, very heavily on their counsel and take their counsel's advice." **Male lawyer-mediator – voluntary and mandatory – in fifties**

The findings here on lawyers controlling what transpires during mediations correlate with various U.S. studies indicating lawyers' domination of mediations (Gordon 1999, pp. 227–28; Gordon 2000, p. 383; Wissler 2002, p. 658). For instance, in Metzloff et al.'s study of North Carolina court–ordered mediations, it was found that lawyers often took over mediation sessions, with parties regularly remaining separated from the negotiations (Metzloff et al. 1997, pp. 119, 123–25). Likewise, in Wisconsin, lawyers were found to control clients' mediation participation.[5] As such, assertions about disputants' levels of process control (Baruch Bush 1997, p. 17) are questioned. Indeed, the findings portray lawyers as the primary gatekeepers for conflicts, largely determining what interests are addressed during mediations (Reich 2002, p. 188).

At the same time, not unique to litigation, to mediation, or to the jurisdiction, there was evidence of unspoken economic conflicts between lawyers and clients.

"If you settle cases at mediation, your fees are going to be a lot less than if you settle after discovery... or pre-trial. These are undercurrents, but they can't be ignored... They're there... This case is not an injury where the person hasn't reached maximum medical recovery... This case is worth $100,000 today... at pre-trial, and... at trial. It's not going to change... We don't want this lady to go through discovery... *or* trial. So we have competing economic interests at the same time too." **Mandatory mediation – no settlement – infant death case – specialist, male plaintiff lawyer – in forties**

"What incentive does a lawyer have for getting rid of a case?... When you look at the economics and what drives the legal profession... It is about winning cases, for plaintiff, defense or otherwise. From lawyers' perspectives, it's about being able to produce as many billable hours as possible in the interests of securing your position within a firm and making partners... as happy as possible. I have not heard a lawyer ever say to me that s/he would like to go home next year making less than they make this year." **Male, specialist plaintiff and physician lawyer – in forties**

---

5 Meschievitz (1990, pp. 17, 135). Of course, this may not always be the case. McEwen et al.'s research in two U.S. states found that divorce lawyers' attendance at mediation did not interfere with meaningful client participation. However, their data derived from structured interviews with divorce lawyers alone, excluding any litigant data or mediation observations (McEwen et al. 1995, pp. 1322, 1358, 1373, 1394). Thus, arguably, their findings must be viewed from the perspective of lawyers' perceptions.

"I've done plaintiffs' work; I've done defense work; and there's a particular dynamic at play... There were new defense lawyers for the insurers saying 'We're the new guys and we're going to show them that we're very, very good'. How do you do that as a lawyer? You take the file through the process." **Male, specialist plaintiff and hospital lawyer – in forties**

A further aspect of what went on during mediations related to the grandstanding or performing by lawyers on all sides – what I have termed lawyers' "representations."

Representations

The individual effectively projects a definition of the situation when he enters the presence of others... It is in the individual's interests to control the conduct of others... by influencing the definition of the situation which the others come to formulate, and he can influence this definition by expressing himself in such a way as to give them the kind of impression that will lead them to act voluntarily in accordance with his own plan (Goffman 1971, pp. 15, 23).

Legal actors' representations contributed a further aspect to what went on during mediations, very much affecting disputants' experiences. As seen in Figure 21, the strong effects of lawyers' personalities and demeanors on mediations including their grandstanding or "representations" (for fellow lawyers and/or disputants) were noted by a material number of mediation actors.[6] Drawing on Goffman's work on "performances," this finding relates to self-presentation and managing others' impressions. Performances are defined as "all the activity of an individual on a given occasion marked by his continuous presence before a particular set of observers, which serves to influence in any way any of the other participants." Front performances are "that part of the performance which... functions... to define the situation for those who observe... including one's... rank, clothing, sex, age, facial expressions, bodily gestures, etc." (Goffman 1971, pp. 26, 32, 34). Yet, as Goffman aptly notes and what I found to be a regular feature of what occurs during mediation processes, was that "there is hardly a legitimate everyday vocation or relationship whose performers do not engage in concealed practices which are incompatible with fostered impressions... Somewhere in... his activities there will be something he cannot treat openly" (Goffman 1971, p. 71). Indeed, as will be seen, the litigation-track mediation phenomenon was replete with actors' intrigues and concealed intentions.

The "representations" finding was further supported by contemporaneous observation notes of mediations where it was regularly recorded that lawyers acted and spoke quite differently between themselves or to mediators once they left the presence of lay disputants.[7] For example,

---

6 Forty-three percent of physician lawyers, 50% of hospital lawyers, 77% of plaintiff lawyers, 87% of plaintiffs, and 75% of mediators.
7 The parallel deployment of different discursive codes in the sense used by Bernstein (Bernstein 1971) has been widely noted and subjected to commentary and theoretical speculation in the

"One of the biggest problems in mediation is lawyers tend to posture... You have to... say 'Come on, we don't need *that*... we know their case'. They don't have to posture for the sake of their clients. Let's just sort of work *it out*." **Male lawyer-mediator – infant fatality – in fifties**

"PLAINTIFFS MAY GET ASKED OUT OF THE MEDIATION ROOM... I favor it because... it's very hard to be candid and businesslike *number*-crunching if you're being forced to perform for your client." **Male, specialist plaintiff lawyer – in fifties**

"I decided to bring the lawyers into the room by themselves... and I was surprised at the dialogue that happened when the lawyers no longer needed to perform for their clients... It's fascinating when I get the lawyers together, because they can really be direct and upfront with each other." **Female non-lawyer-mediator – mandatory – in forties**

"The mediator has to be really... smart... to be able to control the various personalities and egos... Because lawyers *are*... grandstanding like mad." **Male physician defendant – fatality – in fifties**

"My fellow had given a fellow a wrong substance to drink. It was caustic and burned his oesophagus. It was nasty... I did not make any issue of liability. I went to the mediation fully intending to settle. And the plaintiff's lawyer stood up and grandstanded in front of his client about what a crummy hospital this was, and that they tried to hide records. It was completely nonsense. The mediation failed and I was furious... I didn't know why the plaintiff's lawyer did that. It didn't help his case at all... His guy was eighty years old. Like why are you dragging him through the process?" **Female hospital lawyer – mandatory – in forties**

In addition to lawyers performing for their own clients, opponent lawyers' representations were also noted.

"One of the big things about defense lawyers in mediations is that some of them will try and get very aggressive in a courtroom-like manner. They may humiliate, embarrass, degrade plaintiffs at mediation. Or try to... So what is supposed to be a process to resolve disputes becomes a forum to have a fight." **Male, specialist – plaintiff lawyer – voluntary – in fifties**

As for disputants' representations in front of lawyers, it was interesting to note that though numerous plaintiff lawyers stressed the importance of preparing plaintiffs on what to expect at mediation and about their opportunities to speak, only one plaintiff mentioned anything relating to "performing" for lawyers and no attorneys mentioned this. Nevertheless, as will be seen later, disputants were very much "watched" by lawyers during mediations.

disputing literature, for example, Bloch (1974, pp. 55–81), Comaroff (1975, pp. 149–55), and Comaroff and Roberts (1981, pp. 84–86).

Perceptions during mediations   163

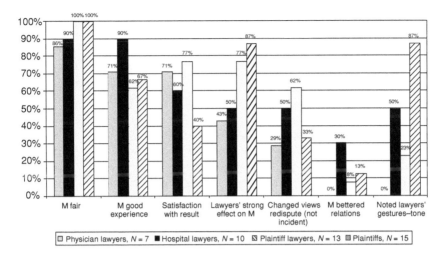

Figure 21. Surface perceptions of mediations – all actors. (*Note:* "M" stands for mediation.) Effects of lawyers' personas and nonverbal communication were important elements within mediation experiences. Yet, views on mediations and their fairness were overall positive, regardless of results. Some actors subsequently changed their dispute views. However, there was little evidence of ameliorated relations between disputants.

Surface findings

There were a number of surface findings from questionnaire and interview responses that stood out. For instance, irrespective of mediation type, most actors in each group expressed feelings of optimism prior to mediation.[8] Moreover, as seen in Figure 21, regardless of views on results the majority of mediation players perceived mediations as both fair and good or positive experiences.[9]

Voluminous procedural justice studies have confirmed that for disputants, assessments of legal procedures' fairness and thus procedural justice are at least as important as views on substantive issues or outcomes.[10] Views on fairness are

---

8   This was particularly interesting in light of chapter three's findings on lawyers' attitudes toward mandatory versus voluntary mediations. Ninety percent of hospital lawyers and 62% of plaintiff lawyers were "optimistic" or "somewhat optimistic." Physician lawyers did not fully answer this questionnaire question, but during interviews noted feelings of optimism prior to mediations.
9   Eighty-six percent of physician lawyers, 90% of hospital lawyers, and 100% of plaintiffs and their lawyers said that mediation was "fair" or "very fair." Similarly, 71% of physician lawyers, 90% of hospital lawyers, 62% of plaintiff lawyers, and 67% of plaintiffs felt mediation was a good/positive experience. In comparison, 71% of physician lawyers, 60% of hospital lawyers, 77% of plaintiff lawyers but only 40% of plaintiffs were satisfied with their mediation results/outcomes irrespective of whether settlement was reached. Although physician responses were not included in the chart (as 78% of physician interviews related to pre-litigation College mediations), it was noteworthy that most medics also felt that mediations were both good and fair experiences (78%).
10 Thibaut and Walker (1975, 1978); Casper (1978, 1988), Barrett-Howard and Tyler (1986), Lind and Tyler (1988, p. 65), and Tyler (1988).

affected by opportunities for voice or expression (with the belief that arguments are seriously considered regardless if later rejected), process control, participation, trustworthiness, interpersonal respect, and neutrality. These elements are particularly important as procedural justice or injustice experiences may have serious consequences for people's satisfaction with and perceptions of their legal experiences, the legitimacy of law and legal authority, their support for legal institutions, and their compliance with individual legal decisions or outcomes – a critical issue in mediation, where voluntary compliance is key for its success in settling disputes (Lind and Tyler 1988, pp. 64, 69–70, 93–94, 207–9; Tyler 1997, pp. 887, 889).

The findings here on mediation "satisfaction" correlate with numerous other studies on the topic. For instance, in the Ontario ADR Centre evaluation, covering different civil case types, 90% of parties interviewed stated that they were either very or somewhat positive about mediation (Macfarlane 1995). Likewise, a U.S. review of sixty-two studies evaluating over one hundred court mediation programs indicated that overall 70% of parties were satisfied with mediation and its outcomes (although disputants were more likely to express satisfaction if their cases settled) and more than 80% of parties felt the process was fair (Shack 2003). This was also the case in Wissler's Ohio survey of court-linked mediation participants (1,224 lawyers and 725 parties) where the vast majority felt mediations were fair and good experiences (Wissler 1998, p. 28).

Interestingly, although relations between disputants generally did not appear to be exacerbated (Simanowitz 1998, p. 64), only a minority of actors felt that they had been ameliorated through mediation.[11] This finding is contrary to assertions about mediation's ability to repair relationships such as Lon Fuller's classic articulation of mediation that "the central quality of mediation [is] its capacity to reorient the parties toward each other... by helping them achieve a new and shared perception of their relationship... redirecting their attitudes and dispositions toward one another" (Fuller 1971, pp. 308, 325–26; Riskin 1985, p. 26; Gitchell and Plattner 1999, pp. 444–45). Yet, the present finding correlates with recent U.S. survey data on this topic. Analyses of outcomes of sixty mediated cases involving different dispute types were studied in various states. Notwithstanding a number of methodological weaknesses, the data indicated that in cases where disputants had prior relationships, mediation rarely repaired relations (Golann 2002, p. 301, 304, 331–32, 336).

The issue of lawyers' personality effects on mediations (mentioned by material numbers in all groups), including their verbal and nonverbal communication, is

---

11 No physician lawyers, 30% of hospital lawyers, 8% of plaintiff lawyers, and 13% of plaintiffs – which were those who received apologies – felt that relations had been improved. Thirty-three percent of physicians (most of whom underwent College pre-litigation mediations) felt mediation bettered relations with complainants.

further explored later together with the findings on actors changing their views about their disputes.[12] Yet these issues were only part of what emerged when legal and lay actors' recounted their mediation experiences.

6.2 Favored and disfavored mediation elements – legal actors

To best elucidate what began as over a thousand pages of data solely on recounted mediation perceptions, what each actor group considered favorable and objectionable within their mediations is examined. In addition to providing some insight into the little known area of how lawyers actually negotiate (Menkel-Meadow 1984, p. 762, n. 24), this exploration results in a picture of two worlds of perception and reality coexisting during mediations: one of legal actors and the other of lay disputants (plaintiffs in particular). Somewhere in between are mediators' understandings of "what went on." For lawyer-mediators this provides further evidence of their move away from the legal world. For example,

> "All wanted to say the things that caused them grief... They wanted to get it out. They 'feel' better... and I think that's the way mediation should be. You should facilitate the whole catharsis of them trying to get it all out." **Male, senior lawyer-mediator – voluntary – in sixties**

> "I think the greatest benefit is the emotional aspect and the transformation that can result from the parties having an opportunity to vent and to hear what each has been through... to really focus on the psychological interests of the parties... Number two is a transformation of what the parties see as the merits of their case, credibility." **Female, senior lawyer-mediator – in forties**

Favored elements

For lawyers, mediation's favored elements far outweighed those disfavored. Of greatest importance was the opportunity for direct tactical communication with all involved in the dispute. Figure 22 highlights the main findings.

Direct tactical communication

For legal actors, mediation appeared to be a key vehicle for tactical communication. There were marked similarities between lawyers' perceived mediation advantages, regardless of whom they represented. Most defense lawyers stressed the importance of communicating directly with plaintiffs (or via mediators) to highlight weaknesses or risks in their cases, litigation realities, and/or how they reached certain numbers – overall, to lower plaintiffs' expectations. This was in part because defense

---

12 Twenty-nine percent of physician lawyers, 50% of hospital lawyers, and 62% of plaintiff lawyers changed their views in some way. However, only 33% of plaintiffs did.

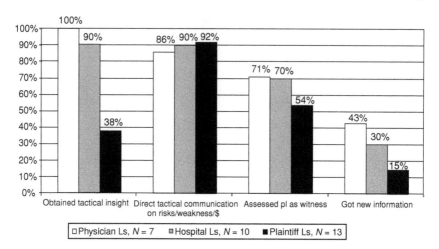

Figure 22. Mediation's favored elements – legal actors. (*Note:* "pl" stands for plaintiff and "$" for money.) Legal actors of all camps described similar tactical benefits deriving from mediation. These were very different from the benefits described by disputants.

lawyers were often dubious as to whether plaintiffs' lawyers were doing this.[13] For instance,

> "It's very helpful for plaintiffs to... see what is being said about the case... I don't know how much their counsel is communicating with them... Frankly I don't think plaintiffs' lawyers explain how cold trial is... to their clients... So I like mediation... because if they don't say it, I do." **Female physician lawyer – in thirties**

> "Mediation is my only chance probably in the whole case... to tell plaintiffs 'Here's how *litigation* works... You have to persuade us there was fault'... to recognize these are things they need to succeed. Often their lawyers never have that conversation with them... And I see lots of times at the end, they're nodding, they're agreeing with me. And suddenly their lawyer is out of the picture. So in effect, *mediation* can also act as a counterbalance to conflicting financial interests between plaintiff lawyers and plaintiffs... Lots of times I... undermine their own lawyer... It's an invaluable adversarial tool." **Male hospital lawyer – in forties**

As with defense lawyers, the vast majority of plaintiff lawyers (92%) expressed the advantage of having their clients hear directly from others at mediation about their cases' risks, weaknesses, and why it was felt their disputes were worth X amount. This was perceived as easing plaintiff attorneys' jobs vis-à-vis their clients, who tended not to want to hear these things from their own lawyers.[14] For example,

13 Eighty-six percent of physician lawyers and 90% of hospital lawyers mentioned this. Hospital lawyers also felt that having direct communication with plaintiff lawyers was advantageous. "Direct communication" was among the most utilized codes within the entire dataset.
14 These findings correlate with Macfarlane's study of commercial litigators in Ontario where frequent mediation benefits noted by lawyers related to "reality checking" for clients in hearing opponents, their counsel, and/or mediators (Macfarlane 2002, p. 263).

"Mediation was a great vehicle for... learning about risks, which was more difficult for me to tell the plaintiffs... They never felt their case had weaknesses... So there was a role for defense counsel and perhaps the mediator to help them understand that." **Male, specialist plaintiff lawyer – voluntary – in thirties**

"Most clients, no matter what their lawyer tells them, have a somewhat sugar-coated view of their situation. Coming to mediation allows them to hear... somebody else's take... The problem is that sometimes when their own lawyer tells them about weaknesses in their case, there's a tendency for them to say 'Well I didn't hire you to point out my weaknesses. You're supposed to be arguing my strengths'.... *So* I meet with a lot of resistance. At mediation... the process brings you down to maybe a little more realistic level *together*." **Male plaintiff specialist lawyer – voluntary – in fifties**

"As a way of perhaps easing the explanation to the client that there may be another side to this story... *Mediation* can be useful in your own client relations." **Male, generalist plaintiff lawyer – mandatory – in forties**

"I think usually plaintiffs come out of mediations with a greater understanding of the complexities of the case. And they see maybe it isn't all black and white." **Male, generalist plaintiff lawyer – in forties**

Defense lawyers (50%) also mentioned this benefit when their own clients attended mediation.

"Plaintiff lawyers have the same issue that we do, which is sometimes your assessment of the case is not attractive to your client... So if you can get your client to listen to opposing counsel on their position and all the difficulties they're going to face, sometimes it's helpful for your client to know you're not the only one saying the gloom and doom." **Female hospital lawyer – in twenties**

"*Being at mediation* brought home the risk to the doctor from what they've alleged, and the intensity with which they've alleged it... made it more real, not just on paper." **Male physician lawyer – fatality – mandatory – in fifties**

"At mediation my client learned probably that it would be a more difficult case to try than he had previously thought." **Female hospital lawyer – voluntary – in forties**

In addition to tactical communication, legal actors also favored obtaining various forms of strategic insight at mediations.

Obtaining strategic insight

Only a minority of attorneys discussed obtaining new information at mediation (e.g., effects of injuries on plaintiffs).[15] However, virtually all defense lawyers

---

15 Forty-three percent of physician lawyers, 30% of hospital lawyers, but only 15% of plaintiff lawyers said they learned new information at mediation. One hundred percent of defense physician lawyers and 90% of hospital lawyers compared with only 38% of plaintiff lawyers said that they obtained new insights into the disputes at mediation.

described gaining new insight into disputes. This insight related primarily to strategic intangibles such as who was "in charge" between co-plaintiffs, the internal dynamics and any lack of communication between plaintiffs and their lawyers, and learning about plaintiffs' motivations. This was irrespective of satisfaction with mediations or whether settlement ensued. For example,

> "*The mediation* was very helpful... I got a sense of who I was dealing with, the plaintiffs or their lawyer. That's helpful for my strategy as to what's going to happen next... It was very helpful for me to know that this woman could never handle trial... It made me realise that... if I can't get the right number, I'll go to trial and they'll have to cave because she can't handle it. It's all very crass to say it that way, but it's a huge tactical benefit for me... I also saw the dynamic between the plaintiff spouses, and I *now* know her husband is very reasonable. That's also important to know, who in the piece is the soft person." **Female physician lawyer – mandatory – surgical error case – in thirties**

> "I obtained more information than I had when I walked in... I knew that what they were saying to me is what they were going to say in the box at trial... So I knew the approach they were going to take... That's a benefit that probably accrues more to the defense than to plaintiffs." **Male physician lawyer – voluntary – in fifties**

> "Sometimes we don't know if our problem is the lawyer or the client, or a combination. You're able to sort that our fairly quickly at mediation... *and* get a sense of who's the real decision-maker." **Female hospital lawyer – in forties**

> "You're always gaining more knowledge about your opponent's case... your strengths, weaknesses... I want to find out as much as I can. It might help me ultimately win the case... So I'm not there innocently just trying to resolve it. That's my primary objective. But if I can't, I want to learn as much as possible... to give me a leg up if we are going to fight it out." **Male hospital lawyer – in forties**

Comparing the insights described by legal versus nonlegal, non-disputant actors at the same mediations foreshadowed the later findings on the diversity of mediation perceptions between those in the legal world and litigants outside it. For instance, in the child operation case,

> "WHAT DO YOU FEEL YOUR SIDE GOT OUT OF MEDIATION... A chance to see them and hear the family's story... Viewing them more as a mom and dad... How they talked about their son... *rather* than angry parents out to get something... And to tell them that we've taken it seriously and to have that dialogue with them... and to apologize... They said that meant the most to them." **Female hospital representative (nonlawyer) – in forties**

In contrast,

> "It was useful to hear the emotional underpinnings of their experience... to make a credibility call on what was likely motivating them, emotion versus money... I

understood the dynamic between the parents better... I think the father was... dominant... He was the one that had to be convinced if they were going to sign off on this... and that was something I didn't fully appreciate... I also appreciated that the optics of the event were such that... if we were to go to trial, they appeared genuine and credible. So I learned that." **Male physician lawyer – in forties**

Similarly, in the vasectomy case,

"They could not afford another *child*... It became also a religious issue. They both are practicing Catholics... They had done this horrible thing that goes against everything they believe... This came out in mediation when the husband spoke." **Female non-lawyer-mediator – in thirties**

"We heard a lot about the abortion, and how that affected them... *But* it was interesting to watch... the whole dynamics between the plaintiffs... It has given us a bit of a theory of the case... He has no idea what happened... So we learned stuff." **Female hospital lawyer – in twenties**

A further important aspect of the mediation "insight" defense lawyers described related to evaluating plaintiffs through seeing and hearing them, in order to assess how they would be perceived at witnesses should cases continue to trial.[16] Importantly, only 13% of plaintiffs mentioned being aware that this was occurring while they recounted the consequences of the tragedies they endured. Lawyers' assessments of parties may have assisted in precipitating earlier settlements or abandonment of cases, with lower legal costs. Hence, they need not be regarded as sinister. However, for analytical purposes, I termed this phenomenon "the red riding hood syndrome," reflecting disputants' needs to tell their stories at mediation simultaneously feeding into lawyers' concomitant needs to obtain strategic information at mediation.

"The whole point of the mediation *was* for the plaintiff to tell us... and for us to assess... what her damages really were... *and* how we think she would do as a witness should this go to trial." **Female hospital lawyer – in twenties – near-death case – mandatory**

"Plaintiffs explaining at mediation why they need to be compensated... really has a huge impact... If you think your case is iffy on liability and you see this person who's a very sympathetic person... it's going to have an impact on how aggressively you're going to defend." **Female hospital lawyer – in twenties**

"If the other party conduct themselves horribly in terms of how they might fare as a witness, then I suppose I've learned something." **Male physician lawyer – in forties**

---

16 Seventy-one percent of physician lawyers, 70% of hospital lawyers, and 54% of plaintiff lawyers mentioned this.

Most plaintiff lawyers also referred to their clients being "assessed" but often as an advantageous tactical tool for them. For instance,

> "The best part of mediation is to... allow the person that's making the settlement decision see the plaintiffs, understand their concerns, hear their emotions... to see they are well-spoken, presentable, make a sympathetic impression... will do well at trial. That is very important in presenting the case... I always ask plaintiffs to speak... on how this has affected them or speak to an issue that I know the other side wants to hear." **Male, specialist plaintiff lawyer – in thirties**

The child fatality voluntary mediation highlights well the red riding hood syndrome.

> "It was a very warm, caring experience for me... THE TWO LAWYERS... I felt their compassion and their caring. And that was healing for me." **Female plaintiff – mother – in fifties**

> "It was a terrible loss they suffered... It's sad to listen to parents speak of hopes and dreams they had for their child and then talk about the pain and anguish they've suffered in the years since he died. DOES IT AFFECT THE DEFENSE? Oh ya, but not in an emotional way... I would say to my clients 'This is my view as to how this is going to play in front of a jury... my view as to how credible these people are going to be as witnesses'." **Male physician lawyer – in thirties**

Similarly, in the fatality do not resuscitate (DNR) case-mandatory mediation,

Female hospital lawyer – in twenties

> I got new insights on what happened *and* an opportunity to evaluate the credibility of the plaintiffs and the physician.

Male physician lawyer – in fifties

> I got advance discovery. I got a sense of who these people were... and how to approach them strategically... Most important from our side was that it's clear the plaintiffs aren't about to be reasoned out of their belief system... and that their motivations for this lawsuit are largely emotional, but money is also a factor.

Plaintiff – widow – in seventies

> I spoke for a long time... I told them everything... I wanted to say for over a year... How I was hurt, how I felt my husband was neglected... I am very happy that I explained... I would like that they explained what happened... There should be questions and answers. Maybe we would have achieved something.

Plaintiff – son – in forties

> I had my three minutes of glory... I made my point... and I feel good... I said my father had told me "I want to live to see your wedding, my grandchildren"... I think mediation was a great thing to have... It would have been a lot better if we would have had an open forum... I wanted to confront *them*. But I was also looking forward to getting an answer back... The lawyer wouldn't let him answer... I thought we would have had a heart to heart, the two of us.

These findings support Menkel-Meadow's argument that U.S. lawyers as advocates try to manipulate mediation processes to achieve conventional party maximization goals (Menkel-Meadow 1991, p. 5; 1997a, p. 408). Interestingly, the fact that the strategic assessment of disputants (particularly plaintiffs) had a direct affect on defense lawyers' strategies, including whether or how much they would offer in settlement, highlights the reality that the results of many mediated cases on the litigation track may turn on issues completely outside the law. Likewise, lawyers' disfavored elements at mediation had more to do with strategy than law. Yet they also had material effects on mediation experiences and case results.

Objectionables

As for objectionable elements within mediations, interestingly defense lawyers did not mention much other than not having adequate information prior to certain mandatory mediations. For plaintiff lawyers, there was one main objectionable factor: the uneven flow of information. Most plaintiff lawyers did not feel they obtained any new information from the defense at mediation (85%), with the majority also stressing defense lawyers' guardedness (54%). Likewise, as compared with virtually all defense lawyers, only a minority of plaintiff lawyers (38%) felt they learned new insights at mediation (Figure 22). This was primarily through hearing their own clients speak or hearing evaluative mediators' views. Defendants' (and/or their lawyers') relative silence at many litigation-linked mediations was recurrent in the interview and observation data, particularly as compared with College (pre-litigation) mediations. This finding was similar to that in Metzloff et al.'s research in North Carolina, where doctors were mostly passive during joint sessions (Metzloff 1997, p. 125). For example,

> "There was not a lot of information coming from the other side at mediation. The plaintiffs didn't get any new information from the defense... The physician said very little. I mean it was so little, I can't remember anything of any significance that he said." **Male, specialist plaintiff lawyer – in forties – fatality – mandatory**

> "A lot of lawyers don't let their parties talk at mediation." **Male, senior lawyer-mediator – in sixties – voluntary**

> "It's not like you get any statements out of the doctors because they sit there, silent as dummies because their lawyers tell them not to talk. WAS THAT THE CASE HERE? Always the case... that's been true for virtually all of the mediations I've been to where a doctor was present. They're window dressing... Clearly the doctor was told "you leave it up to the lawyer"... The doctor didn't communicate anything. He sat and stared... *after* the plaintiff told him what he thought... occasionally whispered something to his lawyer. And the lawyer would make a comment... If the doctor spoke, I'd find out information. But because there seems to be this rule that you sit there quietly and your lawyer will speak for you, there isn't that much tactical benefit to the plaintiff." **Male, generalist plaintiff lawyer – in forties – mandatory**

"Where the doctor was there, the lawyer did all the talking." **Male hospital lawyer – voluntary – in forties**

"I was a little bit surprised because the impression I was given by *my lawyer* is that I would not be requested to answer questions, and that my position will be just listening and observing." **Male defendant physician – in fifties – mandatory – fatality**

"I do a lot of these mediations with doctors... I have only good experiences... Once the lawyers are involved I find doctors do not communicate." **Female non-lawyer court-linked voluntary/mandatory/College mediator – in forties**

This state of affairs was exacerbated further when defendants did not attend mediations, as doctors' mere presence resulted in at least some insight or information being obtained by the plaintiffs' side (*chapter four*).

"We put our theory of liability straight on the table... What the doctor's theory of liability is, I have no clue." **Male, specialist plaintiff lawyer – infant fatality – mandatory – defendant absent – in forties**

"DO PLAINTIFFS OBTAIN TACTICAL ADVANTAGES? No, not usually. Occasionally a mediator will ask a question or make a statement that might remind you that something could be done to better prepare your case... Generally, I feel vulnerable at mediation in that sometimes in order to effectively present your case... you're tipping off... the defense. And generally the physician lawyers give away very little." **Male, specialist plaintiff lawyer – defendant absent – in fifties – voluntary**

Defense lawyers' failure to provide information to plaintiffs' sides at mediation appeared to have been related, at least in part, to their lack of faith in mediation's confidentiality (*chapter five*). Thus, the unequal information flow at mediation may simply have been another consequence of strategy (something little mentioned by disputants). Nevertheless, it was striking that all legal actors (regardless of allegiances, cases, or mediation types) spoke of the positive and negative attributes of mediations utilizing the same paradigm. Lawyers' tendency to take control, disregarding litigants' empowerment and underlying needs (Currie 1998, p. 220) and instead offering their own perceptions of litigation and court realities (Welsh 2004b, pp. 137, 139), can be viewed as distorting informalism and mediation's original ideals (Thornton 1989, p. 756; Welsh 2001a, pp. 788–89, 791–92). Nevertheless, a very different picture of mediation emerged when speaking to disputants.

6.3 Favored and disfavored mediation elements – disputants

Disputants' spoke of favorable and objectionable elements within mediations utilizing a very different paradigm to that of legal actors. With their disparate conceptions of the meaning of mediation, few plaintiffs discussed anything tactical. Observation data offered some insight into how two worlds could coexist concurrently during mediations. For example, in the hospital fall-fatality voluntary mediation, the plaintiffs' side read out a personal and posthumous statement, which included, "We lost our mother after watching her suffer for three years. We want the nurse to know she changed our lives profoundly forever." The female plaintiff (in forties) described mediation as,

> "It's our voices, and it was our mother... It was good because it gives them a chance to hear us, instead of our lawyer. They don't know how we feel, really. Only we can express that... So it was much more personal."

Yet at the same time, the observation notes of their mediation highlighted how the dispute swiftly altered in its very nature from being personal to the family to being an impersonal legal actors' confrontation as soon as the lawyers moved rooms to caucus with the mediator privately. This helped to explain the very different version of the same mediation described by the hospital lawyer. She said, "What we were really discussing *at mediation* were issues around assessment of damages... *and* resolve a lot of... technical... and causation issues."

Overall, the data on disputants' favored and disfavored mediation elements suggested that legal and lay actors experienced the same mediations quite differently.

Favored elements

Disputants' views of litigation-track mediation were less favorable to those of lawyers. This appears to have been linked to parties' expectations and objectives for the process (*see chapter five*).[17] Only 53% of plaintiffs felt they received acknowledgments of their harm (including three who received apologies – speaking positively about them), which most sought. Moreover, most claimants did not receive the fault admissions, apologies, or answers they were seeking at mediation. Likewise, the bulk of disputants did not feel they learned any new information (80% of plaintiffs; 89% of physicians).[18] Most, however, did speak of obtaining new insights (60% plaintiffs; 89% physicians). The insights plaintiffs described related to litigation risks and weaknesses in their cases as articulated by defense lawyers, the power of defense lawyers, and "realistic" financial expectations as articulated by mediators. Nevertheless, only 33% of plaintiffs said they changed their views about their disputes. None changed their views about the incidents that precipitated their claims. These findings offer insight into disputants' perspectives in terms of how they perceive information provided to them during mediations – something little spoken of in the literature.[19] Consequently, the most talked about mediation

---

17 Interestingly, in noting the lack of research on parties' expectations and objectives for mediation and possible links to their subsequent mediation experiences, Wissler similarly found that parties' assessments of the process were overall less favorable to those of lawyers (Wissler 2002, p. 691).
18 Similarly, in Wissler's study of mandatory mediation of general civil cases in nine Ohio courts – deriving primarily from questionnaire data from lawyers, parties, and mediators – mediation was found to only "moderately" improve disputants' understandings of their cases and of opponents' views (Wissler 2002, pp. 642, 644–46, 664, 692).
19 In Metzloff et al.'s North Carolina study, it was similarly found that mediators often impressed on disputants the risks inherent in trials in order to deflate expectations. However, although based

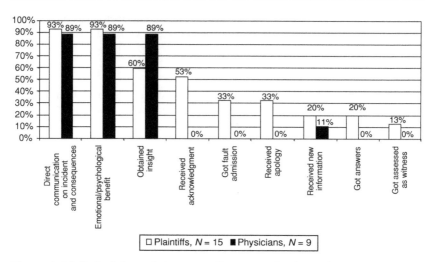

Figure 23. Mediation's favored elements – disputants. The things disputants favored at mediations bore little resemblance to those favored by legal actors. The bulk of disputants spoke of extralegal communication, emotional and psychological relief, receiving acknowledgments, and obtaining insight. However, most plaintiffs did not receive the answers, apologies, or admissions they sought.

advantage related to disputants expressing themselves to opponents (i.e., "being heard") and the emotional and psychological relief it brought. Figure 23 sets out the main findings on disputants' favored mediation elements.

In recounting mediation experiences, 93% of plaintiffs and 89% of physicians discussed the importance of expressing themselves and "being heard." This illustrated plaintiffs' need to communicate with and effectively provide information to defendants and/or their lawyers. Additionally, most plaintiffs (73%) said they corrected misinformation at mediations. For cases that did not settle, plaintiffs recurrently mentioned that being heard was probably the best thing that happened at mediation.

Despite evidence that mediation was more difficult emotionally for female versus male plaintiffs (see Section 6.4), this finding – which applied equally to males and females – questions Grillo's assertion that mediation can be detrimental to women in that it requires them to talk in a setting they have not chosen (Grillo 1991, pp. 1549–50). Indeed, the opportunity to tell one's story and express one's views is a powerful factor in people perceiving procedures as just. Feelings of justness and fairness as well as process control are enhanced in dispute resolution processes where parties additionally feel that those in power are giving due consideration to their perspectives and views (Lind and Tyler 1988, pp. 101, 106, 215–16). The

on observations and survey data of lawyers and mediators, their findings did not include data from litigants themselves (Metzloff et al. 1997, pp. 109, 117, 122).

need for disputants to communicate their stories, be "heard," and the resulting positive therapeutic benefits have been found in various studies.[20] For instance, in Wissler's research involving 144 civil cases that underwent voluntary and mandatory mediation, the "opportunity to express oneself" was among the criteria plaintiffs used to judge their mediations (Wissler 1997, pp. 567, 582, 598). The following quotes are illustrative of this finding:

"WHAT WAS THE MOST IMPORTANT THING FOR YOU... I was there and able to express. That is the key. That becomes your forum." **Male physician defendant – fatality – College – in fifties**

"I needed to be there. I wanted to have a voice... I needed to be able to share my pain. I didn't think they would really understand if I couldn't have shared my words." **Female plaintiff – in fifties – child fatality case – voluntary**

"It's important that you be heard, even if it doesn't affect the overall thing. That's your chance to get it all out... I mean, had I been in court and wasn't allowed to say some of the things, it would have been less sense of satisfaction... even if we'd have gotten more money... I wanted somebody to hear it." **Female plaintiff – voluntary – hospital fall – fatality case – in forties**

"I had psychological relief because our side was being heard... Whatever little time we spent there, at least we got our point across... Even though nothing got resolved, it was important that at least they understood." **Female plaintiff – in thirties – vasectomy mediation – mandatory**

"I wanted to speak. Yes. Because it was in here and I wanted to get it out." **Male co-plaintiff – loss-of-sight case – voluntary – in fifties**

Consequently, regardless of views on mediation experiences or results, all plaintiffs said it was important for them to have participated. This was consistent with Mulcahy's findings in Britain (Mulcahy 1999; Mulcahy et al. 2000, pp. 75–79), where notwithstanding emotional difficulties, all plaintiffs wanted to attend mediation. However interestingly, not all legal actors appreciated the importance of mediation participation and "voice" for plaintiffs. For instance,

"WHAT DO YOU THINK YOUR CLIENT GOT OUT OF MEDIATION, IF ANYTHING Besides money? YA. Oh, I don't think she got anything *else*. I'd like to think there was something beneficial to be involved. But it's not usual that I say 'Gee, they're happy they were involved'." **Male, specialist plaintiff lawyer – in fifties**

Despite mediation's advantages for disputants, there were some elements of mediations that disputants found objectionable.

---

20 Pennebaker (1995, p. 6), Des Rosiers et al. (1998, pp. 433, 435, 438), and Welsh (2004, pp. 595, 619–20, 666, 671, 820).

Objectionables

Plaintiffs were often more critical of their mediation experiences than legal actors. This was not surprising, considering plaintiffs' articulated mediation aims (*chapter five*, figure 15), which were regularly not met. Other than defendants' absences and the values of settlements or offers, there were two main objectionable elements of mediation for plaintiffs: lack of information and negative aspects of mediation's transparency, including issues of hierarchy, the focus on money, and nonverbal communication from defense lawyers.

Unequal information flow:

> The requirement that both sides of the conflict should be equally heard always needs to be stressed because it is not obviously guaranteed, as it is in a court of law (Hampshire 1999, p. 90).

As with their lawyers, plaintiffs recurrently stated they had not received any information or the answers they sought at mediation. This was irrelevant of whether mediations were mandatory or voluntary. For instance,

> "WHEN THEY PUT FORWARD THEIR SIDE, HOW DID YOU FEEL? They didn't put anything forward. They didn't have anything to say." **Male plaintiff – voluntary mediation – fatality – in fifties**

> "IF YOU COULD CHANGE ANYTHING... I'd make it compulsory for the opposing side to tell their story... I wanted to hear their side of it in order for there to be justice... closure... to see where they are coming from... If I know where they're coming from, I will more understand them... But when there's absolutely nothing at all coming from them... " **Male co-plaintiff – in fifties – loss-of-sight case – voluntary**

> "They really didn't say very much." **Plaintiff – mother – child fatality – voluntary mediation – in fifties**

Whether physician defendants attended mediations also seemed to have little effect.

> "The doctor didn't say much. So I didn't learn much. I wanted him to speak... I wanted his explanation... But he didn't explain... He didn't respond." **Male plaintiff – in forties – mandatory – bladder operation case – defendant present**

> "I thought mediation would be a total open forum. Like, I got a question, you answer my question... You want to ask me anything, I can ask you anything... That's what I wanted... But I felt it was just a one way flux of information... from our side, and then limited information was coming back... The doctor spoke so briefly... He could have told me what transpired... Give me a brief synopsis. Tell me 'something...' If we had an open forum... maybe the two sides would grasp better... That's what we're all here about. We're here to rectify our problems." **Male plaintiff – in forties – fatality – mandatory – defendant present**

"The question isn't merely about money... These mediations like, you're just there trying to settle. There's no answers.... Why did I have to be put through this?... I wasn't given no answers, nothing... I wanted to hear their side... Whatever explanation they had would give me a little bit of ease." **Male plaintiff – in thirties – vasectomy case – mandatory – defendant absent**

Observation notes from another mandatory mediation with the defending physician present confirmed this trend. The doctor did not speak at all throughout the joint sessions, while the legal actors did most of the talking. Interestingly, defense lawyers said little about the "information flow" issue. Instead, some explained,

"Even if the doctor is there, I wouldn't want him or her to be saying much. I'll speak for you and I'll communicate the hurt you're feeling if you need it communicated. I'll communicate my position for the doctor, and I think I'll do a better job of it in any event... The doctors can't communicate that as well as an objective someone sitting beside them... The more emotional somebody is, the less likely I am to recommend they open their mouth... Not because I'm afraid they're going to say the wrong thing. But because I don't think it's going to be productive... Because this isn't an opportunity for them to feel better." **Female physician lawyer – in thirties**

"As a lawyer [he chuckles], I like the evaluative approach where the doctor is participating silently with his/her own counsel as an active force in the process." **Male physician lawyer – in forties**

Although plaintiffs in the present study did participate during mediations to various degrees, this finding for defendants in litigation-track mediations accords with U.S. knowledge, where in the few studies that mediation observations were conducted, it was found that parties were generally little involved in the process (Hensler 2003, p. 192). This problem for plaintiffs was compounded by other things they saw and heard during mediations.

Negative transparency effects of mediation:

Performers... must take care... lest the audience impute unintended meanings *to their performances* (Goffman 1971, p. 73).

A second prominent perceived negative element of mediation for parties related to issues consequential to mediation's transparency, offering disputants a rare view into the legal world of strategy and money. A paucity of in-depth empirical data exists on disputants' perceptions of the negotiating elements inherent within case processing (Relis 2002, pp. 174–77). Therefore, the findings here on the effects of mediation's transparency for litigants, allowing more visible settlement procedures, are particularly important in adding to the knowledge in this area.

Hierarchy

First, most plaintiffs (53%) discussed perceiving a social hierarchy at mediations. This was especially prevalent in mediations without defendant physicians present, where plaintiffs were enclosed in rooms surrounded by lawyers who had nothing personal to lose.

> "I felt small." **Female plaintiff – in thirties – mandatory**

> "If I was... at the same prestigious level of a lawyer or a surgeon... I think they would be a little bit more concerned... Unfortunately that's the thing I got from mediation... I just feel there's hierarchy at that whole mediation thing." **Male plaintiff – in thirties – mandatory**

> "We have a saying in Jamaica, 'Hold down and take away'. The stronger man holds the weak man down and takes away from him. That's the impression I got. They have the power. So we have to surrender to the *lawyers*." **Male plaintiff – in fifties – voluntary**

One plaintiff did not perceive hierarchical issues as negative.

> "I felt nice because I *had* three guys around me. They are professionals, and just me alone. I *am not* a professional... So the guys *are* more intelligent than me... The mediator as well. Everybody listened... I had a good feeling." **Male plaintiff – mandatory – in forties**

The focus on money

Most plaintiffs (53%) also noted negative learning experiences relating to how their disputes were handled by lawyers. Mediation made transparent to them the disparity of what their cases meant to them as compared with what they meant to the legal actors involved. For example,

> "DID MEDIATION AFFECT THE PLAINTIFFS' UNDERSTANDING OF THE CASE? Negatively, yes. They think it's a game. That's what the dad said. 'This is just a game'." **Male, specialist lawyer – in forties – infant fatality case – mandatory**

> "It's almost a little bit of a game." **Female plaintiff – in forties – parent fatality – voluntary**

> "The damage that has been done to my wife, no money can ever repay her for it. It hurts me, having to see these lawyers at mediation, how they take it very lightly to the extent where it's just dollars and cents. It's much more than dollars and cents. It's my wife's eyes... Money cannot heal emotion, scars. Money cannot bring real contentment. You know, apologize, say something... There are other things attached to this thing." **Husband – co-plaintiff – loss-of-sight case – voluntary – in fifties**

> "It becomes a competition... like 'Ok, we'll start at a thousand dollars; we'll start at forty'... I'm like 'It's not about the money. It's about the principles, where you didn't apologize to us, and I don't want this to happen to somebody else'... It infuriated me... EVEN THOUGH YOU SETTLED? Ya... It's insulting... They just want to get it over with. 'Okay, how much can we give you... You know your legal fees will be...' I shouldn't care about how much my lawyer's bills are. It should be about the principle. It should be about what they are supposed to pay me... It's not about legal fees. It's

about somebody being accountable for their actions and what they've done... Let's make sure they don't screw up and then we don't have to go to court." **Male plaintiff – in thirties – child operation case – mandatory**

> "The truth of what really happened, and how we can change it and make it right *was my aim*. But that's not what mediation is about... My experience was that it was deciding on what dollars... I didn't know that until I was very near the end of the process. Then it became very, very clear." **Female plaintiff – in fifties – child fatality – voluntary**

Cobb's research into community mediations found that discourse in mediation resulted in victims' rights being transformed into needs, with relationships being framed as monetary arrangements. In examining a break-in and rape case, Cobb describes how the focus at mediation moved from the violence to the cost of the screen through which the attacker came. Consequently, Cobb argues that "mediation processes contribute to the erasure of any competing morality by folding that competing morality into the morality of mediation itself" (Cobb 1997, pp. 397, 400–401).

It could be argued that the conflicting interests and desires of lawyers and disputants (Kritzer 1998, p. 796) resulted in things being offered to plaintiffs at mediation in ways that often did not deal with their needs as they perceived them. The current findings also provide evidence supporting procedural justice research that litigants can view negotiations that concentrate on money alone as trivializing issues of importance to them (Lind et al. 1990, pp. 965–67), negatively affecting perceptions of procedural justice.[21] Thus, as Menkel-Meadow argues, in negotiating solutions to cases lawyers must look beyond the money demanded to ascertain what parties' "real" needs and aims are (Menkel-Meadow 1984, pp. 760, 771, n. 72).

The DNR-fatality-mandatory mediation illustrates well the transparency phenomenon and makes evident the clash between the legal and extralegal worlds at mediation.

Male plaintiff specialist lawyer – in forties

> I told the mediator "Counsel for the defense and I have discussed this matter. These are the issues. It's a difficult point of law... It probably has to be litigated, and we're not going to be able to do very much here." Her response was "Well, have you looked at the human cost of litigating this issue out?" That's a fair question. I went to close my notebook, and the mediator then turned to my client and said "Can you tell me how the death of your husband made you feel." And two hours later we were still there... We heard a lot of valid, but largely human interest information from the plaintiffs, which really didn't cut the knot, which was the legal issue that needed to be determined... at trial.

---

21 Welsh (2001a, p. 860). Interestingly, in Merry's research of small claims litigants and their court and mediation experiences, she similarly found that their consciousness of law and the legal system changed subsequent to their experiences in the legal system in terms of how they spoke of rights and entitlements. This occurred after litigants observed contradictions between what happened to them and what they expected from the legal system (Merry 1990a, pp. 5, 170).

Plaintiff – son – in forties

> The two lawyers started going on their own little thing about legalities, which really didn't matter... We wanted to have our own format... They're pulling out little verses "X versus Y"... I respect my lawyer and everything he's done, but it doesn't make a difference about his legalities... The lawyers, forget them. Let them be there, but let the two people ask each other questions... That should have happened... We could have resolved all that right there. This is my father we're talking about. This is our family. There's not a dollar value to it. Why don't you say you're sorry, come clean and walk away?

Female non-lawyer court-assigned mediator – in forties

> I asked them to talk about the human costs around this. There was a whole other story that came out *than what was on the documents*... This was not about money... I really believed that if the doctor had a chance to really explain... what he was trying to do... that the money would have just fallen away... The parties appeared to be genuinely interested in settlement... But I'm not so sure about their lawyers... There was a legal point the lawyers were thinking would be really fun to take to the courts... I asked who's going to be paying for that legal point? What is this really all about?... We totally missed what we were really there about. To me, it was to create some healing between the physician and family. And that didn't happen.

Defense lawyers' nonverbal communication

Although less mentioned by legal actors,[22] a final aspect of mediation's transparency related to most plaintiffs' (87%) perceptions of defense lawyers' nonverbal communication (see Figure 21), the majority viewing it negatively (53%). As Goffman notes, "Some unmeant gestures occur in such a wide variety of performances... A performer may accidentally convey impropriety or disrespect by momentarily... yawning, make a slip of the tongue... Secondly the performer may act in such a way as to give the impression that he is too... little concerned with the interaction" (Goffman 1971, p. 61). For example,

> "I told the doctor's lawyer my situation... and what I had gone through... And he just put his hands up like that. HOW DID YOU FEEL... Like he don't care... I'm the one that was hurt in this, but he don't care... He had no remorse... He just put up his hands, putting his eyes up in the air like 'What are we doing here'? Like 'Unless you can tell me something else, let's get out of here'.... He was so blunt." **Male plaintiff – in thirties – vasectomy case – mandatory – defendant absent**

This finding was particularly prominent in the child operation mandatory mediation.

> "I wasn't happy with mediation at all. WHAT DIDN'T YOU LIKE? The gentleman who was representing the doctor... He was just rude... very abrupt, just horrible. Even at

---

22 No physician lawyer, 50% of hospital lawyers, and 23% of plaintiff lawyers mentioned nonverbal communication.

the end, everybody shook our hands but him. He just got up and walked out... I don't think he cared either way... It seemed like we were wasting his time... *The hospital lawyer, she* seemed really apologetic... sincere... The apology meant a lot." **Plaintiff mother – in thirties**

"The doctor's lawyer was pompous and arrogant... I felt we were just annoying him, being a minor thorn in his morning, not really affecting his career... He did say at the beginning 'We're sorry but...' But it wasn't sincere. It was more like routine for him... probably his opening speech every time he sits down. Where*as* the apology from the hospital seemed sincere, and it meant a lot." **Plaintiff father – in thirties**

Interestingly, the male physician lawyer (in fifties) had only praise for the mediation.

"I thought the mediation was exactly what should have happened. It happened in the right way. And inch by inch, I thought it was excellent... The flow of the mediation moved towards being able to, you know, uh, get rid of some of the feeling and get a little more rational about what the numbers should be... I think they got an apology from the hospital that was sincere... I think that had a benefit... *though* I don't think it was at all relevant to the mediation... Maybe there was some goodwill that had some relevance to them wanting to settle it. But I doubt it had a significant role in what happened."

As most negative perceptions related to male defense lawyers' conduct, gender issues pertaining to both lawyers and disputants were subsequently examined.

6.4 Gender disparities

Notwithstanding the small numbers, perhaps the most interesting findings in the analysis of litigation-track mediation experiences relate to gendered differences between actors – both legal and lay.

Legal actors

There were gendered disparities in the way lawyers recounted mediation experiences. Most male lawyers (though not all) spoke predominantly about tactical issues when explaining what occurred at mediations. Although there were too few female plaintiff lawyers for meaningful analysis, on the defense side female lawyers more often than males spoke of plaintiffs' perspectives in describing mediations, for example, speaking about plaintiffs being heard, wanting apologies, things they said to plaintiffs to address extralegal needs, and plaintiffs' reactions. For instance,

"We explained to *the plaintiffs* why we were taking the position that things were worth certain things. We did get an opportunity at the very beginning... to explain to her that it is rather uncomfortable to sit around a table and quantify someone's loss. It's very unnatural, and it sounds terrible... And she shouldn't take offence by it. That's what the justice system has to do. But... nothing that anybody says should be taken to be an insult to her, or to be not recognizing that she has suffered. I said that to her at the beginning of mediation. I think she mildly appreciated that." **Female physician lawyer – in thirties – mandatory – operation error case**

"*To* actually listen to what *plaintiffs are* saying and try and find a way to acknowledge what they're saying without compromising your own position... It's important that we demonstrated to the plaintiffs that we're committed to listening to their concerns and we want them to listen to us." **Female hospital lawyer – in twenties – vasectomy case – mandatory**

"There was a lot of bitterness... a lot of sadness, I think, and a lot of unexplained. And they needed to be able to tell their story. We needed to be able to explain what our role was... what we were hoping to achieve at mediation... To hear this from us, as opposed to their own counsel... Often plaintiffs need to understand that a number has to be put to their suffering, to their pain... And *mediation's* the only way we have an opportunity to explain that, or to apologize." **Female hospital lawyer – in twenties – near-death case – mandatory**

Female defense lawyers' sensitivity during mediations was remarked on by 40% of plaintiffs, whereas only 13% of plaintiffs mentioned this in relation to male lawyers. For instance,

"The lawyer did apologize ahead of time for anything that she may say that would upset us... She didn't want us to feel bad about anything. I think that was important too." **Female plaintiff – in forties – voluntary**

"What was nice too... was the hospital lawyer mentioned she had just lost her *family member*. And she talked about it. It was like she had some understanding of what it's like... She had compassion." **Female plaintiff – in fifties – voluntary**

In comparison, 27% of plaintiffs remarked on male defense lawyers' insensitivity during mediations. This was never mentioned about female attorneys. For instance, in the loss-of-sight voluntary mediation,

"They don't care. It's obvious they did not... from what the lawyer didn't say. All he said was... 'We are here to sign a check'." **Male plaintiff – in fifties**

"MOST IMPORTANT THING AT MEDIATION? Well, perhaps ego gets in the way, but that the plaintiffs would see me and perhaps walk away with the impression that they may not want to see me in a courtroom." **Male physician lawyer – in fifties**

This was recurrent over a number of cases involving male lawyers alone. For example,

"At mediation the physician lawyer offered us a settlement called a 'nuisance value'... If he thinks that's a nuisance, my father's death... You know, you could have used better terminology. Say 'This is the only money allowed in our budget'. Everyone has a value.

It doesn't matter what your age is. And he's telling me my father has no value to his life... If people have compassion, then the rest will all just fall *away*." **Male plaintiff – in forties – parent fatality – mandatory**

"*The defense lawyers*... they didn't want to hear my story... They don't want to spend too much time listening to you. I got that sense... from them that it was difficult for them... painful... to even... listen to me... what it was like. It's like... they're just looking at the wound and then getting a dollar sign... Men especially, they're not going to be good at that." **Female plaintiff – in fifties – child fatality – voluntary**

"They weren't about to waste time. They wanted to get to business... They were really interested in what I was expecting financially. What were the things I needed, monetarily. They weren't going into... They'd heard it all... They weren't interested in listening to me... If there had been all females around the table, they would have understood where I was coming from on a lot of issues, like where I was emotionally; and what I felt was 'really' important to me, like the fact that I had to give up babysitting my grandchildren... like walking in the woods... That was important... *in helping reach closure*... besides the fact that I'm uncomfortable... Men maybe don't get... they're not on the same wavelength... I was comfortable with them... *But* mediation is a lot more than dollars and cents." **Female plaintiff – in sixties – loss of limb – voluntary**

This finding supports Kolb and Coolidge's work, which notes that whilst both sexes tend to equally be able to recognize others' feelings, females – generally found to be more empathetic than males – should have an advantage in eliciting negotiating partners' interests and intentions as they tend to be more personally responsive (Kolb and Coolidge 1988, p. 7). Indeed, the skills of empathy, conflict management, and cooperation are thought to be advantageous in negotiations (Kolb 2000, p. 348).

The findings here also correlate with Tannen's sociolinguistic work on gender. Tannen's work illustrates gender differences inherent in conversational styles and suggests that most women speak and hear a language of connection and rapport whereas most men listen and communicate in a language of independence and status preservation through exhibiting knowledge and skill. Thus, the same scene can appear and be interpreted very differently by different genders. In drawing on Tannen's research, Menkel-Meadow posits that women, who use emotional language and articulate needs with ease, might actually be better at "mediation talk" than some men (Tannen 1990, pp. 13, 38, 42, 77; Menkel-Meadow 1997b, p. 1427).[23] More generally, utilizing Gilligan's findings, Menkel-Meadow

---

23 Other studies have similarly found differences in female versus males' communication styles, with women being more collaborative and men more quickly resorting to legal categories (Davis 1991, p. 1676; Evans 2001, p. 164; Payne 2001, pp. 104–12). In contrast, Bogoch's small-scale analysis of seven lawyer–client conversations in Israel found little difference between male and female lawyers' speech patterns (Bogoch 1997, pp. 677, 683, 705). However, her research focused solely on lawyers and their own clients.

additionally suggests that females' different moral reasoning to males, being more often motivated by an ethic of care rather than a more abstract, individual rights-based stance to case resolution, may result in women having a greater natural inclination for mediation and a greater sense of empathy with the opposing side (Gilligan 1982, pp. 25–29; Menkel-Meadow 1985, pp. 43, 52–53). Others too have speculated (but noted the lack of empirical evidence) that women may be temperamentally better suited to mediation than males (Subrin 2003, pp. 207–8) and may be more sensitive to contextual issues such as relational facets of disputes for parties, despite this often conflicting with their professional education and adversarial training (Menkel-Meadow 1987, p. 45; 1994a, p. 639; Stempel 2003, pp. 310–11; Klein 2005, pp. 772, 777, 792). The present findings offer empirical evidence from participating actors themselves in support of these views.

The gender findings on legal actors were paralleled by those relating to plaintiffs.

Plaintiffs

There were five main gender disparities in plaintiffs' discourse on what transpired during mediations and the negotiations inherent within them, offering insight into how males and females experience the process. First, the data highlighted females' greater emotional needs for mediation than males. Yet, this was accompanied by female plaintiffs more often than males experiencing emotional difficulties in undergoing mediation, as well as females' greater sensitivity to others' perceptions at mediations.[24] Additionally, the data indicated that female plaintiffs were more accepting of what went on during mediations, while being less astute than males as to what was occurring tactically. Overall, the data support several aspects of the literature on informal dispute resolution process dangers for women (Grillo 1991, pp. 1602–4). Figure 24 sets out the findings.

First, in speaking of their mediation experiences, most females (67%) but no males mentioned fears or worries prior to mediation. At the same time, as foreshadowed in chapter five, in discussing what transpired at mediations female plaintiffs more often than males mentioned their emotional need for the psychological and emotional elements of the process (89% of females versus 17% of males). However, once at mediation the data suggested that the process was more emotionally arduous for women than for men. All females' discourse (100%) included references to mediation being emotionally difficult for them in some respects. This was virtually absent from males' discourse. The following case studies involving co-plaintiffs illustrate these gender findings.

---

24 This was found in similar proportions in chapter five when plaintiffs spoke about their aims for mediation.

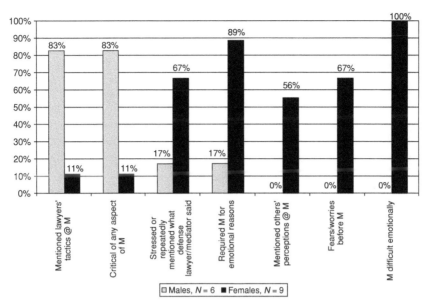

Figure 24. Plaintiffs' gender disparities at mediation. (*Note:* "M" stands for mediation.) The gender data on plaintiffs' experiences in mediation showed marked differences between males and females, highlighting females' greater emotional needs for mediation coupled with their greater emotional difficulties in undergoing mediation. Females were also more accepting of whatever occurred and less tactically aware than males of what went on.

Child fatality mediation – voluntary – settled

"HOW DID YOU FEEL PRIOR TO MEDIATION? I had no problem with it... I had no concerns whatsoever... From my perspective *mediation* was an information gathering." **Plaintiff – father – in fifties**

"I met fear... a little scary for me. So you just pray before going in... Your pain and the consequences of this is big... I knew my husband would have the most to say, and that was ok... It took me about three days after the mediation *to come out of grief*, even though it's a good process. So I'm caught in this pain cycle, and it takes me some time." **Plaintiff – mother – in fifties**

"The husband was enthusiastic *to attend*. She, I believe... probably didn't want to come... She's had trouble re-living this... The husband was more comfortable... with the process." **Specialist plaintiff lawyer – male – in fifties**

Vasectomy dispute mediation – mandatory – not settled

"I wasn't at all nervous. No.... ANY FEARS OR WORRIES BEFORE? No... DID YOU SPEAK? Yes... I was the only one speaking." **Male co-plaintiff – in thirties**

"HOW INVOLVED WERE YOU? Um, not very involved, because, I guess I was scared, and I didn't know what to say... Even though I didn't say anything, I think they must have known how much it hurt... DID YOU SPEAK AT ALL? No, I didn't because... I couldn't... because if I did [long pause]. DID YOU WANT TO?... Ya, I would have liked to, but I was too nervous. It was emotional... Having them talk about you, just like a knife went through your heart... But it was important for me to attend, even though nothing got solved." **Female co-plaintiff – in thirties**

The degree to which disputants participate and raise issues of personal importance to them is critical in mediation (Metzloff et al. 1997, p. 123). Thus, despite most plaintiffs (93%) ultimately discussing the importance of expressing themselves or being heard (Figure 23), these gender findings provide a more nuanced understanding of the opportunities provided by mediation as compared with formal adversarial processes in terms of allowing all disputants to tell their stories. Likewise, they question unqualified assertions that mediation environments accord with women's strengths, empowering them and allowing them to speak on their own terms (McCabe 2001, pp. 459–60, 471). Similar to the present findings, in Pearson and Thoennes divorce mediation research, notwithstanding both sexes being positive and "satisfied" overall with mediation (including mandatory mediation), women more often than men reported concerns about the process, feeling ill at ease in expressing their feelings during mediations, and more frequently felt pressured by opponents. In comparison, males felt relaxed and comfortable (Pearson and Thoennes 1988, pp. 440–41, 449).

The present findings might be explained by Tannen's sociolinguistic research that suggests that females are most comfortable talking when they feel safe among friends and equals. Whereas men feel comfortable speaking when there is a need to establish and preserve their status in groups. Tannen also found that most women preferred to settle disputes without direct confrontation, whereas many males viewed confrontation positively as necessary in order to negotiate their status.[25] Thus, this finding suggests that women may not be taking full advantage of mediation's opportunity to speak for themselves and share their experiences (McCabe 2001, pp. 460, 472–73). This is particularly worrying, as power has been found to be manifested through language at mediation (Kandel 1994, pp. 879–88).

In line with other research suggesting that females tend to speak and advocate their positions less than males in group settings, possibly feeling they have less ability to affect results, Kolb and Coolidge posit that how individuals behave in various environments relates to how they identify the situations they are in and their "sense of place" there. Negotiation contexts, which represent opposing interests and conflict, may be perceived as "foreign" by many women as they are frequently at variance with at least certain females' qualities, values, how they speak, and how they may have been socialized. Therefore, females may feel uncomfortable in those situations. Consequently, women may be negatively impacted in terms of their abilities as negotiators to communicate their goals and interests (Kolb and

---

25 Tannen (1990, pp. 75, 94, 150). This finding accords with research into sexual violence cases where female plaintiffs felt unable or did not want to face their alleged wrongdoers, as it was too difficult for them psychologically and emotionally (Des Rosiers et al. 1998, pp. 433, 435, 438).

Coolidge 1988, pp. 6–8, 10). In fact, others have argued that as mediation becomes integrated into formal legal processes, women will suffer the same inequalities that they do in formal legal systems (Rifkin 1984, p. 22; McCabe 2001, pp. 463, 467–68).

There were also indications that female plaintiffs were more sensitive to others' perceptions during mediations.

> "Going in and thinking 'Well, what do they think? That we're after money? Do they think that money is really going to settle this type of thing, and is going to make it okay'?" **Female plaintiff – in forties – voluntary**

> "I think my lawyer was disappointed I wasn't more forceful in things at mediation." **Female plaintiff – in sixties – voluntary**

> "I sensed my lawyer's tension and his desire to settle. I think my husband only sensed it after I told him." **Female plaintiff – in fifties – voluntary**

Additionally, there was evidence that female plaintiffs were more accepting at mediations than males. Only 11% of females were critical of any aspects of their mediations as compared with 83% of males. This was especially noticeable between co-plaintiffs within the same mediations. For example,

Loss-of-sight case – voluntary mediation – not settled

Female plaintiff – in fifties

> WHAT HAPPENED? Surprisingly nothing happened. Our lawyer spoke... *My husband spoke*... DID YOU SPEAK? Um, no. YOU NEVER SPOKE? No, no... After our lawyer spoke, then my husband had the floor.
>
> The doctor's lawyer, he showed compassion... very professional. He said he sympathized with my anguish, and that sort of cushioned it... He said "Mrs... I like you a lot. And I hope not to ever see you in court"... As if to say "If I ever get you in that witness stand I'm going to tear you to shreds. You better get it resolved here because if I see you in my court, you wouldn't like me as much as you do." That was my interpretation... So I admired him... I wish he was my lawyer... DID YOU GET AN EXPLANATION? No, he didn't say much at all. It was my lawyer and my husband doing the talking.

Still, the plaintiff was pleased with the mediation experience.

> SOME PEOPLE WANT TO HAVE THEIR DAY IN COURT. My day was at the mediation. I did not need to go to court for my day. It was already there.

Male co-plaintiff – in fifties

> WHAT HAPPENED... The impression I got is that they were working on a schedule... They didn't recognize what I was saying. From when they left the office, they already knew what they were going to say and offer... And although I gave my thoughts, it's like "Forget that. This is what we have planned." It made no difference to them what I said.

> When asked to go to the other room... We were completely locked out... I felt left out... Why did we show up at this thing in the first place when we were not given the privilege to be there and hear what took place between the lawyers?... Our lawyer, he came in and said "These people are saying this..." My perception of it was that he doesn't care about us... trying to minimize the whole thing... I think he could have done a lot more... being unable to counter their theory.
>
> And the doctor's lawyer could express remorse somehow... At least it would say he's a human being... What my wife is going through, it's "real." It's not fabricated. It's a real loss... I lost the wife I had before... *But* it was like "I'm here to write a check"... They tried to appear as if they are doing a favor... If they recognized my position, they wouldn't have acted so callous*ly*. The offer and how they didn't make an apology, absolutely no remorse.

Loss-of-limb case – voluntary mediation – settled subsequently

Male physician lawyer – in forties

> DO YOU THINK MEDIATION ASSISTED THE PLAINTIFF... No, because she was kept out of the process. She came in. She was asked twenty minutes worth of questions, and then she was shuttered off to a room for the next four hours... She was told to by the mediator... At the end, they went in and talked to her about the numbers.

Male plaintiff specialist lawyer – in fifties

> I think she acquiesced to pretty much what was going on around her.

Female plaintiff – in fifties

> I guess it gave me a chance to say what I wanted to say... It was important for them to hear my side of the story... That was the most important thing that happened... *and* I felt important.
>
> There were certain things they wanted to talk about, so I went into the mediator's office. I don't know what they talked about... My lawyer said "We're going to ask you to leave," so I did. HOW DID YOU FEEL ABOUT THAT? Fine... Obviously there were things they wanted to talk about, and they didn't want me there. Heaven only knows what it was.
>
> The only thing I found negative was that I didn't know if I was giving the answers my lawyer wanted me to give.

A final difference seen between male and female plaintiffs related to their perceptions of the tactical goings-on during mediations. Male plaintiffs generally appeared to be more tactically astute in terms of legal actors' conduct during mediations. In recounting their mediation experiences, 83% of males as compared with only 11% of females spoke of defense lawyers' tactics. For instance,

> "I think they're all in fear of repercussions... that anything they say will come and fight them in future... The lawyer wouldn't let *the doctor* answer... I think both lawyers are afraid to give up information... They want to control that information

flow at mediation... Lawyers... they're keeping control of their environment... The physician lawyer is... from a large firm. So it's a power struggle between the two legal firms, who puts a notch on their belt.

The lawyers were there also... to find out exactly who's the weaker, who's going to be more vulnerable... The physician lawyer's not looking at the facts. He's looking at tactics... to see who he could prey on... because eventually when it does go to trial, 'I want to win this thing'... That's what I felt." **Male plaintiff – in forties – fatality case – mandatory (never mentioned by female co-plaintiff)**

"The surgeon's lawyer... he knew the ball was in his court and he played it to his advantage... I knew they were going to have me there and low ball us... and try and deter us from going to court, because... court costs... blah, blah... I knew how they were going to approach it." **Male plaintiff – in thirties – mandatory (never mentioned by female co-plaintiff)**

These findings resuscitate the significance of the feminist critiques of informal justice processes including mediation relating to female disputants' disempowerment. There has been much theoretical debate on the issue, principally argued in the family law arena.[26] Grillo's work has been among the most cited in this regard. Although accepting that formal processes are no better for women, Grillo argues (in the context of mandatory Californian custody mediations, though speaking of all mediation) that mediation as a process, which stresses compromise over rights, is dangerous for women or those who operate in the female mode as their relational sense to others may result in them being more acquiescing at mediations, resulting in agreements that do not serve their needs. Yet, this is masked by informal processes.[27] Thus, underlying Grillo's argument is the premise that women are too cooperative (McCabe 2001, p. 477).

Numerous family mediation studies have highlighted behavior and bargaining differences between males and females (Evans 2001, p. 147). Additionally, although no substantive gender injustice was found within mediations at the U.S. Metro Court, disputants' interviews and mediator questionnaires in 603 disparate small claims mediations suggested that female claimants tended to yield on demands earlier than males, indicating greater willingness to concede their claims.[28] However, few empirical studies have tested whether females are actually disadvantaged at mediation or whether gender differences hinder women's ability to mediate

---

26 Rifkin (1984, p. 22), Delgado et al. (1985, pp. 1360–61), Rosenberg (1991, pp. 492–93), Nader (1993, p. 4), Brinig (1995, p. 4), Cobb (1997, p. 397), Palmer and Roberts (1998, p. 139), Rack (1999, pp. 217, 224), and McCabe (2001, pp. 478, 481).
27 Gilligan (1982, pp. 62–63), Grillo (1991, pp. 1549–51, 1583–84, 1602–4, 1610), Bryan (1992, p. 523), Menkel-Meadow (1997b, p. 1420; 2000, p. 13), and McCabe (2001, p. 476).
28 Rack (1999, pp. 236, 288–89, 292, 294). In the same vein, qualitative and quantitative research into conversation patterns of lawyers and clients indicate that female clients are more cooperative than male clients, exhibiting features that stress connection and involvement (Bogoch 1997, pp. 677, 683, 705).

successfully. Of the extant research, little evidence has been found to suggest that women ultimately fare worse than males.[29]

The present research does not examine case outcomes and does not purport to make any comprehensive claims. Indeed, one must bear in mind the caveat of universalizing the female gender. Equality feminists argue that gender differences are overemphasized. Diversity feminists posit that differences within groups such as ethnicity and socioeconomic status problematize any single conceptualization of the "female gender." Moreover, in negotiation settings, gender can interact with power, status, and demographic characteristics.[30] Yet, in injecting actors' meanings and understandings into the debate, the present findings tend to support the view that although women do not perceive they are disadvantaged, gender differences may hinder some females' abilities to mediate – at least with regard to the present dataset (which, though small, includes plaintiffs of different ethnicities and socioeconomic groupings).[31]

The findings here also inform some of the inconclusive and conflicting research and theoretical debates in negotiation theory on whether gender affects actors' objectives, perceptions, and behavior in negotiation situations (including mediation). Research indicates that gender may have a significant impact.[32] However, most of the empirical work to date from various disciplines does not actually study negotiations relating to ongoing litigation, as is the case here (Kolb and Coolidge 1988, pp. 2, 10–11, 18–19; Menkel-Meadow 2000a, pp. 358, 360–61, 364; Kolb 2003, pp. 101–2). Still, meta-analyses have demonstrated a small but significant probability that during negotiations women are generally more cooperative than men. Other research suggests that females are more likely to avoid and do less well in competitive settings than males.[33]

---

29 Goldberg et al. (1992, p. 141), Nader (1993, p. 13), King (1994, p. 84), Brinig (1995, p. 33), and LaFree and Rack (1996, p. 769). Dingwall et al.'s research in England, examining tape recordings of thirty divorce mediations (statutory and voluntary), found no systematic gender biases (Dingwall et al. 1998, pp. 277, 280, 284). Similarly, a predominantly quantitative study in New Mexico comparing the effect of gender (and ethnicity) on monetary outcomes of 323 court and 280 mediated small claims cases of various dispute types found only limited support that gender disparities were greater in mediation than in adjudication (LaFree and Rack 1996, pp. 767, 789).
30 Kolb and Coolidge (1988, p. 1), Watson (1994a, pp. 203, 205–6), Menkel-Meadow (1997b, p. 1426; 2000a, pp. 357–60, 362–65), Roberts (1997, p. 157), and Kolb 2000, p. 350).
31 Of course, as neither mediation results nor the effects of legal representation in safeguarding female disputants' rights were tested, the data in the present study can only reflect tendencies in disputants themselves.
32 Walters et al. (1998, p. 1), Stamato (1992, p. 377), Stuhlmacher and Walters (1999, pp. 653, 673), Kolb (2000, p. 348), Evans (2001, pp. 166, 180), and Riley and McGinn (2002, p. 7). Drawing on empirical research, Kolb and Coolidge similarly argue that it seems there are material differences in how males and females negotiate and the techniques they employ in attempting to reach agreements (Kolb and Coolidge 1988, pp. 1–2).
33 Studies have shown that women in negotiations are more likely to be conciliatory than men (Hinshaw and Forbes 1993, p. 876; Rack 1999, p. 224). Additionally, psychological studies and empirical research suggest that women are more risk-averse and have a lower preference for competition than men (Kolb and Coolidge 1988, p. 1; Craver and Barnes, 1999, 300–301, 312, 345; Kolb 2000, p. 348; Menkel-Meadow 2000a, pp. 360–61; Evans 2001, p. 157, n. 68).

Sociological and psychological studies relating to pay differentials suggest that females accept lower salaries and are at least as satisfied with their pay as males despite typically earning less for the same work. On this basis, Babcock and Laschever as well as Kolb and Williams argue that females feel less comfortable with overt competition and negotiation than men, are more accepting of what they are offered, and are more reluctant to request or negotiate change or additional benefits for themselves.[34] Thus, females are more likely than males to expect less and be satisfied with less, tending to view their circumstances as more fixed with others being more in control. Scholars additionally posit that females tend to feel less competent than males as negotiators, often wary of adversely affecting existing relationships during competitive situations.[35] Therefore, women are generally understood to find it difficult to advocate their own interests, instead promoting harmony in negotiation. They are seen to undervalue their positions, viewing them in terms of how they affect others, and they are overly preoccupied that others involved in their negotiations are content.[36] This is despite empirical findings indicating that women and men achieve comparable results in negotiation exercises (Craver and Barnes 1999, p. 347; Farber and Rickenberg 1999, p. 292).

Although males and females clearly do not consistently act in this way, some scholars explain differences by saying that females may view negotiation as a male-oriented task and therefore avoid it or tend to perform under their potential.[37] Babcock and Laschever explain these disparities in relation to the different socialization of males and females deriving from societal gender-based expectations, with boys being brought up to be competitive, while girls are not. Males are taught to welcome competition and focus on their own needs. Women are expected to be more cooperative, avoid conflict, and have greater orientation toward others' needs. Therefore, requesting things in negotiations and being assertive may clash with normative expectations of women and thus what is viewed as "acceptable" for females as compared with males behaving the same way in the same situations (Kolb and Coolidge 1988, p. 6; Babcock and Laschever 2003, pp. 62–64, 86, 102–4, 106–7, 120). Consequently, males – having greater expectations – are more assertive and competitive, resulting in them obtaining better results (despite being less focused on problem solving and relationships). In contrast, females are more accepting, dislike competition, are overly concerned with others, and are better at listening to

---

34 Kolb and Williams' work similarly suggests that women are more accepting of job terms than males, with others expecting them to behave this way during negotiations (Kolb and Williams 2000, p. 10).
35 Watson (1994b, p. 118), Farber and Rickenberg (1999, pp. 291–92), Babcock and Laschever (2003, pp. 1–4, 19–20, 23, 41–43, 62, 114, 116–19, 140–41), and Klein (2005, p. 787). In a simulation study of New York University law students it was found that although both sexes fared comparatively equally, females were less confident than males in their abilities to negotiate (Riley and McGinn 2002, pp. 5–6) (Stamato 1992, p. 377).
36 Kolb (1993, pp. 139, 141), Watson (1994b, p. 118), Kolb and Williams (2000, p. 42), and Kolb et al. (2004, pp. 139, 141).
37 Farber and Rickenberg (1999, pp. 283, 291–93, 283), Evans (2001, p. 164, n. 115–17), and Babcock and Laschever (2003, pp. 79–81).

them and seeking agreements that take into account others' needs.[38] Socialization theory is the most frequent explanation for differences in negotiation expectations, perceptions, and conduct. However, as Menkel-Meadow notes, socialization theory has not been tested (Menkel-Meadow 1994a, p. 83; 2000a, p. 362).

Within the theoretical debates, various scholars have pointed out that negotiation theories themselves are gendered, reasserting and subordinating female tendencies to those of males as behavioral characteristics described are generally more regularly associated with maleness (e.g., individual agency) (Kolb and Putnam 1997, pp. 232, 236–37, 247). Going further, Cohen asserts that these arguments bifurcate our understandings rather than expand on them in that by focusing on male–female distinctions or similarities in explaining negotiation behavior found in empirical studies, feminist theoretical debates are themselves based on the premise that gender differences exist and that male–female distinction determine individuals' conduct. For instance, Kolb and Williams argue that even with the same access to personal and organizational power and resources, females will not negotiate in the same way as males although they may not all be as empathetic and cooperative (Kolb and Williams 2000, pp. 23–24). In this way, Cohen asserts that these writings reinforce gendered analytical groupings and falsely circumscribe individuals' true communicative and behavioral abilities. Instead, gender should be viewed as multiply-determined in light of the complexity of human behavior (Cohen 2003, pp. 172–76, 178, 183, 186, 189).

In terms of what actually occurs in negotiations and mediations, it has been argued that power and status are materially responsible for individuals' conduct during negotiations. Thus, it has been found that women in positions of power are not necessarily more cooperative or compassionate than males (Watson 1994a, pp. 191, 203, 205–6). Adding to this, scholars such as Menkel-Meadow assert and demonstrate that gender and status result in complex dynamics affecting negotiating behavior, as gender, power, and status interact with other demographic characteristics such as ethnicity, profession, and socioeconomic positions. Together, these result in diverse negotiation expectations, goals, and conduct. Moreover, different conduct during negotiations may be affected by the gender composition of each negotiation team, with behavior possibly altering continuously. Thus, although certain females may be more cooperative and males more competitive in certain circumstances, the effect and significance of gender varies in diverse negotiation circumstances, with sex not always being a determinant factor for individuals' perceptions or behavior (Menkel-Meadow 2000b, pp. 357–60, 362–65). Kolb too speaks of moving away from the treatment of gender identities as fixed, and instead focusing more on negotiation contexts and interactions themselves (Kolb 2000, p. 350). Moreover, Kolb and Williams argue not only that gendered

---

38 Gender differences in negotiation have also been explained in terms of access to power resulting in better-negotiated results. Thus, as males generally have greater access to power, they achieve superior outcomes. A further theory suggests that it is gender expectations that result in stereotypical gendered behavior in negotiations (Menkel-Meadow 2000a, p. 363).

negotiation theories should not be universalized, but also that training women in substantive as well as nonverbal, parallel, or "shadow negotiation" techniques can reduce gendered differences in negotiation conduct and results (Kolb 2000, p. 350; Kolb and Williams 2000, pp. 11, 20–21, 31; Menkel-Meadow 2001, pp. 261, 271). Their work on "shadow negotiations" advocates the need to make explicit the unspoken hidden expectations, contexts, agendas, and perceptions of parties and issues inherent in all negotiations irrespective of participants' genders.

Yet in so doing, in terms of the present findings, with the disparity of legal, lay, and gendered actors' perceptions and understandings coexisting at mediations, one tended to wonder whether they were undergoing the same process at all.

6.5 Chapter conclusion

This chapter has highlighted mediation as providing an arena within which confrontations and representations are carried out. This affected disputants' mediation experiences and often case results (Goffman 1971, pp. 17–18, 26, 34). The confrontations were chiefly between legal actors, affected by their personalities and firms' hierarchies. There were also notable representations aimed at disputants by lawyers on all sides, attempting to influence and manage impressions – yet behaving quite differently when disputants were not present in the room. At the same time, universal yet subliminal conflicts were evident between lawyers and clients, including conflicting financial interests inherent in all lawyer–client relationships and issues of lawyer influence and control over what transpired at mediations. Still, throughout these goings-on, things looked good on the surface. Most actors were optimistic about mediating (regardless of mediation type), reinforcing their needs for communication. Moreover, although few felt that relations had been ameliorated, the majority felt that their mediations were both fair and good experiences irrespective of results.

However, delving deeper into what each actor group perceived as positive and objectionable during mediations revealed different and incongruous realities and perceptions of what took place, and highlighted mediation as host to the confluence of the conflicting worlds of tactics and strategy versus that of human needs and desires. There were diverse perceptions of lawyers' presence and power, the flow of information (and related inequalities), tactical versus extralegal goings-on, nonverbal communication, learning of positive/negative "truths," healing, and disappointments. Mediation was also seen to be a forum for dual communication, almost antithetical in nature. As such, the data invited the reader into three worlds coexisting during mediations: that of lawyers, another of disputants, and a third on gender lines.

Mediators' descriptions of what transpired lay between those of lawyers and parties – further solidifying the evidence of lawyer-mediators' move away from the legal world. Thus, adding a new angle to understandings of mediation processes, the data not only indicated that mediators mediated between cases' opposing sides, but also that they simultaneously stood in between and mediated actors' different perceptions, senses of reality, practices, and representations – those of lawyers who wanted to take control and equally those of parties who sought relief, satisfaction, catharsis, and so on (Menkel-Meadow 2006). This is further evidenced in chapter seven.

Attorneys' descriptions of what happened at mediations were remarkably similar irrespective of their disparate allegiances. In speaking of mediation's favorable elements, they spoke almost wholly utilizing a tactical, adversarial paradigm (different to how most law schools teach mediation – Golann 2002, p. 302). As such, mediation was perceived as a key vehicle for strategic communication. Both defense and plaintiff lawyers stressed the importance of direct communication with plaintiffs about risks, weaknesses, and litigation realities. This was aimed at lowering plaintiffs' expectations. Likewise, the strategic assessments of plaintiffs as trial witnesses were discussed favorably by legal actors on all sides. Defense lawyers talked about the tactical insight they obtained at mediations. This included gaining views into the internal dynamics of the relationships between plaintiff lawyers and clients, as well as between co-plaintiffs, and understanding plaintiffs' motivations. On the same lines, plaintiff lawyers spoke of the paucity of tactical insight they gained at mediation due to defense sides' perceived guardedness and the consequent inequality of information flow.

Yet, these issues were absent from most disputants' descriptions of the same mediations. Compared with lawyers' strategic discourse outlining what went on tactically, disputants described mediations as very personal encounters. The most talked about favored elements (irrelevant of settlement) related to the importance disputants ascribed to expressing themselves, offering human, extralegal information and the psychological and emotional relief this brought. This finding adds empirical support to the literature discussing disputants' needs to speak at mediation about nonlegal issues they deem important and relevant to their cases.[39] It also supports the position that seriously hurt plaintiffs required mediation to release their emotions, discuss their anxieties, and ask questions.[40] Of course, answers proved to be a rare commodity. Indeed, the majority of plaintiffs' articulated mediation aims (including the information they sought – *chapter five*) were not met – something unrecognized by most legal actors.

Nevertheless, hearing plaintiffs speak at mediation about their life situations served to sensitize lawyers to the human realities of disputes. However, plaintiffs'

---

39 Meschievitz (1991, p. 198), Galton (1994, p. 119), Metzloff et al. (1997, p. 123), and Gitchell and Plattner (1999, p. 443). Procedural justice studies have repeatedly found that people seek opportunities to be listened to, irrespective of whether these result in favorable outcomes. Thus, the opportunity to speak has value in itself regardless of actual influence on decisions. Voice or "process control" relates to the degree to which legal procedures allow parties a chance to express their opinions on how end results or decisions should be reached. Heightened process control has been found to increase judgments of procedural justice and influence evaluation of legal authorities (Tyler et al. 1985, pp. 72–75, 79).
40 Phillips (1992, p. 583), Dauer and Marcus (1997, p. 206), Johnson (1997, p. 49), Polywka (1997, p. 81), and Caldon (1999, p. 3).

emotional and psychological needs to participate, express themselves, and be heard during mediations represented a double-edged sword, as they resulted in lawyers utilizing this information in ways quite different than virtually all plaintiffs recognized – that is, to inform lawyers' strategies. Perhaps this lack of recognition by plaintiffs symbolized disputants' refusal to enter the legal world. Indeed, although plaintiffs received and digested the tactical information fed to them by legal actors at mediation, only a minority changed their views about their disputes. None changed their views about the initiating incidents. Sarat and Felstiner found that divorce lawyers' and clients' conversations included persistent battles for each one's views of "reality" to be accepted. Their observation data indicated that lawyers' dispute interpretations generally prevailed (Sarat and Felstiner 1988, pp. 741–42, 766–67; 1995b, p. 406). Expanding on this, the present findings suggest that despite surface appearances and notwithstanding hearing lawyers' (their own and those of opponents) or mediators' descriptions of "reality" months or years later during mediations, most plaintiffs retain their own versions of reality in terms of the original meaning they ascribe to disputes and their extralegal resolution objectives.

Additionally, through mediation's window into a legal world most had never seen before, plaintiffs were frequently negatively affected by what they perceived as lawyers' impersonal handling of their tragedies and consequent disputes. This finding is consistent with the procedural justice literature, arguing that litigants may feel that negotiations which focus on money alone trivialize issues they view as important and can negatively affect perceptions of procedural justice (Tyler et al. 1985, p. 72; Welsh 2001a, p. 860). It has been posited in the context of small claims and poverty law cases that transformed legal descriptions of conflicts commonly alter the nature of disputes and may hold little meaning for litigants, resulting in remedies that do not deal with their needs as they perceive them (Hosticka 1979; Conley and O'Barr 1990). The findings here shed further light on this issue, which has generally been neglected (Cunningham 1992, p. 1300). Interestingly, both this finding and that of parties' negative perceptions of lawyers' nonverbal communication were more often associated with male legal actors than with females.

Thus, emerged the final coexisting world at mediation, where gender appeared to influence the way that conflict and its resolution were viewed and understood. For legal actors, females seemed to experience mediation more "extralegally" than males. Male attorneys generally described what transpired wholly tactically, while females' discourse more often additionally included extralegal information, describing plaintiffs' perspectives in recounting "what went on." Female defense lawyers' extralegal sensitivity was sensed by plaintiffs, who tended to perceive female attorneys more positively than their male counterparts in terms of showing compassion and understanding. Adding to the dearth of empirical data on the topic, these findings provide important insight from legal and lay participants into how they perceive and experience conflict resolution processes (Menkel-Meadow 1997b, p. 1427; Stempel 2003, pp. 310–11; Subrin 2003, pp. 207–8; Klein 2005, p. 792).

For plaintiffs, although demographics may well have been influential, overall their gendered mediation experiences highlighted females' potential vulnerabilities. Despite having greater emotional needs for mediation than males (possibly deriving more emotional benefit), female plaintiffs generally suffered more emotional hardship in attending while also being more sensitive to others' perceptions during mediations. There was evidence of some females speaking and partaking less during mediations than males. Importantly, female plaintiffs were less aware of mediation's tactical occurrences while being far more accepting than males of whatever transpired. Although not taking into account the effects of legal representation in safeguarding female disputants' rights, these findings support feminist scholars' arguments that females may be more acquiescing or cooperative at mediations than males.[41] The findings also serve to inform the feminist critiques of mediation generally and the literature on the internalization of females' disempowerment (Ricci 1985, p. 49; Kandel 1994, p. 882).

Having heard the perspectives of all actors, what can one distil as the essence of mediation? Mediation was, for the most part, not about obtaining factual information per se. It was about gaining intangible insight through both verbal and nonverbal communication. It was clear that all actors were seeking to communicate and for others to agree with their positions. Yet, the nature of that communication for legal versus lay actors was almost antithetical. Thus, the communication during mediation was both transmitted and received on different planes. However, as Schutz notes, "successful communication is possible only between persons, social groups, etc, who share a substantially similar system of 'relevances' or 'coinciding interpretive schemes'" (Schutz 1982, pp. 322–23; Tamanaha 1993, pp. 84–85). Thus, these findings serve to limit the unqualified praise of the communication that occurs during mediations.[42] Moreover, with legal and lay actors' scant awareness of each other's mediation aims and perceptions, mediations were shown to be composed of discrete, boundaried slices of perception rather than constituting shared experiences. All experience is personal, but shared experiences entail awareness of the experiences of others (Raz, Interview, September 29, 2004). As such, this chapter's findings serve to question some widely entertained premises about mediation.

Further issues relating to "what went on" during mediations are explored from a final angle in the next chapter, which examines actors' perceptions of mediators and the styles they employed in attempting to resolve these cases. Perhaps unsurprisingly, there too parallel worlds emerge between legal, lay, and gendered actor groups.

---

41 Grillo (1991, pp. 1549–51, 1583–84, 1602–4, 1610), Bryan (1992, p. 523), Menkel-Meadow (1997b, p. 1420; 2000, p. 13), Kolb and Williams (2000, p. 42), McCabe (2001, pp. 476–77); Riley and McGinn (2002, p. 5), Babcock and Laschever (2003, pp. 1–4, 19–20, 23, 41–43, 62, 114, 116–19, 140–41), and Kolb et al. (2004, pp. 139, 141).

42 Reeves (1994, p. 18), Brown and Simanowitz (1995, p. 153), Dauer and Marcus (1997, pp. 199, 205, 218), and Forehand (1999, pp. 907, 926).

CHAPTER SEVEN

Parallel views on mediators and styles

"Party self-determination and informed consent dictate that knowledgeable choices should be made about which process to select for resolving one's dispute. Choice entails having distinct options among an array of possibilities. Self-determination is among the pillars of the mediation process."

Love and Kovach (2000, p. 300)

In line with the chronological ordering of the chapters relating to litigation-track case processing events from contextual and pre-mediation issues (*chapters two to five*) to those of actual mediations (*chapters six and seven*), this chapter examines a final facet of the mediation experience for the actors involved: that of mediators and their styles.[1] For those actors whose cases settled due to mediation, the process and all it entailed represented the end of case processing. Even for those cases that did not settle, mediation was likely to have been the last such gathering of all or most actors involved in these disputes prior to trial, bilateral lawyer settlement, or case abandonment.

Actors' perceptions of mediations were intertwined with their views on mediators. Mediators were often perceived as the core of mediations – even synonymous with "mediation" itself. However, there were material differences in views on mediators' performances.[2] This reflected not only subjective perceptions but also objective realities in mediation, as will be seen. What gave certain mediators "the power" to make mediation worthwhile, while others were left to try to make the best of things? In exploring perceptions of mediators and style, this chapter offers a final view of the discontinuities inherent in mediation's legal and extralegal worlds.

---

1 See chapter six, footnote 1, for details on respondents in chapters six and seven. There were a total of seventeen mediators in the dataset. Ten mediators were male (seven lawyers, three non-lawyers), and seven mediators were female (three lawyers, four non-lawyers).
2 At the time of data collection, there was no central umbrella organization stipulating necessary mediator qualifications and no single accreditation system for mediators in Ontario. This reflected the lack of consensus on what qualities, standards, and training were necessary in a good ADR provider (Pepper 1998, p. 435). One in thirty mediators were accredited, but no formal credentials were necessary in the private sector. For mandatory court-linked mediations, mediators had to be on the government roster and therefore had to meet certain criteria.

In the voluntary mediations, mediators were chosen by the instructing lawyers. This was similarly the case in the mandatory court-linked mediations if opposing attorneys could agree on a mediator (on or off the court roster) within the designated time limits. However, this often proved difficult, resulting in court-roster mediators (a mix of lawyers and non-lawyers) frequently being assigned by the court. Although disputants played no part in choosing mediators, questionnaire data suggested that most actors were pleased with the mediators they had. Moreover, notwithstanding the lack of consensus over whether or not mediators are able to remain completely neutral, irrelevant of mediation results or experiences, virtually all actors also perceived their mediators as "neutral" or "unaligned".[3] However, looking deeper, it became clear that legal and lay actors viewed mediators through entirely different lenses, marking a pronounced disparity in mediator wants and how they perceived and judged their mediators. Moreover, unknown to disputants' legal actors' views on preferred mediator background and style were extremely similar across camps, portending their agendas for mediators.

Yet, the line between styles was sometimes blurred. Both interview and observation data in several cases highlighted the fact that notwithstanding mediators stressing that they were conducting solely facilitative mediations, some utilized evaluative techniques as well, either overtly or subliminally (e.g., by offering "suggestions" or through perceived body language). Likewise, evaluative mediations contained facilitative elements. Other empirical mediation research has similarly found that mediators do not maintain consistent styles (Golann 2000, pp. 61, 78–79; McDermott and Obar 2004, pp. 92, 95). This finding accords with scholarship stating that the two styles are not always clearly divided and might best be viewed as a continuum.[4] Indeed, it is accepted by many that mediation includes elements of both styles.[5] In fact, several mediators and legal actors in the present study noted that most mediators or "good mediators" used a combination of styles. As Gulliver notes, mediators do "not necessarily nor even usually adopt a single role and strategy... They commonly altered their tactics to adapt to changing circumstances" (Gulliver 1979, p. 226). Nevertheless, notwithstanding the lack of consensus on what precisely constitutes each mediation technique,[6] for purposes of analysis respondents were provided with the following definition:[7]

---

3 (Gulliver 1979, pp. 213–14, 217–19; Mulcahy et al. 2000, p. 67). This was seen in both questionnaire responses and interviews. This finding accords with Macfarlane's study on various dispute types where most lawyers and litigants (76%) also felt mediators behaved neutrally (Macfarlane 1995).
4 Goldberg et al. (1992, p. 244), Lande (1997, p. 850, n. 40), Stempel (2000, pp. 371–72), and Levin (2001, p. 269).
5 Birke (2000, p. 310), Lande (2000, p. 321), Guthrie (2001), and Nolan-Haley (2002, pp. 276–80).
6 Lande (1997, pp. 849–56), Lowry (2000, p. 48), and Mcdermott and Obar (2004, pp. 80–81, 93). Rights-based mediation has additionally been called "early neutral evaluation" (Goldberg et al. 1992, p. 243).
7 Physician lawyers perceived 57% of the mediations as evaluative and 43% as facilitative; hospital lawyers perceived 50% of mediations as evaluative, 30% facilitative, and 20% a mix of both styles. Plaintiff lawyers perceived 46% of their mediations as facilitative, 31% evaluative, and 23% a mix.

Evaluative or rights-based mediation can be described as when the mediator makes an expert diagnosis on the basis of the information s/he receives from parties and arrives at an understanding of what parties need to go forward, i.e. prescribes a solution. The mediator then tries to sell that to the parties. So in effect it is a model of expert consultancy (following a professional, legal, medical model). Facilitative or interest-based mediation can be described as a limited intervention to improve or enable bilateral party communication. So in some ways they can be seen as completely different methods of communication.[8]

This chapter first examines a number of contextual realities and surface findings relating to mediators and mediation styles. This is followed by an exploration into legal actors' views on mediators' backgrounds and the techniques they employ, including attorneys' preferences for evaluative, rights-based mediation. Lawyers' reasoning behind their views is also analyzed, offering further evidence of the different meaning of case processing and mediation for legal actors as compared with parties. Next, I examine the data relating to those actors with facilitative, interest-based style preferences. In the final section, two gender findings are discussed, one relating to how mediators' conduct was interpreted by plaintiffs of different genders, and the other relating to mediators' own genders. The gender findings provide final support to the gender theme present throughout the book.

7.1 Contextual realities and surface findings

There were a number of contextual goings-on that related to mediators. First, within the mediators' world, a competitive reality existed between mediators, each pressured to perform and obtain the same or better settlement rates than their colleagues. Linked to this were the issues of mediators' client bases and the number of cases they mediated annually. This resulted in another interest situation occurring during mediations, as there was an unspoken awareness of the possibility of mediators precipitating future work from lawyers. Consequently, this added an additional layer of "performance" or "representation" into the mediation phenomenon: that of mediators performing for lawyers. This was quite separate to their presentations for disputants. Indeed, some of the observation data suggested that mediators, whether consciously or not, attempted to win favor with both lawyers and disputants, for example, by recounting their settlement rates, qualifications, or by describing personal achievements. Yet, at the same time there were also unspoken power struggles

---

8 Riskin's "grid" gave formal recognition to facilitative and evaluative mediation styles (Riskin 1996, pp. 13, 17, 48), later renaming them "directive" and "elicitive" styles (Riskin 2003, pp. 1–2). Bush and Folger suggest there are three models of practice: problem-solving (based on a psychological/economic view of conflict), harmony, and transformative (a form of facilitative mediation, utilizing a social/communicative paradigm that assumes that human transformation is more important to disputants than settlement) (Bush and Folger 1994, pp. 81–95; Folger and Bush 1996, p. 263.) Mediator behavior has also been described in terms of bargaining and therapeutic modes (Silbey and Merry 1986, pp. 19–25; Nolan-Haley 2002, p. 276).

occurring during mediations between mediators and lawyers. As will be seen later, the matter ultimately came down to whether legal actors willingly devolved power to their mediators. For instance,

> "The control of process is in the hands of the lawyers... As a mediator you've got to be unflappable... Lawyers sometimes try to make us look stupid in front of their clients... I'm the one who takes the flack." **Senior, male lawyer-mediator in observed voluntary mediation – in sixties**

> "I don't let the lawyers run the show. It's not their show. Mediation is not litigation. It's not their show... I want to hear from the lawyers. I want to include them. But the first thing I do is hear from the parties, because it's their process." **Female non-lawyer-mediator – twenty years' experience – voluntary/mandatory/College mediations – social work background – in forties**

Finally, there was the issue of mediators representing a new interest or potential information source for disputants within lawyer–client relationships. For example,

> "It would be really nice if... the mediators actually had a chance to speak to the lawyers' clients and hear from them what's really important to them. I've never had that chance... I haven't heard too many mediators say they've been able to contact the real clients. It's always been through the lawyers." **Female non-lawyer mandatory mediator – ten years' experience – social work background – in forties**

> "The lawyers both spoke about an interesting legal issue in this case. And the lawyers' enthusiasm... was picked up by the mediator saying 'Maybe what's motivating you to keep this case running are the interests of the lawyers on a neat legal issue that could go to the Supreme Court'. It probably wasn't bad to put that out on the table for the clients. Be aware your lawyers may be taking you in a direction that is way beyond what you want." **Male physician lawyer – mandatory mediation – in fifties**

> "I didn't try to override anything the plaintiff's lawyer was saying... In caucus... I was allowed to give my view of the risks, which I asked the lawyer first... He allowed me to speak freely." **Male lawyer-mediator – voluntary mediation – in sixties**

> "DID YOU HAVE ANY VIEWS ABOUT HOW MEDIATION CAN AFFECT LEGAL COSTS? Not really. I really appreciated it, because that came from *the mediator*. *He said* 'They may offer you more money, but you're going to end up with less money because your legal fees are going to escalate. We're going to have to pay witnesses....' Until he actually said that, I didn't know. My lawyer hadn't told us." **Female plaintiff – in forties**

Having considered the contextual goings-on, I then examined surface findings relating to mediators and style prior to delving deeper into questions of "why."

For many legal actors, the mediator "was" the mediation experience. Indeed, when asked to describe their mediations, mediators were the first thing mentioned by a material proportion of respondents.[9] For instance,

> "HOW DO YOU FEEL ABOUT MEDIATION'S RESULT? Excellent... I think it was directly related to the mediator's style and approach... The flexibility on both sides was properly tapped into by the mediator, that allowed us to move forward." **Male physician lawyer – in fifties**

> "HOW WOULD YOU DESCRIBE THE MEDIATION? I'd say the mediator provided some leadership on certain critical issues... He influenced the parties in terms of how they assessed their position." **Male hospital lawyer – in forties**

This finding was similar to that in Macfarlane's survey evaluation of the Toronto ADR Center, where for various case types the perceived competence of the mediator was recurrently found to shape lawyers' and disputants' perceptions and assessments of the process (Macfarlane 1995). Yet, the data in the present study additionally suggest that it was the legal actors who largely held the keys to power for mediators, directly affecting mediation experiences for their disputing clients.

> "It's the lawyers that decide who will be the mediator and therefore what type of mediation they want.... The parties just go along with what the lawyers choose... The litigants and their wants just fall through the cracks." **Male lawyer-mediator – in sixties**

> "Mediation is only as good as the *lawyers* willing to permit the mediator to drive them to resolution." **Male, specialist plaintiffs' lawyer – obstetrics accidents – in fifties**

> "It's very important for the mediator to figure out what the clients want. I don't think the mediator can set the agenda... You've chosen the mediator for a particular reason and that particular style. If you haven't chosen the mediator, then the mediator needs to spend some time trying to figure out what kind of mediation you want." **Female physician lawyer – in thirties**

Indeed, lawyers were repeat players in mediations as well as the "buyers" of mediators' services (Lande 1997, p. 847, n. 32). As such, their desires inevitably affected mediators and mediations, as will be seen later. Nevertheless, on a superficial level all appeared very positive in relation to the issue of mediators and their style. Figure 25 sets out the findings.

---

9 For example, 40% of hospital lawyers, 46% of plaintiff lawyers, and 33% of plaintiffs.

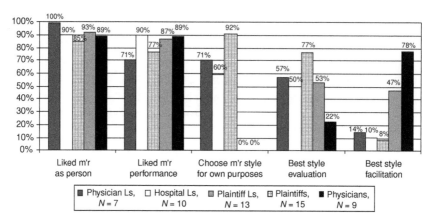

Figure 25. Surface perceptions of mediators and style. (*Note:* "L" stands for lawyer and "m'r" for mediator.) Although disputants had no input into mediator choices, on the surface most legal and lay actors liked their mediators and were pleased with their performances. However, disparities in style preferences suggested that more was occurring beneath the surface.[10]

On the face of it, most mediation actors liked their mediators as individuals, regardless of views on their performances, the mediations themselves, or if settlements resulted. Most actors were also positive about mediators' performances.[11] This accorded with much of what is known generally in terms of mediation satisfaction. For instance, in Wissler's Ohio study of court mediation participants (1,224 lawyers, 725 parties) virtually all lawyers surveyed rated mediators as effective, and nearly all actors felt mediators (who were all lawyers) were neutral and understood them (Wissler 1998, p. 28).

In terms of what was liked about mediators, all lawyers in the present study discussed learned skills (e.g., analytical and persuasive) as well as inherent abilities to gauge what was occurring with participants during mediations. Several plaintiff lawyers also mentioned natural intangibles relating to mediators' characters such as energy, empathy, understanding, warmth, and compassion toward disputants. They also spoke positively of mediators who shared their own similar life stories. This offered further evidence of lawyers reconceptualizing their roles. For instance,

> "The mediator had some experience with the same type of injury that the plaintiff was going through, so was able to share. He had . . . empathy, understanding and insight

---

10 Twenty-nine percent of physician lawyers and 20% of hospital lawyers preferred a mix of the two styles. Additionally, 20% of hospital lawyers and 15% of plaintiff lawyers said that "it depends" or that they did not know which style they preferred.
11 One hundred percent of physician lawyers, 90% of hospital lawyers, 85% of plaintiff lawyers, 93% of plaintiffs, and 89% of physician defendants liked their mediators. Mediators' performances were liked by 71% of physician lawyers, 90% of hospital lawyers, 77% of plaintiff lawyers, 87% of plaintiffs, and 89% of physician defendants.

into what they're coping with... In a very dignified way he shared of himself, and was very positive actually, emotionally positive." **Male, specialist plaintiffs' lawyer – in forties**

"*That mediator* is... compassionate... realizes the trauma, stress and unending poking and probing of the family during the litigation process and re-done at the mediation process." **Male, specialist plaintiffs' lawyer – in forties**

"The mediator... appreciated the human element, made everybody feel welcome and fully heard." **Male, specialist plaintiff lawyer – in thirties**

Disputants' perceptions of mediators were similarly almost always positive. Virtually all plaintiffs liked their mediators as well as mediators' performances.[12] Mediators were described as warm, caring, fair, fatherly, very understanding, respectful, and protective. In fact, two female plaintiffs cited divine intervention when their mediators recounted similar personal life tragedies. Thus, it appeared that plaintiffs generally wanted or at least were pleased with mediators who served their human needs – rarely mentioning their strategic interests. For example, in response to the question, "WHAT WERE YOUR VIEWS ABOUT THE MEDIATOR?"

"I found him to be a very calming person... I felt like I could trust him... I honestly felt that this was the kind of person who was not going to let anything *happen* or let anyone say anything... I mean he's just phenomenal... I have a lot of respect for him... I think he did a wonderful job, and his personality sort of takes the edge off. He jokes... He's got a light-hearted attitude... It was personal and I felt he got some sense of our family." **Female plaintiff – in forties**

"It's as if I knew him before. Isn't that strange?... He made you feel so very comfortable about being in that room... It was as if I knew him for a long time... He had that about him... A very fair person... not judgmental... very respectful... He's a very kind person... It was just his mannerism... extremely warm... a very understanding individual... He was listening. You could see it." **Female plaintiff – in fifties**

Little is known about those mediator attributes that are important to litigants. The only study found relates to non-litigated U.S. school mediations. Correlating with the findings here, it was similarly noted that disputants particularly viewed as important mediators' understanding and sensitivity as part of other procedural fairness criteria (Welsh 2004a, pp. 595, 619). Indeed, the procedural justice literature indicates that parties' assessments of whether procedures are fair and just are affected by how mediators as third parties interact with them, especially with regard to treating them respectfully and evenhandedly. Disputants feel more positive about

---

12 As most of the physician data related to College mediations, plaintiffs' data from litigation-linked mediations has been focused on primarily. Only two plaintiffs (13%) were somewhat critical of mediators' performances, citing too many irrelevant stories or the fact that the mediator did not speak to them sufficiently about their case's strengths and weaknesses.

third-party dispute resolution processes, results, and mediators if they feel the decision maker considered their arguments seriously. This is regardless of whether the result incorporates their positions.[13]

Yet, as Gulliver warns, mediators are never utterly neutral or mere catalysts, and frequently introduce into resolution processes their own interests, values, concerns, and perceptions that are not completely coincident with those of either disputing party. Thus, they may fundamentally influence negotiation processes and results (Gulliver 1979, pp. 213–14, 217–19). In Dingwall's study of British divorce mediation, entailing interviews and observations, mediators' influence and active roles appeared to affect party control (Dingwall 1988, pp. 150, 153). Hence, the choice of mediator is a fundamental issue for mediations, with direct effects on mediation experiences.

As for style preferences, as seen in Figure 25, most legal actors preferred evaluative techniques. However, the findings were less clear for disputants. As virtually all were first-time litigation and mediation participants, they had little to compare with the style they received. Nevertheless, it was intriguing that most plaintiffs (67%) felt that whatever style they experienced, regardless of which one it was, was "the best." This included cases where no settlements resulted.[14] Thus, it may have been that disputants were pleased with any style that included the chance for communication with opposing sides and authoritative third parties.

Further examination of the reasons why actors did and did not like elements of mediators' performances and styles put into context the seemingly clear surface findings on lawyers' and disputants' satisfaction with their mediators overall. This is explored in the following sections.

7.2 The legal evaluative world on style

> "What a mediator can do, what he chooses to do, and what he is permitted to do by the disputing parties are all much affected by who he is... and why he is there at all (Gulliver 1979, p. 213) as mediators need to inspire the confidence of all parties (Polywka 1997, p. 82)."

There were two mediator attributes most important to legal actors: their professional backgrounds and the mediation style they employed. These issues were virtually never spoken of by disputants.

---

13 Tyler (1987, p. 371), Lind et al. (1989, pp. 22–23; 1990, p. 958), and Welsh (2001a, p. 823).
14 Plaintiffs perceived 67% of their mediations as facilitative and 33% as evaluative. Fifty-three percent said they preferred an evaluative style and 47% preferred facilitative styles. All but one physician underwent facilitative mediations. Seventy-eight percent said they preferred facilitative mediations; 22% preferred evaluative styles. For the minority of plaintiffs who said they preferred the style they did not have, most (80%) underwent mediation that did not result in settlement. Thus, this may have been a factor in their style dissatisfaction.

The importance of background

Most lawyers, regardless of camp, wanted expert lawyer-mediators (or retired judges) with knowledge and practical legal experience in the substantive legal area of the dispute.[15] This resulted in attorneys' respect. In effect, this meant that mediators had to be within lawyers' own group. Interestingly, although not part of the general topic guides, all three physicians who mentioned mediator backgrounds felt that mediators needed to be part of "their" group, that is, medics themselves in order to truly understand the issues and resolve these cases.

> "That is very interesting that you say they use retired judges who have dealt with a lot of medical cases and are well respected. They may be well respected as judges, but when they are evaluating specific facts... they still don't know as much medicine as they would need to know to be able to mediate many of these cases. So they are not that expert in that... The mediator has to have a reasonable knowledge of medicine... and know the rules of mediation. That doesn't take a lawyer to do that. It takes physicians to understand the nuances of medicine; because it is so subtle. It is a whole language unto its own." **Male defendant physician – in fifties**

> "How does someone with no knowledge make a decision or a recommendation? The mediator should have medical knowledge. It is difficult enough to assess the pros and cons of a medical report with medical knowledge, let alone without medical knowledge." **Male physician mediator – in seventies**

Yet, for legal actors the issue of mediators' legal backgrounds often appeared to be as important as their actual performances during mediations. Interestingly, this was yet another issue almost never mentioned by disputants, who in this way were utterly unaware of things highly influential on their mediation experiences.

> "The key is the mediator... the respect, the knowledge, the credibility. We often use retired judges in our mediations... because of their expertise and having heard so many similar cases." **Female hospital lawyer – in twenties**

> "It should be a legal person... a retired judge or a practicing lawyer, have a lot of experience... in the specialty... It's not some form of elitism *that* lawyers are better. It's a legal fight; and there are so many legal factors that go into what makes up a resolution that you really do need a lawyer, hopefully a lawyer that has a specialty in the area." **Male, specialist plaintiff lawyer – in forties**

> "We need somebody who's familiar with how one assesses damages and approaches issues of liability... I don't want to go to mediations and have to draw pictures for the mediators and explain to them why it is we're talking about an issue... We need

---

15 One hundred percent of physician lawyers, 90% of hospital lawyers, and 92% of plaintiff lawyers felt mediators not only had to be lawyers, but had to have experience and expertise in the substantive legal area of the dispute.

> someone whose opinion on these things carries some weight by virtue of experience in the field... someone who's got the credentials and presence to sell it to the parties." **Male, specialist plaintiff lawyer – in fifties**

> "If I've got to get a mediator up the learning curve... it's going to be two and a half hours that'll be gone.... You need specialist mediators for specific cases... medical, construction, engineering... a breed of people who understand what the cases are about, how they're litigated... the economic assessment of damages... if they're going to be of any value to anybody." **Male, specialist plaintiff and physician lawyer – in forties**

> "Ex-judges or senior counsel mediators... come with a great background of knowledge and experience in this area... *Their* feedback is very... valuable... because that's what our *insurer* clients need... They have heard from us... about our views of the case. We might be wrong... Likewise, if we're being perfectly reasonable it's helpful to hear that to have a sense you're on the right track... If we go back and tell *our clients* that a certain retired-judge-mediator has told us XY&Z, they really listen." **Female hospital lawyer – in forties**

Thus, although not mentioned outright by most attorneys, the reality appeared to be that unless mediators had the backgrounds lawyers were seeking, the consequent mediations were in some respects doomed from the start.[16] Again, this was never mentioned by disputants.

> "My *insurer* client's not going to care what a psychologist who's never done a medical malpractice case but has his/her mediator training thinks... I mean, I'll go ask my mother what she thinks about the case too. It's not going to mean anything to me." **Male physician lawyer – in thirties**

> "Although I found the *court-mandatory* mediators to be quite helpful in facilitating discussion, typically they don't have the expertise that anyone would probably think their view carried a whole lot of weight." **Female hospital lawyer – in twenties**

Menkel-Meadow argues that mediators "who engage in some prediction or application of legal standards to concrete facts... are 'practicing law'." Thus she similarly advocates the use of legally trained mediators with legal expertise at mediation (Menkel-Meadow 1996a, pp. 60–61; Palmer and Roberts 1998, p. 340). Others have additionally argued that for medical disputes, mediators with subject-matter expertise are required both for their substantive knowledge and to lend credibility to the process (Johnson 1997, p. 54; Gitchell and Plattner 1999, p. 447; Mulcahy et al. 2000). Indeed, being a lawyer-mediator was not necessarily enough for the legal actors in the present study.

---

16 Macfarlane's interview study of commercial litigators in Ottawa and Toronto similarly found that lawyers were sceptical about court-roster mediators' qualifications (Macfarlane 2002, pp. 280, 284).

"The mediator attempted to evaluate, but was not qualified to do so... He gave his view on damages and we basically said 'We know what the damages are because this is what we do all the time. Thanks for you input but... you're not going to sell us on what you think this is worth or what a judge is going to think'." **Female hospital lawyer – in twenties**

Hence, it became clear that mediators' backgrounds were viewed by legal actors overall as necessary to assist them with advice on what arguments would and would not be accepted in courts and, if relevant, on what amounts of damages were reasonable, that is, what courts would decide. Having the desired background provided mediators with the most important attribute for legal actors: credibility. Credibility was of particular importance because of most lawyers' desired mediation style.

The significance of style

"Outside the mandatory program, lawyers are choosing evaluative mediators, mediators they're more comfortable with. You'll very rarely see a lawyer choose a non-lawyer as a mediator... because counsel just want their own opinions verified or disavowed. *Lawyers* play a larger role in evaluative mediation. Whereas in facilitative mediation they tend to be in the background and the parties tend to have much more control. I think lawyers feel that it goes against the grain. They're not used to it." **Male lawyer-mediator – in fifties**

"What you're mediating, what you're trying to resolve is, I mean you're taking bets on the outcome of the case at trial." **Male, generalist plaintiff lawyer – in forties**

Directly linked to mediators' backgrounds was the style they employed. The bulk of lawyers in each actor group noted that they predominantly chose mediators because of their style.[17] Most legal actors preferred evaluative, rights-based mediators to facilitative, interest-based mediators (Figure 25). Lawyers' views of mediators have been studied to some extent, overall correlating with the findings here. For instance, this finding accords with Metzloff et al.'s U.S. study of medmal mediation, where most lawyers surveyed (70%) put much value on mediators' practice backgrounds and expertise and wanted evaluative mediators to assess cases' merits (Metzloff et al. 1997, pp. 144–45). Others too have noted that medical lawyers' preferences are generally for evaluative mediators who make judgments about the issues, consequently influencing what disputants perceive as acceptable settlement ranges (Gitchell and Plattner 1999, pp. 431, 449). Therefore, it might be argued that attorneys' preferences related to the specific case type.[18] That being said, Macfarlane's survey data

---

17 Seventy-one percent of physician lawyers, 60% of hospital lawyers, and 92% of plaintiff lawyers mentioned choosing mediators for their style.
18 In Macfarlane and Keet's research involving a ten-year mandatory mediation program for various case types, although mediators there were generally non-lawyers employing facilitative techniques, few attorneys viewed this as problematic. Still, a minority of lawyers did prefer evaluative

from Canada involving disparate dispute types also indicated that most lawyers (54%) felt that neutral evaluation would have been helpful (Macfarlane 1995). Likewise, in her later research involving interviews with commercial litigators in Ottawa and Toronto, preferences for evaluative mediators were strong particularly due to the impact on disputants of hearing evaluative opinions. Approximately half of the lawyers wanted lawyer-mediators to offer expert opinions on cases, reflecting their understanding of mediation's main purpose as being a means of determining case value. Some lawyers additionally said that credible mediators could sway their clients' views (Macfarlane 2002, pp. 285, 310). In U.S. court-connected mediations, it has likewise been found that mediators were selected for their ability to value cases and assess strengths and weaknesses (Welsh 2001a, p. 789). McAdoo's research into various dispute types found that most lawyers wanted lawyer-mediators with the necessary background to perform evaluative mediation (McAdoo and Hinshaw 2002, pp. 473, 524). Other commentators have similarly noted that U.S. lawyers are generally choosing lawyer-mediators with knowledge and substantive experience, enabling them to assess parties' legal arguments, value cases, and lower disputant expectations (Gordon 1999, p. 228; Welsh 2001b, pp. 4–5, 25–27; 2004b, p. 137; McAdoo 2002, pp. 429–30; Menkel-Meadow et al. 2006, p. 580).

These findings are unsurprising in that evaluative mediations are closer to traditional lawyering, generally adopting the adversarial system's norms in structuring and resolving conflict. In contrast, facilitative mediations create disparate (or opposed) narratives of disputes (Reich 2002, pp. 188–92; Rubinson 2004, p. 848), though often leading to the emergence of a common view. Accordingly, U.S. lawyers have been found to look down on facilitative mediators (Lande 1997, pp. 850–51; Stempel 1997, pp. 973–75). This is notwithstanding the fact that the validity of mediator evaluations has not been tested empirically (Levin 2001, p. 295).

Interestingly, in the present study, when proffering views in favor of evaluative styles, attorneys made little mention of disputants. The discourse on reasons why each style was favored adds yet another angle to the discontinuity between the legal and the extralegal worlds in case processing and mediation, highlighting completely different understandings of what mediation "is."

Physician lawyers gave the following reasons why they preferred evaluative styles: respected mediators' opinions could sway opponents as well as their paying insurer clients; both sides' lawyers (including non-specialist plaintiff attorneys) and clients' expectations could be deflated by mediators' views on weaknesses/risks; expert lawyer-mediators' views provided knowledge and advice on how courts would react to the issues; and they were more likely to reach settlements. For instance,

> "The evaluative ones are far more beneficial... I don't need somebody to facilitate the process... We needed *this evaluative retired-judge mediator* to say 'You're never going

mediation, and some wanted more choice over mediators' style and expertise (Macfarlane and Keet 2004–5, pp. 693–95).

to get two hundred thousand dollars for this'... bringing some reality to plaintiffs' money expectations, or look at me saying 'He's going to get it'. IN WHAT WAY DO YOU THINK EVALUATIVE IS BETTER FOR PLAINTIFFS, NOT THEIR LAWYERS? Oh. Well, because I think it's more likely to achieve a settlement. I mean if I've got *this ex-judge-mediator* telling me this is what he thinks the numbers are going to be, that's going to have a whole lot more sway when I go back to my *insurer* client... as opposed to me saying 'Well, we had this mediation and the plaintiffs have sort of now convinced me that this may be the right number'." **Male physician lawyer – in thirties**

"I much prefer an evaluative approach... Each side can make their pitch and have some feedback from somebody with expertise and skill in the area... and can facilitate the thinking through of positions and the risks... It helps you sort of say 'Maybe I'm not seeing it right, objectively'. But it also reminds *defendant* doctors... there's no certainty here even when I think s/he is a good lawyer... WHAT ABOUT FROM THE DEFENDANT'S PERSPECTIVE? You see, I, I, you have to ask the physicians. I don't think that serves their interests... Do I know that for sure? I don't. I don't think there was any relief from that kind of opportunity." **Male physician lawyer – in fifties**

"I take cases to *this mediator* that are indefensible, that I'm going to pay money on, or I've got a plaintiff who has unrealistic expectations on the other side. Because... he has a particular skill at um, at you know, bringing some reality to a plaintiff's expectations about money." **Male physician lawyer – in thirties**

Hospital lawyers gave similar reasons on why they sought evaluative mediations: they assisted in educating nonspecialist plaintiff lawyers on medical litigation realities (i.e., swaying their views); they deflated plaintiffs and their lawyers' expectations when hearing weaknesses and risks from mediators; hospital lawyers themselves obtained an extra objective view on the issues and numbers; they resulted in quicker settlements. For example,

"You are going there to obtain the mediator's point of view, have them assess the case and give you assistance." **Male hospital lawyer – in forties**

"In *these* actions... it is key to have some evaluation from someone considered authoritative... *for* plaintiffs and/or their lawyers... to hear from someone other than me... they're on the wrong track... misconstrued the evidence... As they're suspicious of me." **Female hospital lawyer – in forties**

"People are probably looking for a little bit of help from the mediator... who's really experienced in the area. It's a big time saver... causes parties to reassess their positions." **Male hospital lawyer – in forties**

"I think that the voluntary mediations... when there are *mediator* experts are 'very', very effective. That's why they're going there, to obtain the mediator's point of view, and to have them assess the case and give you assistance in both parties maybe coming to their own agreement... The purpose one goes there, to pay the fees, and to take the benefit of their knowledge and expertise." **Female hospital lawyer – in twenties**

Almost mirroring defense counsel, plaintiff lawyers' reasons as to why they preferred evaluative mediation included that they wanted expert lawyer-mediators' advice themselves on how courts would react generally and what arguments would be accepted; it assisted in impasses, in identifying solutions, and it achieved faster settlements. Evaluative mediators also helped them with advising and/or reinforcing their views with their clients (e.g., deflating expectations). As Palmer and Roberts note, "devices such as early neutral evaluation serve to reduce unrealistic expectations, which lawyers may themselves have recklessly created or nourished" (Palmer and Roberts 1998, p. 228).

> "We came here to seek some guidance from a qualified mediator." **Male, specialist plaintiff lawyer – in fifties**

> "It was actually useful to have someone else's take on it. WAS IT OF BENEFIT TO YOUR CLIENTS... It probably helped me more than them." **Male, specialist plaintiff lawyer – in forties**

> "To me the evaluative form is very important. When I tell my client to compromise a case, they say 'Why should I?... I don't have as much experience as some... So it's nice to get some confidence... and know the other side is hearing the same story." **Male, generalist plaintiff lawyer – in forties**

> "I'm a big fan of evaluative mediation... You're talking about how much money a case is worth. The issue is not what's truly just or morally right. The issue is what the courts award... We needed down to earth, practical guidance on amounts... Secondly to teach the parties... or confirm that the amounts *advised* by the lawyers are relatively accurate of... court *awards*." **Male, specialist plaintiff lawyer – in fifties**

> "It has to be evaluative... *The defense lawyer* and I need to hear from an objective person... give you a gut reaction as to whether or not you're going to take a fall on that issue." **Male, specialist plaintiff lawyer – in forties**

> "I want to 'know' what this case is going to be doing if it goes to trial... from someone whose opinion I can trust." **Male, specialist plaintiff lawyer – in thirties**

The following voluntary, evaluative mediation of a child fatality case illustrates actors' perceptions of most attorneys' preferred style.

Male, specialist plaintiff lawyer – in fifties
> The mediator did his usual good job of displaying the right kind of sympathy to the parties who've been hurt, and gets them to the point where he says "I know it's not enough money, but our damn court system is stingy."

Male physician lawyer – in thirties

> It was important for the plaintiffs to tell their story so that they knew *the mediator* listened and understood the position they were coming from... So he'd have credibility in saying "You've suffered a terrible loss, but this case isn't worth millions of dollars... *This* is the right amount of money and you need to put this behind you."

Plaintiff – mother – in fifties

> The three lawyers were all pretty quiet... The *mediator* was really conducting it... the mediator was... warm... sensitive... *But* my experience was that it was deciding on what dollars... It was the *mediator* saying "That's the fair amount." It was clear the lawyers would listen to him... They were seeking his wisdom.

Plaintiff – father – in fifties

> *The retired-judge-mediator* directed the physician lawyers to approach the insurers and tell them this was a fair settlement and encouraged them strongly to accept it.

Interestingly, Wissler's survey of court-linked mediation participants in four Ohio counties (649 mediators, 1,224 lawyers, and 725 parties) calls into question whether mediators with extensive training and expertise in the subject matter of disputes have higher settlement rates. Although mediators who have substantive expertise were rated by lawyers as being more effective, that expertise did not increase settlement rates. The only mediator qualification that increased the likelihood of settlement was whether the mediator previously had mediated more than fifteen cases. The number of hours of training, years in legal practice, and whether the case was in a substantive area of the mediator's law practice did not increase the likelihood of settlement or progress toward settlement (Wissler 1998, p. 28). This was similarly noted in Wissler's later work, encompassing over 1,200 court-linked mandatory mediated cases where all mediators were attorneys. Again, this was despite the fact that lawyers were generally of the view that expertise in the subject matter was an important mediator qualification (Wissler 2002, p. 699). Likewise, in Pearson and Thoennes divorce mediation research, the degree of mediator experience was found to be key, as mediators who had mediated at least six cases offered major improvements in terms of outcomes (Pearson and Thoennes 1988, p. 436).

Of course, the value of obtaining settlements should not be underrated. As noted by a prominent retired judge mediator, "Settlement provides not only the money but piece of mind... Get it settled. Get on with your life. Put it behind you. Stop worrying about... the lawsuit... trial... how you're going to pay your lawyer if you lose." Yet, if third parties somehow impose their views, even non-coercively, on disputants is this really mediation? Moreover, looking at the findings in chapter two on plaintiffs' articulated litigation aims, chapter four on why disputants felt defendants should attend mediations, and chapter five on parties' mediation objectives, the question reemerged: Were these mediated disputes related to arguments over money alone?

7.3 The extralegal facilitative world on style

> "In the court-linked mediations... basically I had no role as a mediator, to tell you the honest truth. Yes I could facilitate, but I sat back and I watched the two lawyers trade until they traded in a way that both felt comfortable. You need to hear from the parties. Anybody can trade... I'll give you a hundred. I'll give you fifty. Let's saw off at 75. That can happen in five minutes or five hours. It's not a process... If you actually think about what the mediation process is... I think a legally focused mediation is really not; I wouldn't call it mediation. It shifts the definition in such a way that it takes away from what the process was meant to do." **Senior, female non-lawyer-mediator – twenty years' experience – in fifties**

In examining actors' pro-facilitative discourse, I entered the world of the extralegal. As subjective factors such as anger and confusion often motivate plaintiffs to file these suits, it has been argued that facilitative styles as opposed to other ADR methods that focus on the legal merits of disputes are best for these case types. Furthermore, facilitative, interest-based mediations are said to enable far more satisfying and thorough resolutions for parties, as they do not restrict party input and work against the issues being too narrowly defined – as is often the case with evaluative mediations where lawyers have larger roles (Currie 1998, pp. 222–23; Meschievitz 1991, p. 214; McDermott and Obar 2004, p. 105). Interestingly, in speaking of facilitative mediation, respondents in the present study mentioned all the issues that disputants (particularly plaintiffs) had said they were seeking from both litigation (*chapter two*) and mediation (*chapter five*). Pro-facilitative reasoning included talk about disputants being heard and being able to understand things and communicate with opponents for their own needs, allowing for questions and answers, and about how it addresses the emotional elements in cases. The following quotes highlight some of the issues that were mentioned:

> "Where somebody really wants some kind of verbal satisfaction, information or acknowledgment, facilitative has a much better role." **Female, senior physician lawyer – in fifties**

> "I think mediation should be facilitative... Absolutely... because... most of the time the plaintiff wants to get some understanding of what happened... We are looking for satisfaction for both sides. And that is quite different than a court of law." **Male physician defendant – in fifties**

> "I think the facilitative elements helped in that we were able to hear their side, their story, and that we had an opportunity to speak as well. The apology would not have come out with an evaluative approach." **Female hospital lawyer – in twenties**

> "With the facilitative approach there was always an open ear and time to hear what plaintiffs wanted to say... no limitations on issues or concerns that the plaintiffs personally felt needed to be talked about or addressed... *Plaintiffs*' comments... become part of the mix of information that weaves itself towards a settlement.... *The plaintiffs*'

view was very important to the resolution of this case... taken into account." **Male, specialist plaintiff lawyer – in thirties**

Consequently, it appeared that facilitative mediation assisted in resolving disputants' self-described extra-legal needs and objectives particularly in relation to communication and voice, whereas evaluative mediation more often served legal actors most in terms of litigation strategy and numbers.[19] Indeed, in facilitative mediation disputants focus on their underlying interests and needs rather than on the potential outcomes of litigation (Goldberg et al. 1992, p. 244; Stitt et al. 1999, p. 3). In line with this conclusion, it has been argued that disputants' interests in procedural fairness (which is said to be more important than obtaining analyses of legal outcomes or having control over results) endorse facilitative mediation. In contrast, lawyers' process interests lie in evaluative mediation (Reich 2002, pp. 183–86, 223–24). This conclusion is also reminiscent of Conley and O'Barr's research where it was found that litigants in court needed to tell their story, with many viewing litigation as a type of therapy. Thus, communication opportunities in court were sometimes of greater importance to litigants than results (Conley and O'Barr 1988, pp. 186–87).

Findings in some mediation studies support this conclusion, with various scholars noting that when disputants' expectations of voice are met, this is perceived as the greatest gain in mediation (Price et al. 2001, p. 101; Welsh 2001a, pp. 838–46; Sally 2003, p. 103, n. 77). In Mcdermott and Obar's quantitative study utilizing questionnaire data from mediators and disputants involved in 645 employment cases, both plaintiffs and defendants rated facilitative mediation more favorably than evaluative mediation on both procedural and distributive measures (being more likely to report they obtained what they wanted). This was notwithstanding the fact that under certain circumstances evaluative mediation resulted in higher monetary settlements (though legal representation played a major role in both styles). Having a full chance to present one's views was among the top four reasons for the difference. As a result, Mcdermott and Obar posit that the reason for the findings may be that facilitative mediations address intrinsic and nonfiscal gains as opposed to being focused on money (Mcdermott and Obar 2004, pp. 75–76, 79, 89–90, 92, 96–98, 101–2, 107–8). Likewise, in Wissler's Ohio court-mediation survey consisting of 144 cases that underwent voluntary and mandatory mediation, it was found that the "opportunity to express oneself" was among the criteria plaintiffs used to judge their mediations (Wissler 1997, pp. 567, 582, 598). Other research findings, albeit using experimental data with university students, also suggest that disputants prefer facilitative mediation over evaluative mediation as these are in line with their preferences for process control, including control over the relaying of their views (Shestowsky 2004, pp. 211, 239, 245).

That being said, further studies resulting in similar findings indicate that differences between mediation styles are less important. In McGillis' community

---

19 Of course, any resulting satisfactory settlements in either type of mediation would assist both.

mediation research it was found that style did not influence results or disputants' perceptions of the mediation process (Love and Boskey 1997, p. 84; McGillis 1997, p. 84). Similarly, a study on school mediations found that distinctions between evaluative versus facilitative (or transformative) styles were far less important to disputants than issues relating to procedural fairness. These include disputants' needs to participate, express themselves on issues perceived as significant, be heard, and be considered.[20] At the other end of the spectrum, in Wissler's Ohio court-mediation study of various case types, parties tended to have more favorable appraisals of mediators, the process, and the outcome if mediators evaluated cases' merits (without recommending particular settlements) (Wissler 1998, p. 28). Other research suggests that participants have greater perceptions of fairness with evaluative mediation (Lande 2000, p. 332; Wissler 2001, p. 35; 2002, pp. 679–80, 684–85).

Nevertheless, in terms of lawyers' transformations, for pro-facilitative attorneys (as well as those who were in favor of a mix of styles) their interest-based preferences and explanations added further evidence to the gradual move of those in the legal world away from conventional legal thought in terms of how lawyers conceptualize their cases. Lawyer-mediators staunchly against evaluative, rights-based mediation and pro-facilitative approaches offered further evidence of the reconceptualization phenomenon in the world of legal actors. For example,

> "The parties benefit tremendously in facilitative mediation because there is no catharsis with an evaluative approach. They're coming and listening to someone they see as an authoritative figure 'tell them'. I don't think that's what parties need. I think it's very important in the process not just to get a settlement, but to help contribute to something positively, to the future life of the litigant." **Male, retired judge – mediator – in seventies**

> "Evaluative mediation from a lawyer's point of view is very, very important... in settling a case. Unfortunately, it sucks when it comes to settling the plaintiff's and sometimes the defendant's difficulties that arise from these cases... Evaluative will get the case settled, but it won't get the job done. The parties will not feel as good as if they had control, made the settlement themselves and had a chance to vent... I'm convinced that the parties themselves benefit more from the facilitative. I strongly believe that." **Male lawyer-mediator – in fifties**

Reasons proffered by respondents in favor of facilitative mediation were almost antithetical to legal actors' reasons for evaluative mediation preferences, strongly indicating disparate visions and understandings of cases and how they should be resolved. Interestingly, no non-lawyer-mediator said anything positive about evaluative mediation. For example,

> "I don't believe in the evaluative model... You may get a settlement. Do you get an agreement? I've been in mediations where there was settlement and the issue

---

20 Ury (1988, p. 12), Baruch Bush (1997, pp. 18, 20–21), Wissler (1997, pp. 567, 582), Forehand (1999, pp. 909, 919), and Welsh (2004, pp. 595, 619–20, 666, 671, 820).

supposedly worked out. And I leave feeling a pit in my stomach... *as* in my mind it was not successful because the issues weren't really looked at and there were some really bad feelings left underneath... They've got it on paper. People got what they've got financially. But they're as angry as hell. And I have been in mediations whereby in some ways there has been no settlement, but the issue's gone away. All the human issues were dealt with, and they were fine. I have seen that happen." **Female non-lawyer-mediator – ten years' experience**

> "I think mediation is about offering people a process of communication and problem solving... the possibility to understand that for them to really resolve this, A, B, C and X will be addressed... 'X' may be a legal issue... money... But let's offer them an opportunity... that if there are other interests, those interests might also be satisfied. So at the end of the day... there are no pieces that are still outstanding... The differences between a trading scenario versus a facilitative scenario are fairly significant." **Female non-lawyer-mediator – twenty years' experience (social work background) – trains lawyers for voluntary/court-linked mandatory/College mediations – in fifties**

In fact, examining the discourse overall on the matter, the style issue emerges not only as another facet of the discontinuity between legal and extralegal interests and needs in case processing and mediation, but almost as a clash between them. This conclusion is further supported by lawyers' explanations of why they did not favor facilitative, interest-based mediators' styles. Lawyers' negative attitudes toward court-allotted mediators' performances appeared largely to be due to the fact that the majority used predominantly facilitative, interest-based styles.[21] Legal actors disliked facilitative techniques because they felt that they were inappropriate, took longer to reach settlements and did not offer opinions. Facilitative mediations were also called "groupie things" and "airy-fairy." For example,

> "When one is dealing with an argument over an amount of money, a touchy feely mediator isn't going to be a lot of help." **Male, specialist plaintiff lawyer – in fifties**

> "It was like 'What is it that 'you' want? Is there something you want to say to the doctor'? This kind of groupie thing...." **Male physician lawyer – in forties – describing a facilitative mediation of a fatality case – non-lawyer-mediator**

> "I don't think it's appropriate for plaintiffs to be venting *at mediation*... Go see a therapist if you want to vent... I can't stand mediators' strategy where they come in and go 'Tell me what you want to say'. I just don't like the concept... I always think it's odd. It's a job of the solicitor to talk to clients about expectations. I don't think this is an opportunity for you to state your case in life, for you to have your voice heard... I don't want my clients to have to come and say 'You know, here's where I stand. This is

---

21 The only mediators who were not liked by plaintiff lawyers were facilitative mediators. Defense physician lawyers' questionnaires indicated that virtually all who liked mediators' performances were those where mediators made suggestions for substantive solutions or discussed how a court would respond to the issues – both suggesting an evaluative approach.

what I did'.... I just don't like the emotional component. I think there's other places for it." **Female physician lawyer – in thirties**

"On the interest-based mediations... I don't think the mediator serves a significant role. In fact, on those I'm usually happy if the mediator does just about nothing. Because I can control it... I am more interested in going to somebody who can evaluate... We know we're not going to get some airy fairy sort of thing." **Male hospital lawyer – in forties**

Thus, clashes often resulted when courts allotted facilitative mediators to cases, as most lawyers viewed mediation as a process within the legal, tactical domain being encroached on by what was often perceived as an extralegal process outside the province of the law and lawyers' fields of operation. Unlike evaluative styles operating in the shadow of the law, facilitative mediation was frequently viewed by lawyers as an illegitimate form of resolving "their" cases. This reality highlights the difficulties facing ADR methods like facilitative mediation, fighting for inclusion in the "law," and for legitimacy in the eyes of the legal profession. Although the findings suggest that in terms of legal actors the struggle was still uphill, for disputants facilitative mediation was certainly perceived as part of their legal quest.

Legal actors' reasons in favor of evaluative mediation were valid. They were valid in the world of litigation, risks, strategy, and numbers. What was strange, however, was that almost no disputants spoke in the same way. One would think that even without legal backgrounds, disputants would be cognizant of at least some of these mediation style issues from their lawyers. Yet, these types of conversations did not seem to have occurred much, if at all. In fact, no lawyer ever mentioned disputants' style choices or having discussed mediation style issues with clients. As one male specialist plaintiff lawyer noted, "The most important thing to do is to talk *to clients* about the mediator 'that's been chosen', their role and qualifications, and your experience with them." Indeed, not a single disputant mentioned the issue of mediator or style choice. Thus, it appeared that most disputants simply "got whom they were given" without being aware of the differences in mediators or their styles, nor what it would mean in terms of their mediation experiences or results. Although this was not a focus of the topic guide interview questions, when explaining the two styles to plaintiffs a few said things to this effect:

"I think it should be plaintiffs to decide style. Yes, the lawyers should educate the plaintiffs and let the plaintiff know the difference between the two techniques, and let the plaintiffs decide. The plaintiff is the one who is at the disadvantage here. They have the problem. It's not the lawyer; it's not the defense... Let *plaintiffs* have a say in this whole thing instead of these two lawyers who have never experienced what the plaintiff experienced... and they are making that decision." **Male plaintiff – loss-of-vision case – in fifties**

"As a client, I was only told 'This is the mediation. We have to go to this mediation'.... If I would have known that I could have had another type of mediation... I would have said to my lawyer 'I don't want this type of mediation, I want ... ' I don't know why that wasn't offered, and I will ask him eventually about it. I think that would have been the best thing for our case." **Male plaintiff – fatality case – in forties**

"I definitely think parties themselves should decide whether they want evaluative or facilitative mediation." **Female plaintiff – hospital accident case – in forties**

Although some disputants may very well have chosen evaluative mediation if asked, plaintiffs obtaining any respite for their extralegal needs appeared to have done so serendipitously in mediations where lawyers sought evaluations of their strategic positions. That is not to say that disputants did not benefit from evaluative mediation as well. However, they benefited within the legal actors' world.

7.4 Gendered mediator experiences

There were two prominent gender findings immersed within the mediator data: one relating to plaintiffs and the other to female mediators.

Overpowered female facilitative mediators

On the gender front, the data suggested that the combination of gender and lack of "lawyer status" tended more often to result in female non-lawyer-mediators being overpowered by attorneys at mediations than males. Interestingly, although no lawyers mentioned this directly, 33% of plaintiffs said this had occurred, resulting in the lawyers in some respects taking charge. There were female mediators in all five cases where plaintiffs described this had occurred (with only one having legal qualifications but not perceived as an experienced practitioner). The remaining 67% of plaintiffs who had male lawyer-mediators did not perceive them as being overpowered by the attorneys. Likewise, most of the mediators plaintiff lawyers said they were not pleased with were female non-lawyer facilitative mediators. In all three of those mediations, actors' discourse indicated that it was the lawyers who "ran the show." Finally, there was no evidence that any male non-lawyer-mediator in the dataset was overpowered by legal actors at mediations. The DNR-fatality-mandatory mediation provides one illustration of this occurrence.

DNR fatality – post-discovery – mandatory court-linked mediation
Female non-lawyer-mediator – ten years' experience – trained mediators, ran victim – offender/community mediation program – in forties

My sense is the lawyers aren't too trusting of *mediation*... I mean, pretty well every case I walk in they tell me "This isn't meant for mediation"... The lawyers kept saying "What are we going to accomplish here today?" ... *both lawyers*, in terms of "How can we get through this quickly?"
   I would really like to work with the lawyers... rather than being seen as... to help them do their job, actually to help the clients... together... I do believe that the lawyers

are doing what they're doing believing it's in the best interests of their clients. *But* I do have the best interests of their clients at heart.

I look at the healing. I don't look at the money... We didn't have enough of the defendant speaking... for the chance of healing... I'm taking responsibility for it... because I was sensing real resistance from his lawyer. In fact, if I could have just removed the two lawyers, it would have happened.

Plaintiff – son – in forties

Mrs... beautiful lady, nice... very compassionate... She was trying. She was doing a great job... *But* the lawyers controlled her... Whatever the lawyers wanted, they maneuvered her into it. She had no power or clout. She really wanted to work it, but she couldn't because these two guys were there, like two pit bulls... The hospital lawyer, she just stayed pretty quiet. But the others both, you know, overpowered her... I saw it as a struggle of dominance between the plaintiff and doctor's lawyers... But here's a social worker *mediator* telling you "Look, I figured it out in 15 minutes."

I really felt for the mediator. My heart went out to her... One day I'd love to meet her and say "I really appreciate everything you've done"... If only she would have had more power on the two lawyers... *If* they'd respect her... I think we would have had a lot more resolved... She would have had the power to ask everyone the questions... And I think the two lawyers would have to listen a little bit better, and say "Well, you know, maybe she has a point here"... *So* the lawyers would know their strategy game was not going to work.

They didn't respect her... because they went on their own thing of talking about... *this* case... The lawyers were like they are at a trial argument. It's not a trial argument here, my friend... She tried to intervene a few times but she just got cut right down. She should have a big baking spoon to hit both of them over the head.

Plaintiff – widow – in seventies

Mostly the lawyers spoke during the mediation... The mediator was *a* very nice lady, very gentle and very, very professional... She was very attentive to me and didn't interrupt me while I spoke for a long time... She showed sympathy to me... *But* the mediator had no chance.

Male defendant physician – in fifties

I think the mediator did a good job. She tried to be objective... she put weight on one issue and another... When things were not very clear she was there jumping on it just to try to see if she can make the other person change their position, by making it sound that what they're saying is not really quite valid... She was not judgmental... She was quite clear at the end... She talked to us... Then she talked to them... And then she came up with her conclusions.

Male, specialist plaintiff lawyer – in forties

It was probably facilitative, interest-based... because the mediator was not a lawyer, or at least was not prepared to make an assessment of the merits of the legal position... DID THE FACILITATIVE ELEMENTS BENEFIT YOUR CLIENTS AT

ALL? In terms of result, not at all. In terms of an exercise in venting emotions I thought it was helpful for one of the plaintiffs. It didn't get the case resolved though. SO THE FACILITATIVE ELEMENTS REALLY ONLY HELP THE PARTIES AS OPPOSED TO THE COUNSEL? In my view, I think that's true.

She asked us to look at the human risk, the human suffering element. And I got to tell you, and I mean this not in a disrespectful way. In my books, that's not going to make it on this kind of case... because the *insurers* assess cases on the basis of expert opinions... And you can't sort of sit there and say "Look, the human interest is ..." A check isn't going to happen.

She was a decent, sympathetic person. She was intelligent. She'd obviously read the material. She got the message from me in short order that the physician lawyer and I had figured out what this case was really about, and that there was likely going to be a trial... She responded to my view in an appropriate fashion. I think she would have been equally justified in saying "Well, experienced counsel have discussed this case and there doesn't seem very much that I can do. Let's go home." In many ways I would have preferred that... But on the other hand, at an entirely different level, the human level – not that I'm necessarily supposed to think about that – she gave my client an opportunity to have her say about the fact that her husband is gone, and that this was terrible for her. Is there a value to that? It's not a question I can answer. I mean, maybe there is.

Male physician lawyer – in fifties

I was as disappointed in this mediation as I'd expected to be... because of the style of the mediator... I didn't like the mediator AT ALL. Well, I didn't dislike her personally. I just didn't think the style was what we needed. I didn't think the approach was one that I wanted to see. On the other hand, she had some success.

WHAT HAPPENED... The mediator was a social worker. It was much more, you know "What would you like out of this, and what would you like to say, and what would you like to hear?"... directed to counsel, and then to each party. Much more of "Let's try to diffuse the emotions... See if we can come to some issue"... much more emphasis on trying to dialogue... So we got into something like that [he makes a face].

DO YOU THINK IT HELPED THE DISPUTANTS? No, I don't... She had no expertise in the area. So it wasn't like there was any validation to the plaintiff's position being reasonable... I suspect there was probably... some emotional benefit... But if this is to be placed on you in circumstances where this is not really what it's all about, it's unacceptable.

Of course, this begged the question, "What was this all about?" The following case provides a further example of this phenomenon.

Vasectomy dispute – mandatory court-linked mediation

Female non-lawyer-mediator of twelve years – in thirties

If I was in the plaintiffs' position, I would have questioned the lawyers, "Why did we come here? What was the point?... The male plaintiff was quite verbal about expressing himself, and emotional... I think it only helped him tell his story and how devastating this was... I don't think they got much out of it, unfortunately... because the lawyers were so focused on the *impending* discoveries... Maybe my facilitators' approach didn't work this time. Maybe I should have really pushed it. I don't think it would have made a difference.

Male plaintiff – in thirties

The mediator was good... DID SHE HAVE A BIG PART IN THE MEDIATION? Not really... I just spoke my part for a brief moment and... the lawyers did the talking.

Female plaintiff – in thirties

I don't think the mediator did much talking... She just... let both sides' *lawyers* talk; that's it... She was a nice person and she did her job... She sympathized and I think she got the feeling of what we were there for.

Male, generalist plaintiff lawyer – in forties

She was fine for as far as it went... She wanted the plaintiffs to tell their story, and *was* happy to let the lawyers say as much as they wanted.

Female hospital lawyer – in twenties

YOUR VIEWS ON THE MEDIATOR? She was fine... She was lovely. But... really it's the opportunity to have the discussion... Probably if we'd all been put in a room we could have done exactly the same thing... without the mediator... THIS WAS SOLELY FACILITATIVE. DID ANY FACILITATIVE ELEMENTS BENEFIT YOU? No.

Overpowering scenarios were more commonly associated with female non-lawyer facilitative mediators than with male mediators, either lawyers or nonlawyers. This included female mediators of substantial credentials and experience.[22] Perhaps this can be explained by sociolingual research, which suggests that all else being equal, women are not as likely to be listened to as men regardless of how they speak or what they say (Tannen 1994, p. 284). Regardless of the reasons, by stunting mediators' abilities these scenarios appeared ultimately to detrimentally affect disputants most.

Mediators and female plaintiffs

A mediator establishes what may be a risky relationship of informality and apparent intimacy with the parties (Grillo 1991, p. 1589).

A second gender finding within the discourse on mediators related to plaintiffs. The data suggested that female plaintiffs tended to be more affected by what mediators said or did during mediations than male plaintiffs. This particularly related to mediators' extralegal gestures or conduct. Furthermore, females tended to be less

---

22 Interestingly, Kolb's research found that there is a tendency for female mediators to be assessed as less effective than males, even when the results they achieve are superior (Kolb 1991, pp. 64–93).

questioning or critical of information provided by mediators. Sixty-seven percent of female plaintiffs versus 17% of males stressed or repeatedly mentioned things mediators had said during mediations (*chapter six*, figure 24). This included references to how mediators acknowledged photos of deceased loved ones, mediators' personal stories, and case risks or weaknesses they spoke about. This trend was particularly noticeable between co-plaintiffs of different genders who had undergone the same mediations. For example, in the loss-of-sight voluntary mediation (no settlement):

Female plaintiff – in forties

> I think the mediator was more or less a godsend. REALLY? Yes, because he was full of empathy. He mentioned about his wife *who is in a similar situation to me*... He was very kind, very, very kind. I said to my husband... "This has got to be divine intervention to have him as our mediator."
> DID HE SAY "I THINK YOU SHOULD GET...?" Oh no. He did not interfere with... As a matter of fact, he did not talk about money at all... However... he told me about all these wonderful things the blind institute offers... a kind of grandfather-type. And probably at that particular time I needed to hear someone with a compassionate tone... I felt his warmth... I felt him actually reaching out to me... DID HE LIVE UP TO YOUR EXPECTATIONS? And then some.

Husband – co-plaintiff – in fifties

> He empathised... It was nice that the mediator talked about his wife who lost her sight. That was good... All well and good. But, you know, my wife lost her sight. That is a reality; and it's not her doing. It's the doctor's doing... *Yet the mediator made* no mention of disciplining the doctor. He didn't mention anything about the doctor... ANYTHING ABOUT YOUR CASE? He didn't give any view, nothing at all. WOULD YOU HAVE WANTED THAT? Well definitely, definitely.

Likewise, in the child fatality voluntary mediation (settled), the issues recounted by the female plaintiff (in fifties) relating to the mediator were not mentioned by the male co-plaintiff (in fifties):

> I loved every minute of *the mediation*... *The mediator* was especially good in helping me feel comfortable... I put a picture of *my son* on the table... I didn't know if the mediator would want it there... and he commented that it was a lovely picture right off the bat. So right from the word go it was a good process for me.
> It was really remarkable because *the mediator*... had a life experience with his own family, and he knows what the *grief* is like... He also had a brother that died... So he has two life experiences that put him in a special place to hear our story and to understand it. That was just amazing when I found that out... It was an incredible experience for me, in ways beyond the legal part... He was just a wonderful, wonderful person and he really shared with us a lot of his own life experiences... I felt everything that day was relevant, every story *the mediator* told... They were just amazingly

relevant... It was as if he was brought to us that day, that he was God's chosen one to deal with the case.

We knew that the *mediator* said that amount was a horrible amount. So we knew he didn't like what he had to tell us as far as the dollars... I... had a *real* sense... of what the next cost was going to be if we don't settle... because of what *the mediator* said... mainly because *he* shared with us some other cases... He did it in a very subtle... way... Then after you listen to that story... you thought "Hmn, I wouldn't want that happening"... I just had a sense "You are the... one person that could really understand our pain... and be able then to give... good advice."

WHAT WAS THE MOST IMPORTANT THING THAT HAPPENED AT MEDIATION? Um, meeting *the* mediator. REALLY? Ya. NOT ACHIEVING SETTLEMENT, OR SPEAKING YOUR SIDE, OR Well, I felt the presence of God through *the mediator*... It was just, it was a very warm, caring experience for me.

Male – father co-plaintiff – in fifties

WHAT HAPPENED... It went pretty much as I expected it... We went through some uh, familiarization, which was not really relevant to the case; in fact, quite a lot of familiarization. And then *the retired-judge mediator* wanted to know how this had impacted on us, and we went through that process... It was necessary, but not relevant really to the case. It was basically a process of putting everybody at ease... *The mediator then* came up with... some numbers by traditional methods, and... I told him that I didn't feel that that was going to settle the matter... If we had continued on the traditional method that *the mediator* presented, I'm quite sure that it would not have gotten settled because here you're trying to put numbers on things that were wrong, put numbers on a life.

WHAT FOR YOU WAS THE MOST IMPORTANT THING THAT HAPPENED DURING MEDIATION? You know, I didn't really view the thing as being of particular significance to me.

A similar trend was seen in other cases with female plaintiffs alone. This finding was linked to the comparable finding in chapter six relating to female plaintiffs tending to be more accepting than males of whatever transpired at mediations. Leaving aside the protections of legal representation, these issues could clearly have material effects on disputants in terms of both mediation experiences and case results.

Indeed, it is known that mediators may exert influence at various levels, for example, in reformulating information, stressing certain issues and ignoring others, or in offering suggestions (Roberts 1997, p. 129). Grillo posits that because mediation resembles a therapeutic environment in some respects, female disputants may be particularly influenced by what mediators say (Grillo 1991, pp. 1590–91).

These findings correlate with research in California. Kelly and Duyree's study of 184 respondents in divorce/custody mediations in two Californian settings found no gender differences in perceptions of mediators or mediations on the surface. However, similar to the present findings on females tending to be more influenced by and less critical of mediators (and the process) than males, Kelly and Duyree found that while both genders rated fairly positively mediators' skill, women were significantly more likely to agree that mediators were skilful. They also rated mediators' abilities considerably more highly than did men. Likewise, although few gender differences in perceptions of mediations were found, where significant differences appeared, women rated mediation experiences more favorably than did men (Kelly and Duyree 1995, pp. 37, 41–42, 45; Palmer and Roberts 1998, pp. 139–41).

7.5   Chapter conclusion

"There is a difference between simple settlement of case issues and the more difficult task of healing from genuine resolution of underlying conflict when disputants are changed in their attitudes." (Christiansen 1997, pp. 67, 75–76).

In examining actors' perceptions of mediators and their styles, this chapter has presented a final window into litigation-track mediation's parallel and complex worlds. For most lawyers and parties the mediator "was" the mediation experience. Adding another layer to the performance or representation theme in chapter six, mediators were seen to perform in front of their legal and lay mediation clients, either stressing their settlement rates and achievements, or in other ways endearing themselves to disputants and lawyers (who were potentially mediators' repeat clients). However, concurrently, unspoken and subliminal power struggles existed between mediators and attorneys, as mediators represented a new information source for litigants and sometimes a new interest intruding on lawyer–client relationships. Yet, mediators' ultimate influence was largely contingent on whether lawyers would willingly devolve power to them.

Disputants in the present study were not privy to mediator or style options, being left to accept both the mediators who had been chosen and the styles they employed. As such, the data revealed another way in which legal actors appeared to perceive mediation as a vehicle for them primarily, and parties only secondarily. Notwithstanding arguments that lawyers may not make better mediator choices due to their different interests from their clients (Lande 1997, p. 847, n. 32) and that disputants should be educated in advance and given the choice of different mediation types prior to undergoing the process (Levin 2001, p. 295), little mention was made by anyone of this occurring. Still, on the surface nearly all legal actors and disputants liked their mediators as individuals and perceived their mediators as unaligned. Most were also pleased with mediators' performances.

Yet, delving deeper into what participants liked about their mediators' performances, it was seen that most lawyers and parties viewed mediators through entirely different lenses – highlighting a discontinuity of preferences. The findings on lawyers' preferences correlate with other research (Metzloff et al. 1997, pp. 144–45; Welsh 2001a, p. 789; Macfarlane 2002, p. 285; McAdoo and Hinshaw 2002, p. 473). However, little data have been available on mediator attributes important to litigants. Lawyers across camps had similar wants and agendas for mediators.

This was something unknown to disputants. Most lawyers preferred evaluative mediation and chose mediators for their style. Lawyers spoke predominantly of tactical assistance by experienced specialist lawyer-mediators, while disputants spoke mainly of mediators' human attributes, rarely mentioning any strategic requirements or tactical benefits they derived from mediators.

Legal and lay actors' discourse also empirically informs the debate on facilitative versus evaluative mediation styles and illustrates the different understandings of what case mediation "is," adding another facet to the parallel worlds' thesis. Most lawyers, regardless of camp, sought qualified evaluative mediators to assist them with their strategic agendas in terms of giving them advice on how courts would react to issues and to assist with their clients (e.g., by deflating expectations) and opponents (e.g., to sway their views). This finding indicates that some forms of mediation have little to do with uncoerced decision making or facilitative consensual decision making, as lawyers were effectively seeking advisory opinions. Interestingly, it appeared that most parties liked best whatever style they experienced. In fact, disputants seemed to judge their mediation experiences not by their style, but by the perceived opportunities to express themselves and to dialogue with opposing sides and mediators. Nevertheless, in comparing actors' pro-facilitative discourse they spoke in a different language, premised upon very different understandings of the meaning of disputes, case processing, and conflict resolution. Thus, reasons in favor of facilitative styles were almost antithetical to reasons for evaluative preferences.

Actors' pro-facilitative discourse encompassed disputants' self-described extralegal needs and aims for litigation and mediation (*chapters two and five*). Thus, in this way facilitative mediation appears to assist disputants more, whereas evaluative mediation appears to serve lawyers' needs most in terms of litigation strategy and tactical assistance.[23] It has been argued that attorneys' process interests favor evaluative mediation and compete with the frequently different ones of disputants, which endorse facilitative mediation. Yet, with mediation being lawyer driven and lawyers being mediators' main customers, it is lawyers' process interests that are likely to be satisfied (Reich 2002, pp. 183, 186, 223–24). Indeed, this chapter has demonstrated that legal actors ultimately dominated the style game in their approval of evaluative and general disapproval of facilitative mediations – with consequent effects for disputants.

Conceptually, as evaluative mediations entail expert understandings occupying the dominant role, whereas in facilitative mediations lay understandings are dominant, this chapter's findings can also be viewed within a paradigm of struggle for dominance between mediation's legal and extralegal actors. Within this struggle, the discourse of the minority of legal actors in favor of facilitative styles additionally provided evidence of their gradual move away from conventional legal thought

---

23 It was intriguing that disputants' discourse overall lacked any talk of "rights." Thus, the present findings in some respect additionally support arguments on the inadequacy of rights' discourse in being able to fully resolve all issues in disputes for parties (Brown and Simanowitz 1995, p. 154)

and practice. Lawyer-mediators describing facilitative styles favorably provided yet further evidence of legal actors' reconceptualization of cases and their roles within them.

Finally, the chapter's gender findings provide further indications of female plaintiffs' potential vulnerabilities during mediation processes, adding empirical evidence to the feminist literature on females' disadvantage in informal justice processes (Grillo 1991, pp. 1549–51, 1583–84, 1602–4, 1610). Female plaintiffs tended more than males to be affected by mediators' words and actions (particularly their extralegal gestures and conduct). Yet at the same time they were less critical or questioning of mediators' behavior or the information they provided. This was consistent with the findings in chapter six on female plaintiffs being overall more accepting of all aspects of their mediation experiences. As for female mediators, the confluence of legal and nonlegal worlds at mediation at times resulted in non-lawyer female mediators being overpowered or disempowered by male legal actors involved in the cases. Although discussed by parties, few lawyers mentioned this. Still, many articulated their disdain for both facilitative styles and non-lawyer-mediators. As with the findings in chapters four to six, this scenario often left disputants to contemplate "what could have been."

Chapter eight, the conclusion chapter, summarizes the key findings, making the argument about the differentially experienced parallel worlds of those who participate in case processing and mediation of legal disputes.

CHAPTER EIGHT

Conclusion: The parallel understandings and perceptions in case processing and mediation

"An important measure of a civilization is the quality of justice received by its citizens" (Gold 1991, p. 267). Yet... "procedures of conflict resolution within any state are always being criticized, are always changing and are never as fair and as unbiased as they ideally might be."

Hampshire (1999, p. 35)

Following upon the research question posed in chapter one, "How do professional, lay, and gendered actors understand and experience litigated case processing leading up to and including mediation in legal disputes?," three recurrent themes have been important throughout the book: (1) the parallel worlds of understanding and meaning prevalent for legal actors versus lay disputants, (2) the reconceptualization of legal actors consequent to involvement with the extralegal dimensions of mediation processes, and (3) the parallel understandings and meanings of gendered actors in both lay and professional groups. In support of these themes, the data and findings throughout the book inform both the empirical-based discourse and the theoretical debates in various literatures.

First, the research has provided empirical data from disputants themselves on how they perceive and address legal disputes and their resolution – offering insight into the little known, yet critical area of litigants' hidden agendas for both formal litigation and mediation processes (Conley and O'Barr 1988, pp. 182–84, 196–97; Guthrie 2001, p. 165) (*chapters two and five*). Additionally, the findings on the negative transparency effects of mediation add to the scant knowledge on how litigants actually feel during negotiations and what factors affect their perceptions (*chapter six*) (Relis 2002, p. 175). The data also enrich comprehensions of mediator attributes and styles important to parties, comparing them with those of lawyers (*chapter seven*). These findings are valuable at a time when mediation, which is increasingly becoming institutionalized in numerous jurisdictions, is at a stage of development where there is still no consensus on what the goals of the process or suitable methods should be (Waldman 1998, p. 169; Levin 2001, p. 295, n. 143; McDermott and Obar 2004, p. 78; Welsh 2004a, p. 662).

Second, in providing a comparative view of attitudes of disputants and legal actors within the same or similar cases, the data illustrate through actors' perceptions the sharp disparity inherent in the notion of "mediating for a settlement (or abandonment)" versus "mediating a dispute." Legal representation of disputants during non-adversarial ADR procedures represents a material transformation in the practice of law (Kovach 2003, pp. 400, 403–4). Yet, there are little data on lawyers' roles in representing parties at mediation (Sternlight 1999, p. 275). Thus, as Hensler notes, "We need thick descriptions of... what ADR... means to and for lawyers" (Hensler 1999, p. 15). Similarly, Stempel notes, "ADR has been surrounded by large doses of rhetoric about freedom and self-determination, but ADR, in practice, reflects insufficient examination of the degree of freedom actually in evidence" (Stempel 2003, p. 353). It has been suggested that "in light of the tensions inherent in lawyer-disputant relationships, disputants' views on mediation might diverge from those of their lawyers" (Welsh 2004a, pp. 601–2). Indeed, in juxtaposing divergent actors' views within the same and similar cases, the findings here reveal the very different perspectives and goals of disputants and lawyers during case processing and mediation, something questioned by scholars (Wissler 2002, pp. 642, 645, 691). The data additionally add a novel angle to the discourse in the lawyering theory and dispute resolution literatures, particularly relating to the ways in which attorneys and the legal system understand and address litigants' problems and needs (Sherwin 1992a, pp. 42–43, 48, 51).

Moreover, by looking at the micro-elements of case processing and conflict resolution, the findings uncover important realities about the macro-elements of formal and informal justice processes. These findings suggest that something is occurring within the processing of litigated disputes that is not being captured, revealing inherent problems with the core workings of the legal system. This, in turn, has added a rider to the theoretical critiques on informal justice, as will be seen.

Third, the reconceptualization findings, based on lawyers' own discourse, add to the scant empirical knowledge on transformations within lawyers themselves simply through experience of mediation processes or in becoming mediators. The study also adds to the small body of literature examining mediation from the perspective of the mediator. Fourth, as no systematic empirical studies have examined gender-based differences in lawyers and parties, the gender findings on legal actors add important insight to the limited empirical knowledge on how the diverse genders actually practice law (Menkel-Meadow 1994a, pp. 89, 91, 95; Stempel 2003, p. 312), including ADR. Likewise, the disputant findings inject actors' meanings into the predominantly structure-oriented debate on whether mediation disadvantages women. Fifth, the data inform the debate on facilitative, interest-based versus evaluative, rights-based mediation styles, which has lacked empirical evidence including disputants' views (McDermott and Obar, 2004, p. 78). Finally, as the dataset comprises participants' views in both voluntary and court-linked mandatory mediations, the findings add to the debate on mediation mandating (e.g., Grillo 1991, pp. 1551, 1581; Welsh 2001a, pp. 787–89; Nader 2002, p. 141). Yet more than simply answering a call for more research to compare court-connected mediation with private mediation (Wissler 2002, p. 689, n. 227), the present findings offer insight into the issues from actors' perspectives.

Of course, in addition to the limitations noted in chapter one, one should not ignore the fact that as with most such research, the findings here derive from a particular study in a particular geographic, jurisdictional, and cultural location and cover one dispute type. Thus, extrapolating to other case types and legal systems should not be done without qualification. Certainly, to assume direct parallels would be oversimplifying matters particularly in view of the plethora of different cultural precepts and norms between societies in different countries. Still, within each of the recurrent themes in the book, the findings have offered a more nuanced understanding of legal and sociolegal constructions of professionals, disputants, males and females. They have also extended the limits of previous studies as well as modified and clarified some of the important generalizations developed in the disciplines. Each of the themes is examined next, summarizing the chapters' findings and their import, and supporting the conclusions reached about the differentially experienced worlds of those who participate in legal case processing and mediation. In addition, the practical application of the findings as well as recommendations for future research are discussed in Sections 8.5 and 8.6.

8.1 Parallel lay versus legal worlds of understanding and meaning in case processing and mediation

Grounded in interpretive theory, this work has shown case processing and mediation to be both constraining and enabling for its actors, both setting limits and providing the means for interaction (Giddens 1984, p. 25; Mouzelis 1991, p. 27). Yet, the recurrent parallel worlds' theme findings have reflected often antithetical currents of understanding and meaning attached to cases and their litigated and mediated resolutions, thereby challenging the notion that litigants and their lawyers understand and want the same things in case processing. Legal actors on all sides inhabit a tactical and strategic universe, while lay plaintiffs and defendants reside in an extralegal world based on psychological needs, feelings, and emotions. Thus, in each chapter there were remarkable similarities in perceptions and comprehensions of the diverse facets of disputes, case processing, and mediation by actors on opposite ends of cases. Consequently, I offer a new theory, in which the identities of attorneys and litigants are reinvented to demonstrate this reality and in order to serve as a basis for meaningful reform. My theory necessitates revising conceptions about formal and informal justice case processing to reflect legal and lay actor groups' divergent understandings, needs, and aims. Underlying each actor group's disparate positions is an unlikely conceptual alignment between plaintiffs and defendants, distancing them from legal actors in their cases (including their own representatives). Lawyers are also notionally aligned, regardless of which side they are on. Each "new" conceptual group – that is, (1) attorneys on all sides, and (2) disputing plaintiffs and defendants – ascribes similar meanings to cases and their resolution, wants similar things, and wants communication. However, these "new" groups do not necessarily want the same things nor do they speak the same "language." Thus, actors involved in case processing create competing meanings of what conflict and its resolution entail. Although legal actors have significant impact on how cases are conceptualized within the legal system, overall the meaning of disputes and their resolution is contingent on the position of the actors concerned.

Stuart Hampshire offers one explanation for the recurrent finding that legal actors generally held similar views, regardless of camp. He posits that "those who operate within various institutions in pursuit of their own particular ends naturally come to share certain professional attitudes and customs and a common professional morality... Most lawyers... feel a certain solidarity in the face of outsiders, and in spite of other differences they share fragments of a common ethic in their working life, and a kind of moral complicity" (Hampshire 1999, pp. 48–49). On this level, it can be argued that utilizing legal representatives to assist disputing individuals in resolving their conflicts is laden with difficulties as epistemologically legal actors and lay disputants occupy different, though parallel, worlds of meaning and understanding of disputes and how to resolve them. These parallel worlds evolve in tandem, yet never really converge. Moreover, there is little awareness between groups of the disparities prevailing.

The following paragraphs summarize the findings supporting the parallel worlds' thesis of legal and lay actors' different understandings, aims, perceptions, and experiences in case processing and mediation. The macro-meanings of these findings as well as relevant literature are discussed further in Section 8.3.

Litigation aims and mediation objectives

First, while legal representatives' conduct in processing cases is premised on basic understandings of what those who commenced these suits want, chapter two revealed fundamental misconceptions about plaintiffs' aims – something that goes to the core of the practice of law and approaches to the resolution of disputes. Overall, legal actors, regardless of whom they represented, understood that plaintiffs sued solely or at least predominantly for money – as that was all the system could provide. Yet, highlighting the first facet of the discordant understandings of lay disputants and legal actors, plaintiffs' discourse rarely correlated with lawyers' comprehensions of this basic premise. Virtually all plaintiffs vehemently stressed they sued not for money, but for extralegal principles, such as desiring defendants' acceptance of responsibility, that what occurred should never happen again, answers, explanations, apologies, and acknowledgments of their harm. Only a minority (35%) said pecuniary recompense was even a secondary aim. This was notwithstanding evidence of plaintiffs' lawyers conditioning their clients about the civil justice system's monetary "realities" and translating extralegal aims into legal categories and ultimately into money. This resulted in some plaintiffs' discourse on their aims of principle becoming intertwined with pecuniary recompense. These lawyer and clients "conditioning" conversations, together with evidence of some plaintiffs ceasing to discuss their extralegal agendas with their lawyers may have cemented attorneys' own understandings that financial compensation was all or primarily what their clients were seeking. Plaintiff lawyers may have then transmitted this misunderstanding or incomplete understanding to defense lawyers in their subsequent conversations and negotiations.[1] This contributed to meanings in the legal world becoming manifestly different to disputants' conceptions of their cases.

The findings on mediation aims in chapter five thus evinced significantly diverse, often conflicting, mediation objectives and agendas of legal actors and lay disputants. Regardless of camp and with little faith in mediation's confidentiality, legal actors' articulated mediation aims were replete with tactics, strategy, and pecuniary aspirations. For legal actors mediation was not about information sharing for educational or psychological purposes. Mediation was about relaying tactical information to opponents to strategically assist lawyers in highlighting their strengths and opponents' case weaknesses (as in traditional advocacy) in an effort to achieve financial settlement or case abandonment. Apart from the few plaintiff lawyers who included some extralegal objectives in their discourse, what lawyers had planned for mediation contained little of what disputants sought.

Plaintiffs and defendants also discussed very similar aims for mediation, conceptually aligning them against mediation's legal actors (often including their own lawyers). Besides the ubiquitous desire to resolve their disputes, parties' articulated objectives were extralegal – with none saying that they aimed solely for pecuniary settlement. Parties sought psychological and emotional closure, and wanted to be heard, seen, understood, and acknowledged. Specifically, most wanted mediation to include at least a qualified apology (whereas only a small minority of attorneys aimed for this), the provision of explanations (virtually no legal actors desired this), and to hear the other side's point of view (only a small minority of lawyers had this as a mediation objective). This accorded with the findings on litigation aims (*chapter two*) and highlighted the indivisibility of plaintiffs' legal and extralegal needs, something rarely mentioned by legal actors. Thus, overall, both legal and lay actors wanted communication at mediation, seeking for others to agree with their perspectives. Yet, each spoke essentially different languages – even most lawyers and their clients.

Mandatory versus voluntary mediations

Views on mandatory versus voluntary mediations represented another facet of the parallel worlds' thesis (*chapter three*). Perceiving mediation as a forum where tactical strategies play out, mandatory mediations were generally viewed negatively by lawyers predominantly due to their early timing. Thus, legal actors usually had low expectations and little intention to resolve their cases at mandatory mediations. Yet, despite any expectation management by their attorneys, disputants perceived both voluntary and mandatory mediations similarly, simply as a stage in litigation.

---

1 Ceasing to discuss extralegal issues with their counsel was similarly found with U.S. divorce lawyers and clients (Felstiner and Sarat 1992, pp. 1460, 1463–64).

Consequently, plaintiffs and defendants exhibited the same needs, positive attitudes, high expectations, and eagerness regardless of mediation type.

Defendants' attendance and the meaning of mediation

Lawyers' versus parties' discourse on defendants' mediation attendance (*chapter four*) represented a further facet of legal versus extralegal actors' diverse understandings, needs, and meanings ascribed to case processing, mediation and case resolution, further supporting the unlikely conceptual alignment between plaintiffs and defendants, and distancing them from legal actors in their cases.

Although attorneys discussed reasons both for and against defendants' attendance at mediation, the data indicated that plaintiff and defendant lawyers were regularly agreeing "not to invite" defendants to mediations. This angered most plaintiffs who thought defendants did not want to face them. Talk of defendants' attendance in all lawyer groups was directly linked to issues of settlement and the effect of defendants' attendance on lawyers' strategic agendas. Defendants' presence was often perceived as dangerous (by causing "raised emotions") or unnecessary (as any settlement monies would not come from physicians) for legal actors. Any talk of mediation being a venue for disputants' extralegal enterprises was discussed only secondarily or as a serendipitous effect. As such, the discourse on defendants' attendance and on attorneys' mediation aims (*chapter five*) revealed lawyers' unspoken understandings of mediation's purpose and meaning. For most legal actors, mediation was a strategic litigation vehicle for money talk and financial settlement or case abandonment, not a forum for fault talk or extralegal communication. Yet, this ignored the indivisibility of disputants' legal and extralegal needs in case processing – something made plain by parties' views on defendants' attendance at mediation. Plaintiffs' and defendants' discourse on defendants' presence at mediation was starkly different to that of lawyers. All proffered psychological, therapeutic, and educational reasons for mediating together. This made clear that far from a forum where tactical strategies played out, for disputants mediation was a place to treat human needs and preserve human dignity. It was a place for both verbal and nonverbal communication, information sharing, human interchange, closure, and most importantly "feeling better about their situations." No mention was made of monetary settlement or the obvious fact that any settlement monies would not come from physicians themselves.

Mediation perceptions and assessments

In chapter six, attorneys' and parties' discourse on "what went on" during actual mediations revealed different and incongruous realities and perceptions of what took place. This highlighted mediation as host to the confluence of the conflicting worlds of tactics and strategy versus that of human needs and desires. Mediation was also seen to be a forum for dual communication, almost antithetical in nature. Notwithstanding each actor's need to communicate, the communication that occurred between legal and extralegal actors was transmitted and received on different planes, resulting in very different insight obtained from participants within the same mediations. Thus, although interacting together, lawyers and litigants perceived things in completely different ways, often not really communicating at all.

When examining what attorneys on all sides favored about their mediation experiences, their discourse reflected their understandings of mediation as being a key vehicle for tactical communication aimed at lowering parties' expectations. This included having litigants hear about case weaknesses and the risks and realities of the litigation system. Defense lawyers also spoke of obtaining strategic insight at mediation by assessing how plaintiffs would fare as trial witnesses and viewing the internal dynamics between plaintiffs and their lawyers and co-plaintiffs. In the same vein, plaintiff lawyers spoke of the paucity of tactical insight they acquired due to defense lawyers' guardedness. This highlighted the issue of the unequal information flow generally occurring at mediations. Yet, in recounting the positives and negatives of their mediation experiences, attorneys seemed to be unaware that most of plaintiffs' extralegal mediation aims had not been realized.

In contrast to lawyers' highly strategic accounts, disputants depicted the same mediations as very personal encounters, providing emotional and psychological descriptions and interpretations of what went on. Parties' favored mediation elements sharply differed to legal actors' focus on tactical issues. What nearly all plaintiffs and defendants valued was the opportunity to express themselves, be heard, and offer extralegal communication. This resulted in emotional relief. As for disfavored aspects, apart from the dearth of information they received, what plaintiffs particularly did not like related to what they saw through mediation's window into the legal world. Consequent to the verbal and nonverbal communication of some legal actors, plaintiffs perceived lawyers as "playing a game" or impersonally handling their tragedies. In some respects it could be argued that lay disputants refused to enter the legal world. Indeed, the vast majority did not recognize what I have termed the "red riding hood syndrome" relating to plaintiffs' strong emotional and psychological needs to tell their stories, express themselves, and be heard feeding into legal actors' needs to evaluate them strategically. Furthermore, notwithstanding any tactical information transmitted by lawyers at mediation, only a minority of plaintiffs changed their views about their disputes. None changed their views about the initiating incidents.

Mediators and their styles

The examination of perceptions of mediators and their styles presented a final facet to the parallel worlds' theme (*chapter seven*). There were gross disparities in how legal versus lay actors within the same mediations conceived, perceived, and assessed their mediators. What legal actors liked was described almost wholly in terms of the tactical assistance they provided to lawyers. Most attorneys sought evaluative mediators with legal practice experience within the specialist dispute area in order to assist them with their case strategies. Yet, distant from the lenses through which lawyers judged mediators, when describing what they liked, parties predominantly spoke of mediators' encouragement of communication and human attributes of warmth, caring, and protectiveness, rarely mentioning tactical requirements or benefits. Nor did disputants speak much of mediators' backgrounds – being unaware that in many respects mediations were doomed from the start when lawyers did not perceive mediators to have the requisite experience. Interestingly, for most disputants almost anything mediators did was perceived positively. Several plaintiffs recounted how their mediators were "heaven-sent or fated" to them when mediators discussed similar life experiences.

Likewise, most legal and lay actors' explanations of why each mediation style was favored represented yet another facet of the discontinuity between the different comprehensions of what case resolution and mediation "was." The majority of lawyers perceived mediation as a process within the legal, tactical domain. Thus, facilitative mediation (especially with non-lawyer-mediators) was often viewed as almost an illegitimate way of dealing with their cases in that it was an extralegal process outside the province of the law and lawyers' fields of operation. In contrast, little disparity was found in disputants' discourse relating to evaluative and facilitative mediations, with most parties liking best whatever mediation style was employed. Although virtually all were first-time litigants with little to compare to, this appeared to be because disputants judged their mediations very differently to legal actors. Similar to other court and mediation studies' findings, parties seemed to assess their mediations according to the opportunity they had to express themselves and to communicate with opponents and mediators, regardless of the style it was conducted in. In effect, this meant that at times essentially different processes yielded the same evaluations from disputants.[2]

Lawyers' reasoning in favor of evaluative styles did not include any extralegal talk pertaining to disputants' perspectives on their cases, nor to the extralegal communication parties sought at mediation. Evaluative mediation by qualified mediators was perceived by attorneys irrelevant of camp as an assistance in the persuasion of opponents and lawyers' own clients (e.g., in swaying views or by deflating expectations). Additionally, legal actors favored evaluative mediation because they themselves sought advice from knowledgeable mediators as to what arguments would be accepted by a court and how much if any compensation was reasonable. Thus, evaluative, rights-based mediation was seen to principally assist legal actors with their strategic missions, as it operated in "the shadow of the law" where expert understandings occupied the dominant role.

In sharp contrast to most lawyers' views on evaluative mediation, pro-facilitative discourse was spoken in a different language and was premised on very different understandings of the meaning of disputes and conflict resolution. Facilitative mediation was seen to serve disputants' extralegal needs as reasoning in favor of

---

2 Conley and O'Barr (1988, pp. 186–87), Ury (1988, p. 12), Baruch Bush (1997, pp. 18, 20–21), Love and Boskey (1997, p. 84), McGillis (1997, p. 84), Wissler (1997, pp. 567, 582), Forehand (1999, pp. 909, 919), and Welsh (2004, pp. 595, 619–20, 666, 671, 820).

facilitative styles included all of plaintiffs' articulated desires and objectives for both litigation and mediation (*chapters two and five*). As facilitative mediation allows lay understandings to occupy a dominant position at mediations, disputants' interests in procedural fairness and process control also endorse it. This correlates with assertions that facilitative mediation focuses on nonmonetary outcomes (McDermott and Obar 2004, p. 108) and that facilitative styles imply a "changed and diminished role for lawyers" (Roberts 1993, pp. 462–63). Yet, with mediation being lawyer driven and lawyers being mediators' main customers, the findings indicated that it was regularly lawyers' process interests that were likely to be satisfied (Reich 2002, pp. 183, 186, 223–24). Indeed, legal actors ultimately dominated the style game in their approval of evaluative and general disapproval of facilitative mediations – with consequent effects for disputants.

8.2 The reconceptualization of legal actors

Notwithstanding the coexisting parallel worlds of legal and lay actors in case processing, the chapters repeatedly provided evidence of mediation experiences resulting in many practicing lawyers gradually reconceptualizing their cases and their roles within them, with extralegal considerations becoming inherent within lawyers' thinking and discourse. I argued that this subtheme is a consequence of mediation's extralegal attributes being thrust upon the legal world, resulting in lawyers viewing their cases at least in some respects on a more extralegal, human, or holistic basis. It has been asserted that the advent of ADR has resulted in a decline in rights' discourse within the legal domain and a move toward more of an emphasis on human needs and interests to instead evaluate conflict and resolution.[3] The reconceptualization findings empirically support this view. Indeed, in the present study, talk of "rights" was almost wholly absent from respondents' discourse about their cases and their mediations.

The first hint of lawyers' reconceptualization was seen when attorneys discussed defendants' attendance at mediation (*chapter four*). Despite non-attendance norms, the talk of most attorneys in each camp was peppered with extralegal pro-attendance reasons on why defendant physicians' attendance could be beneficial to disputants. A few lawyers even spoke wholly within an extralegal paradigm. Then in chapter five, within lawyers' discourse on mediation objectives, notwithstanding the diversity of mediation aims between legal and lay actors there was further evidence of the legal world undergoing a process of change. Conventional legal thought and practice appeared to expand to increasingly include psychological and emotional extralegal considerations relating to parties. For instance, plaintiffs' lawyers instructed their clients to "tell their stories" for reasons not limited to law and strategy, marking some recognition of the indivisibility of plaintiffs' legal and extralegal needs. Several

---

3 Rifkin (1984, p. 27), Silbey and Sarat (1989, pp. 483, 491), Cobb (1997, pp. 413, 436–37), Alberstein (2002, p. 322), Silbey (2002, p. 177), and Hensler (2003, pp. 195–96).

plaintiff lawyers' own mediation objectives included extralegal elements. There was also some evidence of defense lawyers rethinking their cases once having heard plaintiffs' extralegal realities at mediation. Indeed, for practicing attorneys overall, notwithstanding their experiencing mediation predominantly tactically, the data suggested that hearing plaintiffs recount their situations sensitized them to the human realities of these disputes. New relationships were also formed at mediations between defense counsel and plaintiffs, relationships that were nonexistent prior to the advent of mediation. This may have contributed to the reconceptualization of legal actors on the defense. Finally, in chapter seven it was seen that a number of plaintiff lawyers specifically noted mediators' "warmth" and "compassion" toward plaintiffs as attributes that pleased them. Again, these attributes did nothing for the legal issues in their cases. Likewise, the discourse of the minority of attorneys in favor of facilitative, interest-based mediation styles provided further evidence of their gradual move away from conventional legal thought and practice.

A second element supporting the reconceptualization subtheme throughout the chapters relates to the differences in discourse of practicing attorneys versus lawyers who had become mediators. It has been posited that mediators are a "product of the tension between the lawyer and the therapist" and that they combine legal with psychological, psychoanalytical, and philosophical knowledge (Alberstein 2002, pp. 322–23). Indeed, throughout the chapters it was clear that something had changed within lawyer-mediators' understandings of cases and ways of looking at the world. This highlighted an increasing gap in comprehensions and meanings between lawyers who remained practitioners and those who became mediators, the latter moving more swiftly to the "extralegal world" in terms of how they viewed disputes and the way they should be resolved. This finding was strengthened when comparing the discourse of lawyer-mediators to non-lawyer-mediators (e.g., of social work backgrounds) on various aspects of case processing – where frequently no discernable differences could be found.

In particular, lawyer-mediators' discourse on defendants' attendance included far more extralegal considerations relating to disputants than that of practicing attorneys (*chapter four*). In fact, all spoke with an extralegal focus – a world away from what practicing lawyers were saying. Moreover, no differences were found when comparing lawyer-mediators' discourse on defendants' attendance with that of non-lawyer-mediators. Then, in chapter six further evidence of a move away from traditional legal thinking was seen when exploring lawyer-mediators' discourse on what they viewed as favorable and objectionable within their mediation experiences – again extremely different from the perspectives of practicing attorneys at the same mediations. Lawyer-mediators' pro-facilitative and anti-evaluative explanations in chapter seven evidenced a final element of their swifter reconceptualization to that of practicing lawyers as they spoke a completely different language in relation to how cases should be resolved.

It was as if in conceiving conflict and its resolution, human beings who studied and practiced law entered a "legal world" premised on rules, norms, and strategies.

Yet, these same individuals who later mediated or even simply experienced mediations seemed to return to the extralegal world in terms of their conceptions and understandings of "what disputes were about" and how to resolve them. Thus, I argue that mediation experience plays a role in transforming legal actors, representing part of the shift in what lawyers "are" and how they present themselves.

The literature

In terms of the use of mediation as a mechanism for transformation, Menkel-Meadow asks, "What, if any, transformative potential does mediation have to change people, situations and political and social structures?" "Can mediation be used to transform individuals, organizations, systems and our society" (Menkel-Meadow 1995c, pp. 217–18)? There has been a fair amount of discourse in the theoretical literature on both sides of the Atlantic about the expansion of ADR slowly transforming and expanding the practice of law, the values inherent within it, and thus the traditional model of the lawyer.[4] Although some are skeptical of ADR's ability to transform legal actors (Hensler 2003, p. 193), scholars have speculated that mediation's incorporation into formal court and litigation-track processes will materially alter attorneys' representational roles and reduce adversarial behavior to allow for the necessary nonadversarial (or less adversarial) roles of lawyers involved in mediation (Lande 1997, pp. 841, 879–80; Kovach 2003, pp. 403–4). Although concerned about adversarial co-option of the mediation process, Menkel-Meadow too notes this transformation in positing that growing numbers of U.S. lawyers are looking to new forms of lawyering, some quite alien to the traditional conception of the lawyer's role (Menkel-Meadow 1999, p. 802). However, little empirical evidence exists from actors themselves on the actual transformations of practicing lawyers who partake in mediation processes nor on any changes in attorneys who become mediators. Only three studies were found that alluded to the effects of mediation experience on practicing lawyers.

Metzloff et al.'s research into court-ordered medmal mediation in North Carolina found that lawyers were enthusiastic about mediation notwithstanding low success rates. This was explained by the fact that numerous attorneys felt that mediation provided the potential for a "better" resolution of disputes (Metzloff et al. 1997, p. 142). McEwen et al.'s findings on divorce lawyers, although admittedly not definitive, similarly suggest that involvement in mediation may change lawyers' attitudes outside mediation as well. Interviews with Maine divorce lawyers revealed that subsequent to the introduction of mandatory mediation they perceived their own practices as having become less adversarial (McEwen et al. 1994, pp. 149, 151, 177–79, 181; McEwen 1995, pp. 1367–68).

Finally, Macfarlane's interviews with commercial litigators involved in various dispute types who had participated in at least ten mandatory mediations in Ottawa

---

4 Roberts (2002, pp. 25–27), Nolan-Haley (1998, pp. 1372–73; 2002, pp. 237, 299), and Macfarlane (2001, p. 191).

and Toronto indicated that mediation experiences affected lawyers' practices and resulted in their strategies being changed. In speaking of their cases and mediations, some lawyers gave markedly greater importance to emotional and psychological dimensions of disputes. Additionally, although many viewed mediation simply as another part of litigation, there was evidence of lawyers behaving more conciliatory than adversarial. Thus, similar to the findings in the present study, Macfarlane's research reveals fundamental changes in how some lawyers think about conflict and resolution subsequent to experience in mediation (Macfarlane 2002, pp. 244, 252, 264, 297–99, 320).

As to the transformations of lawyers who become mediators, the data here resonate with the conclusions reached in assessments of the San Francisco Community Boards Mediations ("SFCB") of neighborhood disputes. There it was found that mediation was most salient, transformative, and important for mediators, and not for disputants. Interestingly, interviews and longitudinal questionnaire data revealed that the SFCB mediations in fact failed in their objective of community amelioration and transformation. Indeed, it was found that the mediators themselves were more transformed by their training in mediation ideology and techniques, and by mediation experiences than were the disputants involved in the cases before them.[5] Most mediators felt participation in the program had profoundly affected their lives in terms of them being better able to handle their own conflicts as well as help others solve problems. Additionally, mediators' own feelings of community had improved through their shared mission and relationships with others on the program. Thus, the authors concluded that the SFCB mediations had the potential to help its mediators as much or more than the disputants who attended to resolve their cases (Dubow and McEwen 1993, pp. 162–64).

However, the SFCB program and its mediators were quite different to the lawyer-mediators in the present study, making the findings here even more noteworthy. First, the focus of the SFCB mediations was not only to resolve individual cases, but also to enhance neighborhood relations by parties communicating and expressing their problems and feelings, as well as understanding how opponents experienced disputes. Thus, mediators' training focused more on the expression of feelings than on dealing with the issues in conflict. Moreover, mediators' success was gauged more by the degree to which communication about feelings was established than by case resolutions. Second, different to the lawyers-mediators in the present study, SFCB mediators reported that they joined the program largely for personal development.[6]

---

5 Generally, three to five trained volunteer, community member mediators met face to face with parties using questioning and listening techniques to assist disputants reach their own voluntary agreements (Dubow and McEwen 1993, pp. 127–28, 132–33, 139, 144, 149, 156–57; Merry and Milner 1993, pp. 125–66; Menkel-Meadow 1995c, pp. 219–20, 230–31; 2006).

6 Mediators underwent a four-step training process. This was viewed as an important facet of the program as mediators were also community members assisting in ameliorating the neighborhood in terms of dealing with conflict peacefully. Mediators had generally undergone higher education, were predominantly female (60%), and under the age of 45 (83%) (Dubow and McEwen 1993, pp. 132–33, 144, 149–51, 156–59, 163; Menkel-Meadow 1995c, p. 232).

In sum, mediation may be viewed as transformative. It is educational in terms of learning about oneself and others and how to interact with them, learning diverse modes of conceiving problems and transforming them into opportunities, and creatively resolving conflicts (Menkel-Meadow 1995c, p. 240). Consequently, I argue that with mediation increasingly becoming the norm within formal courts and litigation, the parallel worlds of legal actors and lay parties in case processing may converge or at least move somewhat closer to one another.

8.3   Parallel worlds' findings – macro-meanings

Lay individuals desire different things from the legal system than they are typically given. What they want reflects a psychological paradigm. Yet, this is fundamentally different from the paradigm of legal decision-making that legal actors are socialized into in law school, and which dictates discussions in the legal field (Tyler 1997, pp. 872–84).

The parallel worlds' findings illustrate the ideological dissonance that exists between how plaintiffs and defendants versus the justice system, through its actors, view disputes and their resolution.[7] The data additionally challenge dominant understandings of how litigation-track case processing leading up to and including mediation works in practice and circumscribe the unfettered praise of mediation[8] and opportunities for empowerment and disputant self-determination.[9] Damaska posits that "the reactive state, reluctant to embrace any philosophy of the good life allows individuals to be sovereign in the management of their own concerns. Transposed to the administration of justice, this sovereignty requires that a party be recognized as the master of his lawsuit, entitled to conduct it as he pleases." Yet, the findings here show that this is not always the case, with most counsel not seen to "zealously advance clients' interests only as the latter defined them" (Damaska 1986, pp. 104, 142).

Disputants' situations were surely even worse prior to the advent of mediation, when they were even more comprehensively in the control of their legal representatives.[10] Nevertheless, the present findings suggest a system where cases are no longer wholly "owned" by disputants, in some sense being co-opted from them, with decisions resulting in fundamental consequences for parties being taken out of their hands. As Felstiner et al. note, as a result of lawyers' monopoly on legal dispute processing coupled with the obscure nature of legal discourse and processes

---

7 This has similarly been found for other case types (Hunting and Neuwirth 1962, automobile accident cases; Merry 1990a, family and neighbourhood disputes; Felstiner and Sarat 1992, divorce; Baldwin 1997, small claims).

8 For example, Meschievitz (1991, p. 198), Reeves (1994, p. 17), Brown and Simanowitz (1995, p. 153), Christiansen (1997, p. 72), Dauer and Marcus (1997, p. 199), Polywka (1997, p. 81), Gitchell and Plattner (1999, p. 459), and Saravia (1999, p. 139).

9 Goldberg et al. (1992, pp. 154–55), Baruch Bush and Folger (1994, pp. 2–3, 81), Baruch Bush (1997, pp. 29–30), Kovach (2001, pp. 935, 939, 942–43, 952), and Welsh (2001b, pp. 15–18).

10 Indeed, Damaska has also noted "when the management of a lawsuit is entrusted to lawyers, the parties fade into the background" (Damaska 1986, p. 218).

including mediation and the inevitable dispute transformations that occur, "disputants' 'property' interests in disputes are appropriated by lawyers and the state" (Felstiner et al. 1980–81, pp. 648–49). Merry too speaks of a fundamental paradox in that using the law symbolically empowers individuals in relation to others involved in their disputes. Yet, it increases their dependence on state institutions and comes at the price of domination by the state in the form of courts. To this, I would add "agents of the courts and court-linked processes." Thus, when plaintiffs move into the court system, they lose control over this power and become vulnerable to "the intervention of the rules and practices of the legal system and to the groups with the power to generate them." These groups then shape problems in their discourses, naming and pointing toward solutions that constrain how problems are understood (Merry 1990b, p. 181).

Indeed, although the disputes discussed here themselves had not changed from parties' perspectives, conceptually their nature and dynamics had irreversibly evolved. By invoking the legal system with mediation as its part, an outer realm was created around inner-core disputes. Although based on these inner-core disputes, the outer realm was larger, containing numerous "outsider entities" being actors with diverse, often competing, understandings, interests, and conceptions of "the good." These were quite foreign to the original disputes themselves. Yet they became factors within the core disputes, diluting them and altering them, sometimes beyond recognition. This resulted in many of disputants' visions and needs for resolution not being realized. Thus, the findings modify Gulliver's argument that the process of negotiation (or mediation) is in one sense the gradual creation of order or coordination between the parties (Gulliver 1979, p. 114) as the parallel worlds' findings suggest that order may be created on one plane, for example, that of legal actors, but not necessarily on the other of lay disputants.

Moreover, although the data highlight diverse locations of power within the system of case processing and dispute resolution, supporting Foucault's view of power circulating at different levels within "a specific domain formed by relations of power" (Foucault 1981, p. 82), they also illustrate how power is interlinked with knowledge (Rabinow 1986, pp. 6–7) and how lawyer–client interactions operate under "conditions of unequal power generated by unequal knowledge and experience" (Sarat and Felstiner 1995b, p. 404). Consequently, it is lawyers' values that are primarily served within the system. In this way, the present findings support Abel's assertion that "informal institutions for conflict resolution . . . empower those who create and operate them (Abel 1982, pp. 5, 12; Hensler 1999, p. 17). Hence, far from the view of ADR being part of a communitarian vision of justice and social unity (Morris 1999, p. 272), the present findings on legal actors' understandings and desires dominating case processing and mediation suggest that it is lawyers' power that is focal, with legal actors exercising "hegemonic elements of control".[11]

---

11 This differs from Nader's argument that it is court-sponsored mediation which represents hegemonic elements of control (Nader 2002, p. 141).

Yet, viewing lawyers as a collectivity, their interests (being themselves to "continue in existence") must matter only inasmuch as they protect and advance individuals' interests and concerns. This is because they act as proxies in the name of individuals, not in their own names. If the interests of collectivities conflict with individuals' interests the system is then shown to become concerned with itself. Of course, this is not always a bad thing as systems must maintain themselves, and the motivations within a system need not be the same to make it work well.[12]

The formal versus informal justice debates

The parallel worlds' findings additionally inform the formal versus informal justice theoretical debates. As Palmer and Roberts note, "The informalism critiques of Abel and Fiss, though delivered from very different standpoints in ideological terms, amount to an endorsement of superior court adjudication" (Palmer and Roberts 1998, p. 29). Bentham viewed settlement as compromise, which represented a denial of justice (Bentham 1843, p. 35). Fiss too argues that informality and ADR are antithetical to the achievement of social justice and that "settlement is not preferable to court as justice may not be done"... whereas judges "can employ a number of measures to lessen the impact of distributional inequalities" (Fiss 1964, pp. 1075–78, 1085, 1089). Similarly, Auerbach posits that "only when there is congruence between individuals and their community with shared commitment to common values, is there a possibility for justice without law" (Auerbach 1983, pp. 16, 120). In a different vein, Abel asserts that informal institutions focus on process not outcome. Yet, within the formal system "the aggrieved can demand state redress as of right rather than depend on paternalistic constructions of what is best" (Abel 1982, pp. 294, 308).

The present findings overall show the critiques of Abel, Fiss, and Auerbach to be fully justified. However, they additionally add an important rider, particularly to the Fiss criticism: We must not lead our critique of informalism to end in glorification of the formal justice system as that too is shown to be just as defective. Menkel-Meadow notes the phenomenon of "litigation romanticism," arguing that "litigation is no more likely than alternatives... to produce complete fairness" (Menkel-Meadow 1995a, p. 1173; 1995b, p. 2669; 2004, p. 23). The parallel worlds' findings support this view, indicating that during both formal and informal justice processes with all the benefits legal representation can offer, litigants are throughout dominated by lawyers and dependent on their expertise and paternalistic constructions of what is best.[13] Yet, this is often incongruous with disputants' own understandings and goals.

---

12 Raz (Interview, September 29, 2004) and Raz (2004). Even if one was to argue that the civil justice system is more about the regulation of society than being a vehicle in the service of disputing individuals, I would argue that in view of the public's misconceptions of the function of the legal system, there must at least be greater public education about what the civil justice system is actually for.

13 Rifkin (1984, p. 30) and Rack (1999, p. 295). Legal representation has been found to provide numerous benefits. These include protection against opponents' extreme demands and settlement pressure (McEwen et al. 1995, pp. 1320, 1373, 1394), stronger bargaining power, enhancement of settlement chances, higher monetary results (Bingham et al. 2002, pp. 342, 372; McDermott

The role of the legal system

> "*Suing is not* going to make you feel better...Nothing about the justice system is designed for therapy." **Female defense lawyer – in thirties**

"The operations of the legal system hinge on law's ability to sharply distinguish between the legal and the extra-legal" (Banakar 2003, pp. 7–8, 74). Yet, in highlighting the indivisibility of plaintiffs' and defendants' legal and extralegal needs and agendas during formal case processing, the parallel worlds' data show that this is ultimately misleading. It has been argued that the legal system ignores persons in favor of rules and undervalues the human element (Noonan 1993, pp. 9–14; Barton 1999, p. 927; Klein 2005, p. 777). But, is it a proper function of the legal system to address disputants' extralegal needs and objectives? Some argue that the law should be concerned with individuals' concerns, that is, all the human pursuits that give life meaning. Others reject this stance, believing that the law must exercise restraint and should not impinge on these issues. There are principles of concern for the public that do not relate to individuals (Raz 2004). Thus it has been argued that disputants expect the legal system can deliver more than it is actually able to and consequently their desires may be unrealistic (Merry 1990a, p. 179; Felstiner and Sarat 1992, pp. 1459–60).

Banakar describes the law as "much more than a system of legal rules, decisions and doctrines. The reproduction of legal knowledge, and thus the legal system, is also dependent on patterns of legal practice, or forms of participation in and observations of legal processes... Thus, the law needs also to be understood as a field of practice or an on-going process" (Banakar 2003, pp. 134–35). But what should the law and its practice be concerned with? Based on the premise that the law and its workings must exist for the benefit of laymen rather than legal or institutional actors, the parallel worlds' thesis implicitly argues that conceptions of the meaning and role of law and the justice system must evolve and be broadened to include litigants' extralegal needs and objectives. Menkel-Meadow too argues that in this "era of poststructural, postmodern knowledge, the attributes of the adversary system as the 'ideal type' of a legal system must be re-examined as human disputes have not only legal implications, but often a host of other concerns e.g. emotional, interpersonal and moral. Thus, the objectives of the legal system and the methods utilized to reach those objectives require rethinking as well as a 'cultural change'" (Menkel-Meadow 1996b, pp. 5, 7, 14, 19, 21–27, 42). If justice system processes are viewed solely as legal and financial mechanisms, many fundamental issues within cases will not be addressed or resolved (Vincent et al. 1994, p. 1612). Thus, on a policy level, a rethinking of civil justice assumptions and objectives is urgently necessary.[14]

---

and Obar 2004, pp. 77, 102, 105), and protection of clients' legal rights (McEwen et al. 1994, pp. 171–72).

14 Des Rosiers et al. (1998, pp. 433, 442). In analyzing observations from small claims court hearings as well as interviews with litigants, Conley and O'Barr present evidence of the "invalidity

Perhaps Western modes of conflict resolution may learn from Eastern models. For instance, in exploring the expansion of extrajudicial mediation in China for most conflicts between individuals, Palmer illustrates China's clearly different ethos for the resolution of disputes involving legal representation. In China, wider social issues are taken into consideration when resolving cases. For instance, Palmer describes the case of the "unhappy customer" who through mediation was allowed to return a tape recorder despite store policy to the contrary on the basis that it adversely affected his marital relationship (Palmer 1987, pp. 220, 223–26). As Palmer notes, mediation not only defends important principles of law, policy, and justice but also promotes social unity and stability and the restoration of harmony between disputants (Palmer 1987, pp. 240, 244, 259).[15]

Does the legal system need redefining to help the polity genuinely resolve its disputes – or is it the role of its agents, the legal actors that must be reinvented?

The role of lawyers

One may argue that disputants' extralegal objectives are not within the legitimate fields of lawyers' operations. As Raz asserts, when we deal with institutions, we want a certain distance, an impersonal contact with people acting in an official, professional capacity (Raz, Interview, September 29, 2004). Yet, as lawyers have achieved over generations a near monopoly over dispute management (Palmer and Roberts 1998, p. 25), if attorneys do not work to assist disputants with these issues once they enter the justice system, who else is in the position to? Who else has the power to? Thus, as Hampshire argues, developing procedural fairness should be lawyers' priority (Hampshire 1999, pp. 40, 79).

The parallel worlds' findings support those who have previously urged lawyers to integrate clients' legal and nonlegal interests,[16] as well as those who advocate a general "ethic of care" to be part of lawyers' practices.[17] The data also resonate with the interdisciplinary literature and approach to lawyering of "therapeutic jurisprudence" whose tenets are argued to be akin to the philosophy of ADR (Kovach 2001, p. 971). That literature posits that lawyers' actions should strive to achieve

of the law's operating assumptions that civil litigants come to court to pursue discrete economic objectives and that people define their problems in financial terms, and are thus prepared to accept monetary solutions." They, therefore, find that "dissatisfaction occurs when litigants seek intangible benefits from legal procedures that were designed to process rational economic demands, when plaintiffs insist on pursuing non-economic goals" (Conley and O'Barr 1990, pp. xi, 126).

15 Of course, this model is not without its problems. For instance, mediators being more active can result in concomitant problems relating to coercion (Palmer 1989, p. 170).
16 Binder and Price (1977, pp. 22, 185–86), Lehman (1978, pp. 1079–80), Margulies (1990, p. 213), Pepper (1995, pp. 1602–4), Riskin and Westbrook (1997, pp. 86–95), Nolan-Haley (1998, p. 1386), and Mnookin et al. (2000, p. 169).
17 Gilligan (1982, pp. 8, 33), Shalleck (1992, p. 1078), Ellman (1993, p. 2667), Kovach (2001, pp. 966–67), and Kovach (2003, p. 418).

and maintain the psychological or physical well-being of the individual (Stolle et al. 1997, pp. 50–51; Winick 1997, p. 192). Similarly, in highlighting the need for lawyers to be reoriented to a different set of assumptions about legal problems, Menkel-Meadow advocates a broader social welfare approach for lawyers to determine what underlying conflicts may be at issue in disputes (Menkel-Meadow 2004, p. 19–20). In arguing for an expansion of what lawyers should do, Menkel-Meadow posits that "lawyers create a particular epistemic understanding of what they can know and do out of the adversary and advocate's conception of their work that frequently shuts them off from other ways of knowing, being, and doing" (Menkel-Meadow 1999, pp. 785, 787–89, 797).

The complicity of the adversary system

It has been argued that the incorporation of nonadversarial, problem-solving mediation within adversarial litigation (consisting of different philosophies, paradigms, and goals for dispute resolution) has resulted in lawyers missing the "human dignity dimension" and consequently not adequately serving clients' human needs and interests.[18] Many contend that the behavior of most lawyers is a direct result of the contentiousness and adversarial culture inherent in the adversary system (Maute 1987, pp. 18–19; Kovach 2001, p. 949). In speaking of adversarial negotiation, Menkel-Meadow posits that by encouraging competitive strategies important information may not be communicated and parties may arrive at unsatisfactory and inefficient solutions (Menkel-Meadow 1984, pp. 775–76). Riskin too argues that most lawyers are trained to operate according to a "philosophical map" premised on rights and rules, disputants being adversaries, and dispute resolution meaning the application of law to facts, placing people and occurrences into legal categories. This results in an "underdevelopment of emotional faculties" making it difficult for attorneys to be sensitive to parties' emotional needs (Riskin 1982, pp. 14, 43–46; Guthrie 2001, pp. 155–56).

Thus, lawyers have been accused of obstructing communication and generally interfering with the development of mediations, which could help the parties (Fineman 1988, pp. 754–55), often leaving clients in the dark (Nolan-Haley 1998, pp. 1372–73). Menkel-Meadow too asserts that lawyers, co-opting some of ADR's goals, may be utilizing ADR not to obtain "better" outcomes, but simply for strategic purposes as a further weapon within the formal adversarial process . . . for perceived client advantage. Consequently, lawyers may have corrupted mediation without changing their attitudes, viewing mediation as another step in the litigation game. Thus, what is necessary is for lawyers to reconceptualize their roles and move away from an adversarial way of being (Lowry 1983, pp. 252–54; Menkel-Meadow 1991, pp. 3, 5; 1997a, pp. 408, 418, 427).

18 Menkel-Meadow (1997a, pp. 429, 453; 1999, p. 789; 2004, p. 7), Nolan-Haley (1998, pp. 1370–71), and Sternlight (1999, pp. 269, 274).

Lawyers' psyches and legal education

Yet, the different ways that lawyers and parties see the world of disputes can also be viewed in the context of empirical studies that have demonstrated divergences in psychological makeup or attributes of disputants and legal actors generally (Korobkin and Guthrie 1997, pp. 81–82, 84). For instance, some have found that individuals who are very competitive or lack collaborative proclivities are drawn to the study of law (Daicoff 1998, pp. 548, 585; Kovach 2001, p. 950). Lawyers have additionally been found to be predominantly left-brain dominant, suggesting analytical orientation (Strong 1998, pp. 761–62; Guthrie 2001, p. 157). Likewise, research has shown that law students and lawyers, subsequent to law school entrance screening processes and educational training, tend as human beings to be rational, logical, and analytical individuals, with far less interest or focus on feelings, emotions, or interpersonal concerns than those who do not choose the legal profession.[19] Thus, lawyers will often focus exclusively on or emphasize money issues in contrast to disputants' tendencies to be more emotional (Felstiner and Sarat 1992, p. 1456; Nelken 1996, p. 423; Sternlight 1999, pp. 323–24, 326, 342). Therefore, Guthrie concludes that "whether because of their innate personalities, their legal training, the realities of law practice, or some combination thereof, lawyers are... analytically oriented, emotionally and interpersonally underdeveloped... and adversarial" (Guthrie 2001, pp. 160, 162–63). This can result in them causing harm to disputants (Sternlight 1999, p. 271). Consequently, some advocate the use of separate nonadversarial "settlement counsel" or "collaborative counsel" to represent parties at mediations (Kovach 2001, pp. 975–76).

Yet, although it has been argued that certain personality traits would be difficult to alter (Daicoff 1998, pp. 566, 594), other scholars assert that legal education and changes in ethical rules for lawyers are key in transforming attorneys' orientations to a problem-solving paradigm from an adversarial one.[20] This should result in behavioral transformation, focusing on relationship and communication skills as well as listening, empathizing, and problem-solving skills (Guthrie 2001, pp. 180–82; Rosenberg 2004, pp. 1228, 1234). This approach responds to calls for lawyers to include nonadversarial skills within their repertoire for mediation representation.[21] In essence, what these writers are advocating is something more akin to what disputants are seeking, as found in the present study: extralegal consciousness and considerations in their daily work. This issue is further discussed in Section 8.5.

---

19 Hafner and Fakouri (1984, pp. 236–41), Janoff (1991, pp. 228–29, 234), Bell and Richard (1992, p. 152), Nelken (1996, p. 422), Daicoff (1997, p. 1405), Korobkin and Guthrie (1997, p. 87), Silver (1999, pp. 1198–1200), and Guthrie (2001, pp. 158–59).
20 Kovach (1997, p. 619; 2003, p. 429), Menkel-Meadow (1997a, pp. 409–10, 428; 2004, p. 9), and Nolan-Haley (1998, pp. 1372–73).
21 Sternlight (1999, p. 271), Lawrence (2000, pp. 425–26), Menkel-Meadow (2002b, pp. 83, 110), and Rubinson (2004, p. 834).

8.4 Gendered parallel worlds

The chapters' findings repeatedly evidenced the fact that disparate worlds also exist throughout case processing and mediation on a further level within most actor groups – on gender lines. Indeed, gender appeared to influence the way conflict and its resolution were understood, interpreted, and experienced. This was seen in relation to female legal professionals' extralegal sensitivity and female disputants' disempowerment as compared with their male counterparts. The gender findings inject insight from actors' perspectives during case processing into the conflicting, and often inconclusive research in conflict resolution and negotiation theory on whether males and females have different understandings, objectives, perceptions, and behavior in these contexts. The data additionally offer frequently elusive first-hand evidence of the interpretive understandings of the experiences of females versus males involved in the legal system.[22]

In utilizing actors' own discourse as the study's primary data, the findings highlight female attorneys' strengths as well as the potential vulnerabilities of female plaintiffs involved in these cases in the legal system. In this way, the findings offer insight into the paradox noted by Menkel-Meadow that females are on the one hand claimed to be disempowered in negotiations and mediations while at the same time are said to be better at communicating and collaborative problem solving (Menkel-Meadow 2000a, p. 365). Others too have commented on this issue (Kolb and Coolidge 1988, p. 2). The data here show both assertions to be correct, with the former relating to female plaintiffs and the latter relating to female lawyers.

Extralegal sensitivity of female lawyers

The third most used code in the entire dataset (of 2,639 codes) was "female legal actor mentions extralegals." This finding was seen throughout virtually all chapters. There were too few female plaintiff lawyers for meaningful analysis. However, in examining perceptions of plaintiffs' litigation aims (*chapter two*), female defense attorneys generally evinced greater sensitivity than males to claimants' extralegal needs, desires, and realities relating to litigation. Similarly within the mediators' group, talk of plaintiffs' extralegal litigation aims was more prevalent with female mediators than with males, who more often spoke of plaintiffs' monetary aims being primary.

There was also evidence that gender had an effect on the meaning legal actors' ascribed to case mediation (*chapter four*). For instance, female lawyers in all groups took greater account of disputants' extralegal needs when discussing whether defendants should attend. When looking at all lawyers combined or simply all defense lawyers, females' discourse more often than males highlighted an understanding that mediation was not only a tactical forum, but also a forum to resolve extralegal

---

22 Kolb and Coolidge (1988, pp. 10–11, 18–19), Stamato (1992, pp. 378, 380), Menkel-Meadow (2000a, pp. 358, 360–61, 364), McCabe (2001, p. 459), and Kolb (2003, pp. 101–2).

issues – evidencing a diverse layer of meaning ascribed to the mediation process. Similarly, when examining all lawyers combined or all defense lawyers, males more often discussed tactical reasons against having physicians present at mediation than did females. Even in the mediators' group, no females, but 44% of males, included within their discourse strategic reasons against defendant attendance at mediation. In chapter five on mediation aims, talk of plaintiffs' extralegal mediation aspirations was more frequently associated with female lawyers than with males, who more often spoke of plaintiffs' monetary objectives. Female defense lawyers also spoke more of their own extralegal mediation aims than did males. Indeed, it was only females who wanted to relay extralegal information to plaintiffs and communicate their perspectives. For defense hospital lawyers especially, females also more often aspired to hear plaintiffs' perspectives than did males. Similarly their discourse highlighted a greater desire to be understood by plaintiffs.[23]

Finally, in chapter six female defense lawyers provided different visions of what occurred at mediations as compared with their male counterparts, seemingly experiencing mediation more "extralegally." Most males tended to describe what transpired wholly tactically, whereas females' discourse more often additionally incorporated extralegal information. This included their impressions of plaintiffs' perceptions of the process, accounts of plaintiffs' need to be heard, plaintiffs' reactions, plaintiffs wanting apologies, as well as things they said during mediation to address plaintiffs' extralegal needs. Thus, perhaps unsurprisingly, plaintiffs more often perceived female defense lawyers more positively than males, remarking on their compassion and understanding of their concerns. Moreover, no females, but a number of male defense lawyers (27%), were perceived negatively in terms of their handling plaintiffs' tragedies impersonally and uncaringly.

These findings expand on the extant literature in a number of respects. On a general level, only limited empirical data exist on how the diverse genders actually practice law and whether females contribute to an emphasis on needs versus rights (Menkel-Meadow 1994a, pp. 89, 91, 95). Moreover, no systematic empirical studies have looked at gender-based differences in lawyers and parties (Stempel 2003, p. 312). In relation to mediation in particular, notwithstanding Goldberg et al.'s comment that "disputing may be influenced by the... gender of those involved" and that "gender-based differences may affect the dynamics of mediation sessions" (Goldberg et al. 1992, p. 139), commentators have noted the lack of empirical knowledge on female versus male legal actors in mediations.[24] Thus, arguably, the present findings offer an important view through the gendered lenses of lawyers

---

23 Also, although only a tentative finding due to the small number of female defendants in the sample, there was some evidence that compared with males, female defendants were more often better equipped to offer plaintiffs greater psychological redress at mediations. Additionally, it may have been that female defendants themselves obtained more emotional benefit from mediation than did males.
24 Menkel-Meadow (1997b, p. 1427), Stempel (2003, pp. 310–11), Subrin (2003, pp. 207–8), and Klein (2005, p. 792).

and parties on perceptions of how legal actors understand, experience, and behave during case processing leading up to and including mediation.

Gilligan's findings relating to divergences in males' versus females' moral development – with males inclined to view conflict resolution and moral problems from a hierarchal, independent, rights-oriented perspective and females tending to seek relational compromises and avoid win–loss, rights-based solutions utilizing an "ethic of care" – have been widely cited, and have played a key role in shaping feminist legal thought (Gilligan 1982, pp. 25–29). Nevertheless, Gilligan's work has been controversial, with some not at all subscribing to her views (DuBois et al. 1985, pp. 74–75; Bartlett 1990, p. 871, n. 174). Some scholars view differences as emphasizing separate but equal power paradigms (Rhode 1994, p. 44). Others assert that to treat gender as a difference tends to obscure power inequalities (MacKinnon 1987, p. 8). It has also been suggested that differentiations will encourage negative distinctions of women (Williams 1982, p. 196; Vogelstein 2003, pp. 157–58) or that Gilligan's findings simply reflect the repressive realities of the current gender regime (Williams 1989, p. 802). Feminist legal theorists and postmodernists argue against generalizing on the basis of gender, as the notion of women lawyers driven by an ethic of care is an essentialist one and variations within genders detract from this argument (Epstein 1988, p. 83; Bowman 1999, p. 173). Postmodernists in particular argue that as there are no common features or experiences that all women share, a homogeneous "women" categorization should not be utilized.[25]

Yet, at least in the context of this particular dataset, the present findings support Gilligan's thesis (which has been elaborated on by various scholars) in that overall during case processing female lawyers tended to look not only to the legal substance of cases, but were also inclined to focus more than male attorneys on the connections of the individuals involved. Thus, female lawyers appeared to utilize a more contextual form of perception and reasoning in dealing with their cases. They also tended to stress others' needs in these cases more often than male lawyers (Kolb and Coolidge 1988, p. 4). Thus, the data additionally offer empirical support to those who have argued that female lawyers tend to interpret events differently to males (e.g., in recounting mediation experiences) and in attempting to resolve disputes tend to utilize sensitivity, compassion, and care more often than male attorneys.[26] Applying Gilligan's work to law students, Janoff found that while females commenced law school with more of a "care" inclination than males (who had a greater "rights" inclination), they shifted to rights perspectives after one year of law school (Janoff 1991, pp. 218, 228–29, 232–34, 238). This was similarly found by

---

25 Cahn (1992, pp. 1050–54), Patterson (1992, pp. 302–3), Brown (1996, p. 185), and Eichner (2001, pp. 6, 30).
26 Gilligan (1982, pp. 62–63, 173), Menkel-Meadow (1985, pp. 39, 43, 46, 49; 1989, pp. 312–13; 1994, p. 75), Hill (1990, p. 342), Maslow Cohen (1990, p. 664), Neumann (2000, pp. 353–57), and Maute (2002, p. 161). It should be noted, however, that as this research did not look at litigation or mediation outcomes or negotiating skills of lawyers, the present findings do not comment on the litigating or negotiating acumen of female lawyers.

Taber et al. (1988, p. 1251). Thus, the present findings could mean that mediation's influence may be bringing female lawyers back to their "ethic of care."

Disempowered female plaintiffs

The second strand of the gender findings throughout the chapters relates to disputants, where the potential for female plaintiffs' disempowerment could be discerned in a number of respects: First, females regularly exhibited unease in discussing the compensatory element within their litigated claims. This was not seen with male plaintiffs (*chapter two*). Likewise, no males but most females (73%) were initially not inclined to face perceived wrongdoers at mediation due to emotional difficulties, with a number of female plaintiffs additionally expressing concern over how their behavior or reactions to defendants at mediation would be perceived by others (*chapter four*). Virtually all recanted later on reflection, viewing defendants' absences as a lost opportunity for understanding and closure. In light of the array of emotional and psychological benefits described by both plaintiffs and defendants who did mediate together, this may be seen as an element of female disadvantage. For instance, if plaintiffs were given the choice, females might be more likely than males to refuse or acquiesce in lawyers' decisions on defendants' non-attendance at mediation. Certainly, without defendants present, plaintiffs' articulated litigation and mediation aims could not be fully realized.

In speaking of mediation objectives (*chapter five*), female plaintiffs exhibited greater concern than males over how their aims as well as they themselves would be perceived at mediation by others present. Likewise, females more often than males stressed the integrity of their missions as well as wanting to be seen as individuals. Female plaintiffs were also seen to seek and need greater emotional recompense at mediation than males. This was similarly the case with the limited data obtained from female versus male defendant physicians. Thus, arguably females may have the potential to derive greater psychological or emotional benefit from mediation than males.

Yet, the discourse on mediation experiences suggested that conflict resolution was also perceived and experienced differently by plaintiffs of different sexes, highlighting further potential vulnerabilities for females (*chapter six*). For instance, although females had greater emotional needs for mediation, they suffered greater emotional hardship in undergoing mediation. They were more sensitive to others' perceptions during the process, with evidence of some female plaintiffs partaking or speaking less than males. Moreover, females were less aware than males of mediation's tactical goings-on. But perhaps of greater concern, female plaintiffs' discourse showed them to be far more accepting than males of whatever transpired during mediations.

Lastly, in chapter seven it was seen that mediators' conduct was interpreted differently on gender lines, providing further indication of female plaintiffs' potential vulnerabilities at mediation. Females tended more than males to be influenced by communications and information conveyed by mediators (and possibly opponents' lawyers) during mediations. Females also tended to be more influenced by mediators' extralegal gestures and words. Equally, just as with mediation experiences overall, female plaintiffs more than males tended to be more accepting and less critical of mediators' behavior and the information they provided.

In terms of the literature, one must bear in mind the caveat of universalizing the female gender in light of disparities among females themselves as well as the fact that gender can interact with power, status, and demographic characteristics in actual negotiation settings.[27] Nevertheless, these findings inform and expand on various strands of the feminist literature relating to formal and informal justice processes as well as the negotiation theory literature. For instance, the data here on female plaintiffs being less at ease than males in discussing the compensatory elements in their litigated claims (*chapter two*) are reminiscent of and expand on Babcock and Laschever's work relating to research on gender and pay differentials. Finding that females feel less comfortable than males in discussing or requesting compensation for their work in excess of whatever is offered to them, Babcock and Laschever posit that this is due to women feeling less at ease in conflict and negotiation contexts for various reasons (*see Section 6.4*) (Babcock and Laschever 2003, pp. 1–3, 19–20, 23, 33, 41–61, 64).

Likewise, the data indicated that female plaintiffs tended to be more concerned than males with how their aims and conduct would be and were perceived during mediations, and that mediation was more emotionally difficult for women plaintiffs, with some speaking less during the process (*chapters four to six*). These findings provide a more nuanced understanding of the opportunities provided by mediation as compared with formal adversarial processes in terms of allowing all disputants to tell their stories. They also circumscribe unqualified arguments that mediation environments accord with women's strengths, empowering them and allowing them to speak on their own terms. Indeed, the findings suggest that women may not be taking full advantage of mediation's opportunity to speak for themselves and share their experiences (McCabe 2001, pp. 459–60, 471–73). This was similarly found in Pearson and Thoennes' divorce mediation research in four U.S. cities, where women more often than men reported concerns about the process and feeling ill at ease in expressing their feelings during mediations. In comparison, males felt relaxed and comfortable (Pearson and Thoennes 1988, pp. 440–41, 449).

In this way, the findings here additionally add empirical evidence to the strand of the feminist critique of informal justice processes relating to the internalization of disempowerment. This could result in women not stating their own interests with sufficient assertiveness or too readily deferring to opponents' or mediators' requests (Ricci 1985, p. 49; Kandel 1994, p. 882). Indeed, in line with communication and negotiation studies as well as sociolingual research, the data here suggest that

---

27 Kolb and Coolidge (1988, p. 1), Watson (1994, pp. 191, 203, 205–6), Menkel-Meadow (1997b, p. 1426; 2000a, pp. 357–60, 362–65; 2001, p. 261), Kolb (2000, p. 350), and Kolb and Williams (2000, pp. 11, 20–21, 31).

women in actual litigation and mediation contexts may tend to be less eager, less self-confident, and less comfortable than men to undergo mediation and speak in groups. This may be because female plaintiffs perceive negotiation and mediation contexts – which represent opposing interests and conflict – as "male" or "foreign" (Tannen 1990, pp. 75, 94, 150; Walters et al. 1998, p. 20; Evans 2001, p. 166). Consequently, women more often than men may be negatively impacted in terms of their abilities to advocate their positions and to communicate their goals and interests (Kolb and Coolidge 1988, pp. 6–8, 10).

As for female plaintiffs feeling less inclined or able than males to face defendants at mediations (*chapter four*), this finding correlates with and expands on research into sexual violence cases where female victims felt incapable or did not want to face alleged perpetrators in litigation or mediation, as it was too difficult for them psychologically and emotionally (Des Rosiers et al. 1998, pp. 433, 435, 438). This finding is also in line with research that suggests that most women prefer to settle disputes without direct confrontation, compared with many males who view confrontation positively and as something necessary to negotiate their status (Tannen 1990, pp. 75, 94, 150). Yet, female claimants may be contributing to their own disadvantage in this respect, as without defendants present at mediation many of plaintiffs' expressed extralegal litigation and mediation aims cannot be realized.

Female plaintiffs also tended to be more accepting or cooperative and less critical than males at mediations, both in terms of what transpired generally and in relation to mediators' conduct and influence (*chapters six and seven*). These data inform and expand on the knowledge in this area, in terms of both jurisdiction and case type and particularly in the context of litigation-track mediation. The theoretical debates on this issue have been principally argued in the family law arena.[28] The findings here resuscitate the significance of the feminist critiques of informal justice processes including mediation relating to female disputants' disempowerment. Feminist scholars have long posited that females may be more acquiescing or cooperative in negotiation settings including mediation.[29] For instance, although accepting that formal processes are no better for women, Grillo argues (in the context of mandatory Californian custody mediations) that mediation as a process – which stresses compromise over rights – is dangerous for women or those who operate in the female mode, as their relational sense to others may result in them being more acquiescing at mediations, resulting in agreements that do not serve their needs. Yet, this is masked by informal processes.[30] However, few

---

28 Rifkin (1984, p. 22), Delgado et al. (1985, pp. 1360–61), Rosenberg (1991, pp. 492–93), Nader (1993, p. 4), Brinig (1995, p. 4), Cobb (1997, p. 397), Palmer and Roberts (1998, p. 139), Rack (1999, pp. 217, 224), and McCabe (2001, pp. 476–78, 481).
29 Grillo (1991, pp. 1549–51, 1583–84, 1602–4, 1610), Bryan (1992, p. 523), Menkel-Meadow (1997b, p. 1420; 2000, p. 13), Kolb and Williams (2000, p. 42), McCabe (2001, pp. 476–77), Riley and McGinn (2002, p. 5), Babcock and Laschever (2003, pp. 1–4, 19–20, 23, 41–43, 62, 114, 116–19, 140–41), and Kolb et al. (2004, pp. 139, 141).
30 Gilligan (1982, pp. 62–63), Grillo (1991, pp. 1549–51, 1583–84, 1602–4, 1610), Bryan (1992, p. 523), and Menkel-Meadow (1997b, p. 1420; 2000, p. 13).

empirical studies have tested whether females are actually disadvantaged at mediation or whether gender differences hinder women's ability to mediate successfully. In injecting actors' meanings and understandings into the debate, the present findings tend to support the view that although women do not perceive they are disadvantaged, gender differences may hinder some females' abilities to mediate.[31]

These findings also inform some of the inconclusive and conflicting research and theoretical debates in negotiation theory on whether gender affects actors' objectives, perceptions, and behavior in negotiation situations (including mediation). Research indicates that gender may have a significant impact on negotiations.[32] Scholars have posited that females tend to feel less competent than males as negotiators, and are often wary of adversely affecting existing relationships.[33] Babcock and Laschever as well as Kolb and Williams additionally assert that females more than males tend to feel less comfortable with overt competition and negotiation situations, and are more accepting of what they are offered.[34] Other research similarly suggests that females are more likely to avoid and do less well in competitive settings than males.[35] Moreover, meta-analyses have demonstrated a small but significant probability that during negotiations women are generally more cooperative than men. Therefore, women are generally understood to undervalue their positions, viewing them in terms of how they affect others, and are overly preoccupied that others involved in their negotiations are content.[36] That being said, most of the empirical work to date from various disciplines does not actually study negotiations relating to ongoing litigation and litigation-track mediation, as is the case here (Kolb and Coolidge 1988, pp. 2, 10–11, 18–19; Menkel-Meadow 2000a, pp. 358, 360–61, 364; Kolb 2003, pp. 101–2).

---

31 Although lawyers were involved in virtually all mediations studied, as neither mediation results nor the effects of legal representation in safeguarding female disputants' rights were tested, the data here can only reflect tendencies in disputants themselves.
32 Stamato (1992, p. 377), Walters et al. (1998, p. 1), Stuhlmacher and Walters (1999, pp. 653, 673), Kolb (2000, p. 348), Evans (2001, pp. 166, 180), and Riley and McGinn (2002, p. 7). Drawing on research, Kolb and Coolidge similarly argue that it seems there are material differences in how males and females negotiate and the techniques they employ in attempting to reach agreements (Kolb and Coolidge 1988, pp. 1–2).
33 Watson (1994a, p. 118), Farber and Rickenberg (1999, pp. 291–92), Riley and McGinn (2002, p. 5), Babcock and Laschever (2003, pp. 1–4, 19–20, 23, 41–43, 62, 114, 116–19, 140–41), and Klein (2005, p. 787).
34 Kolb and Williams' work suggests that women are more accepting of job terms than males, with others expecting them to behave this way during negotiations (Kolb and Williams 2000, p. 10).
35 Studies have shown that women in negotiations are more likely to be conciliatory than men (Hinshaw and Forbes 1993, p. 876; Rack 1999, p. 224). Additionally, psychological studies and empirical research suggest that women are more risk-averse and have a lower preference for competition than men (Kolb and Coolidge 1988, p. 1; Craver and Barnes 1999, pp. 300–301, 312, 345; Kolb 2000, p. 348; Menkel-Meadow 2000a, pp. 360–61; Evans 2001, p. 157, n. 68). In a simulation study of New York University law students it was found that although both sexes fared comparatively equally, females were less confident than males in their abilities to negotiate (Stamato 1992, p. 377; Riley and McGinn 2002, p. 6).
36 Kolb (1993, pp. 139, 141), Watson (1994a, p. 118), Kolb and Williams (2000, p. 42), and Kolb et al. (2004, pp. 139, 141).

Finally, in relation to the findings on female versus male plaintiffs' more favorable assessments of mediators, the data correlate with Kelly and Duyree's California study of divorce and custody mediations where it was found that while both genders rated fairly positively mediators' skills, women were significantly more likely to agree that mediators were skilful. They also rated mediators' abilities considerably more highly than did men (Kelly and Duyree 1995, pp. 37, 41–42, 45; Palmer and Roberts 1998, pp. 139–41).

8.5 Practical application of the findings

What are the principal implications of these findings for the field? On a superficial level, the data should assist lawyers and litigants involved in litigation and mediation, as all respondents were deeply interested in their opponents' approaches, strategies, and tactical maneuvers. However, more generally the findings should be significant in reorienting attorneys, law students, those involved in conflict resolution, and others to realities that are occurring within legal practice and case processing, causing them to ask, How can we engage in a system of change? Consequently, four specific areas of application are relevant.

First, as the problems uncovered here derive partially from narrow, adversarial approaches to disputes, changes are urgently necessary within legal education. Education in the law and legal practice generally entail educating students to view problems objectively from the perspective of rights and rules, filtering out any extralegal considerations as irrelevant (Menkel-Meadow 1994a, p. 96; Eyster 1996, p. 756; Klein 2005, p. 777). Therefore, core law school curricula, mandatory continuing legal education and ethical rules for attorneys must provide far greater emphasis on litigants' extralegal dispute realities, needs, and objectives during case processing. Various changes have occurred in North American law schools to include new approaches to lawyering aimed at supplementing adversarial teachings. These include "therapeutic jurisprudence" (dealing with emotional and psychological implications of the legal system and attempting to apply law in a more therapeutic way; Ferris 2004, pp. 185–86), "holistic lawyering," and "collaborative lawyering." However, much more remains to be done as these educational approaches have existed for a number of years. Yet, they remain on the periphery of legal education and practice.[37] Thus, these or similar approaches must be included in mainstream legal education regardless of jurisdiction.

Changing the focus of legal education, training and ethical rules should result in a broadening of the meaning of legal cases from that dictated by narrow, adversarial paradigms. It should also precipitate a reevaluation of the operating economic premises of the civil justice system. Indeed, the findings here suggest disproportionate views by lawyers as to the importance of money for disputants.

---

37 Menkel-Meadow (1997a, p. 427), Brest (2000, p. 20), Sander and Mnookin (2000, p. 21), Kovach (2001, pp. 972–76), and Riskin (2002, pp. 8, 10, 14, 16–21, 23).

Thus, changes are also necessary in relation to perceptions and understandings of "money" within the civil justice system. The findings here must generate further recognition of the importance of looking beyond the monetary elements of claims to understand plaintiffs' motivations, needs, and aims during litigation and litigation-linked processes such as mediation. More attention should be paid by attorneys to the possibility that litigants seek things other than or more than money from the legal system. Thus, educational changes should aid in precipitating the necessary cultural change within legal practice, generally, and in altering attorneys' orientations to focus more on problem solving as opposed to money alone.[38] As Menkel-Meadow notes, "Good resolutions of conflicts... in the law can occur when people realize that valuing different things differently is good. Money need not be a proxy for everything" (Menkel-Meadow 2000b, p. 36). The reconceptualization findings in this book indicate that training in or simply experiencing mediation may also assist in the cultural transformation necessary for the legal world and its actors.

Second, and in a similar vein, this research should affect the way lawyers on all sides interact with disputants during case processing and conflict resolution, addressing parties' extralegal needs to a greater extent. As these findings derive in part from issues of failed communication, direct dialogue early on in litigation between defense lawyers and plaintiffs concerning plaintiffs' litigation and mediation aims is necessary. This could occur during early litigation-track mediations, which present opportunities for litigants to articulate their extralegal needs and objectives in a confidential environment. Assuming plaintiffs partake in a meaningful way, this would serve to sensitize defense attorneys and defendants to case realities from plaintiffs' perspectives and may affect the way all sides' lawyers subsequently deal with these cases (whether or not they are resolved through mediation or continue on the formal litigation track). Certainly, attorneys should ensure that defendants are present at all mediations to address issues of material significance to both plaintiffs and defendants, regardless of their direct legal value. Third, the gender findings throughout the chapters additionally emphasize the need for lawyers to exercise particular care in ensuring that female plaintiffs obtain the most they can out of case processing and mediation.[39] In terms of pragmatic incentives for these changes in law firms, apart from altering ethical rules for lawyers, it may be helpful that when entertaining partnership bids, partners should consider anonymous

---

38 Kovach (1997, p. 619; 2003, p. 429), Menkel-Meadow (1997a, pp. 409–10, 428; 2004, p. 9), and Nolan-Haley (1998, pp. 1372–73). Others too have discussed behavioral transformation of attorneys, focusing on relationship and communication skills as well as listening, empathizing, and problem-solving skills (Guthrie 2001, pp. 180–82; Rosenberg 2004, pp. 1228, 1234).
39 In response to arguments that the legal system lacks the resources and expertise to address litigants' extralegal needs, Conley and O'Barr suggest (in the context of small claims cases) that these demands on the system are frequently minimal and that what is necessary is often to simply "pay attention to what litigants say rather than act on assumptions about their objectives and concerns." In this way, the legal system and its actors "may precipitate substantial increases in litigant satisfaction, utilizing minimal resources and time" (Conley and O'Barr 1990, p. 131).

client assessments (e.g., of the applicant attorney's clients over the previous three to five years) of whether their case understandings and goals were attended to and how they were addressed by their lawyers.

Finally, and perhaps more immediately, until transformations in case conceptions and legal practice are more commonplace, an important result of these findings should be the future conceptual separation of the entities of parties and their lawyers (*see Section 8.1*), who are regularly assumed by others involved in their cases to have the same preferences and desires during formal and informal justice processes. This may alter formats of mediations and approaches taken by mediators. For instance, it has been suggested that mediators should meet with parties separately prior to mediation to assist disputants to both comprehend the process and organize their plan of action according to their needs. A similar suggestion has been made for judges in courts in terms of their focusing more on litigants' own articulated objectives and concerns (Conley and O'Barr 1990, p. 131; Welsh 2004a, pp. 600–1, 658).

8.6 Recommendations for future research

There are numerous possible avenues for future research. However, three main recommendations stand out: First, notwithstanding access difficulties, clearly more data from disputants and lawyers embroiled within formal courts and informal justice conflict resolution processes would be a great advantage. Moreover, similar studies could be done utilizing other dispute types to strengthen the validity of these findings. Second, due to the small numbers of female defendants in the dataset, more research on female versus male defendants' understandings, aims, and experiences in litigation and conflict resolution processes would also be beneficial. Likewise, further research into female versus male legal professionals' understandings, aims, and practices within ongoing court and informal justice processes is necessary. Third, it would be particularly valuable if similar research would be done in other jurisdictions and other cultures to test whether they too suffer from similar problems relating to the use of legal representatives in formal courts and informal justice processes or whether the present findings are solely or predominantly a product of Western adversarial legal systems and legal education.[40]

The findings and conclusions reported in this book seek to provide a rich source for debate among scholars, students, attorneys, trainers, mediators, and others interested in issues related to human conflict and its resolution. Although research in itself cannot settle any specific problem and is restricted in its ultimate applied applications, this study has provided solid data that can shed light on issues that are

---

40 The author is currently undertaking large-scale empirical research throughout India, comparing legal, lay, and gendered actors' perspectives relating to the permeation of international human rights laws and norms as well as actors' understandings, aims, and experiences in formal courts versus informal justice processing of violence against women cases.

often debated on supposition and conjecture. I hope that the dissemination of these findings will propel the consideration of the issues brought to light further so that the processing of disputes, be they mundane or life-altering, will not in essence remain "rough justice" for the justice system's most important actors: the disputants themselves. As Hampshire notes, "Fairness in procedures for resolving conflicts is the fundamental kind of fairness... acknowledged as a value in most cultures, places, and times... an invariable value, a constant in human nature" (Hampshire 1999, p. 4).

Bibliography

Abel, R. (1974). "A Comparative Theory of Dispute Institutions in Society." *Law and Society Review* **8**(2): 217.

Abel, R. (ed.) (1982). "The Contradictions of Informal Justice," in *The Politics of Informal Justice: The American Experience*, Vol. 1. New York, Academic Press, pp. 267–320.

Abel, R. (ed.) (1995). "What We Talk about When We Talk about Law," in *The Law & Society Reader*. New York, London, New York University Press, pp. 1–12.

Abel, R. (2005). Comments on manuscript. Unpublished. On file with author.

ADR-Chambers (1998a). *ADR Chambers.* http://www.adrchambers.com (last viewed August 8, 2008).

ADR-Chambers (1998b). *ADR Chambers: Mediation.* Canada, ADR Chambers. http://www.adrchambers.com/mediationintro.htm (last viewed August 8, 2008).

Alberstein, M. (2002). *Pragmatism and the Law: From Philosophy to Dispute Resolution.* Aldershot, Ashgate.

Alexander, N. (2002). "Global Trends in Mediation." *World Arbitration and Mediation Report* **13**: 272.

Alfieri, A. (1991). "Reconstructive Poverty Law Practice: Learning Lessons of Client Narrative." *The Yale Law Journal* **100**: 2107.

Anderson, V. A. (2003) "Alternative Dispute Resolution and Professional Responsibility in South Carolina: A Changing Landscape." *South Carolina Law Review* **55**: 191.

Attorney-General-of-Ontario (1999). *Regulation to Amend Regulation 194 of the Revised Regulations of Ontario 1990 Made under the Courts of Justice Act.* Ministry of the Attorney General of Ontario. http://www.attorneygeneral.jus.gov.on.ca/english/courts/manmed/notice.asp (last viewed August 8, 2008).

Auerbach, J. (1983). *Justice without Law?* New York, Oxford, Oxford University Press.

Babcock, L. and S. Laschever (2003). *Women Don't Ask: Negotiation and the Gender Divide.* Princeton, NJ, Princeton University Press.

Baldwin, J. (1997). *Monitoring the Rise of the Small Claims Limit: Litigants' Experiences of Different Forms of Adjudication.* Oxford, Clarendon Press.

Bales, R. F. (1951). *Interaction Process Analysis*. Cambridge, MA, Addison-Wesley Press, Inc.

Banakar, R. (2003). *Merging Law and Sociology*. Glienicke, Berlin, Madison, WI, Galda+Wilch Verlag.

Bandura, A. (1977). *Social Learning Theory*. Englewood Cliffs, London, Prentice-Hall.

Bandura, A. and R. Walters (1963). *Social Learning and Personality Development*. New York, Holt, Rinehart and Winston.

Barrett-Howard, E. and T. Tyler (1986). "Procedural Justice as a Criterion in Allocation Decisions." *Journal of Personality and Social Psychology* **50**: 296.

Bartlett, K. T. (1990). "Feminist Legal Methods." *Harvard Law Review* **103**: 829.

Barton, T. D. (1999). "Therapeutic Jurisprudence, Preventive Law, and Creative Problem Solving: An Essay on Harnessing Emotion and Human Connection." *Psychology, Public Policy and Law* **5**: 921.

Baruch Bush, R. (1997). "What Do We Need a Mediator For?: Mediation's 'Value-Added' for Negotiators." *Ohio State Journal on Dispute Resolution* **12**: 1.

Burns, T. (1992). *Erving Goffman*. London. Routeledge.

Bush, R. B. and J. Folger (1994). *The Promise of Mediation: Responding to Conflict through Empowerment and Recognition*. San Francisco, CA, Jossey-Bass.

Bell, S. and L. Richard (1992). "Anatomy of a Lawyer: Personality and Long-Term Career Satisfaction," in *Full Disclosure: Do You Really Want to Be a Lawyer?* Princeton, NJ, Peterson's Guides, pp. 150–62.

Bentham, J. (1843). "Scottish Reform," in *The Works of Jeremy Bentham* (S. J. Bowring, ed.) Vol. 5. Edinburgh, William Tate, pp. 1–54.

Bernstein, B. (1971). *Class, Codes and Control*. London, Routledge and Kegan Paul.

Bethel, C. A. and L. R. Singer (1982). "Mediation: A New Remedy for Cases of Domestic Violence." *Vermont Law Review* **7**: 15.

Bibas, S. and R. A. Bierschbach (2004). "Integrating Remorse and Apology into Criminal Procedure." *Yale Law Journal* **114**(October): 85.

Binder, D., P. Bergman and S. Price (1991). *Lawyers as Counselors: A Client-Centered Approach*. St. Paul, West Coast Publishing Company.

Binder, D. and S. Price (1977). *Legal Interviewing and Counseling: A Client Centered Approach*. St. Paul, MN, West Publishing Company.

Bingham, L., K. Kim and S. S. Raines (2002). "Exploring the Role of Representation in Employment Mediation at the USPS." *Ohio State Journal on Dispute Resolution* **17**: 341.

Birke, R. (2000). "Evaluation and Facilitation: Moving Past Either/Or." *Journal of Dispute Resolution* **2000**: 309.

Bloch, M. (1974). "Symbols, Song, Dance and Features of Articulation: Is Religion an Extreme Form of Traditional Authority?" *European Archives of Sociology* **15**: 55.

Boettger, U. (2004). "Efficiency Versus Party Empowerment – Against a Good-Faith Requirement in Mandatory Mediation." *Review of Litigation* **23**: 1.

Bogoch, B. (1997). "Gendered Lawyering: Difference and Dominance in Lawyer-Client Interaction." *Law and Society Review* **31**: 677.

Bourdieu, P. (1977). *Outline of a Theory of Practice*. Cambridge, Cambridge University Press.

Bourdieu, P. (1990). *The Logic of Practice*. Cambridge, Polity.

Bowman, C. (1999). "Women and the Legal Profession." *American University Journal of Gender, Social Policy and Law* **7**: 149.

Brest, P. (2000). "Skeptical Thoughts: Integrating Problem Solving into Legal Curriculum Faces Uphill Climb." *A. B. A. Dispute Resolution Magazine* **20**(Summer): 20.

Brinig, M. (1995). "Does Mediation Systematically Disadvantage Women?" *William & Mary Journal of Women & the Law* **2**(Fall): 1.

Brown, H. and A. Simanowitz (1995). "Alternative Dispute Resolution and Mediation." *Quality in Health Care* **4**(2): 151.

Brown, W. (1996). "Constitutions and 'Survivor Stories': In the 'Folds of Our Own Discourse' the Pleasures and Freedoms of Silence." *University of Chicago Law School Roundtable* **3**: 185.

Bruner, J. (1992). "A Psychologist and the Law." *New York Law School Law Review* **37**: 173.

Bryan, P. (1992). "Killing Us Softly: Divorce Mediation and the Politics of Power." *Buffalo Law Review* **40**: 441.

Bush, R. A. B. and J. P. Folger (1994). *The Promise of Mediation: Responding to Conflict through Empowerment and Recognition*. San Francisco, CA, Jossey-Bass.

Bush, R. B. (1997). "What Do We Need a Mediator For?: Mediation's 'Value-Added' for Negotiators." *Ohio State Journal on Dispute Resolution* **12**: 1.

Cahn, N. R. (1992). "Theoretics of Practice: The Integration of Progressive Thought and Action: Styles of Lawyering." *Hastings Law Journal* **43**: 1039, 1050–54.

Caldon, D. T. (1999). *Medical Malpractice Disputes in the Age of Managed Care*. Malibu, CA, Strauss Institute for Dispute Resolution, Mediation Information and Resource Center (MIRC). www.mediate.com/articles/caldon.cfm?plain=t (last viewed August 9, 1999).

Cameron, J. (1999). "Adjusting the Scales of Justice." *Canadian Insurance* June 18, 1999.

Campbell, C. (1976). "Lawyers and Their Public," in *Lawyers in Their Social Setting* (D. MacCormick, ed.). Edinburgh, Green & Son Ltd., p. 209.

Casper, J. (1978). "Having Their Day in Court: Defendant Evaluations of the Fairness of Their Treatment." *Law and Society Review* **12**: 237.

Casper, J. E. A. (1988). "Procedural Justice in Felony Cases." *Law and Society Review* **22**: 483.

Christiansen, V. (1997). "The Role of Reconciliation in the Mediation Process: Lessons from a Traditional Chinese Village." *Dispute Resolution Journal* **52**(Fall): 66.

Clement, J. A. and A. I. Schwebel (1993). "A Research Agenda for Divorce Mediation: The Creation of Second Order Knowledge to Inform Legal Policy." *Ohio State Journal on Dispute Resolution* **9**: 95.

CMPA (1999). *What Is the CMPA?* The Canadian Medical Protection Association. www.cmpa.org/english/whatis-e.cfm (last viewed August 12, 1999).

Cobb, S. (1997). "The Domestication of Violence in Mediation." *Law and Society Review* **31**(3): 397.

Cohen, A. (2003). "Gender: An (Un)Useful Category of Prescriptive Negotiation Analysis?" *Texas Journal of Women and the Law* **13**: 169.

Comaroff, J. L. (1975). "Talking Politics: Oratory and Authority in a Tswana Chiefdom," in *Political Language and Oratory in Traditional Society* (M. Bloch, ed.). London and New York, Academic Press, pp. 141–61.

Comaroff, J. L. and S. Roberts (1981). *Rules and Processes: The Cultural Logic of Dispute in an African Context.* Chicago, IL, University of Chicago Press.

Conley, J. and W. O'Barr (1988). "Hearing the Hidden Agenda: The Ethnographic Investigation of Procedure." *Law and Contemporary Problems* **51**(4): 181.

Conley, J. and W. O'Barr (1990). *Rules Versus Relationships: The Ethnography of Legal Discourse.* Chicago, IL, University of Chicago Press.

CPSO (1999a). *General College Information.* The College of Physicians and Surgeons of Ontario. http://www.cpso.on.ca/about_the_college/geninfo.htm (last viewed August 8, 2008).

CPSO (1999b). *Complaints Against Md's.* The College of Physicians and Surgeons of Ontario. http://www.cpso.on.ca/Info_Public/factcomp.htm (last viewed on August 8, 2008).

Craver, C. B. and D. W. Barnes (1999). "Gender, Risk Taking and Negotiation Performance." *Michigan Journal of Gender and Law* **5**: 299.

Crawford, M. (1996). "Rent-a-Judge Business Taking Flight in Ontario." *The Financial Post, Toronto,* **8**.

Cunningham, C. (1989). A Tale of Two Clients: Thinking about Law as Language. *Michigan Law Review,* **87**: 2459.

Cunningham, C. (1992). "The Lawyer as Translator, Representation as Text: Towards an Ethnography of Legal Discourse." *Cornell Law Review* **77**: 1298.

Currie, C. (1998). "Mediation and Medical Practice Disputes." *Mediation Quarterly* **15**(3): 215.

Daicoff, S. (1997). "Lawyer, Know Thyself: A Review of Empirical Research on Attorney Attributes Bearing on Professionalism." *American University Law Review* **46**: 1337.

Daicoff, S. (1998). "Asking Leopards to Change Their Spots: Should Lawyers Change? A Critique of Solutions to Problems with Professionalism by Reference to Empirically-Derived Attorney Personality Attributes." *The Georgetown Journal of Legal Ethics* **11**: 547.

Damaska, M. (1986). *The Faces of Justice and State Authority: A Comparative Approach to the Legal Process.* New Haven, CT, Yale University Press.

Daniel, A. E., R. J. Burn and S. Horarik (1999). "Patients' Complaints about Medical Practice." *Medical Journal of Australia* **170**: 598–602.

Dauer, E. and L. Marcus (1997). "Adapting Mediation to Link Resolution of Medical Malpractice Disputes with Health Care Quality Improvement." *Law and Contemporary Problems* **60**(1–2): 185.

Davis, P. (1991). "Contextual Legal Criticism: A Demonstration Exploring Hierarchy and 'Feminine' Style." *New York University Law Review* **66**: 1635.

Deason, E. (2001). "Reply: The Quest for Uniformity in Mediation Confidentiality: Foolish Consistency or Crucial Predictability?" *Marquette Law Review* **85**(Fall): 79.

Delgado, R., C. Dunn and D. Hubbert (1985). "Fairness and Formality: Minimizing the Risk of Prejudice in Alternative Dispute Resolution." *Wisconsin Law Review* **6**: 1359–404.

Des Rosiers, N., B. Feldthusen and O. Hankivsky (1998). "Legal Compensation for Sexual Violence: Therapeutic Consequences and Consequences for the Judicial System." *Psychology, Public Policy and Law* **4**(1–2): 433.

Dingwall, R., D. Greatbatch and L. Ruggerone (1998). "Gender and Interaction in Divorce Mediation." *Mediation Quarterly* **15**(4): 277.

Dingwall, R. (1988). "Empowerment or Enforcement? Some Questions about Power and Control in Divorce Mediation," in *Divorce, Mediation and the Legal Process* (R. Dingwall and J. M. Eekelaar, eds.). Oxford, UK, Clarendon, pp. 150–67.

Dispute-Resolution (1999). Dispute Resolution Home Page. www.dispres.com (last viewed September 17, 1999).

DuBois, E. C., M. C. Dunlap, C. J. Gilligan and C. J. Menkel-Meadow (1985). "Feminist Discourse, Moral Values, and the Law – A Conversation." *Buffalo Law Review* **34**(1): 11.

Dubow, F. L. and C. McEwen (1993). "Community Boards: An Analytic Profile," in *The Possibility of Popular Justice: A Case Study of Community Mediation in the United States* (S. Merry and N. Milner, eds.). Ann Arbor, MI, University of Michigan Press, pp. 125–68.

Duryee, M. (1992a). "Mandatory Mediation: Myth and Reality." *Family and Conciliation Courts Review* **30**: 507.

Duryee, M. (1992b). "Mandatory Court Mediation: Demographic Summary and Consumer Evaluation of One Court Service." *Family and Conciliaiton Courts Review* **30**: 260.

Easterbrook, J. (1996). "Resolving Health Care Disputes." *Solicitors Journal* **140**(16): 410.

Edwards, H. T. (1986). "Commentary: Alternative Dispute Resolution: Panacea or Anathema?" *Harvard Law Review* **99**: 668.

Eichner, M. (2001). "On Postmodern Feminist Legal Theory." *Harvard Civil Rights – Civil Liberties Law Review* **36**(Winter): 1.

Ellman, S. (1993). "The Ethic of Care as an Ethic for Lawyers." *Georgetown Law Journal* **81**(August): 2665.

Engel, D. (1984). "The Oven Bird's Song: Insiders, Outsiders and Personal Injuries in an American Community." *Law and Society Review* **18**(4): 551.

Epstein, C. F. (1988). *Deceptive Distinctions: Sex, Gender, and the Social Order.* New Haven, CT, Yale University Press.

Evans, M. (2001). "Women and Mediation: Toward a Formulation of an Interdisciplinary Empirical Model to Determine Equity in Dispute Resolution." *Ohio State Journal on Dispute Resolution* **17**(1): 145.

Ewick, P. and S. Silbey (1998). *The Common Place of Law.* Chicago, IL, Chicago University Press.

Eyster, M. J. (1996). "Clinical Teaching, Ethical Negotiation, and Moral Judgment." *Nebraska Law Review* **75**: 752.

Farber, H. S. and M. J. White (1994). "A Comparison of Formal and Informal Dispute Resolution in Medical Malpractice." *Journal of Legal Studies* **23**(2): 777.

Farber, S. R. and M. Rickenberg (1999). "Under-Confident Women and Over-Confident Men: Gender and Sense of Competence in a Simulated Negotiation." *Yale Journal of Law and Feminism* **11**: 271.

Fassnacht, G. (1982). *Theory and Practice of Observing Behavior.* London, Academic Press.

Felstiner, W., R. Abel and A. Sarat (1980–81). "The Emergence and Transformation of Disputes: Naming, Blaming Claiming." *Law and Society Review* **15**(3–4): 631.

Felstiner, W. and A. Sarat (1992). "Enactments of Power: Negotiating Reality and Responsibility in Lawyer-Client Interactions." *Cornell Law Review* **77**: 1447.

Ferris, L. (2004). "Using Therapeutic Jurisprudence and Preventive Law to Examine Disputants' Best Interests in Mediating Cases About Physicians' Practices: A Guide for Medical Regulators." *Medicine and Law* **23**: 183.

Fineman, M. (1988). "Dominant Discourse, Professional Language, and Legal Change in Child Custody Decisionmaking." *Harvard Law Review* **101**: 727.

Fiss, O. (1964). "Against Settlement." *Yale Law Journal* **93**: 1073.

Flick, U. (1992). "Triangulation Revisited – Strategy of Validation or Alternative?" *Journal for the Theory of Social Behavior* **22**(2): 175.

Folberg, J., D. Golann, L. Kloppenberg and T. Stipanowich (2005). *Resolving Disputes: Theory, Practice, and Law.* New York, Aspen Publishers.

Folberg, J. and A. Taylor (1984). *Mediation: A Comprehensive Guide to Resolving Conflicts without Litigation.* San Francisco, CA, Jossey-Bass.

Folger, J. P. and R. A. B. Bush (1996). "Transformative Mediation and Third-Party Intervention: Ten Hallmarks of a Transformative Approach to Practice." *Mediation Quarterly* **13**: 263.

Forehand, S. (1999). "Note & Comment: Helping the Medicine Go Down: How a Spoonful of Mediation Can Alleviate the Problems of Medical Malpractice Litigation." *Ohio State Journal on Dispute Resolution* **14**: 907.

Foucault, M. (1981). *The History of Sexuality.* Harmondsworth, Penguin Books.

Fuller, L. L. (1971). "Mediation: Its Forms and Functions." *South California Law Review* **44**: 305.

Fuller, L. L. (1978). "The Forms and Limits of Adjudication." *Harvard Law Review* **92**: 353.

Galanter, M. (1974). "Why the 'Haves' Come Out Ahead: Speculations on the Limits of Legal Change." *Law and Society Review* **9**: 95.

Galanter, M. (1986). "The Day after the Litigation Explosion." *Maryland Law Review* **46**: 3.

Galanter, M. and M. Cahill (1994). "'Most Cases Settle': Judicial Promotion and Regulation of Settlements." *Stanford Law Review* **46**(6): 1339.

Galton, E. (1994). *Representing Clients in Mediation*. Dallas, TX, American Lawyer Media.

Garfinkel, H. (1984). *Studies in Ethnomethodology*. Cambridge, Polity.

Gaskell, G. and M. Bauer (2000). Social Research Design Course – Mi421. London, London School of Economics Methodology Institute. Unpublished lecture series.

Gatter, R. (2004). "Institutionally Sponsored Mediation and the Emerging Medical Trust Movement in the U.S." *Medicine and Law* **23**: 201.

Geertz, C. (1973). *The Interpretation of Cultures*. New York, Basic Books.

Genn, H. (1995). "Access to Just Settlements: The Case of Medical Negligence," in *Reform of Civil Procedure: Essays on "Access to Justice"* (A. Zuckerman and R. Cranston, eds.). New York, Oxford, Oxford University Press, Clarendon Press, pp. 393–412.

Genn, H. (1999). *Paths to Justice: What People Do and Think about Going to Law*. Oxford, Hart.

Giddens, A. (1984). *The Constitution of Society: Outline of the Theory of Structuration*. Cambridge, Polity Press.

Gilkerson, C. (1992). "Poverty Law Narratives: The Critical Practice and Theory of Receiving and Translating Client Stories." *Hastings Law Journal* **43**: 861.

Gilligan, C. (1982). *In a Different Voice: Psychological Theory and Women's Development*. Cambridge, MA, Harvard University Press.

Gitchell, R. L. and A. Plattner (1999). "Mediation: A Viable Alternative to Litigation for Medical Malpractice Cases." *Depaul Journal of Health Care Law* **2**(3): 421.

Glasser, C. and S. Roberts (1993). "Dispute Resolution: Civil Justice and Its Alternatives: Introduction." *Modern Law Review* **56**(3): 277.

Goffman, E. (1961a). *Asylums*. Harmondsworth, Penguin.

Goffman, E. (1961b). *Encounters: Two Studies in the Sociology of Interaction*. Indianapolis, IN, Bobbs-Merill.

Goffman, E. (1971). *The Presentation of Self in Everyday Life*. Harmondsworth, Penguin.

Goffman, E. (1974). *Frame Analysis: An Essay on the Organization of Experience*. New York, Harper and Row.

Golann, D. (2000). "Variations in Mediation: How – and Why – Legal Mediators Change Styles in the Course of a Case." *Journal of Dispute Resolution* **2000**: 41.

Golann, D. (2002). "Is Legal Mediation a Process of Repair – or Separation? An Empirical Study, and Its Implications." *Harvard Negotiation Law Review* **7**(Spring): 301.

Gold, N. (1991). "Considering Dispute Resolution: A Research Prospectus," in *A Handbook of Dispute Resolution: ADR in Action* (K. Mackie, ed.). London, New York, Routeledge and Sweet&Maxwell, pp. 267–77.

Goldberg, S. B., F. E. A. Sander and N. H. Rogers (1999). *Dispute Resolution: Negotiation, Mediation and Other Processes*. Gaithersburg, MD, Aspen Law & Business.

Goldberg, S., F. Sander and N. Rogers (eds.) (1992). *Dispute Resolution Negotiation, Mediation, and Other Processes*. Boston, Little Brown and Company.

Gordon, E. (2000). "Attorneys' Negotiation Strategies in Mediation: Business as Usual?" *Mediation Quarterly* **17**(4): 377.

Gordon, E. E. (1999). "Why Attorneys Support Mandatory Mediation." *Judicature* **82**: 224.

Griffiths, J. (1986). "What Do Dutch Lawyers Actually Do in Divorce Cases?" *Law and Society Review* **20**: 135.

Grillo, T. (1991). "The Mediation Alternative: Process Dangers for Women." *Yale Law Journal* **100**(6): 1545.

Gulliver, P. (1979). *Disputes and Negotiations: A Cross-Cultural Perspective*. London, Academic Press.

Guthrie, C. (2001). "The Lawyer's Philosophical Map and the Disputant's Perceptual Map: Impediments to Facilitative Mediation and Lawyering." *Harvard Negotiation Law Review* **6**(Spring): 145.

Guthrie, C. (2002). "Symposium: Procedural Justice Research and the Paucity of Trials." *Journal of Dispute Resolution* **2002**: 127.

Habermas, J. (1981). *The Theory of Communicative Action*. Boston, Beacon, Cambridge, Polity.

Hafner, J. and M. E. Fakouri (1984). "Early Recollections of Individuals Preparing for Careers in Clinical Psychology, Dentistry, and Law." *Journal of Vocational Behavior* **24**: 236.

Hampshire, S. (1999). *Justice Is Conflict*. London, Duckworth.

Harnick, C. (1997). *Improving Access to Our Courts: Notes for Remarks by Attorney General Charles Harnick*. Canadian Bar Association – Ontario. Stitt Feld Handy Houston. http://www.adr.ca/news/harnick013197.asp (last viewed August 13, 1999).

Hart, H. M., Jr. and A. Sacks (1994). *The Legal Process: Basic Problems in the Making and Application of Law*. Westbury, NY, Foundation Press.

Hensler, D. (1999). "A Research Agenda: What We Need to Know about Court-Connected ADR." *Dispute Resolution Magazine* **6**(1): 15.

Hensler, D. (2003). "Our Courts, Ourselves: How the Alternative Dispute Resolution Movement Is Re-Shaping Our Legal System." *Penn State Law Review* **108**(Summer): 165.

Hickson, G., E. Clayton, P. Githens and F. Sloan (1992). "Factors That Prompted Families to File Medical Malpractice Claims Following Perinatal Injuries." *JAMA* **267**(10): 1359.

Hill, E. (1990). "Alternative Dispute Resolution in a Feminist Voice." *Ohio State Journal on Dispute Resolution* **5**: 337.

Hinshaw, L. and G. Forbes (1993). "Attitudes toward Women and Approaches to Conflict Resolution in College Students in Spain and the United States." *Journal of Social Psychology* **133**: 865.

Hobbs, T. and G. Gable (1998). Coping with Litigation Stress. Physician's News Digest. http://192.41.26.254/law/198.html (last viewed August 20, 1999).

Hosticka, C. (1979). "We Don't Care about What Happened, We Only Care about What Is Going to Happen: Lawyer–Client Negotiations of Reality." *Social Problems* **265**: 599.

Hughes, S. H. (1998). "A Closer Look: The Case for a Mediation Privilege Has Not Been Made." *Dispute Resolution Magazine* **5**(Winter): 14.

Hunting, R. and G. Neuwirth (1962). *Who Sues in New York City?* New York, Columbia University Press.

Janoff, S. (1991). "The Influence of Legal Education on Moral Reasoning." *Minnesota Law Review* **76**: 193.

Johnson, S. M. (1997). "A Medical Malpractice Litigator Proposes Mediation." *Dispute Resolution Journal* **52**(2): 42.

Jones, G. T. (2003). "Fighting Capitulation: A Research Agenda for the Future of Dispute Resolution." *Penn State Law Review* **108**(Summer): 277.

Kandel, R. (1994). "Power Plays: A Sociolinguistic Study of Inequality in Child Custody Mediation and a Hearsay Analog Solution." *Arizona Law Review* **36**: 879.

Kelly, J. and M. Duyree (1995). "Women's and Men's Views of Mediation in Voluntary and Mandatory Mediation Settings." *Family and Conciliation Courts Review* **30**(1): 35.

Kelly, J. B. (1989). "Mediated and Adversarial Divorce: Respondents' Perceptions of Their Processes and Outcomes." *Mediation Quarterly* **24**(December): 71–87.

King, C. (1994). "Are Justice and Harmony Mutually Exclusive? A Response to Professor Nader." *Ohio State Journal on Dispute Resolution* **10**: 65.

Klein, K. (2005). "A Judicial Mediator's Perspective: The Impact of Gender on Dispute Resolution: Mediation as a Different Voice." *North Dakota Law Review* **81**: 771.

Kolb, D. M. (1991). "Women's Work: Peacemaking Behind the Organizational Scene," in *The Dialectics of Disputing: New Perspectives in Organization Conflict* (D. Kolb and J. Bartunek, eds.). Newbury Park, CA, Sage, pp. 64–93.

Kolb, D. M. (1993). "Her Place at the Table: Gender and Negotiation," in *Negotiation: Strategies for Mutual Gain* (L. Hall, ed.). Newbury Park, London, Sage, pp. 138–51.

Kolb, D. M. (2000). "More Than Just a Footnote: Constructing a Theoretical Framework for Teaching about Gender in Negotiation." *Negotiation Journal* **16**(4): 347.

Kolb, D. M. (2003). *Negotiation Overview. Reader in Gender, Work and Organization* (R. J. Ely, E. G. Foldy, and M. A. Scully, eds.). Maldon, MA, Blackwell Publishing, pp. 101–7.

Kolb, D. M. and G. G. Coolidge (1988). "Her Place at the Table: A Consideration of Gender Issues in Negotiation," in *The Program on Negotiation Working Paper Series 88-5*. Boston, Harvard Law School.

Kolb, D. M. and L. L. Putnam (1997). "Through the Looking Glass: Negotiation Theory Refracted through the Lens of Gender," in *Workplace Dispute Resolution: Directions for the Twenty-First Century* (S. E. Gleason, ed.). East Lansing, Michigan State University Press, pp. 231–47.

Kolb, D. M. and J. Williams (2000). *The Shadow Negotiation: How Women Can Master the Hidden Agendas That Determine Bargaining Success*. New York, Simon & Schuster.

Kolb, D. M. and J. Williams (2003). *Everyday Negotiation: Navigating the Hidden Agendas in Bargaining*. San Francisco, CA, Jossey-Bass.

Kolb, D., J. Williams and C. Frohlinger (2004). *Her Place at the Table: A Woman's Guide to Negotiating Five Key Challenges to Leadership Success*. San Francisco, CA, Jossey-Bass.

Korobkin, R. and C. Guthrie (1997). "Psychology, Economics and Settlement: A New Look at the Role of the Lawyer." *Texas Law Review* **76**: 77.

Kovach, K. (1997). "Good Faith in Mediation: Requested, Recommended or Required: A New Ethic." *South Texas Law Review* **38**: 575.

Kovach, K. (2001). "New Wine Requires New Wineskins: Transforming Lawyer Ethics for Effective Representation in a Non-Adversarial Approach to Problem Solving: Mediation." *Fordham Urban Law Journal* **28**(April): 935.

Kovach, K. (2003). "Lawyer Ethics Must Keep Pace with Practice: Plurality in Lawyering Roles Demands Diverse and Innovative Ethical Standards." *Idaho Law Review* **39**: 399.

Kovach, K. and L. Love (1998). "Mapping Mediation: The Risks of Riskin's Grid." *Harvard Negotiation Law Review* **3**: 71.

Kritzer, H. (1984). "The Dimensions of Lawyer-Client Relations: Notes Toward a Theory and a Field Study." *American Bar Foundation Research Journal* **9**(2, Spring): 409–25.

Kritzer, H. (1990). *The Justice Broker: Lawyers and Ordinary Litigation*. New York, Oxford University Press.

Kritzer, H. (1998). "Contingent-Fee Lawyers and Their Clients: Settlement Expectations, Settlement Realities, and Issues of Control in the Lawyer-Client Relationship." *Law and Social Inquiry* **23**: 795.

Lacey, N. (2002). Theoretical Paradigms in Legal Research Lecture Series. London, London School of Economics. Unpublished.

LaFree, G. and C. Rack (1996). "The Effects of Participants' Ethnicity and Gender on Monetary Outcomes in Mediated and Adjudicated Civil Cases." *Law and Society Review* **30**: 767.

Lande, J. (1997). "How Will Lawyering and Mediation Practices Transform Each Other?" *Florida State University Law Review* **24**: 839.

Lande, J. (2000). "Toward More Sophisticated Mediation Theory." *Journal of Dispute Resolution* **2000**: 321.

Lande, J. (2002). "Using Dispute System Design Methods to Promote Good-Faith Participation in Court-Connected Mediation Programs." *UCLA Law Review* **50**: 69.

Lawrence, J. (2000). "Mediation Advocacy: Partnering with the Mediator." *Ohio State Journal on Dispute Resolution* **15**: 425.

Lees, D. (1998). "Justice out of Court: With Our Legal System Clogged with Civil Litigants and Costs Spiralling out of Control, Canadian Firms Have Learnt a Lesson from Their U.S. Counterparts: Mediation Really Is the Better Way." *The Financial Post* 22–34.

Lehman, W. (1978). "The Pursuit of a Client's Interests." *Michigan Law Review* **77**: 1078.

Lemert, C. and A. Branaman (eds.) (1997). *The Goffman Reader*. Malden, Blackwell Publishers.

Levin, M. S. (2001). "The Propriety of Evaluative Mediation: Concerns about the Nature and Quality of an Evaluative Opinion." *Ohio State Journal on Dispute Resolution* **16**: 267.

Liebman, C. B. (2000). "Mediation as Parallel Seminars: Lessons from the Student Takeover of Columbia University's Hamilton Hall." *Negotiation Journal* **16**: 157.

Lind, E. A. (1998). "Procedural Justice, Disputing, and Reactions to Legal Authorities," in *Everyday Practices and Trouble Cases* (A. Sarat, M. Constable, D. Engel, V. Hans and S. Lawrence, eds.). Evanston, Northwestern University Press, pp. 177–98.

Lind, E. A., R. I. Lissak and D. E. Conlon (1983). "Decision Control and Process Control Effects on Procedural Fairness Judgments" *Journal of Applied Social Psychology* **13**: 338.

Lind, E. A., R. MacCoun, P. A. Ebener, W. L. F. Felstiner, D. R. Hensler, J. Resnik and T. Tyler (1989). *The Perception of Justice: Tort Litigants' Views of Trial, Court-Annexed Arbitration, and Judicial Settlement Conferences*. Santa Monica, Rand Institute for Civil Justice.

Lind, E. A., R. J. Maccoun, P. A. Ebener, W. L. F. Felstiner, D. R. Hensler, J. Resnik and T. R. Tyler (1990). "In the Eye Of The Beholder: Tort Litigants' Evaluations of Their Experiences in the Civil Justice System." *Law and Society Review* **24**: 953.

Lind, E. A., L. Kray and L. Thompson (1998). "The Social Construction of Injustice: Fairness Judgments in Response to Own and Others' Unfair Treatment by Authorities." *Organizational Behavior and Human Decision Processes* **75**: 1–22.

Lind, E. A. and T. Tyler (1988). *The Social Psychology of Procedural Justice*. London, Plenum Press.

Love, L. P. and J. B. Boskey (1997). "Should Mediators Evaluate? A Debate between Lela P. Love and James B. Boskey." *Cardozo Online Journal of Conflict Resolution* **1**: 96.

Love, L. P. and K. K. Kovach (2000). "ADR: An Eclectic Array of Processes, Rather Than One Eclectic Process." *Journal of Dispute Resolution* **2000**(2): 295.

Lowry, L. R. (2000). "Training Mediators for the 21st Century: To Evaluate or Not: That Is Not the Question!" *Family and Conciliation Courts Review* **38**: 48.

Lowry, M. (1983). "Law School Socialization and the Perversion of Mediation in the United States." *Windsor Yearbook of Access to Justice* **3**: 245.

Macaulay, S. (1979). "Lawyers and Consumer Protection Laws." *Law and Society Review* **14**: 115.

Macfarlane, J. (November 1995). *Court-Based Mediation of Civil Cases: An Evaluation of the Ontario Court (General Division) ADR Centre*. Toronto, Queen's Printer for Ontario.

Macfarlane, J. (2001). "What Does the Changing Culture of Legal Practice Mean for Legal Education?" *Windsor Yearbook of Access to Justice* **20**: 191.

Macfarlane, J. (2002). "Culture Change? A Tale of Two Cities and Mandatory Court-Connected Mediation." *Journal of Dispute Resolution* **2002**(2): 241.

Macfarlane, J. and M. Keet (2004–5). "Civil Justice Reform and Mandatory Civil Mediation in Saskatchewan: Lessons from a Maturing Program." *Alberta Law Review* **42**: 677.

MacKinnon, C. (1987). *Feminism Unmodified: Discourses on Life and Law*. Cambridge, MA, London, Harvard University Press.

Macleod, L. H., E. H. Fleischmann and A. Demelo (1998). "The Future of Alternative Dispute Resolution in Ontario: Mechanics of the Mandatory Mediation Programs." *Advocates' Quarterly* **20**: 389.

Maiman, R. J., L. Mather and C. A. McEwen (1992). "Gender and Specialization in the Practice of Divorce Law." *Maine Law Review* **44**: 39.

Manning, P. (1992). *Erving Goffman and Modern Sociology*. New York, Polity Press.

Margulies, P. (1990). "'Who Are You to Tell Me That?': Attorney-Client Deliberation Regarding Nonlegal Issues and the Interests of Nonclients." *North Carolina Law Review* **68**: 213.

Maslow Cohen, J. (1990). "Feminism and Adaptive Heroinism: The Paradigm of Portia as a Means of Introduction." *Tulsa Law Journal* **25**: 657.

Mather, L. and B. Yngvesson (1980–81). "Language, Audience, and the Transformation of Disputes." *Law and Society Review* **15**(3–4): 775.

Mather, L. M., C. A. McEwen and R. J. Maiman (2001). *Divorce Lawyers at Work: Varieties of Professionalism in Practice*. New York, Oxford University Press.

Maute, J. (1987). "Sporting Theory of Justice: Taming Adversarial Zeal with a Logical Sanctions Doctrine." *Connecticut Law Review* **20**: 7.

Maute, J. (2002). "Lady Lawyers: Not an Oxymoron." *Tulsa Law Review* **38**(Fall): 159.

McAdoo, B. (2002). "A Report to the Minnesota Supreme Court: The Impact of Rule 114 on Civil Litigation Practice in Minnesota." *Hamline Law Review* **25**: 401.

McAdoo, B. (2007). "All Rise, the Court Is in Session: What Judges Say about Court-Connected Mediation." *Ohio State Journal on Dispute Resolution* **22**: 377.

McAdoo, B. and A. Hinshaw (2002). "The Challenge of Institutionalizing Alternative Dispute Resolution: Attorney Perspectives on the Effect of Rule 17 on Civil Litigation in Missouri." *Missouri Law Review* **67**(Summer): 473.

McCabe, K. (2001). "A Forum for Women's Voices: Mediation through a Feminist Jurisprudential Lens." *Northern Illinois University Law Review* **21**: 459.

McDermott, E. P. and R. Obar (2004). "'What's Going on' in Mediation:An Empirical Analysis of the Influence of a Mediator's Style on Party Satisfaction and Monetary Benefit." *Harvard Negotiation Law Review* **9**(Spring): 75.

McEwen, C. (1995). "Bring in the Lawyers: Challenging the Dominant Approaches to Ensuring Fairness in Divorce Mediation." *Minnesota Law Review* **79**: 1317.

McEwen, C., L. Mather and R. Maiman (1994). "Lawyers, Mediation, and the Management of Divorce Practice." *Law and Society Review* **28**: 149.

McEwen, C., N. Rogers and R. Maiman (1995). "Bring in the Lawyers: Challenging the Dominant Approaches to Ensuring Fairness in Divorce Mediation." *Minnesota Law Review* **79**: 1317.

McEwen, C. A. and R. L. Wissler (2002). "Finding Out If It Is True: Comparing Mediation and Negotiation through Research." *Journal of Dispute Resolution* **2002**: 131.

McGillis, D. (1997). *Community Mediation Programs: Developments and Challenges, National Institute of Justice.* U.S. Department of Justice. www.ncjrs.org/txtfiles/165698.txt (last viewed February 25, 2005).

Menkel-Meadow, C. (1984). "Toward Another View of Legal Negotiation: The Structure of Problem Solving." *UCLA Law Review* **31**: 754.

Menkel-Meadow, C. (1985). "Portia in a Different Voice: Speculations on a Women's Lawyering Process." *Berkeley Women's Law Journal* **1**: 39.

Menkel-Meadow, C. (1987). "Excluded Voices: New Voices in the Legal Profession Making New Voices in the Law." *University of Miami Law Review* **42**: 29.

Menkel-Meadow, C. (1989). "Exploring a Research Agenda of the Feminization of the Legal Profession: Theories of Gender and Social Change." *Law and Social Inquiry* **14**: 289.

Menkel-Meadow, C. (1991). "Pursuing Settlement in an Adversary Culture: A Tale of Innovation Co-Opted or the Law of ADR'." *Florida State University Law Review* **19**(Summer): 1.

Menkel-Meadow, C. (1994a). "Portia Redux: Another Look at Gender, Feminism, and Legal Ethics." *Virginia Journal of Social Policy and the Law* **2**(Fall): 75.

Menkel-Meadow, C. (1994b). "The Future of the Legal Profession: Culture Clash in the Quality of Life in the Law: Changes in the Economics, Diversification and Organization of Lawyering." *Case Western Reserve Law Review* **44**: 621.

Menkel-Meadow, C. (1995a). "Ethics and the Settlements of Mass Torts: When the Rules Meet the Road." *Cornell Law Review* **80**: 1159.

Menkel-Meadow, C. (1995b). "Whose Dispute Is It Anyway?: A Philosophical and Democratic Defense of Settlement (in Some Cases)." *Georgetown Law Journal* **83**: 2663.

Menkel-Meadow, C. (1995c). "Book Review: The Many Ways of Mediation: The Transformation of Traditions, Ideologies, Paradigms, and Practices." *Negotiation Journal* **11**(3, July): 217–42.

Menkel-Meadow, C. (1996a). "Is Mediation the Practice of Law?" *Alternatives to the High Cost of Litigation* **14**(5): 60.

Menkel-Meadow, C. (1996b). "The Trouble with the Adversary System in a Postmodern, Multicultural World." *William & Mary Law Review* **38**(October): 5.

Menkel-Meadow, C. (1997a). "Ethics in Alternative Dispute Resolution: New Issues. No Answers from the Adversary Conception of Lawyers' Responsibilities." *South Texas Law Review* **38**: 407.

Menkel-Meadow, C. (1997b). "What Trina Taught Me: Reflections on Mediation, Inequality, Teaching and Life." *Minnesota Law Review* **81**(June): 1413.

Menkel-Meadow, C. (1999). "New Roles: Problem Solving the Lawyer as Problem Solver and Third-Party Neutral: Creativity and Non-Partisanship in Lawyering." *Temple Law Review* **72**(Winter): 785.

Menkel-Meadow, C. (2000a). "Teaching about Gender and Negotiation: Sex, Truths and Videotape." *Negotiation Journal* **16**: 357.

Menkel-Meadow, C. (2000b). "Mothers and Fathers of Invention: The Intellectual Founders of ADR." *Ohio State Journal on Dispute Resolution* **16**: 1.

Menkel-Meadow, C. (2001). "Negotiating with Lawyers, Men and Things: The Contextual Approach Still Matters." *Negotiation Journal* **17**(3): 257–93.

Menkel-Meadow, C. (2002a). "Ethics Issues in Arbitration and Related Dispute Resolution Processes: What's Happening and What's Not." *University of Miami Law Review* **56**: 949.

Menkel-Meadow, C. (2002b). "The Lawyer as Consensus Builder: Ethics for a New Practice." *Tennessee Law Review* **70**(Fall): 63–119.

Menkel-Meadow, C. (2004). "From Legal Disputes to Conflict Resolution and Human Problem Solving: Legal Dispute Resolution in a Multidisciplinary Context." *Journal of Legal Education* **54**(March): 7.

Menkel-Meadow, C. (November 17, 2006). Comments on manuscript by Carrie Menkel-Meadow to author. On file with author.

Menkel-Meadow, C., L. P. Love and A. K. Schneider (2006). *Mediation: Practice, Policy and Ethics.* New York, Aspen Publishers.

Merriam, S. and R. Caffarella (1991). *Learning in Adulthood: A Comprehensive Guide.* San Francisco, CA, Jossey-Bass.

Merry, S. (1990a). "The Discourses of Mediation and the Power of Naming." *Yale Journal of Law and the Humanities* **2**: 1.
Merry, S. (1990b). *Getting Justice and Getting Even: Legal Consciousness among Working-Class Americans*. Chicago and London, University of Chicago Press.
Merry, S. (1992). "Culture, Power, and the Discourse of Law." *The New York Law School Law Review* **37**: 209.
Merry, S. and N. Milner (eds.) (1993). *The Possibility of Popular Justice: A Case Study of Community Mediation in the United States*. Ann Arbor, MI, University of Michigan Press.
Merry, S. and S. Silbey (1984). "What Do Plaintiffs Want? Reexamining the Concept of Dispute." *The Justice System Journal* **9**(2): 151.
Meschievitz, C. (1990). *Mediating Medical Malpractice Claims in Wisconsin: A Preliminary Report*. Madison, University of Wisconsin – Madison Law School.
Meschievitz, C. (1991). "Mediation and Medical Malpractice: Problems with Definition and Implementation." *Law and Contemporary Problems* **54**(1): 195.
Meschievitz, C. S. (1994). "Efficacious or Precarious? Comments on the Processing and Resolution of Medical Malpractice Claims in the United States." *Annals of Health Law* **3**: 123.
Metzloff, T., R. Peeples and C. Harris (1997). "Empirical Perspectives on Mediation and Malpractice." *Law and Contemporary Problems* **60**(1): 107.
Ministry-of-the-Attorney-General (1999). *Code of Conduct: Ontario Mandatory Mediation Program*. Ministry of the Attorney General. http://www.attorneygeneral.jus.gov.on.ca/english/courts/manmed/codeofconduct.asp (last viewed August 8, 2008).
Mnookin, R., S. Peppet and A. Tulumello (2000). *Beyond Winning: Negotiating to Create Value in Deals and Disputes*. Cambridge, MA, Belknap Press of Harvard University Press.
Mnookin, R. H. and L. Kornhauser (1979). "Bargaining in the Shadow of the Law: The Case of Divorce." *Yale Law Journal* **88**: 950.
Moore, C. W. (2003). *The Mediation Process: Practical Strategies for Resolving Conflict*. San Francisco, CA, Jossey-Bass.
Morris, C. (1999). "The Moulding of Lawyers: ADR and Legal Education." *Windsor Yearbook of Access to Justice* **17**: 271.
Morton, L. and F. Einesman (2001). "The Effects of Mediation in a Juvenile Incarceration Facility: Reduction of Violence Through Transformation." *Cleveland State Law Review* **49**: 255.
Mouzelis, N. (1991). *Back to Sociological Theory: The Construction of Social Orders*. London, Macmillan Press Ltd.
Mulcahy, L. (1999). *Mediating Medical Negligence Claims – An Option for the Future*. Socio-Legal Studies Association Annual Conference, Loughborough, England.
Mulcahy, L., M. Selwood, L. Summerfield and A. Netten (2000). *Mediating Medical Negligence Claims: An Option for the Future?* London, Stationery Office.

Nader, L. (1993). "Controlling Processes in the Practice of Law: Hierarchy and Pacification in the Movement to Re-Form Dispute Ideology." *Ohio State Journal on Dispute Resolution* **9**: 1.

Nader, L. (2002). *The Life of the Law*. Berkeley, CA, University of California Press.

NCC (1995). *Seeking Civil Justice: A Survey of People's Needs and Experiences*. London, HMSO.

Nelken, M. (1996). "Negotiation and Psychoanalysis: If I'd Wanted to Learn about Feelings, I Wouldn't Have Gone to Law School." *Journal of Legal Education* **46**: 420.

Neumann, R., Jr. (2000). "Women in Legal Education: What the Statistics Show." *Journal of Legal Education* **50**: 313.

Nisselle, P. (1999). "Editorial: Angered Patients and the Medical Profession." *Medical Journal of Australia* **170**: 576.

Nolan-Haley, J. (1996). "Court Mediation and the Search for Justice through Law." *Washington University Law Quarterly* **74**(January): 47.

Nolan-Haley, J. (1998). "Lawyers, Clients, and Mediation." *Notre Dame Law Review* **73**: 1369.

Nolan-Haley, J. (2002). "Lawyers, Non-Lawyers and Mediation: Rethinking the Professional Monopoly from a Problem-Solving Perspective." *Harvard Negotiation Law Review* **7**(Spring): 235.

Noonan, J., Jr. (1993). "Persons and Masks of the Law (1976)," in *The Responsible Judge: Readings in Judicial Ethics*. Westport, CT, Praeger, pp. 22–34.

O'Barr, W. M. and J. M. Conley (1990). "Litigant Satisfaction versus Legal Adequacy in Small Claims Court Narratives," in *Language in the Judicial Process* (D. N. Levi and A. G. Walker, eds.), Vol. 97. New York, Plenum.

O'Hara, E. A. and D. Yarn (2002). "On Apology and Consilience." *Washington Law Review* **77**: 1121.

Ontario Ministry of the Attorney General (1999). *Ontario Mandatory Mediation Program: Fact Sheet on the Mandatory Mediation Program*. Ontario Ministry of the Attorney General. http://www.attorneygeneral.jus.gov.on.ca/english/courts/manmed/factsheet.asp (last viewed August 8, 2008)

Palmer, M. (1987). "The Revival of Mediation in the People's Republic of China: (1) Extra-Judicial Mediation," in *Yearbook on Socialist Legal Systems* (W. E. Butler, ed.). Dobbs Ferry, New York, Transnational Publishers, pp. 219–77.

Palmer, M. (1989). "The Revival of Mediation in the People's Republic of China: (2) Extra-Judicial Mediation," in *Yearbook on Socialist Legal Systems* (W. E. Butler, ed.). Dobbs Ferry, New York, Transnational Publishers, pp. 145–71.

Palmer, M. and S. Roberts (1998). *Dispute Processes: ADR and the Primary Forms of Decision Making*. London, Butterworths.

Patterson, D. (1992). "Postmodernism/Feminism/Law." *Cornell Law Review* **77**: 254.

Patton, M. Q. (1990). *Qualitative Evaluation and Research Methods*. Newbury Park, London, Sage Publications.

Pavlick, D. L. (2003). "Apology and Mediation: The Horse and Carriage of the Twenty-First Century." *Ohio State Journal on Dispute Resolution* **18**: 829.

Payne, K. (2001). *Different but Equal: Communication between the Sexes.* Westport, CT, Praeger.

Pearson, J. and N. Thoennes (1988). "Divorce Mediation Research Results," in *Divorce Mediation: Theory and Practice* (J. Folberg and A. Milne, eds.). New York, Guildford Press, p. 429.

Pennebaker, J. (ed.) (1995). "Emotion, Disclosure and Health: An Overview" in *Emotion, Disclosure and Health.* Washington, DC, American Psychological Association, pp. 3–10.

Pepper, R. A. (1998). "Mandatory Mediation: Ontario's Unfortunate Experience in Court-Annexed ADR." *Advocates Quarterly* **20**(4): 403.

Pepper, S. (1995). "Counseling at the Limits of the Law: An Exercise in the Jurisprudence and Ethics of Lawyering." *Yale Law Journal* **104**: 1545.

Phillips, R. A. (1992). "Mediation of Medical Malpractice Disputes." *North Carolina Medical Journal* **53**(11): 582.

Polywka, S. (1997). "Mediation of Clinical Negligence Claims: A Pilot Scheme Endorsed by the NHS Executive in the Anglia and Oxford Region." *Clinical Risk* **3**(3): 80.

Price, K. H., T. W. Hall, K. V. D. Bos, J. E. Hunton, S. Lovett and M. J. Tippett (2001). "Features of the Value Function for Voice and Their Consistency across Participants from Four Countries: Great Britain, Mexico, the Netherlands, and the United States." *Organizational Behavior and Human Decision Processes* **84**: 95.

Rabinow, P. (ed.) (1986). *The Foucault Reader/Michel Foucault.* Harmondsworth, Penguin Books.

Rack, C. (1999). "Negotiated Justice: Gender & Ethnic Minority Bargaining Patterns in the Metro Court Study." *Hamline Journal of Public Law and Policy* **20**: 211.

Raz, J. (2004). *Legal Philosophy Seminar Series.* New York, Columbia University.

Reeves, J. W. (1994). "ADR Relieves Pain of Health Care Disputes." *Dispute Resolution Journal* **49**(3): 14.

Reich, J. B. (2001). "A Call for Intellectual Honesty: A Response to the Uniform Mediation Act's Privilege against Disclosure." *Journal of Dispute Resolution* **2001**: 197.

Reich, J. B. (2002). "Attorney V. Client: Creating a Mechanism to Address Competing Process Interests in Lawyer-Driven Mediation." *Southern Illinois University Law Journal* **26**(Winter): 183.

Relis, T. (2002). "Civil Litigation from Litigants' Perspectives: What We Know and What We Don't Know about the Litigation Experience of Individual Litigants," in *Studies in Law, Politics, and Society* (A. Sarat and P. Ewick, eds.), Vol. 25. London, New York, Oxford, Elsevier Science, p. 151.

Relis, T. (2004). "Lawyers and Clients: Disparate Conceptions of Dispute Resolution in Litigation-Linked Mediation," in *Sociology of Law*. Japan, Japan Association of the Sociology of Law (JASL), University of Tokyo, pp. 24–41.

Relis, T. (2007a). 'It's Not about the Money!': A Theory on Misconceptions of Plaintiffs' Litigation Aims." *University of Pittsburgh Law Review* **68**(2): 701–46.

Relis, T. (2007b). "Consequences of Power." *Harvard Negotiation Law Review* **12**: 445–501.

Rhode, D. (1994). "Gender and Professional Roles." *Fordham Law Review* **63**: 39.

Ricci, I. (1985). "Mediator's Notebook: Reflections on Promoting Equal Empowerment and Entitlement for Women," in *Divorce Mediation: Perspectives on the Field* (C. Everett, ed.). New York, Haworth Press, pp. 49–62.

Rifkin, J. (1984). "Mediation from a Feminist Perspective: Promises and Problems." *Law and Inequality* **2**: 21.

Riley, H. and K. L. McGinn (2002). *When Does Gender Matter in Negotiation?* KSG Faculty Research Working Paper Series. Cambridge, MA, John F. Kennedy School of Government, Harvard University.

Riskin, L. (1982). "Mediation and Lawyers." *Ohio State Law Journal* **43**: 29.

Riskin, L. (1996). "Understanding Mediators' Orientations, Strategies and Techniques: A Grid for the Perplexed." *Harvard Negotiation Law Review* **1**: 7.

Riskin, L. (2002). "The Contemplative Lawyer: On the Potential Contributions of Mindfulness Meditation to Law Students, Lawyers, and Their Clients." *Harvard Negotiation Law Review* **7**(Spring): 1.

Riskin, L. (2003). "Decisionmaking in Mediation: The New Old Grid and the New Grid System." *Notre Dame Law Review* **79**: 1.

Riskin, L. and J. Westbrook (1997). *Dispute Resolution and Lawyers*. St. Paul, MN, West Publishing.

Riskin, L. L. (1985). "The Special Place of Mediation in Alternative Dispute Processing." *Florida Law Review* **37**: 19.

Robbennolt, J. (2003). "Apologies and Legal Settlement: An Empirical Examination." *Michigan Law Review* **102**: 460.

Roberts, M. (1997). *Mediation in Family Disputes: Principles of Practice*. Aldershot, Arena Ashgate.

Roberts, S. (1993). "ADR and Civil Justice: An Unresolved Relationship." *Modern Law Review* **56**: 450.

Roberts, S. (2000). "Settlement as Civil Justice." *Modern Law Review* **63**(5): 739.

Roberts, S. (2002). "Institutionalized Settlement in England: A Contemporary Panorama." *Willamette Journal of International Law and Dispute Resolution* **10**: 17.

Rosenberg, J. (1991). "In Defense of Mediation." *Arizona Law Review* **33**: 467.

Rosenberg, J. D. (2004). "Interpersonal Dynamics: Helping Lawyers Learn the Skills, and the Importance, of Human Relationships in the Practice of Law." *University of Miami Law Review* **58**: 1225.

Rosenthal, D. (1974). *Lawyer and Client: Who's In Charge?* New York, Russell Sage Foundation.

Rubinson, R. (2004). "Client Counseling, Mediation, and Alternative Narratives of Dispute Resolution." *Clinical Law Review* **10**(Spring): 833.
Sally, D. (2003). "Yearn for Paradise, Live in Limbo: Optimal Frustration for ADR." *Penn State Law Review* **108**(Summer): 89.
Sander, F. and R. Mnookin (2000). "A Worthy Challenge: The Teaching of Problem Solving in Law Schools." *American Bar Association Dispute Resolution Magazine* (Summer): 21.
Sander, F. E. A. (1976). *Varieties of Dispute Processing*. National Conference on the Causes of Popular Dissatisfaction with the Administration of Justice, F. R. D.
Santos, B. D. S. (1977). "The Law of the Oppressed: The Construction and Reproduction of Legality in Pasargada." *Law and Society Review* **12**(1): 5.
Sarat, A. (1976). "Alternatives in Dispute Processing: Litigation in a Small Claims Court." *Law and Society Review* **10**: 339.
Sarat, A. and W. Felstiner (1986). "Law and Strategy in the Divorce Lawyer's Office." *Law and Society Review* **20**: 93.
Sarat, A. and W. Felstiner (1988). "Law and Social Relations: Vocabularies of Motive in Lawyer/Client Interaction." *Law and Society Review* **22**(4): 737.
Sarat A. and W. Felstiner (1989). "Lawyers and Legal Consciousness: Law Talk in the Divorce Lawyer's Office." *Yale Law Journal* **98**: 1663.
Sarat, A. and W. Felstiner (1990). "Legal Realism in Lawyer–Client Communication," in *Language in the Judicial Process* (J. Levi and A. Walker, eds.). London, Plenum Press, pp. 133–54.
Sarat A. and W. Felstiner (1995a). *Divorce Lawyers and Their Clients*. New York, Oxford University Press.
Sarat, A. and W. Felstiner (1995b). "Law and Social Relations: Vocabularies of Motive in Lawyer/Client Interaction," in *The Law & Society Reader* (R. Abel, ed.). New York, New York University Press, pp. 403–30.
Saravia, A. (1999). "Notes and Comments: Overview of Alternative Dispute Resolution in Healthcare Disputes." *Journal of Health and Hospital Law* **32**(1): 139.
Schutz, A. (1967). *The Phenomenology of the Social World*. Evanston, Northwestern University Press.
Schutz, A. (1982). "The Problem of Social Reality," in *Collected Papers I. The Problem of Social Reality* (M. A. Natanson and H. L. van Breda, eds.). The Hague, Boston, Martinus Nijhoff.
Scott, L. W. (2006). "The Law of Mediation in Texas." *St. Mary's Law Journal* **37**: 325.
Shack, J. E. (2003). *Bibliographic Summary of Cost, Pace, and Satisfaction Studies of Court-Related Mediation Programs*. Chicago, IL, Center for Conflict, Center for Analysis of Alternative Dispute Resolution Systems (CAADRS) Publication.
Shalleck, A. (1992). "The Feminist Transformation of Lawyering: A Response to Naomi Cahn." *Hastings Law Journal* **43**: 1071.
Shalleck, A. (1993). "Constructions of the Client within Legal Education." *Stanford Law Review* **45**(6, July): 1731–53.

Shapiro, M. (1981). *Courts: A Comparative and Political Analysis.* Chicago, London, University of Chicago Press.

Sherwin, R. (1992a). "Lawyering Theory: An Overview What We Talk about When We Talk about Law." *The New York Law School Law Review* **37**: 9.

Sherwin, R. (1992b). "Preface: Comment." *The New York Law School Law Review* **37**: 1.

Shestowsky, D. (2004). "Procedural Preferences in Alternative Dispute Resolution: A Closer, Modern Look at an Old Idea." *Psychology, Public Policy and Law* **10**(September): 211.

Shuman, D. (2000). "Role of Apology in Tort Law." *Judicature* **83**(4): 180.

Silbey, S. (2002). "The Emperor's New Clothes: Mediation Mythology and Markets." *Journal of Dispute Resolution* **2002**: 171.

Silbey, S. and S. Merry (1986). "Mediator Settlement Strategies." *Law and Policy* **8**: 7.

Silbey, S. and A. Sarat (1989). "Dispute Processing in Law and Legal Scholarship." *Denver University Law Review* **66**: 437.

Silver, M. (1999). "Emotional Intelligence and Legal Education." *Psychology Public Policy and Law* **5**: 1173.

Simanowitz, A. (1998). "Mediation in Medical Negligence." *Clinical Risk* **4**(2): 63.

Stamato, L. (1992). "Voice, Place, and Process: Research on Gender, Negotiation, and Conflict Resolution" *Mediation Quarterly* **9**: 375.

Stempel, J. (1997). "Beyond Formalism and False Dichotomies: The Need for Institutionalizing a Flexible Concept of the Mediator's Role." *Florida State University Law Review* **24**: 949.

Stempel, J. (2000a). "Identifying Real Dichotomies Underlying the False Dichotomy: Twenty-First Century Mediation in an Eclectic Regime." *Journal of Dispute Resolution* **2000**: 371.

Stempel, J. W. (2000b). "The Inevitability of the Eclectic: Liberating ADR from Ideology." *Journal of Dispute Resolution* **2000**: 247.

Stempel, J. W. (2002–3). "Forgetfulness, Fuzziness, Functionality, Fairness, and Freedom in Dispute Resolution: Serving Dispute Resolution through Adjudication." *Nevada Law Journal* **3**(Winter): 305.

Sternlight, J. (1999). "Lawyers' Representation of Clients in Mediation: Using Economics and Psychology to Structure Advocacy in a Nonadversarial Setting." *Ohio State Journal on Dispute Resolution* **14**: 269.

Sternlight, J. (2003). "ADR Is Here: Preliminary Reflections on Where It Fits in a System of Justice." *Nevada Law Journal* **3**: 289.

Stitt, A., L. Feld and H. Houston (1999). *The ADR Spectrum.* Stitt Feld Handy Houston. www.adr.ca/news/adrspect.asp (last viewed August 17, 1999).

Stolle, D., D. Wexler and B. Winick (1997). "Integrating Preventive Law and Therapeutic Jurisprudence: A Law and Psychology Based Approach to Lawyering." *California Western Law Review* **34**: 15.

Strang, H. and L. W. Sherman (2003). "Repairing the Harm: Victims and Restorative Justice." *Utah Law Review* **2003**(1): 15.

Strong, G. (1998). "The Lawyer's Left Hand: Nonanalytical Thought in the Practice of Law." *University of Colorado Law Review* **69**: 759.

Stuhlmacher, A. F. and A. E. Walters (1999). "Gender Differences in Negotiation Outcome A Meta-Analysis." *Personnel Psychology* **52**: 653.

Stulberg, J. (1997). "Facilitative versus Evaluative Mediator Orientations: Piercing the 'Grid' Lock." *Florida State University Law Review* **24**: 985.

Subrin, S. (2003). "A Traditionalist Looks at Mediation: It's Here to Stay and Much Better Than I Thought." *Nevada Law Journal* **3**: 196.

Taber, J., M. Grant, M. Huser, N. Rise, J. Sutton and C. Wong (1988). "Project, Gender, Legal Education, and the Legal Profession: An Empirical Study of Stanford Law Students and Graduates." *Stanford Law Review* **40**: 1209.

Tamanaha, B. (1993). *Understanding Law in Micronesia: An Interpretive Approach to Transplanted Law*. New York, E. J. Brill.

Tanick, M. H. and T. J. Ayling (1996). "Alternative Dispute Resolution by Apology: Settlement by Saying 'I'm Sorry'." *Hennepin Law* **22**(July–August): 112.

Tannen, D. (1990). *You Just Don't Understand: Women and Men in Conversation*. New York, Ballantine Books.

Tannen, D. (1994). *Talking from 9 to 5*. New York, William Morrow.

Teff, H. (1994). *Reasonable Care: Legal Perspectives on the Doctor-Patient Relationship*. Oxford, Clarendon Press.

Thibaut, J. and L. Walker (1975). *Procedural Justice: A Psychological Analysis*. Hillsdale, NJ, Lawrence Erlbaum Associates.

Thibaut, J. and L. Walker (1978). "A Theory of Procedure." *California Law Review* **86**: 386.

Thoennes, N., J. Pearson and J. Bell (1991). *Evaluation of the Use of Mandatory Divorce Mediation*. Denver, Center for Policy Research.

Thornton, M. (1989). "Equivocations of Conciliation: The Resolution of Discrimination Complaints in Australia." *Modern Law Review* **52**(6): 733.

Turner, V. (1974). *Dramas, Fields and Metaphors: Symbolic Action in Human Society*. Ithaca, NY, Cornell University Press.

Twining, W. (1993). "Alternative to What? Theories of Litigation, Procedure and Dispute Settlement in Anglo-American Jurisprudence: Some Neglected Classics." *Modern Law Review* **56**(3): 380.

Tyler, T. (1987). "The Psychology of Disputant Concerns in Mediation." *Negotiation Journal* **3**(4): 367.

Tyler, T. (1988). "What Is Procedural Justice?: Criteria Used by Citizens to Assess the Fairness of Legal Procedures." *Law and Society Review* **22**(1): 103.

Tyler, T. (1997). "Citizen Discontent with Legal Procedures: A Social Science Perspective on Civil Procedure Reform." *American Journal of Comparative Law* **45**(Fall): 871.

Tyler, T. R., J. D. Casper and B. Fisher (1989). "Maintaining Allegiance toward Political Authorities: The Role of Prior Attitudes and the Use of Fair Procedures." *American Journal of Political Science* **33**: 629–52.

Tyler, T. R., K. A. Rasinski and N. Spodick (1985). "Influence of Voice on Satisfaction With Leaders: Exploring the Meaning of Process Control." *American Journal of Personality and Social Psychology* **48**(1): 72.

Ury, W. (1988). *Getting Disputes Resolved: Designing Systems to Cut the Cost of Conflict.* San Francisco, CA, Jossey-Bass.

Vallance, R. (1990). "Preliminary Legal Steps for the Patient," in *Medical Negligence* (M. Powers and N. Harris, eds.). London and Edinburgh, Butterworths, pp. 101–30.

Vidmar, N. (1984). "The Small Claims Court: A Reconceptualization of Disputes and an Empirical Investigation." *Law and Society Review* **18**(4): 515.

Vincent, C., M. Young and A. Phillips (1994). "Why Do People Sue Doctors? A Study of Patients and Relatives Taking Legal Action." *The Lancet* **343**(8913): 1609.

Vogelstein, R. (2003). "Confidentiality vs. Care: Re-Evaluating the Duty to Self, Client, and Others." *Georgetown Law Journal* **92**: 153.

Waldman, E. (1998). "The Evaluative-Facilitative Debate in Mediation: Applying the Lens of Therapeutic Jurisprudence." *Marquette Law Review* **82**: 155.

Walters, A. E., A. F. Stuhlmacher and L. L. Meyer (1998). "Gender and Negotiator Competitiveness: A Meta-Analysis." *Organizational Behavior and Human Decision Processes* **76**: 1.

Watson, C. (1994a). "Gender Differences in Negotiating Behavior and Outcomes: Fact or Artifact," in *Conflict and Gender* (A. Taylor and J. B. Miller, eds.). Cresskill, NJ, Hampton Press, pp. 191–201.

Watson, C. (1994b). "In Theory: Gender Versus Power as a Predictor of Negotiation Behaviors and Outcomes." *Negotiation Journal* **10**: 117.

Weber, M. (1922). *Wirtschaft Und Gesellschaft* (English translation by A. Henderson and T. Parsons, 1957). Tübingen, J.C.B. Mohr (P. Siebeck).

Weckstein, D. (1997). "In Praise of Party Empowerment-and of Mediator Activism." *Willamette Law Review* **33**: 501.

Welsh, N. (2001a). "Making Deals in Court-Connected Mediation: What's Justice Got to Do with It?" *Washington University Law Quarterly* **79**(Fall): 787.

Welsh, N. (2001b). "The Thinning Vision of Self-Determination in Court-Connected Mediation: The Inevitable Price of Institutionalization?" *Harvard Negotiation Law Review* **6**(Spring): 1.

Welsh, N. (2004a). "Stepping Back through the Looking Glass: Real Conversations with Real Disputants about Institutionalized Mediation and Its Value." *Ohio State Journal on Dispute Resolution* **38**: 573.

Welsh, N. A. (2004b). "The Place of Court-Connected Mediation in a Democratic Justice System." *Cardozo Journal of Conflict Resolution* **5**(Spring): 117.

White, J. (1990). *Justice as Translation: An Essay in Cultural and Legal Criticism.* Chicago, IL, University of Chicago Press.

Williams, J. (1989). "Deconstructing Gender." *Michigan Law Review* **87**(February): 797.

Williams, W. (1982). "The Equality Crisis: Some Reflections on Culture, Courts, and Feminism." *Women's Rights Law Report* **7**: 175.

Winick, B. (1997). "The Jurisprudence of Therapeutic Jurisprudence." *Psychology, Public Policy and Law* **3**: 184.

Wise, R. K. (2006). "Mediation in Texas: Can the Judge Really Make Me Do That?" *South Texas Law Review* **47**: 849.

Wissler, R. (1997). "The Effects of Mandatory Mediation: Empirical Research on the Experience of Small Claims and Common Pleas Courts." *Willamette Law Review* **33**: 565.

Wissler, R. (1998). "Study Finds Mediators' Style Can Have an Impact on Outcome of Dispute Resolution." *Dispute Resolution Magazine* **4**(4): 28.

Wissler, R. (2000). "'Attorneys' Use of ADR Is Crucial to Their Willingness to Recommend It to Their Clients." *Dispute Resolution Magazine* **2000**(Spring): 36.

Wissler, R. (2002). "Court-Connected Mediation in General Civil Cases: What We Know from Empirical Research." *Ohio State Journal on Dispute Resolution* **17**: 641.

Wissler, R. L. (2001). "To Evaluate or Facilitate?" *Dispute Resolution Magazine* **2001**(Winter): 35.

Index

Abel, Richard, 13, 41, 239
ADR debates, 20–21

Babcock, Linda and Sara Laschever, 60, 147, 190–191, 249, 251
Bourdieu, Pierre, 1n2

confidentiality, 150–152
Conley, John and William O'Barr, 15, 34, 45, 157n3, 195, 213, 241n14, 253n39

Damaska, Mirjan, 238, 238n10
dispute transformation, 16–17, 35, 35n5, 51–58, 62–63

evaluative versus facilitative mediation styles, 22, 204, 207–217, 223–225

gender theme, 3, 9, 22–26, 58–61, 119–124, 128, 139–141, 145–149, 153–154, 181–193, 195–196, 217–223, 225, 245–252
Giddens, Anthony, 1n2
Gilligan, Carol, 247–248
Goffman, Erving, 160, 193
Grillo, Trina, 189, 222, 250

Habermas, Jurgen, 4, 12n15

informal justice critiques, 14–15, 240

Kolb, Deborah, 183, 187, 191, 192–193, 251
Kritzer, Herbert, 41, 43n9

lawyering theory, 13, 34
lawyers' reconceptualization theme, 9, 17–19, 101, 104, 134–135, 137–139, 154–155, 202–203, 214, 234–238

mandatory mediation, 20, 65–85
Menkel-Meadow, Carrie, 3, 9n14, 15, 21, 41, 64, 171, 184, 192, 206, 236, 241, 243
Merry, Sally, 45, 64, 179n21, 239
Merry, Sally and Susan Silbey, 45
methodology, 26–28
Metzloff, Thomas, 19n29, 160, 174n19, 207, 236

negotiation theory, 190–193, 251–252

parallel worlds theme, 8–12, 17, 46–51, 61–64, 68–84, 86–87, 125–128, 131–136, 141–145, 153, 165–181, 193–195, 204–217, 223–224, 228–234, 238–244
procedural justice, 14, 21, 33n1, 51, 127–128, 164, 174–175, 179, 194n39, 204

Raz, Joseph, 196, 240, 242
research sites, 29–31
respondent demographics, 28–29
Roberts, Simon, 4–5

Sarat, Austin and William Felstiner, 52n17, 195, 230n1
Schutz, Alfred, 1n2

Tannen, Deborah, 186, 220
theoretical framework, 1
therapeutic jurisprudence, 15, 243, 252

Weber, Max, 1n2
Wissler, Roselle, 20, 66, 71, 164, 175, 202, 211, 213–214